Excavations at Tell Um Hammad 1982 - 1984

The Early Assemblages (EB I - II)

For James Mellaart

Excavations and Explorations in the Hashemite Kingdom
of Jordan

Excavations at Tell Um Hammad

1982 - 1984

The Early Assemblages (EB I - II)

Edited by

A.V.G. BETTS

S. W. Helms
and
A. Betts, N. O' Tool

EDINBURGH UNIVERSITY PRESS

Edinburgh University Press
22 George Square, Edinburgh

Printed in Great Britain by
The Alden Press Limited, Oxford

British Library Cataloguing in Publication Data
Excavations at Tell Um Hammad 1982 - 1984:
 The Early Assemblages (EB I - II)
I. Betts, A.V.G.

ISBN 0 7486 0336 0

Contents

List of Illustrations

FIGURES

TABLES

PLATES

8.   (1) stamp seal impressions on a holemouth jar of genre 2 (cf. Fig. 143: 1); (2) stamp
      seal impressions on a holemouth jar of genre 1/2 (cf. Pl. 4: 3; Figs 142, 272);
      (3) 'reed' impressed bands on genre 82 (cf. Fig. 244: 5); (4) stabbed impressions on
      genre 21 (cf. Fig. 197: 1); (5) 'reed' impressed bands (cf. Figs 147, 148: 1-7, 154: 1-6)

Abbreviations

The following abbreviations are used in the text. A list of abbreviated bibliographical references appears at the beginning of the bibliography.

'chalc. moy.'	'chalcolithique moyen'
'chalc. sup.'	'chalcolithique supérieur'
'én. moy.'	'éneolithique moyen'
'én. rec.'	'éneolithique recent'
'én. sup.'	'éneolithique superieur'
'neol. anc.'	'neolithique ancien'
[?]	questionable comparison (pottery)
AH	absolute height (metres below sea level)
av	average
bs	body sherd(s)
C	field catalogue number (pottery)
Chalco	Chalcolithic
EB	Early Bronze (Age)
ext	external
Gx	genre designation (pottery)
H	hybrid(s) [pottery]
hmj	holemouth jar
horiz	horizontal
Ht (ht)	height
int	internal
MB	Middle Bronze Age
misc	miscellaneous
N.T.	New Testament
Neo	Neolithic
ph	phase
PN	Pottery Neolithic
pot. c	pottery catalogue (number)
Prov	provenance (last three digits = deposition number; preceding digit[s] = square number)
PU	Proto Urban (after Kenyon)
R	repertoire
St (st)	stage
Str	stratum (Arad)
TUH	Tell Um Hammad
TUH000: n	Pottery Catalogue Fig. 000: form n
v/gn	excavated volume per phase/total number of recognisable genres
vert	vertical
<x	derived from x

Editor's Preface

A. V. G. BETTS

This is the second in a series of three volumes describing excavations at the sites of Jawa and Um Hammad in Jordan. Tell Um Hammad is a large open settlement in the central Jordan Valley, on the banks of wadi Zerqa near its confluence with the River Jordan. The site was first occupied in the late Chalcolithic period and has an almost continuous stratigraphic sequence up until EB II on the main tell. Um Hammad was largely abandoned during the middle of the Early Bronze Age, but was re-occupied in EB IV when a new settlement was established. A cemetery associated with the Early Bronze Age occupation lies to the south, along the cliffs overlooking the Zerqa river. The cemetery is classified as a separate site, Tiwal esh-Sharqi. Um Hammad was abandoned at the end of the Early Bronze Age, but was briefly re-occupied later when an Iron Age farmstead was built on the main tell.

Tell Um Hammad was first 'discovered' by Nelson Glueck during his pioneering surveys east of the Jordan river. The rich potential of the site was recognised by James Mellaart, who made soundings there in 1953 as part of a research programme to study the nature of fourth and third millennium occupation in the Jordan Valley. Excavations under Svend Helms began in 1982 and continued over two seasons to 1984. Prior to the excavations at Tell Um Hammad, Helms had been working at Jawa, an extensive fortified site on the lower slopes of Jebel Druze. Jawa's massive fortifications and complex water systems were constructed at the beginning of the Early Bronze Age, but the relationship between this early fortified town and village settlements of the same period in Palestine was unclear. While Helms was working at Jawa, Mellaart pointed out to him similarities between some of the Um Hammad pottery forms and those from Jawa; forms which were not parallelled elsewhere in Palestine at that time. A short visit to Tell Um Hammad in 1981 convinced Helms of this connection and he arranged to begin excavations at the site.

Tell Um Hammad is important because it has preserved deep stratigraphy of the period between the Chalcolithic and what has been called the 'walled town' culture of the Early Bronze Age. The depth of occupation and the related structural sequence indicate that this period was much longer than has previously been thought. The Chalcolithic/EB transition has long been the subject of debate, yet despite a wealth of hypotheses, these questions have so far not been resolved. Tell Um Hammad's rich yield of ceramic remains provides the best opportunity yet to answer some of the questions concerning the period. The 'Jawa connection' is also important. The excavations have provided confirmation that the first occupation at Jawa can be related to EB I A, and the direct link between the two pottery assemblages extends the EB I cultural sphere beyond Palestine and into Syria.

I have been closely involved with the work at Tell Um Hammad from the day in 1981 when Helms found the first 'Jawa type' sherd. I worked as Area Supervisor and Lithics Analyst in both seasons and was a member of teams from the Department of Antiquities and the British Museum excavating the Tiwal esh-Sharqi cemetery. Through my involvement with the site, I have become increasingly fascinated by the changing socio-economic patterns throughout Syria/Palestine during the Early Bronze Age. I believe this volume will add considerably to our understanding of the period. I would like to thank the contributors, and all those in Jordan, the U.K., and elsewhere, who made the publication possible.

Preface

S. W. HELMS

The excavations at Tell Um Hammad al-Sharqi took place in the autumn of 1982, and were followed (spring 1983) by a short additional season of clearing EB IV tombs which had been exposed and severely damaged recently. This latter work was carried out under the auspices and with the financial support of the Jordanian Department of Antiquities. A second season of excavations at the occupation site, now also including the western areas (Tell Um Hammad al-Gharbi), was conducted in the autumn of 1984. This work season was preceded by further clearance of the extensive EB IV cemetery by a team from the British Museum (Tubb 1990). In 1986 a post-excavation grant from the British Institute at Amman for Archaeology and History allowed me to process the pottery and other finds in Amman. At this stage the master pottery typology was established and this formed the basis of selection for further technical analyses by N. Vaillant of IFAPO from 1988 onward. Through the kind co-operation offered by IFAPO, then directed by F. Braemer, Vaillant and I were able to view survey pottery at IFAPO Damascus as well as visiting several relevant sites in the Syrian Hawran (e.g. Khirbet Umbachi and Leboué). The British Institute at Amman for Archaeology and History made further grants towards the processing of data for final publication.

The excavations were sponsored and generously supported financially by the British Institute at Amman for Archaeology and History. Additional financial support came from the following: the Ashmolean Museum; Birmingham Museum and Art Gallery; the British Academy; the British Museum; the British School of Archaeology in Jerusalem; Bolton Museum; the Central Research Funds Committee (London University); E. Helms; Manchester Museum; the Palestine Exploration Fund; the Society of Antiquaries of London; and the G.A. Wainwright Fund.

Staff for the two seasons included A. Betts (lithics specialist and area supervisor), M. Darweesh, A. Lowe, C. Maclaughlin, L. McClintock, C.D. Politis, I. Ruben and S. Thorpe. Sa'ad Hadidi represented the Department of Antiquities in 1982 and M. Darweesh in 1984. The team for the 1983 clearance of EB IV tombs included A. Betts, M. Darweesh and M. Jumra.

The then new 'dig house' at Deir Alla was made available to the team during the clearance of EB IV tombs (1983) and also for post excavation work through the generosity of the Department of Antiquities, Yarmouk University, and Leiden University. We are particularly indebted to Dr Adnan Hadidi, Director of Antiquities at the time of the excavations, and Dr Mu'awiyah Ibrahim of Yarmouk University.

Important photographic work was done at the Institute of Archaeology, London University, through the cooperation of P. Dorrell and S. Laidlaw. We are particularly grateful to Professor J.D. Evans for his support during the early stages of the project.

No fieldwork is easy without a 'home base' and this was provided by the British Institute at Amman for Archaeology and History under the direction of A.N. Garrard, and also by the American Center for Oriental Research under the direction of D. McCreery.

James Mellaart, to whom this work is dedicated, has taught us much; he has shared generously not only his ideas but also important empirical data which he collected in Jordan when agricultural development first began seriously to jeopardise archaeological sites. Mellaart passed much of these data on to Albert Leonard (n.d.) who, in the spirit of international scholarly cooperation spawned at the first Conference on the Archaeology and History of Jordan in 1980 (Hadidi [ed.] 1982), shared this material with us. Leonard has also supplied pre-publication drawings and photographs of stamp seal impressions from the site of Kataret es-Samra, which appear for the first time in this volume.

1. Introduction

S.W. HELMS

Tell Um Hammad is not a 'tell' in the normal sense: that is to say, a high and obviously artificial mound containing the remains of many super-imposed settlements, a 'mound of many cities' (Bliss 1894) such as the well-known tells at Deir Alla, Tell Mazar, and Tell es-Sa'idiyah; rather it is a relatively flat, extensive area of sherd scatter along the marl bluffs on the northern edge of wadi Zerqa (Fig. 3). Although we did find surprisingly deep stratigraphy representing several occupation stages, the nature of these occupations was markedly different from that of other Early Bronze Age settlements in the region, settlements which had come to typify the period. Tell Um Hammad was the site of a series of large, unfortified villages in open, flat land, beside irrigable fields and near the permanent water source of the Zerqa River. This difference in itself made the site an important one since, until recently, very few, if any, villages of the Early Bronze Age had been explored: particularly not villages where occupation could be dated in the problematical stages of development between the Chalcolithic period and the so-called 'urban' Early Bronze Age. The emphasis had been on large, usually fortified, sites in easily defensible locations, sites whose massive structural remains, densely built up domestic quarters, and even putative specialised architecture, lead to the notion of a first urban age in the land. The rural hinterland of this new, 'urbanised' stage had been subsumed; its character and relative importance in the economy and demography of the period had, however, remained nebulous. In addition to this, many studies regarding the nature, as well as the actual size, of Early Bronze populations had unaccountably ignored, or underestimated, the presence of non-sedentized peoples who, in view of later written history, as well as more recent ethnographic studies, have played a significant role in the Near East. (For example, two important studies of settlement distribution and size [Broshi and Gophna 1984; Gophna 1984] fail to include mobile populations in their calculations.) Um Hammad and its apparent wealth of early cultural material provided a chance to explore village life in relation to the larger, so-called 'urban' settlements in the region, and a chance to elucidate settlement patterns, particularly during the vexatious 'transition' period (EB I A/B: the second half of the fourth millennium BC) which separated the rural economy of the Chalcolithic period and the 'full', or 'urban' Early Bronze Age.

The site has two names, Um Hammad al-Sharqi ('east', the settlement along the wadi Zerqa bluffs), and Um Hammad al-Gharbi ('west', the settlement[s] on the watershed between the Zerqa and Jordan Rivers [Pl. 1; Figs 3 - 5]). It is likely that both of these settlement areas were joined as one sprawling village during some of the 'cultural' stages, notably during the EB IV period of the later third millennium BC (Betts and Helms in press). A third area of 'sherd scatter' to the south of Um Hammad represents the site's cemetery (mostly for the EB IV period) and is called Tiwal esh-Sharqi (Fig. 4; cf. Helms 1986: Fig. 2).

Um Hammad lies at the southern end of the locally available arable land (Fig. 3: q5), settlements of the protohistorical period being restricted to the almost sterile Dead Sea marls (Fig. 3: q2). Today the fields next to the site are irrigated by a system of canals drawing water from the recently constructed East Ghor Canal. It may be postulated that irrigation also played an important role during the Early Bronze Age. The evidence for this lies in the potential for irrigation which is provided by the Zerqa River, and the topography of the area: aerial photographs pre-dating the construction of the East Ghor Canal (Pl. 2; Fig. 3) show wadi courses, as well as canals, fed by runoff from the hills to the east. One wadi course, perhaps artificially augmented, can be seen in plate 2 taking water from wadi Zerqa well up-stream from Tell Um Hammad (Pl. 2: top right) just east of the large fortified EBA site of Tell Abu Zighan, and flowing along the top of the marl bluffs through the fields separating Um Hammad al-Sharqi and Um Hammad al-Gharbi (Pl. 2: site 199), eventually cutting through the marls in Tiwal esh-Sharqi, to join again with wadi Zerqa. Such augmented (or controlled) natural wadi flow could have been used to irrigate the ancient fields at Um Hammad (see McCreery 1981 for evidence of irrigation at Bab edh-Dhra' during EB I).

Today wadi Zerqa (*sayl al-Zerqa*) discharges an average of 70 million cubic metres annually (gauging station at Deir Alla: *National Water Master Plan*: 12). Maximum flow occurs in January/February, the minimum from July to September. Average annual rainfall is in the region of 278 mm with a standard deviation of about 94 mm (Salah and Dakkat 1974). December and January receive peak rainfall. Summers are dry and very hot in the Jordan Valley: i.e. the region experiences tropical winters, facilitating October/November planting and December/January harvesting. Temperatures range from 15 to 22 degrees (Centigrade) from November to March and from 30 to 33 degrees, commonly reaching 40 degrees, in summer. The relative humidity is 33 per cent in summer and 84 per cent in winter. Ground water resources are classed as medium to bad (offset by the availability of water from perennial sources). The salinity hazard is very high with regard to irrigation (e.g. Fig. 3: al-Mallaha, a small salt lake on the watershed between the Zerqa and Jordan Rivers just north of Um Hammad). Stock watering is classed as medium to bad.

In terms of the amount of available arable land which might be suitable for wadi/canal fed irrigation, the so-called 'Zerqa Triangle' or Zerqa River floodplain (the main EBA nucleated settlement being Tell Abu Zighan), and subsidiary systems on either side of it, can be ranked as a first order sub-region in comparison with other parts of the Jordan Valley. Its crop yield potential may be compared with the sub-regions of the upper Huleh basin (Tell Dan), the area of Beth Shan, and the area almost directly opposite Um Hammad, the wadi Far'ah floodplain (Khirbet Mahruq). Second order sub-regions might include the area about Kinneret, and the east bank of the Jordan River between the Zerqa floodplain and Lake Tiberias (Pella, Tell Handaquq North, Tell es-Sa'idiyah). Third order sub-regions may be identified in the southwestern Huleh basin (Qedesh and Hazor), near Beth Yerah, the Tavor valley, about Jericho, and in the sub-region of wadis Kufrain and Hisban (Tells Iktanu and al-Hammam). Fourth order sub-regions include the narrow Jordan river floodplains north of Lake Tiberias, and between the Beth Shan and wadi Far'ah sub-regions on the west bank of the Jordan River, the area between the Zerqa floodplain and the wadi Kufrain/Hisban sub-region, and the highly saline land immediately north of the Dead Sea. In the Southern Ghor, the sub-region of Bab edh-Dhra' might be regarded as second or third order (i.e. both Jericho and Bab edh-Dhra', on which so much of the current theorizing has been based, are small walled settlements [< 4 hectares] of the EBA, in comparison with the average settlement size of the period which is about 10 hectares, but can be as large as 40 hectares).

The sub-region in which Um Hammad lies may also be regarded as a communication node at the centre of the Jordan Valley, in contrast to sub-regions such as Jericho and, particularly, Bab edh-Dhra', which are much more isolated. Wadi Zerqa represents the most important east-west route linking the Transjordanian uplands with the Jordan Valley. Similarly, wadi el-Far'ah, across the Jordan River to the west, is the main east-west route leading up to the central and northern Palestinian hills. The best north-south route lies along the foothills to the east of Tell Um Hammad.

EXPLORATION HISTORY

Nelson Glueck was among the first to include in his surveys the relatively humble, unfortified occupation sites such as Tell Um

Hammad. In his early reports he speculated on the location of Iron Age establishments (Glueck 1943: 'Israelite towns': Zarethan [?=Tell Um Hammad], Succoth and Zaphon; there was a fortified settlement, perhaps a farmstead, at Um Hammad al-Sharqi during the Iron Age [Fig. 7; Betts and Helms in press]). He also described the earlier remains at the site, which he identified as 'Chalcolithic' (1945a) and MB I - now usually EB IV - (1945b). A fully illustrated report followed in 1951 in which the pottery of Tell Um Hammad (al-Sharqi and al-Gharbi) represented the largest collection from any single site. Glueck stressed the importance of Um Hammad, particularly in terms of the wealth of early occupation, at a time when the debate regarding the protohistory of the Levant had already been under way for at least twenty years and the 'transition' periods such as Chalcolithic to EBA and EBA to MBA had been recognised and variously explained, mainly on the basis of pottery typology, ever since Wright's seminal study (1937).

Mellaart (1962) and de Contenson (1960) continued where Glueck had to stop, the former surveying Tell Um Hammad once again, as well as cutting small sondages at Tell Um Hammad al-Sharqi. It was Mellaart who first properly realized the importance of the site, particularly in relation to the 'transition' from the Chalcolithic to the Early Bronze Age, and who introduced the term 'Umm Hamad esh-Sherqi Ware' to the ceramic typology of the period (Mellaart 1966). (The ware is easily recognized; the repertoire [vessel forms and decoration] is almost identical to Chalcolithic pottery of the Ghassul/Beersheba type.) Mellaart's material from Tell Um Hammad al-Sharqi, as well as finds from other sites in the Jordan Valley, will be published by Leonard (n.d.). The importance of Um Hammad and its characteristic pottery were also given a predominant place in a reconstruction of the 'transition' period by de Miroschedji (1971) who added to Kenyon's 'periodisation' of the early part of the Early Bronze Age the term 'pré-urbaine D': i.e. Kenyon's divisions of 'Proto Urban A, B and C' now with 'pré-urbaine D' standing for whatever might lie behind the distinctive 'Umm Hamad esh-Sherqi Ware'.

The site was resurveyed by Prag as part of a comprehensive study of the second problematical period in the protohistory of the southern Levant, the, by now polyonymous, 'EB IV' period of the later third millennium BC: i.e. among others, the 'Intermediate Early Bronze - Middle Bronze Age (EB-MB), or EB IV/MB I, or 'Intermediate Bronze Age'; etc.). Prag's survey was included in her doctoral dissertation (1971) and in a study of the 'EB-MB' period in Palestine, Transjordan, Syria, and Lebanon (1974), together with her results of the excavations at Tell Iktanu.

The present investigations at Um Hammad began because of the apparently problematical evidence from Jawa in eastern Transjordan (Betts [ed.] 1991). The decision to excavate came as a direct result of seeing pottery drawings by Mellaart which included types remarkably like some of the pottery from Jawa. Several of these pottery forms had been impressed with distinctive designs (stamp seal impressions) which matched almost precisely those at Jawa. It was also noted that Nelson Glueck had published two holemouth jar forms of the common Jawa type (1951), one from Tell Um Hammad, the other from Tell Meghanieh (properly Jebel Mutawwaq), a large site on the upper wadi Zerqa, almost halfway between Um Hammad and Jawa (Betts [ed.] 1991; genre/type AA). A third sherd from Um Hammad, published in the same work, bore a row of characteristic stamp seal impressions related to the designs at Jawa.

I first visited Tell Um Hammad in 1981 and conducted two seasons of excavation at the site in 1982 and 1984. While excavating during the first season (Helms 1984a) some whole vessels of the EB IV period were brought to us by local farmers who later showed us eroded chamber tombs south of the site, at Tiwal esh-Sharqi. Several more of these tombs were cleared by the excavation team during the season of 1982 and, as a result of this, a supplementary season of tomb clearance was conducted in 1983 under the auspices, and with the financial support, of the Department of Antiquities of Jordan (Helms 1983; Betts and Helms in press). A separate season of tomb clearance was undertaken by the British Museum in 1984 (Tubb 1990). During the same season of excavations (1982) at Tell Um Hammad esh-Sharqi it became clear that there was more to Tell Um Hammad than previous exploration had indicated. The westward extent of occupation was surveyed and this showed that the original occupation area (less the cemetery of Tiwal esh-Sharqi) was at least three times larger than its initial recorded extent. A second season of excavation was fielded in 1984 (Helms 1986). There followed a number of preliminary pottery studies aimed at highlighting the significant relationship between Tell Um Hammad in the Central Jordan Valley and far off Jawa at the southeastern end of Jebel Druze (Helms 1987a, 1987b). All material from the excavations was processed in Amman and in Edinburgh, up to 1988.

PERIODS OF OCCUPATION

The following periods of occupation have been identified at Tell Um Hammad (al-Sharqi and al-Gharbi).

Chalcolithic

A few surface finds at Tell Um Hammad al-Sharqi show that this part of the site was occupied during the Chalcolithic period: i.e. in the period identified as 'Ghassul/Beersheba/Abu Hamid', dated in the first half of the fourth millennium BC. The excavations produced no stratified cultural material, although a structural stage pre-dating EB I A was isolated and might represent Chalcolithic occupation. Contemporary larger settlements of this period are known at Kataret es-Samra and Tell Qa'adan (Figs 2, 3).

EB I A

A long and continuous period of occupation has been identified for this period at Tell Um Hammad al-Sharqi. Occupation represents a large (maximum size about 16 hectares) unfortified village along the bluffs overlooking wadi Zerqa. Contemporary, smaller, villages are known at Kataret es-Samra, Tell Mafluq, and Ruweiha (Figs 2, 3). There is some evidence to suggest that Tiwal esh-Sharqi was at this time used as a cemetery; most tombs were probably located along the bluffs south of the occupation site and have long since eroded away.

EB I B

A village, similar in size to that of EB I A, was constructed on the remains of the earlier settlement. The cemetery at Tiwal esh-Sharqi continued to be used; again, most of the tombs must have been located south of the site, along the steep bluffs of wadi Zerqa. The sites of Kataret es-Samra, Tell Mafluq, and Ruweiha were also occupied during this period, as was basal Tell Abu Zighan, a large site on a high spur of the hills on the south side of wadi Zerqa. Tell Abu Zighan was to become a massively fortified settlement during EB II/III.

EB II

A much smaller settlement (about 2 hectares) was built on the ruins of the preceding village. The new occupation might have been no more than a small farmstead. The major, by now heavily fortified, occupation sites in the vicinity were Khirbet Mahruq west of the Jordan River, and Tell Abu Zighan on the east bank.

EB III

Virtually no evidence of this period was found at Tell Um Hammad. A few surface sherds suggest that the site, or rather the area, might at this time have been only sporadically occupied, perhaps in temporary field shelters. The majority of the local population must have lived in the large walled settlement at Tell Abu Zighan.

EB III/IV

By the end of EB III, or at the very beginning of EB IV (the 'transition' is not clearly established: see Betts and Helms in press), the area of Um Hammad experienced gradually intensifying resettlement. Tell Abu Zighan was still occupied at this time. Both areas of Um Hammad (al-Sharqi and al-Gharbi) show signs of the re-establishment of open villages.

EB IV

It is likely that the entire area of Um Hammad (al-Sharqi and al-Gharbi) was settled continuously throughout most, if not all, of the period (Betts and Helms in press). The cemetery was extended from the bluffs of wadi Zerqa almost to the bluffs overlooking the Jordan River in the west. Contemporary settlements and burial zones are known in the vicinity (e.g. Khirbet Abu Nijra [Fig. 3]; burials have been reported from the area along the eastern foothills, south of the Zerqa River).

MBA

A few sherds (MB II A?) have been found at the site, perhaps suggesting the use of fields at this time.

Iron Age

A fortified farmstead was built on the low 'tell' at Tell Um Hammad al-Sharqi and is dated in Iron Age II (Betts and Helms in press).

Recent

The next use of the area, apart from intermittent agricultural development, was the establishment of the Muslim cemetery, probably during the early part of this century. The cemetery is still in use today and has, for that reason, preserved the little that remains of Tell Um Hammad al-Sharqi. Most of the occupation site has been ploughed under.

TELL UM HAMMAD IN EB I A/B - EB II

The long and convoluted debate concerning the protohistorical periods of the southern Levant (i.e. the time before the Middle Bronze Age: Chalcolithic and EBA I - III) may be said to have begun with Petrie's application of his ceramic based 'sequence' dating' to the emerging archaeology of Palestine. From the beginning, and up to the present, both the debate and its archaeological sources were plagued by serious limitations such as historically (and textually) biased motives, skewed data sets, and ever shifting, often diametrically opposed notions of demographic dynamics and socio-political/economic developments which have periodically swung from one extreme to the other: from exclusively internal development to totally foreign impetus.

The major motive for exploration was to become known as 'Biblical Archaeology': that is to say, the quest for Late Bronze Age and Iron Age history in the Holy Land with Biblical texts as a guide. Of all limitations the biblical/historical inclination was, ironically and quite unintentionally, the least negative since the quest for biblical history almost invariably led to the discovery of impressive fortified settlements of the Early Bronze Age, a large number of rich tombs, and even the discovery of the preceding Chalcolithic period. For example, as early as the first decades of the 20th century, the excavations at Jericho (Sellin and Watzinger 1913) laid bare successive EBA settlements whose impressive fortifications were at that time (and later also by Garstang) regarded as the fallen walls of Joshua's divinely inspired, and therefore successful, siege. Kenyon's re-excavations in the 1950s were to correct this attribution and also to form the basis of many hypotheses regarding the first 'urban' stage in Palestine, including the term 'Proto Urban' (= EB I). Ai (et-Tell) was first excavated primarily to test the historicity of the next stage of Joshua's Israelite invasion (Marquet-Krause 1949), a prejudice that was still apparent in the later, exemplary work at the site by Callaway (1972, 1980). Similarly, the search for the 'Cities of the Plain' led to the first excavations of Teleilat Ghassul (Mallon *et al.* 1934) which was to become one of the most famous type-sites of the Chalcolithic period. Similar motives lay behind the first excavations of an EBA 'town' (or 'city') in Transjordan, at Bab edh-Dhra'.

With the ever increasing excavation of large tells in Palestine, many of them with massive EBA remains, a growing corpus of easily published ceramic evidence from EBA burials became available, in contrast to the absence of stratigraphically controlled data from occupation sites. (The material from Kenyon's excavations at the tell of O.T. Jericho did not appear in print until the 1980s.) This reliance on ceramics from mortuary contexts has skewed the evidence available for interpretation up until very recently.

One of the problems regarding notions of shifting demography in the southern Levant, including a plethora of state formation hypotheses, is that interpretations have been based predominantly on what was being reconstructed in other, more economically and, therefore, politically sophisticated regions, notably Egypt and Mesopotamia (e.g. Gordon Childe's precepts for civilization based on Mesopotamia [1950]; cf. now a revival of Childe in Kempinski 1978, 1983 and references there). Diametrically opposed views might be illustrated by two quotations regarding EB I populations and cultures. In one of his explanations of the period (the transition from the Chalcolithic period to EB II) Paul Lapp, pondering upon the apparent plurality of mostly ceramic cultural material, stated that '[t]he postulation of overlapping contemporary cultures in tiny Palestine for a century or more has never been sustained when sufficient archaeological light on a given period became available. To be sure there is overlapping, and each culture assimilates some elements from its predecessor, but there is *no good example of a predecessor persisting for an appreciable period of time alongside the newcomers with its old artifactual tradition*' (1968: 32). At the same time Lapp postulated the introduction of 'population increments', presumably merging rapidly with the indigenous folk, at least in terms of material culture. According to this view, all 'cultures' in Palestine should, therefore, have been sequential, a view which is still most commonly held (despite clear present day evidence in the region to the contrary). Such sequential 'cultures' have often been set into remarkably regular time scales (e.g. Dever on EB IV A, B, and C [1980]; see now Helms 1989). From completely the opposite standpoint, Kempinski has noted with regard to the 'urban' EBA, that '... side by side with the urban centres [there] was a local semi-nomadic population which preserved archaic [EB I B - EB II] pottery types, some of which are to be found later in the EB III/MB I [= EB IV] repertoire' (1983: 240). (We have already noted that Broshi and Gophna [1984] leave out nomadic populations altogether, regarding them as demographically insignificant.) To be fair, these statements are taken out of context and the scholars quoted here have said many other things, all of which may have some truth in them. This is, in fact, the case generally, ever since Wright's masterly first organisation of the early pottery of the Bronze Age (1937): i.e. in the absence of suitable empirical data and, until recently, only a vague idea of socio-economic factors such as tribalism and the relationship between settled and unsettled populations (i.e. both tribally organised; see now Helms 1990: Prolegomenon), all thinkers have, at one time or another, said the same thing, albeit arranged within different structures which changed from time to time, even among individual workers (e.g. Helms 1981, 1984b, 1987a, 1987b). Hanbury-Tenison , regardless of many errors in his 'explanation' of the EB I period, has recently set out a convenient summary of these views and the history of the long debate (1986: 6-32).

The new evidence from Tell Um Hammad, as well as that from Jawa (Betts [ed.] 1991), may resolve some aspects of the debate: at the very least, the new evidence might be used to set out more cogently some apparent realities and this will be attempted here (see Chapter 7). The now undoubted link in terms of both time and (partially), culture between Jawa in eastern Transjordan and Um Hammad in the central Jordan Valley allows us to expand the EB I landscape of the southern Levant to include, for the first time, parts of Syria, and thereby overcome the long-standing bias of looking only to the west of the Jordan River. The nature of the settlement at Um Hammad - an open village and not a deflated, eroded or compressed, and mostly obliterated EB I horizon, as is the case at most fortified sites of the EBA - has preserved a much deeper set of stratified depositions for the period than has been encountered before. Um Hammad (and now perhaps also Tell Shuneh North) is presently the only EB I village of this type to have been excavated (but see also the very shallow occupation at En Shadud: Braun 1985). The wealth of ceramic evidence can be used to test more meaningfully the notion of cultural plurality during the period; it can also serve to test whether there are any cultural links with the preceding Chalcolithic period, thereby helping to resolve the question of the 'transition' from one period to the other. And, finally, since the immediate area of Um Hammad is rich in EBA sites (EB I to EB IV), we may be able to shed further light on changes which took place between EB I and the so-called full, 'urban' Early Bronze Age in one important sub-region of the southern Levant. Whether, in the end, we are able to reduce these new data to a cogent demographic and socio-political-economic hypothesis such as the apparently plausible 'explanation' offered recently by Esse (1989) is debatable. An overview of the entire EBA era (up to the beginning of the Middle Bronze Age) will be essayed in the third and final volume of this series (Betts and Helms in press).

2. Stratigraphy

S. W. HELMS

NATURE OF THE EVIDENCE

Tell Um Hammad al-Sharqi has been seriously damaged in recent years by agricultural and sub-industrial activities. The former, already in progress when Glueck (1951) and, a little later, Mellaart (Leonard n.d.) surveyed the site, has removed almost all occupational material to the west of the track and canal next to the site (Figs 4 - 6) and reduced the stratified depositions in the northern parts of the tell. The latter - mostly the result of cutting access roads to the Zerqa River - has cut away all but a thin crest of the tell to the south and also destroyed or damaged many tombs of the EB IV period (Helms 1983; Tubb 1990; Betts and Helms in press). That any part of Tell Um Hammad al-Sharqi survived at all is due to the establishment of the early modern Muslim cemetery on the presently (and originally) highest remaining parts. Stones for these burials must come from the latest occupation at the site, the Iron Age (Betts and Helms in press). This much, then, is due to human agencies. Natural erosion and deflation and concomitant slippage into the Zerqa flood plain must have removed parts of the eastern flank of the occupation site. How much is hard to say, although stratigraphic analysis (see also 'Architecture') suggests that the general configuration of gullies, as they are now, is probably close to their state in the Early Bronze Age (e.g. Figs 8, 45, 46). It is, therefore, not easy to determine the original size of the various settlements at the site (but see 'Architecture'). It is also not easy to link up separate areas within the site. The deepest stratigraphy, as we noted, lies under the cemetery and on its eastern flank.

EXCAVATION AND EXPLORATION STRATEGIES

The obvious physical restraints of relative preservation dictated excavation strategy. The main objective was to recover a meaningful sample of well-stratified pottery and chipped stone for all stages of occupation and the best point at which to do this was the southeastern edge of the tell, just clear of Muslim burials (square 3 had to be abandoned because of masked burials). The main squares were extended uphill, zig-zagging to avoid burials, to reach the highest point of the preserved tell (Figs 6 - 9) and the eastern limit of the Iron Age settlement (Fig. 7).

A secondary objective was to test the horizontal extent of the various stages and to this end a series of small sondages was cut (Fig. 6: 40 - 54). Three of these sondages were expanded into small squares (i.e. 40 and 50 yielding early material; 41 predominantly later occupation [EB IV]). Observation of surface material along the slopes of wadi Zerqa produced an estimate of the presently preserved depth of occupation here (Fig. 8: dotted line).

RECORDING AND RECOVERY METHOD

The recording system was drastically, and effectively, simplified by digitizing soil depositions, the last three digits in any numerical string being dedicated to excavated soil units, the preceding digits to the square identification. No soil colours were recorded; these are, in any case, useless under varying light and humidity conditions. All pottery, chipped stone, and other 'artefactual' material encountered on sight were recovered. No environmental data were collected; none of the soil was sieved. All recovered material was shipped to Amman and stored pending analyses. The chipped stone material remained intact; the pottery assemblage had to be reduced owing to logistical restraints (see Chapter 4).

TELL UM HAMMAD AL-SHARQI: THE SQUARES

Squares 1, 2 and 4

Squares 2 and 4 represent the deepest excavations at the site and form the basis for the establishment of phases and the construction of the stratigraphic matrix. Squares 1 and 30 can be directly linked in terms of phases. Thereafter (i.e. squares 30 - 32) phases are attributed on the basis of linking structures, similar features, and the analysis of pottery (see Chapter 4), loosely in association with parallel phases in the core squares. The resultant matrix is the basis for the construction of the ceramic master typology according to stages and phases, as well as the relative frequency of occurrence of genres (see Chapter 4).

Stage 1

Phase 0

The earliest structure to be uncovered at the site is a much eroded corner of a room or house in the northwest corner of square 2 (Figs 20, 21: AA, 25a: AA). It is one brick wide in two courses and set on sterile soil, perhaps in a shallow foundation cut (Figs 20, 25a). No artefacts were found in the thin clay layers abutting this wall element. A small rounded pit (P1) was cut into sterile soil to the north; it was also devoid of diagnostic material. On the basis of a few surface finds (e.g. Fig. 252: 5) this phase is classified as 'Chalcolithic', and since it is completely isolated structurally, as well as stratigraphically, from what follows, this horizon is regarded as a stage (1) (see also Fig. 36).

Stage 2

Phases 1 - 2

It is almost impossible to separate the next two phases. Two pits (P2 and P3), or perhaps natural depressions (see below and Figs 45, 46), were slowly filled with occupational tip: they do not appear to represent dwelling areas (see especially Figs 14, 16, 25b). It may be possible to suggest that at least the southern depression was natural and that it was the result of erosion. With reference to figures 8, 45, and 46, it is noteworthy that sterile soil levels correspond with the - 282 metre contour line which not only marks the general limits of occupation at the site, but also bears a significant relation to current erosion patterns. The southern depression (P3), therefore, could easily be an ancient branch of the presently visible gully immediately to the east of the site. On the other hand, the observed contours of the depression and the fissure (Fig. 25a) could suggest a separate entity: i.e. a man-made, or at least -augmented, depression. At any rate, phases 1 - 2 currently represent the earliest stratified occupation at Tell Um Hammad which is associated with recognizable artefacts whereby phases 1 - 2 can be attributed to EB I A.

Both depressions were cut from the same level (phase 1); the lower layers in the deeper pit are also assigned to phase 1. As was noted, this pit in particular filled up slowly. This can best be seen in the west section of square 4 (Figs 16, 26a) where a series of steps in the pit (P3) surface is visible, stepping down from right to left (north-south). It is also evident (and in favour of attributing the lower levels of this pit to phase 1) that structural debris from phase 3, perhaps also phase 2, was found only at the southern end of pit P3 (Figs 14, 16). Some of this material could have come from wall BA.

Wall BA was built on layers of phase 1, a few centimetres above sterile soil (Figs 14, 20): this was established in the profile of a later pit which was cut down from phase 6 (Fig. 28b); the east and south sections of square 4 were not cut to sterile soil. Wall BA consists of six to seven courses of mudbricks and has no wall plaster; nor are there any specially treated floor surfaces at this stage.

The fissure, first noted in sterile soil in pit P3, and a second one in the north-east, continued to be isolated during excavation.

Phase 3

Walls BA, BB, and BC (the last directly on the pit fill) were built at about the same time. At least one layer abutting wall BA is earlier than those linking the wall with wall BB in the east section (Figs 20, 21): hence the attribution of the wall to phase 2 (see above). Wall BC, on the other hand, is clearly built on the pit fill (phase 2); wall BB on layers from which the northern pit (P2) was cut (especially the north section, Fig. 18).

Only wall BC was plastered on its north face, and associated with a hard clay floor (Figs 16, 26b) which was laid between the wall and a lip of the fill in pit P3.

Phase 4

The next phase is clearest in the west section (Figs 16, 17) in relation to wall BC. A re-plastering of wall BC coincides with ash-covered floor levels abutting this wall on the north side (Fig. 27). To the south the layers are rougher, perhaps suggesting an exterior area which is disturbed by pits cut from much higher up (i.e. phases 9 - 10: see below). However, good hard floor surfaces are preserved a little farther east, abutting walls BG and BA. Wall BG is cut in the east by later disturbances, as well as by the fissure; in the west it comes to an end short of the west section, perhaps suggesting a doorway there (but see phases 6 - 7 below). Elsewhere, the relation of phases is less clear (hence phase '4 - 5' in most sections). At this time a second new, well-built mudbrick wall (Figs 20 - 23: BD) was added, abutting walls BB and BC (Fig. 27). Phase 4, therefore, consists of a structural matrix, linked by wall abutments and floors connecting walls BA, BB, BC, and BG. This structural arrangement continues into the next phase.

Pit P3 is no longer in evidence, but pit P2 was still being filled at this time (Fig. 27).

Phase 5

Once again, wall BC shows this phase change (or rather, development) most clearly (Figs 16, 17, 28a). A second re-plastering, this time on the south face, is accompanied by new hard clay floors on both sides of the wall. A similar re-plastering is visible on both faces of wall BD (Figs 20 - 23). The upper parts of wall BA - as they are preserved - were still in use (Figs 14, 20, 28a), although the northern end of the wall was destroyed through the construction of the foundations for wall BM (stage 2/phase 7). Wall BB, however, is no longer part of this phase (Figs 18 and 19 show this most clearly).

Wall BG remains unchanged (see above) and the suspected doorway was still in use. Three new walls (BF, BF" and BH') were now built. Good hard clay floors linked walls BG-BC, BC-BD, and BC-BD-BF (Fig. 28a), some of them split by fissures (a new one in the west). The new walls seem to have been added later in phase 5 (e.g. Figs 16, 17, 22). Later reconstruction to the west of wall BF has removed much of the wall between squares 2 and 4 (see phase 6, etc.). It is, therefore, not known whether wall BF was originally built in two rows of bricks - as elsewhere - all across the area. The north end of square 2 was recut at a later stage (phase 6); the south end of wall BD was also cut off at that time (see below).

Phase 6

Wall BC' was built on wall BC and plastered, this time on the north face. Surfaces link wall BC with wall BG to the south (some of the earlier wall plaster of wall BC may still have been in use), and wall BF (and BH') in the north, although interrupted by a fissure (but see Fig. 28b). A little later, though still in phase 6, wall BH was added. The drawn section (Fig. 16) suggests this stratification of wall BH: however, the relationship between walls in this area is complicated and obscured by alterations in wall BF (noted above) to accommodate the new plan. It is possible that wall BH began in phase 5. This is supported by the location of wall BH' (phase 5) and the structural relationship between it and wall BH (see Chapter 3). Wall BH was provided with a narrow opening (Fig. 28b) and the 'apsidal' space behind the reduced wall BF was filled with black ash.

Elsewhere wall BF abuts a new wall (BE) and shares common surfaces. Wall BE, in turn, is set into wall BD (Figs 20, 21) in the east and has hard clay floors to the north (Fig. 28b). Wall BD itself is still there, but probably served as a bench, curb, or low terrace wall at this stage (e.g. Figs 20 - 23). Surfaces from the bases of walls BF and BE run over the top of wall BA. There is a disturbance in the southern part of square 4 (Figs 14, 15), most likely caused by subsidence owing to the proximity of the Zerqa river marl cliffs to the east. Two small rounded pits were cut from phase 6: one west of wall BF; another east of wall BD (Figs 16, 28b).

Phase 7

From this point on, square 1, and a little later also square 30, can be linked into the stratigraphic matrix. Wall BC' was probably abandoned by this time, although a wall stub could still have been visible on the surface (Figs 16, 17, 29). The section shows what might be a pit (hardly a robber trench) cut during phase 7, or from phase 8 on the southern side of wall BC'. Wall BG, on the other hand, may still have been in use, although this is by no means obvious because of the soil shifts in this area as well as later disturbances. A re-plastering of its north face belongs to the previous phase, but was still in use at the beginning of phase 7. A series of hard clay floors linked wall BG, the upper part of wall BC', wall BF (although interrupted by the fissure there), and two new walls, BF' and BM (see especially Figs 23, 29). Wall BF' was set against wall BF in the west and cut into wall BM in the east. Three vessels, two of them complete, were found on the floor next to wall BF' (Figs 176: 1, 195: 3). (The incomplete vessel was an 'Esdraelon' ware bowl crushed flat on the floor and not reconstructable.) Wall BF continues to be part of the structural matrix, although the 'absidal' wall BH/BH' has gone, but for a stub of wall BH which was left as a divider in the new passage created by wall BJ. Floors link wall BF with the lowest course of this new, curved wall (BJ) which, in turn, is linked to wall BI by later layers in phase 7 (north section). Wall BI was built earlier, at the beginning of phase 7, originally as a reinforcement of wall BE (Figs 18, 19, 29). A bin (BE') was made in the corner of walls BE/BF (a vessel *in situ* [Fig. 224: 13]). The eastern face of wall BE was re-plastered at this time and heavy ash layers on a clay floor (with a complete jar set into a pit: Fig. 197: 4) can be traced along the north and east sections, abutting wall BE there about half way up its preserved height (Figs 20, 21). This level corresponds to a series of floors running off wall BE and over the stump of wall BD to the south. Some of these floors abut a new wall element (BL) which was built at the beginning of phase 7, and then run up against wall BM which was built early in phase 7. Wall BM was built partly on a stone-lined foundation cut and plastered on both sides (Figs 14, 15) and hard floors continue westwards, to be cut by the fissure noted above, as well as by the depression which was filled in phases 9 - 10 (Fig. 15). An internal, diagonal wall (BN) was made at the same time as wall BM (Figs 14, 15, 20, 21). A number of ground stone objects (Fig. 29: S27, 28; see also Chapter 6) was found on the floors between walls BJ and BF, two parts of the same vessel on either side of wall BH.

Wall BF continues southwards into square 1 (Figs 14, 15, 29), as does a projection of wall BJ (BJ'). No reliable layers of phase 7 were excavated here.

Phase 8

Wall BF is now widened (wall BO) in the south and this modified structural element can be traced into square 1 (Fig. 30) where it and wall BF are partly obscured by a later pit (Figs 14, 15). However, both wall elements were preserved to a slightly higher level within square 1 (see also the west section of square 4: Figs 16, 17). To the north, in squares 2 and 4, wall BJ continues in use (as does its southward projection, BJ'), but is widened by the addition of wall element BJ". Similarly, wall BE continues in use for a time and is then overbuilt with a new wall (BK) following a collapse of the earlier wall (clearest in the north section, Fig. 18). Floors to the east are, therefore, at a higher level in this phase. The large pit (stage 3/phases 11 - 12: see below) was cut down along the south face of wall BK (and the later wall, BP: Figs 21, 22). Remnants of phase 8 layers were recovered against wall BM farther south, and within wall BM and also against wall BN. The disturbance and infilling of phases 9 - 10 obscures layers to the west of wall BM and south of wall BF' (south section: Fig. 15). Wall BF' was still in use (Fig. 23).

Phase 9

At this time the southern part of the excavated area was disturbed by a pit, depression or erosion (as was noted above: Figs 14 - 17, 31) over most of square 4, and these deposits were later cut away by the large pit of stage 3/phases 11 - 12. Also at this time, the inner face of wall BJ collapsed and was reconstructed on the same line (Fig. 30: wall BQ). This reconstruction, however, was not a major event since the eastern face of wall BJ/BQ (north section, Fig. 18) appears to have a plaster surface which continues through the phase change. Similarly, the west section (Figs 16, 17) shows that the southern face of wall BJ still stood (and was also plastered up to the end of phase 8). This change also saw the reconstruction of the line of wall BK with a much wider wall (BP) and a short cross wall (BP') dividing the passage between wall BQ and BP (Fig. 31). The relation of wall BF with BP is shown in the internal section (Fig. 24): i.e. only the upper parts of wall BF may have been in use in this area of squares 2 - 4 (but see below: wall BF in the south section). Floors to the east of wall BP slope down towards the northeast corner of square 2 (partly due to the earlier wall debris between phases 7 and 9, partly because of subsidence: the fissure is clearest in the south section, Fig. 20), and up against the eastern section. The southern face of wall BP, in the east section, marks the line of the big pit (stage 3/phases 11 - 12, see below).

The southern part of wall BF and its addition (BO) are cut by the pit of stage 3 (west section square 4, Figs 16, 17). However, in square 1 (Figs 14, 15, 31) layers attributed to phase 10 abutted these walls (internally: the walls are cut by the later pit of phase 20 [Iron Age] in this section) and, therefore, these walls must have been in use during phase 9.

Phase 10

Little can be deduced regarding this phase. The depression in the south was filled up completely (Figs 14, 17), while occupation debris continued to accumulate above wall BJ in square 1, between walls BQ and BP (over wall BP'), and northeast of wall BP. The end of phase 10 (and stage 2) is marked by the total inward collapse of wall BQ and the reconstruction of the line BJ/BQ by wall BR (Figs 16, 31, 51; see also Chapter 3). The entire northern area (square 2) is now sealed by a hard mud floor of phase 13 and its newly aligned structures. Elsewhere, the big pit (phases 11 - 12) has obliterated most of the last phases of stage 2.

Stage 3

Phases 11 - 12

The cuts for the big pit can be seen in the west section (Figs 16, 17), descending from the southern edge of wall BJ and projected upwards in the area disturbed by the Iron Age pit (phase 20). In the east section (Figs 20, 21) the cut runs along the south face of wall BP and the upper part of wall BK. The base of the pit crossed just above wall BL, rises over wall BM and crossed wall BN at the south section, continuing westward into square 1 (Figs 14, 15) to where it is again obscured by another Iron Age pit (phase 20). For most of the excavated area, the pit is sealed by the floor of phase 13 and its walls. This floor is disrupted just above wall BP in the north (Figs 18, 19), and half way along the south section (Figs 14, 15): this is partly the result of erosion, but also of recutting in phase 15. The reconstructed outline of the pit is given in Fig. 32 (see also Chapter 3: Fig. 45).

The fill in the pit was divided into two phases (11/12) on the basis of deposition type. The earliest fill (phase 11) consists of hard clay and brown soils; the later (phase 12) of grey and black ash lenses. Both sets of depositions slope down to the east (Figs 12, 14, 16, 20, 22 - 4, 32).

Phase 13

The floor and its walls (CA, CB) are clearest in the west section of squares 2 and 4 (Figs 16, 17) where the floor slopes up from the south section to wall CA, then down over the north end of the big pit, rising again over the projected stump of wall BQ (obscured by the Iron Age pit of phase 20), and continuing over the hard, levelled mudbrick collapse in the structure defined by wall BQ/BR(BJ), to wall CB. From there it goes on to the north section, on top of the west return of wall BR. Wall CA is two bricks high; only two half bricks of wall CB are preserved in square 2. The floor and wall CB are covered in ashy deposits which continue eastwards in the north section (Figs 18, 19) where they merge indistinguishably with topsoil. In the south (Figs 14, 15) the floor could be traced southward for about 2.00 metres, sloping up and then merging with topsoil. Wall elements of phase 15 appear to have been cut into depositions of phase 13 in some cases. The floor of this phase was cleared all over square 1 and partly in square 30. Walls CA and CE were two bricks high and made a return northeastward in the north section (Figs 12, 16, 32). Wall CC was preserved up to more than five bricks (Figs 12, 14), the floor in all cases running beneath and against the walls. The same ashy deposits as in the other squares were found on the floor, the upper ash layers over the walls, in some cases. Several stone objects were found *in situ* on the floor in the corner of the square made by wall CC. Wall CC has a southwest return with a small doorway in square 30 (Figs 12, 32).

There (in square 30) an upper floor of phase 13 was the lowest excavated surface. Two holemouth jars, one complete, were found on this floor, just inside the entrance (Figs 164: 1, 165: 2). The upper floor of phase 13 was traced almost to the end of square 30 (at the base of later pits cut from phases 15 and 16) and is probably the same surface which was found in association with wall element CF in square 31 (see below).

Stage 4

Phase 14

This phase represents layers over phase 13 which are not associated with any structures: they form a non-structural, occupational interface between two major stages (3 and 4). None of this phase is visible in the east and north sections where the uppermost preserved layers belong to the big pit of stage 3 (Figs 18 - 21). Elsewhere the phase is represented in the west section of squares 2 and 4 (Figs 16, 17), the south section (Figs 14, 15), the west section of squares 1 and 30 (Figs 12, 13), and in the internal section between squares 2 and 4 (Fig. 22). One feature - a clay lined oven - may belong to phase 14 (Fig. 33, square 4).

Phases 15 - 16

These phases constitute a new structural stage (4). The stage is represented only in the west, north, and south sections of squares 2 and 4 (Figs 14 - 19, 22, 23), and includes walls DC', DD, DD'''. The phase is best represented in squares 1 and 30, especially in the west section of square 1 (Figs 12, 13). There, walls DA and DB (about four to six courses of mudbricks) clearly show two phases (phases 15, 16). Walls DA, DA' (a bench?, see Chapter 3: Fig. 41), DB, DC, DC', DC", and DG, as well as DH in square 30 (= its northwest return in square 31, see below) all belong to stage 4, although the surfaces between them were not well-defined and, particularly in the eastern excavated area, were very much disturbed and almost indistinguishable from topsoil, as was noted above. Floor levels between walls DA, DB, DG, and DH were clearest (see especially the west section, Figs 12, 13). These floors were set on ashy deposits, some of which represent phase 14, others the upper layers of phase 13. Phase 16 represents a re-occupation (new floors) after many of the walls had partly fallen down, or had been eroded. The new floors were set on decomposed and eroded mudbrick. A number of floor features was preserved (Fig. 33: two holemouth jars were set into shallow pits (pot. c. 2105, 7843 [Figs 168: 7; 167: 1, respectively]) beside several stone-lined, heavily charred hearths and a number of small, round pits (see also squares 31, 32 below and Chapter 3).

Phases 17 - 19

A new building stage ('EB IV': see also Betts and Helms in press) consists of walls EA and EB in square 30 (Figs 12, 13) which were set into the upper layers of the previous stage (4/15-16). Two superimposed floors with occupational debris were preserved on the north side of wall EA (phase 17 and 18, respectively). To the south lay a thick layer of grey ash which could not be divided into separate phases (hence phases 17 - 18 in that part of the section). A stone lined 'hearth' (EC), however, belongs to phase 17 (west section of square 30) and can be related to similar installations in squares 31 and 32 (e.g. Fig. 34: ED and EF/EG). Phase 18 is the latest phase to be distinguished in squares 1 and 30. Phase 20 consists of pits cut during the Iron Age.

Square 31

The 'hearth' (EP/EG) links up with square 32. The lowest, earliest levels excavated here may belong to phase 10 (Figs 10, 11, lower left): a new surface was reached in one corner of the square, beneath a hard mud floor. This floor is associated with the stone footings of a much-disturbed wall (Fig. 32: CF) running north-south. The wall is cut by a later disturbance. This wall and its occupation layers (including the floor) probably belong to phase 13 and may, cautiously, be related to walls CG, CH, and CI in the adjacent square 32 and, through them, with the walls in the rest of the excavated area (e.g. walls CA-CD). Most of the layers (including the wall) were disturbed by a series of pits cut from layers attributed to phase 15. The next, relatively firm stratigraphic attribution is in phase 15: i.e. wall DI, in the southeast corner (Figs 10, 11, 33) is the same as wall DH in square 30 (Figs 12, 13). More pits, mostly attributed to phase 19, have disrupted all of the stratigraphy from this point on. Only the 'hearth' (Fig. 34: EF) could be used as a link with square 32 and belongs to phases 17 - 18.

Square 32

The earliest occupation layers and structures probably belong to phase 13 and consist of the tops of several mudbrick walls, one of which (CG) appears in the illustrated section (Figs 10, 11). Wall CG (Fig. 32) was found 3.50 metres north where it was overbuilt by the later wall, DJ (phases 15 - 16). A single brick appeared below the corner of walls DJ and DK, and might represent the continuation of the earlier wall. The brick, however, is out of line with the wall. A crosswall (CI) bonded into an upper addition of wall CG, was found running east-west (Fig. 32).

Walls DJ and DK were set directly on top of the previous structure and a series of floors was reached in the area bounded by the angle made by these walls. They probably all belong to phases 15 - 16.

A number of depositions (phases 17 - 18) covered the walls DJ and DK. A stone-paved, heavily charred area (Fig. 34: EG) belongs to phase 17 and may continue in use into phase 18. (The same feature was found in square 31 [Fig. 34: EF] and can be related to similar paved areas elsewhere [Fig. 34: ED, EC; see also Figs 12, 13], as was noted above.) An indistinct surface covered these 'hearths' and ran up to a wide wall of which only the southern face was excavated. This wall (FA) and its associated occupation debris belongs to phase 19, the latest in this area (Figs 10, 11, 34).

The stratigraphic matrix of walls is summarised in Fig. 36, and demonstrates the unbroken occupation at the site throughout stage 2 (i.e. EB I A; see also Chapter 3), a distinct break between stages 2 and 3, as well as a break between stages 3 and 4.

Square 60

An irregular area was cleared of top soil in order to retrieve a plan of stone structures visible on the surface. These belong to the uppermost ancient settlement at the site and can be related to other remains on the main tell (Fig. 7). The overall plan suggests a fortified structure of the Iron Age (II), perhaps with a gate or tower at the northwestern end. Square 60 revealed several structural phases and will be published separately (Betts and Helms in press). It was found that Iron Age occupation layers were set directly on the eroded remains of the 'EB IV' period of phases 17 - 19 (i.e. clearest at the junction of squares 60 and 32 [Fig. 9]). The pits (phase 20) in the eastern area of the excavations (see above) must belong to this stage and represent extramural activities at the site during the Iron Age.

Sondage 40

This marks the northern limit of recent earth moving disturbances (Fig. 6). A bulldozer cut had revealed a long profile which obviously contained occupational debris. This profile was cut back and excavated. Most of the depositions belong to an early stage of 'EB IV' or late 'EB III' (Betts and Helms in press). However, beneath this (Fig. 37) the pattern of occupation with regard to 'periodization' was the same as on the main tell: that is to say, phases 1 - 10, 11 - 13, and 14 - 16 could be identified on the basis of typological analysis. Sterile soil lay at about -280.5 metres, more or less the same as in the main tell (not counting the two pits, or depressions) and also in sondage 50 (-281.7 metres; see below and Fig. 35).

Sondage 41

This sondage was cut into the side of a gully, half way between sondage 40 and the main tell (Fig. 6). Its depositions (about 1.80 metres deep) belong mostly to the 'EB IV' period (Betts and Helms in press). Only one shallow layer could be associated with stage 3/phases 11 - 13. These lay on sterile soil at AH -284.454 metres, over 2.00 metres lower than elsewhere in this area. It was not certain whether these depositions were *in situ*, or represent erosion.

Sondage 50

This area of Tell Um Hammad al-Sharqi was almost completely destroyed by earth moving equipment before the excavations. Most of the area along the modern surfaced road (Fig. 6) was affected, from sondage 40 southwards. The modern cemetery saved the main tell. Areas east of the road (and sondage 50) were also destroyed to make access roads to the Zerqa River floodplain. For some reason, a low mound was left next to the road, and this contained undisturbed occupation layers.

Depth of occupation (less modern tip, Fig. 35: 1) is about 1.50 metres, down to sterile soil. Within this matrix, only two major phases could be recognized: a series of floors with thick ashy depositions (Fig. 35: 7, 8 floors, 3 - 9 depositions); and an ash-filled pit cut from and into sterile soil (Fig. 35: south section) and sealed by compacted clay layers (9 - 11). Very little material was recovered from the lower phase; the upper probably corresponds to phases 7 - 9 (see Chapter 4 for evidence; Fig. 132).

Other sondages (Fig. 6)

Both of the soundings originally made by Mellaart (Leonard n.d.) were cut back and examined. Sondage 44, at the summit of the main tell, produced Iron Age material, then mid-'EB IV', followed by EB II and EB I B: i.e. roughly corresponding to phases 20, 17 - 18, stage 4/phases 14 - 16, and stage 3/phases 13, respectively. Sondage 45, nearby, was cut across a stone wall visible on the surface in 1984 (part of the Iron Age complex: see Fig. 7). The wall was two courses high. No stratified remains were found. Sondage 43, the second of Mellaart's probes, revealed a floor surface which had been cut into sterile soil and pottery which can be broadly related to stage 2 (i.e. EB I A). Nothing later was found here and this tallies with the projected limits of occupation, the level of sterile soil lying at about the -282 metre contour line.

Sondages 46 and 47 delineate limits of occupation along the bluffs overlooking wadi Zerqa to the east. They were cut across the -282 metre contour line. Similarly, Sondage 48 delineated the preserved limits of occupation in the area east of Sondage 50 (see above). All that remained here was a shallow lip of undisturbed occupation; the rest had been cut away by bulldozers. Sondages 49, 51, and 52 to the north of the main tell again confirmed the limit of occupation along the -282 metre contour line. Most of the material recovered from these cuts belongs to stages 2 and 3, with some 'EB IV' material. No diagnostic material of EB II (or of the Iron Age) was found anywhere but on the main tell.

Sondages 53 and 54 were cut at the northern and southern limits of the presently (1984) preserved surface sherd scatter of the main 'tell' along wadi Zerqa (Fig. 5: S43, S54).

STRATIGRAPHIC MATRIX

The stratigraphic matrix is illustrated in figure 36 and summarized below by stages and phases (St/ph) with a list of depositional numbers. Unstratified depositions are labelled '++++'; '[' = no diagnostic pottery.

Square 1

St/ph	Depositions
2/8	88 87 86 84 83 82 81 65 [90 89 = BJ/BF/BO]
2/9	[
2/10	[
3/11	80 55
3/12	79 78 77 76 75 61
3/13	74 73 72 71 70 69 66 63 60 59 57 56 54 53 52 41 39 35
4/14	44 34 33 32
4/15	68 67 46 43 30 29 27 26 25 24 23 20 17 14 10
4/16	[
-/17	[
-/18	[
-/19	[
-/20	85 48 47 18 15 12 11
++++	65 64 62 58 51 50 49 45 42 38 37 36 31 28 22 19 16 13 [9-1 = 4/16--/18]

Square 2

St/ph	Depositions
1/0	[
2/1	160 159 158
2/2	157 156 155
2/3	154
2/4	153 116
2/5	152 151 148 147
2/6	150 149 146 145 142 139 137 136 134 115 106
2/7	144 143 141 138 133 132 131 129 120 119 117 114 113 112 111

	110 109 103 102 100 98 97 91 86 65 57 53
2/8	135 128 127 125 122 121 85 84 76 67 66 61
2/9	123 118 105 104 99 93 92 90 89 88 87 83 81 80 74 73 72 71 70
	64 6362 60 59 58 55 54 52 51 50
2/10	76 75
3/11	126 124 107 96 95 77 56 49 48 47 41 38 33 32 31 30 22 13
3/12	45 44 43
3/13	101 40 36 35 34 27 26 21
4/14	[
4/15	69 68 20 19 18 15
4/16	[
-/17	[
-/18	[
-/19	[
-/20	46 39 37 29 28
++++	79 25 24 23 17 16 14 [11 10-1 topsoil]

Square 4

St/ph	Depositions
1/0	130 129
2/1	128 127 126 66 65 64 61 60 59 58 56 54 53 49
2/2	125
2/3	124 121 104
2/4	123 118 117 114 111 110 109 108 102 86 46 45
2/5	120 116 113 107 105 101 100 99 98 97 57 52 44 42 41
2/6	122 119 106 96 95 85 84 83 82 81 55
2/7	115 112 94 93 92 91 80 79 78 63 62 50 40
2/8	90 89
2/9	[
2/10	51 48 47 43
3/11	87 77 76 75 74 73 72 71 70 69 68 67 38 37 36 35 34 33 32 29 25 24 23 22
	21 20 19 18 17 16 15 13 12
3/12	88
3/13	39 14 11
4/4	[
4/15	30 28 27 9 8 7 5 3 2 1 0
4/16	[
-/17	[
-/18	[
-/19	[
-/20	26
++++	10 4

Square 30

St/ph	Depositions
3/13	20 19 18 17
4/14	16 15
4/15	13 12 9 8 7

| 4/16 | 10 11 14 |
| -/17 | 6 5 [4 3 2 1] |

Square 31

St/ph	Depositions
3/13	21 20 19 18 16
4/14	15 14 13 12
4/15-16	11 10 9 8
-/17-18	4 3 2
-/19	7 6 5 1

Square 32

St/ph	Depositions
4/[14] 16	21 20 19
-/17	18 17 16 15 13 12
-/18	7 6 5
-/19	4 3 2 [1]

3. Architecture

S. W. HELMS

INTRODUCTION

Area excavation was not feasible at Tell Um Hammad al-Sharqi, although enough architectural evidence was recovered to relate structures in some of the major building stages to attested building types in the southern Levant between the 'Chalcolithic' period and EB II, between about the mid-fourth and the first half of the third millennium BC. In the first place, the settlement was not nucleated but open; a settlement which spread without 'urban' constraints along the bluffs overlooking wadi Zerqa. There is, therefore, a certain amount of horizontal stratifications (see also Chapter 2, 'Nature of the evidence') which could only be tested by surface collection of diagnostic artefacts (for the most part pottery) and a series of small sondages. Secondly, it is estimated that well over 50 per cent of the ancient settlement has been destroyed, either by erosion and deflation or by modern agricultural and industrial development. The former processes are particularly relevant along the bluffs; the latter in the area to the west of the modern surfaced road and immediately to the north of the main 'tell' (Figs 4 - 6). In addition to that, a cemetery was established over most of the main 'tell' (Fig. 6) which made excavations there impossible, apart from small sondages. However, the cemetery did serve to protect and, therefore, preserve this part of the site.

The word 'architecture' is probably too ambitious a term for the structures of the fourth millennium BC at Tell Um Hammad: we are dealing with non-nucleated, vernacular building which is not planned, in most cases. This, together with the physical limitations already cited, seriously restricts interpretation which, furthermore, can only be attempted with a limited number of stages. On the other hand, the early settlements at the site probably looked rather like the present day villages nearby (i.e. that on Tell Mintah [Fig. 3]) which are likewise unplanned in any formal sense. The original settlement to the south of Tell Deir Alla (now mostly destroyed) might serve as an ethno-archaeological parallel for some of the characteristic building styles in stage 2 which can be traced far beyond the EB I A landscape of Palestine. The buildings at Deir Alla depart from the architectural norm of the Jordan Valley in being rounded with 'beehive' roofs. Local intelligence has it that the architect was a

Syrian; similar structures are common in northern Syria, along the Euphrates river.

The exposure of the earliest stage (1) is too limited to warrant much discussion except to note that the structure had a square corner. Similarly, architectural remains after stage 4 are almost non-existent in the areas available to clearance at Um Hammad al-Sharqi. The situation regarding later occupation (EB IV) is better in the west, at Um Hammad al-Gharbi (Betts and Helms in press). Iron Age (II) remains are most substantial, although much disrupted by stone robbing for the cemetery.

STAGES 1 TO 4 (CHALCOLITHIC - EB I - EB II)

The four building stages represent clearly separated programmes, at least within the excavated areas. However, this should not be regarded as reflecting a global sequence at the site: i.e. that these stages are absolutely consecutive (or contiguous) throughout the southern Levant, within the sub-region of the Jordan Valley (Helms 1987a; in press), or even at Tell Um Hammad itself.

Stage 1 (Chalcolithic)

A small number of surface finds suggests that a part (or parts) of Tell Um Hammad al-Sharqi was (were) occupied during the later Chalcolithic period (= Ghassul/Beersheba/Abu Hamid, etc.). Stratigraphically, this occupation is preserved in square 2 (Fig. 25) as two wall fragments (AA) and some depositions which, however, yielded no diagnostic artefacts. It is impossible to say more about the nature of this settlement other than that it included at least one mudbrick structure with one square corner. The nearby sites of Kataret es-Samra (Leonard 1983; especially 1989) and Tell Qa`adan (Ibrahim *et al.* 1976; Kafafi 1982: Pls 33, 34) must have been relatively small open villages: the occupation at Um Hammad might have been similar or, minimally, simply a field station ('jiftlik') related to its nearest neighbour, Kataret es-Samra. (See also stage 4 below and the suggestion of a similarly reduced occupation in EB III, though at that time in relation to fortified settlements, not large open villages.)

Stage 2 (EB I A)

It has already been shown (Chapter 2: cf. Fig. 36) that stage 2, as it was in one small sector of the overall settlement, represents a continuous building or, rather, rebuilding programme. In general terms, the stage can be divided into two interrelated episodes, during the first of which the area becomes more congested with time, up to the construction of an 'industrial' installation in phase 9 (Fig. 28b). The second episode begins with the construction of large rectangular units with rounded corners in phase 7 (Fig. 29). This change may, of course, be illusory; it might only be a localized event. In both episodes rectangular and rounded features occur.

Stage 2/7 might be reconstructed as part of a complex of two large rectangular units with rounded corners, separated by straight walls and narrow passages with internal domestic features such as the bin (Figs 29: BE'; 38: a reconstruction). Such units are now well attested in EB I (A) or 'late Chalcolithic' contexts at Byblos (Fig. 42a; Dunand 1973: Fig. 141, *passim*) and the Levantine coast (Fig. 42b; Sidon Dakerman: Saidah 1979), Tell Halif (Seger *et al.* 1990: 2 - 9, Fig. 3), Tell Hesi (O'Connell and Ross 1980: 75), En Shadud and Yiftahel (Braun 1985; 1989a: Figs 4, Upper Register; 5; 6), Meser (Dothan 1957: Fig. 2; see also Braun 1989), Megiddo (Engberg and Shipton 1934: Fig. 2; Loud 1948), Rosh ha-Niqra (Helms 1976a: Fig. 8.3), and Beth Shan (Fitzgerald 1934, 1935), among others west of the Jordan River (see Braun 1989). In the Jordan Valley (see also Hanbury-Tenison 1986: 183ff.) very similar building styles have been found at 'Proto Urban' (= mostly EB I B on the tell, though some tombs are earlier) Jericho (Kenyon 1981), Abu Habil (de Contenson 1960: Fig. 18c), Tell Shuneh North (Mellaart 1962: 132 [Leonard n.d.]: a circular structure with a central pillar base; Gustavson-Gaube 1985, 1986), Tel Teo (Eisenberg 1989: Figs 2B, 6) and even upper Tuleilat Ghassul (Hennessy 1969: Pl. IVb), while related styles (oval rather than rectilinear with rounded corners) have been found in the Jordanian uplands (upper wadi Zerqa) at Tell Mutawwaq (Fig. 42c; Hanbury-Tenison 1986: Fig. 18, bottom; 1989b), and on the Yarmuk River at Pithat ha-Yarmuk (Epstein 1985a), likewise associated with EB I (A) material. Farther east (and north) elongated oval units occur in the later phases of stage I at Jawa (Fig. 42d; Betts [ed.] 1991) and have been reported at a number of sites in Syria (see also Figs 1, 2), notably Khirbet Umbachi and Hebariyeh (Dubertret and Dunand 1954/5: Figs 1, 2, 4; Braemer p.c.: though not EB I A but either EB I B or, more likely, EB IV), at Leboué (Maqdissi 1984; Braemer p.c.: either EB I B or later), and farther north still at Mumasakhin (Nasrallah 1938; Hanbury-Tenison 1986: Fig. 18; but see now Maqdissi [1988, 1990] for an EB IV date). Braun, in his study of such structures, includes an examples from as far afield as Serabit el-Khadim in Sinai (1989a: *passim*; see also *idem*: Fig. 1).

Regarding Jawa, this style of building - that is to say, a single elongated rectangular (or oval) unit with rounded corners - should be separated from the earlier, much more dominant building type there which is sub-circular and can be regarded as a development, or local translation, of a different architectural form altogether: a form which stems from a multi-celled (rectilinear?) unit comprising a main chamber with attached storage facilities (Fig. 43; Betts [ed.] 1991).

This 'architectural' evidence in EB I A is still very vague and incomplete and further speculation is risky. It may, however, be hypothesized that we are dealing with two levels of building programmes: (i) the more formal layout of the units typified by the examples from Byblos and Tel Halif whose distribution currently appears to be along the Levantine coast to the Hebron foothills (and farther south), into the Yezre'el and Jordan valleys; and (ii) a less formal variant - a derivation, an imitation or, simply, an expediency - which appears to exist in the Jordanian/Syrian uplands bordering on the steppe in the east (*badiyat al-sham*). Whether a further distinction in terms of settlement type and economy (perhaps even social structure) is appropriate at this stage is arguable. It might be suggested that the less formal building style (i.e. the stones as bases for rounded or oval tents) represents a steppic adaptation within a more pastorally orientated economy. This is supported, to some extent, by the apparently more complex nature of settlements such as 'éneolithique supérieur' Byblos and EB I (A) Tell Halif, both of which were already in some form of commercial contact with proto-dynastic Egypt (see especially Seger *et al.* 1990). Whether we can see further divisions in such terms is also arguable and probably premature: i.e. (i) a 'proto urban' (to use Kenyon's original term for this period) series of settlements such as Tell Halif and Byblos in the west, and Jawa and other sites in southern Syria in the northeast: two quite separate developments; (ii) 'villages' such as En Shadud, Yiftahel, Tel Teo, Shuneh North, and Tell Um Hammad al-Sharqi (among others) where cultural/economic contact exists with both west and northeast (i.e. the incipient thalassocracy of Byblos and whatever lies behind EB I A Jawa in southern Syria); and (iii) less permanent settlements in the Jordanian/Syrian uplands and steppe lands such as Jebel Mutawwaq (see also Fig. 2) and later EB I A Jawa. At Jawa the simpler, oval units definitely post-date (though still within EB I A) the more formal structures (Betts [ed.] 1991).

The original extent of stage 2 at Um Hammad is calculated to be about 16 hectares (Figs 5, 7). The 'transition' to the next stage (3) is apparently abrupt and absolute, following a collapse of the structures preserved in square 2. The area was excavated, or had eroded (see Chapter 2), to make a large depression (pit) which was filled (phases 11, 12) and then sealed by the floors of the next building programme. But, as was noted above, this total break may be a local phenomenon, both within the site and the sub-region. Pottery analysis, though showing a break in the sequence, indicates some significant technological and stylistic continuity (see Chapter 4).

Stage 3 (EB I B)

The new building programme can be regarded as short-lived: that is to say, the evidence to hand shows only one phase of construction and only two possible sub-phases of occupation; it revealed none of the continuous (therefore lengthy) development of the previous stage. Furthermore, there is a notable difference in the layout of the new settlement (in the excavated areas).

Building units are rectilinear in plan, with square corners, each unit separate from the next (but for those in squares 31, 32 which, however, is an uncertain reconstruction). (See also Dunand [1973: Fig. 146] and the 'transition' to 'proto-urbaine', from rounded to rectilinear plans, as well as Eisenberg [1989: Figs 2: A, B; 6].) Only one doorway with a mudbrick threshold was identified (Fig. 40: square 30) and this was located centrally in the short side of a unit. Internal features consist of a rounded bin (in *pisé*) against a wall just inside this entrance and a stone which may have served as a baseplate for a roof support.

In contrast to the previous stage, these apparently regular units can be compared with the 'architecture' of the later Chalcolithic period of Palestine. By themselves, the proportions and layout of these structures are probably not significantly unique to make such a comparison: but, given the remarkable stylistic relationship of the associated pottery (see also Chapter 4, repertoire R6) with the so-called 'northern Chalcolithic' (e.g. Jawlan/Golan: cf. Dayan 1969; Epstein 1978; also Abu Hamid: *Abu Hamid* 1988; Dollfus and Kafafi n.d.), the comparison becomes compelling. It also poses problems of interpretation (see Chapters 4 and 7).

The almost standard Chalcolithic house in the Jawlan/Golan, as well as in the Jordan Valley, is rectangular and similarly proportioned (Fig. 44a; Epstein 1978: Figs 1, 2a; Pella: McNicoll *et al.* 1982: Pl. 6; Abu Hamid: *Abu Hamid* 1988: Figs 16, 18, 20; Ghassul: Mallon *et al.* 1934: Figs 12, 65; Pl. 15; Shiqmim: Levy [ed.] 1987: Fig. 15.2; among others). Therefore, in architectural (and ceramic) terms, we have what amounts to an anachronistic cultural interlude which could be derived from (or be related to) the indigenous Palestinian/southwestern Syrian Chalcolithic following an EB I A stage at Tell Um Hammad. This chronological (or rather, typologically determinable) sequence is supported by the appearance of 'EB I B' pottery forms in stage 3 which are typical of northern Jordanian and southwestern Syrian repertoires (e.g. 'grain-wash', etc.: see Chapter 4, repertoire R5).

As was noted above, occupation appears to be short, at least in the area where stage 3 was exposed, and perhaps to be perceived as a short interlude. The occupation layers of stage 3 are disturbed by pitting, accompanied by new cultural material (stage 4/14). The extent of the settlement during stage 3 is estimated to be about 16 hectares (Figs 5, 7), roughly the same as the previous stage. If the density of settlement was uniform in comparison with stage 2, the population density would have been slighter than before.

Stage 4 (EB II)

The preserved remains were fragmentary and too close to topsoil to be reliable in terms of plausible reconstruction. Only a general impression of this stage can be presented.

Following the pitting and limited domestic use of apparently open spaces, two interrelated phases of building followed (phases 15, 16). Little can be made of these in architectural terms but for the area in squares 1 to 4.

It is possible to assemble the various wall elements and the many domestic features within and without them, in order to produce a coherent plan of at least one unit which must have been part of a more extensive complex, possibly including a courtyard (Fig. 41). This unit consists of a rectangular space entered on one broad side. There is a bench-like structure against the long wall opposite the door, an internal buttress or partial room divider, a pit in the floor, two stone-lined hearths, and a large holemouth jar set into a pit just inside the door. (Compare the placement of holemouth jars inside a door in stage 3.) A similar configuration is apparent in the square to the east, although the remains of walls there are too fugitive for reconstruction; as was noted above, this area may have been a courtyard.

The type of building is immediately recognisable as the standard EB II/III Palestinian 'house', which is sometimes called the 'Arad house' (Fig. 44b; Amiran 1978: *passim*). The cultural material associated with stage 4 supports this (see Chapter 4). The extent of the settlement is estimated to have been about 2 hectares (Fig. 7): much smaller than in the previous two stages. We are probably dealing with a farmstead ('jiftlik') rather than a village at this stage of the site's settlement history, much like the latest occupation at Um Hammad al-Sharqi in the Iron Age, although that settlement appears to have been fortified (Fig. 7; Betts and Helms in press). The major contemporary (EB II+), nucleated and heavily fortified settlements are on the hillsides on either side of the Jordan River: at Khirbet Mahruq next to the mouth of wadi Far'ah (Yeivin [Z.] 1977: 766 - 68), at Tell Abu Zighan (Tell Handaquq South) at the mouth of wadi Zerqa (Yassine *et al.* 1988; Helms in press), at Tell es-Sa'idiyah (Tubb and Dorrell 1991: though perhaps not fortified in EB II), and at Tell Handaquq North (Mabry 1989).

The settlement of stage 4 appears to have been abandoned: cf. Figure 12 and wall DA whose upper mudbrick courses were eroded and spread on either side of the wall and subsequently (some centuries later) incorporated in the reoccupation of the site in EB IV. There are a few sherds of the EB III period (e.g. in genre 59 [Chapter 4]) at Um Hammad al-Sharqi which suggest an occupation of some kind although no associated structures were found during the excavations. By EB III the site may have been used as a much reduced field station rather like the modern tin huts at the edge of irrigated fields belonging to tenant farmers from Deir Alla, Mu`addi, and other large villages in the area.

CONSTRUCTION METHODS

The excavations were too limited to provide any evidence for roof supports (i.e. base plates for uprights, etc.: but, perhaps, for stage 3 [Fig. 40]). Wall construction consists of the standard variations in mudbrick bonding and coursing. With the possible exception of wall AA in stage 1 and wall BM in stage 2, both of which were built on or in shallow foundation tenches (wall BM partly on a trench lined with stones), all walls were set on level ground without special preparation or footings. Where wall lines were rebuilt (e.g. the sequence of walls BE, BK, BP [Figs 18, 19]), the new brickwork was set directly on the old, though sometimes slightly offset, occasionally leaving the earlier line as a footing above the currently used floor surfaces. Wall bonding consists mostly of abutment (e.g. walls BC-BA [Fig. 26b]), or insertion by cutting into the existing brickwork of the earlier wall (e.g. walls BF'-BM [Fig. 30]). The most intricate bonding preserved is that of walls BE-BD (Figs 20, 21, 28a, b). Existing walls were reused as benches, curbs, or low terrace walls (e.g. wall BD) or cut down to serve as sills (e.g. wall BF [Figs 22, 28, 29]). The two bins (Figs 29: BE'; 32) were made of *pisé* and set against walls; the presence of limestone grinding [?] bowls and stone pounders (Chapter 6: Catalogue Nos 27, 28; Fig. 29) may indicate that the bins were used for internal grain storage. The complete pottery vessel (genre 54, Fig. 224: 13), found inside the bin, may have served as a measure, rather as has been suggested, with various elaborations, for the ubiquitous and more or less contemporary bevelled rim bowls of Syro-Mesopotamia (e.g. Millard 1988; Beale 1978; Chazan and Lehner 1990; the last on evidence from both Mesopotamia and Egypt).

Brickwork consists of a mixture of form-made bricks and more randomly formed ones (see Table 1). Some walls may even have been made in a variation of the *pisé* process: i.e. layers of clay laid in shallow, horizontal courses and allowed to dry before the application of the next course. Brick laying included the combination of half and full bricks in a row (Figs 47, 48: BB, BF', BG, BF'), double rows of bricks (Figs 47, 48: BF, BC, BM) including the rounded corners whose smooth curve was made by plastering, and the addition of half bricks along one side (Figs 47, 48: BD, BJ', BF/BO; 50). Wall BD (Fig. 49) is unique in its structural complexity. It consists of standard brickwork with non-standard (i.e. larger) vertical bricks on alternate sets of courses inside and out. Wall BD was also provided with an inserted, round clay element which may have acted as an engaged column (Fig. 49): a unique feature in Palestinian 'architecture' of the Early Bronze Age (and the preceding Chalcolithic); a feature more at home in Syro-Mesopotamia (e.g. decorated, monumental engaged columns in the Eanna precinct at Uruk IVb [Roaf 1990: 62]). Most walls were plastered (i.e. mud, and sometimes also a form of lime plaster) down to, and some short distance along, the adjacent floors. A few wall elements of stage 4 were built on stone foundations without foundation trenches.

Brick dimensions (when they could be determined) were as follows:

Table 1. Brick dimensions

BA	0.40-0.50 x 0.30 x 0.05-0.10 metres
BB	0.40 x 0.28-0.30 x 0.06-0.09 metres
BC	0.35-0.45 x 0.22-0.30 x 0.12-0.14 metres
BC'	0.40-0.46 x ? x 0.10 metres
BD	0.54-0.56 x 0.30-0.36 x 0.08-0.10 metres (horiz.)
	0.40 x 0.38 x 0.16-0.20 metres (vert.)
BE	0.43-0.52 x 0.28-0.30 x 0.06-0.09 metres
BE'	*pisé* (about 0.15 metres wide)
BF	0.52-0.56 x 30-0.46 x 0.05-0.09 metres
BF'	0.32-0.40 x 0.28-0.35 x av. 0.08 metres
BF"	0.52 x 0.40-0.50 x av. 0.09 metres
BG	0.55 x 0.36-0.45 x 0.08-0.12 metres
BH	0.40-0.48 x 0.65-0.38 x ? metres
BH'	?
BI	? (pisé?)
BJ	0.25-0.45 x 0.35-0.40 x 0.06-0.10 metres
BJ'	0.40-0.58 x 0.20-0.39 x 0.06-0.10 metres
BJ"	0.40 x ? x 0.10 metres
BK	? x 0.40 x 0.06-0.09 metres
BL	? x ? x av. 0.08 metres
BM	av. 0.40 x 0.32 x 0.09 metres
BN	? x ? x 0.04-0.08 metres
BO	av. 0.18-0.20 x 0.36-0.56 x 0.06-0.08 metres

BP	? x ? x 0.06-0.08 metres
BP'	? x 0.04 x ? metres
BQ	? x 0.36 x 0.06-0.08 metres
BR	? x 0.40 x 0.04-0.08 metres
CA	0.50 x 0.36-0.42 x 0.08-0.10 metres
CB	0.25 x 0.42 x 0.08-0.10 metres
CC	0.50 x 0.42 x 0.08-0.10 metres
CD	0.25 x 0.42 x 0.08-0.10 metres
CE	0.50 x 0.42 x 0.08-0.10 metres
CF	stone footings only
CG	?
CH	?
CI	?
EA	? x 0.32 x 0.10 metres

Dimensions (Fig. 52) in stages 2 and 3 (EB I A and EB I B) give the impression that those of stage 3 are more uniform (i.e. 0.50 x 0.40 x 0.10 metres) and half bricks can be clearly distinguished: they were deliberately made. Wall BD apart, the bricks of stage 2 are more randomly formed, although a 'standard' form could be suggested: 0.40-0.50 x 0.30-0.40 x 0.10 metres, similar to the more regular form in stage 3. Dimensions for bricks in stage 4 could not be reliably determined.

4. The Pottery Typology

S.W. HELMS

INTRODUCTION

All diagnostic shapes, including decorated body sherds and bases (plain and decorated), were recorded in the field during the work seasons of 1982 and 1984. These total 8221 entries over the two seasons of excavations. 5543 entries make up the data base for all periods represented at Tell Um Hammad (i.e. EB I, II, III[?], IV, and the Iron Age). 2678 entries comprised undiagnostic body sherds which were discarded in Amman after further analysis. To the overall 'diagnostic' sherd yield should be added 71 complete, or nearly complete, vessels from the Tombs at Tiwal esh-Sharqi (Helms 1983; not counting the 65 vessels found by Tubb [1990]), 103 diagnostic forms from the tomb shafts, and 104 forms from the surface (EB IV) of Tell Um Hammad al-Gharbi (1983). (The later material, including that from the Iron Age, will appear in Betts and Helms in press.) The breakdown of diagnostic material is as follows: EB I/II/[III] 3108; EB IV (and perhaps also some MB II A) 2135; Iron Age 300 (total 5543). With the additional EB IV material the total 'sample' is 8564.

For the earlier range (predominantly EB I, with some EB II and perhaps III) the 3108 diagnostic sherds included material from unstratified depositions (either badly excavated, mixed batches, or material derived from section cleaning and, occasionally, willful destruction and accidents), reducing the meaningful sample even further. This left 2710 entries consisting of 152 unclassified forms or body sherds, and 2558 entries which could be grouped in apparently meaningful entities, or 'genres'. 1379 of these are illustrated in the catalogue, the illustrated 'genres' (Table 3) being cross-referenced to the main data base (2558 entries). Selection from the master typology was made in 1988 by N. Vaillant for further technological and other analyses.

The annotated catalogue appears before the pottery figures in the illustration section: figure number, field catalogue number (C), provenance (Prov: last three digits = deposition number; preceding digits = square number), stage and phase designation (St/ph: see Chapter 2), genre designation (G: see below), and description (see also 'Abbreviations'). The pottery typology is arranged as follows:

(i) The 'Nature of the sample' sets out the physical nature of the sample, its limitations, and the cross-referenced 'genre'/phase data (Tables 2 and 4).

(ii) 'Analysis of genres', including unclassified forms, is accompanied by the comparative study for each genre or unclassified forms using some of the major excavated and published material to hand for Palestine, Transjordan, Lebanon, and Syria. There are important limitations in this last regard. Very few of the major and extensively excavated 'tell' sites have been fully published, particularly with regard to the Chalcolithic/EB I period: the best to hand are Abu Matar/wadi Zoumeili, Jericho, Ai (et-Tell), Arad, and Tell el-Far'ah near Nablus; the rest is limited to ceramic material illustrated in preliminary reports or occasional diagnostic syntheses. The bulk of material on which 'EB I' typologies (and appended hypotheses) have been based comes from tombs and is, therefore, limited (see also 'Introduction'). The 'tell' material often comes from deflated, eroded, compressed, or seriously disturbed contexts, the result of disturbance due to massive reconstruction during EB II/III (even MB II). Similarly, potentially useful comparative material from surface surveys (of which those of Nelson Glueck are still the most exemplary) is limited and necessarily biased, often inadequately illustrated and whole regions of the Levant and the inland zones (i.e. southern Syria) are almost unrepresented, or presented in inappropriate ways (e.g. Hanbury-Tenison 1986; cf. a review of Hanbury-Tenison: Braun 1987). With the probable exception of Tell Shuneh North, no site currently under excavation has the depth of deposition regarding the EB I period comparable to Tell Um Hammad. Thus, much of what is presented here has to be *a priori* internal, with all of the limitations such a constraint implies; it is not the objective here to set Um Hammad up as a type site and then to interpret the whole of the ancient Levant on that basis. On the other hand, the site's location at the centre of the Jordan Valley and at an important cross-roads (wadi Zerqa/wadi Far'ah, etc.) does make Um Hammad a potentially fruitful node in the study of fourth millennium village economies and culture(s). This is borne out by the far-ranging ceramic comparanda, the Jawa connection quite apart. The site, therefore, lies at, or near, the centre of the land in which the apparently complicated change from village to so-called 'walled town' (or 'urbanism', even 'city state' and 'secondary state') occurred towards the end of the fourth millennium, or a little later.

(iii) The analysis of genres and other groupings and their comparanda is followed by a brief survey and correlation of related sites in the immediate region of Tell Um Hammad: e.g. Ruweiha,

Mafluq, Kataret es-Samra, Qa'adan, Tell Abu Zighan, Tell Handaquq North, Tell es-Sa'idiyah al-Tahta, and so forth.

(iv) 'Distribution of genres' discusses the various histograms which may reflect subdivision of genres as well as an interrelationship between genres (i.e. replacement, displacement, imitation, new imports, new inventions, etc.).

(v) This is followed by the reconstruction of repertoires ('Repertoires') and an attempt to localize these in the EB I landscape of Palestine, Transjordan, the coastal Levant, and inland southern Syria.

(vi) A correlation with previous work at the site (Glueck 1951; Mellaart [Leonard n.d.]; Tubb 1990) follows.

(vii) 'Special features' summarizes stamp seal impressions, 'reed' impressions, decorated handles, and 'potter's marks'.

(viii) The section concludes with a brief summary of results.

NATURE OF THE SAMPLE

A total of 8564 sherds and some complete forms was recorded in the excavations at Tell Um Hammad (al-Sharqi and al-Gharbi), including diagnostic body sherds and bases. Of this total 1889 came from Tell Um Hammad al-Sharqi and 1530 from Tell Um Hammad al-Gharbi (Fig. 4). The total number of 'classifiable' forms (genres) is as follows:

Table 2. Total number of 'classifiable' forms (genres)

TUH Sharqi:	(i)	EB I-II (squares 1-4,30-2, 50)	= 2989
	(ii)	EB I-II (squares 40-1)	= 119
	(iii)	EB IV	= 624
	(iv)	Iron Age	= 130
			-----
		total	3862

(EB IV genres total = 2019: i.e. TUH Gharbi = 1395; TUH Sharqi = 624)

The core typology was calculated on the basis of the material from category (i) in Table , and is represented by Table (frequency of occurrence of genres; see also Figs 129-31), in which the total sherd count is 2558 for squares 1-4, 30-1, and 431 for square 50, i.e. those which can be considered as 'stratified'. 1379 sherds and forms are illustrated in the catalogue.

Table 3. Frequency of genres within phases of squares 1, 2, 3, 30-31

gn	1	2	3	4	5	6	7	8	9	10	11	12	13	14	15	t
1	4	1	3	3	--	3	2	--	4	1	4	1	2	--	1	29
2	1	2	5	4	2	15	15	1	12	1	11	1	2	1	5	78
3	3	--	3	2	--	--	2	--	--	--	--	--	--	--	1	11
4	5	4	2	4	3	4	6	--	6	--	3	--	--	--	--	37
5	--	--	--	--	--	2	1	--	--	--	6	--	--	--	--	9
6	--	--	--	--	--	2	6	1	2	2	1	1	2	--	--	17
7	--	--	--	--	--	--	--	--	1	--	--	--	1	--	3	5
8	--	--	--	--	--	--	--	--	--	1	1	--	--	--	--	2
9	--	--	--	--	--	--	--	--	--	--	5	5	--	--	--	10
10	--	--	--	--	--	--	--	--	--	--	27	15	2	2	10	56
11	--	--	--	--	--	--	--	--	--	--	37	7	3	--	2	49
12	--	--	--	--	--	--	--	--	--	--	5	3	--	--	--	8
13	--	--	--	--	--	--	--	--	--	--	--	9	--	--	--	9
14	--	--	--	--	--	--	--	--	--	--	3	--	--	1	7	11
15	--	--	--	--	--	--	--	--	--	--	6	3	1	2	13	25
16	38	40	15	23	13	27	14	10	18	1	33	9	3	1	3	248
17	--	--	--	--	--	--	--	--	--	--	19	3	--	--	5	27
18	--	--	--	--	--	--	--	--	--	--	1	1	--	--	1	3
19	21	0	4	5	1	4	15	4	12	3	11	6	1	--	2	99
20	1	--	--	3	--	2	7	--	1	--	4	--	--	--	1	19
21	--	--	--	--	2	7	4	4	--	--	2	--	--	--	--	20
22	2	10	--	4	--	5	6	4	5	--	10	3	1	--	3	53
23	--	--	--	--	--	--	--	--	--	--	4	--	--	1	1	7
24	--	--	2	--	--	--	1	--	1	--	--	--	--	--	--	4
25	--	--	1	2	2	--	1	--	--	--	1	--	1	--	1	9
26	--	--	--	--	--	--	--	--	1	1	1	--	--	--	--	3
27	--	--	--	--	--	--	--	--	--	--	4	3	--	--	2	9
28	--	--	--	--	--	--	--	--	--	--	5	--	1	--	--	6
29	--	--	--	--	--	--	--	--	--	--	4	2	--	--	1	7
30	--	2	1	--	--	--	--	--	--	--	7	3	--	2	1	16
31	9	11	5	4	8	6	6	2	5	2	10	5	--	--	3	76
32	--	1	--	--	1	--	2	--	--	1	6	5	--	--	1	17
33	--	--	--	--	--	--	--	--	--	--	28	22	1	--	4	55
34	11	7	1	2	1	5	5	1	1	2	3	1	1	1	1	43
35	18	8	4	4	2	12	13	6	11	5	66	17	5	2	9	182
36	25	12	4	3	2	8	11	5	10	5	13	3	--	--	--	101
37	4	1	--	1	1	--	1	--	--	--	--	--	1	--	1	10
38	2	1	1	--	--	--	1	--	--	--	--	--	--	--	--	5
39	8	2	--	--	--	1	--	--	1	--	6	--	1	--	2	21
40	1	1	--	--	--	--	--	--	--	--	--	--	--	--	--	2
41	--	--	1	--	--	--	1	--	1	--	6	3	--	1	--	13
42	--	--	--	--	--	--	--	--	1	--	--	--	--	--	--	1
43	--	--	--	--	--	--	--	--	--	--	1	--	1	--	--	2
44	--	--	--	--	--	--	--	--	--	--	1	7	--	--	1	9
45	22	10	2	17	14	9	22	3	9	1	1	--	--	--	1	111
46	--	1	--	--	--	1	--	--	--	--	--	--	--	--	--	2
47	--	--	1	1	--	--	1	--	--	--	1	--	--	--	--	4
48	15	14	6	9	5	5	7	2	2	1	--	--	--	--	2	68

																Total
49	1	--	1	--	1	--	1	--	--	--	--	--	--	--	--	4
50	--	--	--	--	--	--	--	--	--	--	11	4	2	2	1	20
51	--	--	--	--	--	--	--	--	--	--	--	2	--	--	--	2
52	3	2	--	1	--	2	3	--	2	--	2	4	--	--	--	19
53	7	8	3	4	--	--	2	--	2	--	1	--	--	--	--	27
54	10	4	--	2	2	4	11	4	11	--	9	4	--	1	--	62
55	2	--	--	--	--	--	--	--	--	--	7	-	--	--	--	9
56	--	--	--	1	1	1	--	1	1	1	1	1	--	--	--	8
57	2	--	--	--	--	--	--	--	--	--	--	--	--	--	--	2
58	--	--	--	--	--	--	--	--	--	--	1	--	2	--	3	6
59	--	--	--	--	--	--	--	--	--	--	1	--	2	2	4	9
60	--	--	--	--	--	--	--	--	--	--	--	--	--	--	1	1
61	--	--	--	1	--	2	1	--	--	1	4	--	1	--	--	10
62	--	--	--	--	--	--	--	--	--	--	--	--	--	--	2	2
63	--	--	--	--	--	--	--	--	--	--	1	3	--	--	--	4
64	4	--	--	--	1	1	1	--	2	--	13	--	--	1	--	23
65	2	6	1	--	--	1	2	1	1	1	7	1	1	--	--	24
66	2	2	1	2	--	3	1	1	--	--	--	--	--	--	1	13
67	10	5	3	1	2	4	9	1	2	2	3	--	1	--	--	43
68	--	--	--	1	1	--	--	2	--	--	--	--	--	--	--	4
69	--	--	--	--	1	2	--	--	1	--	1	2	--	--	--	7
70	--	--	--	--	--	1	--	--	4	1	3	--	--	--	1	10
71	--	--	--	--	--	--	--	2	--	--	1	--	--	--	--	3
72	3	2	1	--	1	2	2	--	--	2	9	6	3	1	--	32
73	--	--	--	--	--	--	--	--	--	--	2	2	1	--	1	6
74	--	--	--	--	--	--	--	--	--	--	36	8	4	1	6	55
75	--	--	--	--	--	--	--	--	--	--	1	1	3	1	1	7
76	--	--	--	--	--	--	--	--	--	--	--	1	1	3	--	5
77	[see genres 1/2, 2]															
78	--	--	--	--	--	--	--	--	--	--	--	--	2	2	4	8
79	4	1	--	2	1	--	3	--	11	1	9	--	2	--	--	34
80	[= genre 16]															
81	3	--	--	4	2	3	4	--	6	6	13	--	1	--	1	43
82	--	--	--	--	--	--	--	--	1	1	1	--	--	--	1	4
83	--	--	--	--	--	--	--	--	--	--	4	--	4	--	1	9
84	--	--	--	--	--	--	--	--	--	--	178	83	15	1	26	303
85	2	3	2	3	1	2	5	2	7	--	2	1	--	--	--	30
86	1	2	5	4	--	2	4	2	1	1	--	1	--	--	--	23
87	--	2	2	3	2	1	4	--	1	2	1	1	--	--	--	19
88	--	--	1	1	--	1	3	--	--	1	7	2	1	--	1	18
89	--	--	1	1	--	1	--	2	2	6	1	--	--	--	--	14
90	--	--	--	--	--	1	1	--	--	--	1	--	--	--	--	3
91	--	--	--	--	--	--	--	--	--	--	--	--	--	--	5	5
92	--	--	--	--	--	--	--	--	--	--	2	1	--	--	--	3
93	--	--	--	--	--	--	--	--	--	--	3	--	--	--	--	3
94	--	--	--	--	--	--	--	--	--	--	--	--	--	--	1	1
95	2	6	1	--	--	1	--	--	3	--	--	--	--	--	--	13

gn   248 181 83 122 74 153 207 61 163 53 702 257 76 29 149

Total gn = 2558

The nature of the sample is set out in Table 4 in which the excavated volume per phase is set against the total number of recognizable genres (v/gn). It appears that this 'coefficient' is almost constant for stage 2 (phases 1-10) which, on the whole, represents occupational debris within structures (see also Chapter 2: 'Stratigraphy'). Stage 3, on the other hand, is predominantly represented by a large pit (phases 11 and 12), and only a very shallow occupation above that: the 'coefficient' (v/gn) for phases 11 + 12 comes close to that of stage 2. Stage 4 was very fragmentary.

Table 4. Area and volume excavated per phase in squares 1-4, 30-2

St	ph	area	depth	volume (v)	gen/ph	v/gn
2	1	40.03	0.43	17.21	248	0.07
	2	50.23	0.26	13.06	181	0.07
	3	50.23	0.09	4.52	83	0.05
	4	50.23	0.22	11.05	122	0.09
	5	44.43	0.13	5.78	74	0.08 [av.= 0.07]
	6	50.23	0.19	9.54	153	0.06
	7	66.43	0.23	5.28	207	0.07
	8	66.43	0.09	5.98	61	0.10
	9	66.43	0.18	1.96	163	0.07
	10	66.43	0.04	2.66	53	0.05
3	11	37.23	0.22	8.19	702	0.01*
	12	50.19	0.73	36.64	257	0.14* [11+12v/gn=0.05]
	13	90.15	0.24	21.64	76	0.28*
4	14	30.18	0.17	5.13	29	0.18*
	15	78.32	0.27	21.15	149	0.14*

Totals				189.79	2558	
phase 16		78.32	0.26	20.36 [no genres related]		
EB IV + Iron Age				3.25		
Total				213.40		
Total (actual soil volume)				213.22		

ANALYSIS OF GENRES AND COMPARATIVE STUDY

Introduction

The EB I pottery collected by Glueck (1951), Mellaart (Leonard n.d.) and Tubb (1990) is included in the analysis (see 'Correlation with previous work'; Figs 268-9). Mellaart found more complete vessels than the present project was able to do, despite much more excavations and intensive surface collection. The complete forms are used in the reconstruction of forms throughout. References to the pottery catalogue take the form TUH199: 1-18 (i.e. Tell Um Hammad [al-Sharqi] Figure 199: 1-18).

The pottery catalogue is arranged according to forms (holemouth jars, jars, bowls, etc.: each according to open or closed forms), set out in the relative chronological order in which they appear at Um Hammad (cf. Figs 129-31).

Each genre is described in general and an attempt is made to reconstruct the complete shapes of typical vessels using the parallels cited in the comparative study which is appended to each genre designation, as well as the complete forms from Mellaart's collection (Leonard n.d.). The rim forms are analysed in detail (Figs 53-128). The comparative study strives, in the first instance, to explore the possibility of proto-types in the various Chalcolithic assemblages of Palestine (predominantly those from the Beersheba area which, as we have noted, are the most comprehensively published to date [Commenge-Pellerin 1987], now superseding de Contenson's earlier analysis of 1956). This is followed by parallels from known EB I contexts in Palestine, Transjordan, and southern Syria. A limited number of parallels is given from sites farther afield: notably Jawa, Hama, Byblos, the Amuq area, and Habuba Kabira. Unclassified vessels are discussed in the sequence in which they appear in the catalogue.

Genre 1: holemouth jars (Figs 139 - 41; Pl. 4: 1)

These large, heavy holemouth jars are all 'bag-shaped': that is to say, their widest diameter can be reconstructed as being below their vertical centre point. In most cases, the necks are slightly 'bowed' near the rim. Particular rim shape apart, the genre divides into two main variants: a tall jar (Fig. 53: a); and a more squat form (Fig. 53: b). Most vessels have distinctive slurring or fine grooving on, along, and below the rim (Fig. 139: 1-3), as well as bands of impressed, incised, or moulded decoration on the neck and above the shoulder. About 50 per cent of the vessels is painted with a red pigment (or slip?) which is applied thickly on and along the rim and neck, and allowed to trickle (hence 'trickle-' or 'splash paint') over the body, including the handles, in irregular near-vertical stripes which run down to the base in many cases (Figs 139, 237, 239, 243, 246, 247, and 249; Pl. 4: 1, 2, 3). ('Trickle paint' = clear stripes; 'splash paint' = random patterns: often the two are intermingled.) Many vessels are also given a characteristic surface treatment: they are scored in diagonal or near-vertical patterns all over the external and, sometimes, also the internal surfaces. This patterning is called 'finger streaking' throughout the analysis and appears in several genres; it is one of the criteria, including 'trickle paint' and 'splash paint', for determining repertoires on the basis of production technique and decoration.

Although no complete forms have been found (but see Fig. 53: a, b), it may be assumed that all of the vessels had flat bases (see Figs 245-9). It has been found elsewhere that rim diameters of holemouth jars tend to be equal to those of the bases (see also holemouth jars [genre A] at Jawa in Betts [ed.] 1991: Figs 101, 110-16). Rim forms (Fig. 54) vary from plain, rounded (a, c, d) or rounded, slightly recessed, or rolled along the lip (b), to 'pointed' (h), with intermediate variants being internally recessed (e), distinctly 'bowed' (f), or bulbous (g).

Available ledge handles in the typology can be matched to genre 1 according to fabric and decoration: however, it is not established whether genre 1 ever had ledge-, or any other form of handles. If it did, they would probably appear just above the waist of the vessels (see also bag-shaped jars: e.g. genre 16, Figs 174-86).

The relative crudeness and certain features such as the slightly 'bowed' shoulders, pedestal bases (see Figs 245-6: genre 85), the painted patterns, and impressed bands of decoration on the shoulder cannot be recognized in currently published assemblages of EB I A pottery in Palestine: rather, these features suggest a relationship with Chalcolithic forms which, in some cases, can be seen to stem from Late Neolithic assemblages. These early origins may be illustrated in forms from Jericho (Kenyon and Holland 1983: Fig. 1: 13), and Arad (Amiran 1978: Pls 3: 13; 6: 1, 2 - from Stratum V). Chalcolithic examples come from wadi Rabah (Kaplan 1958: Fig. 5: 7), Abu Zureiq (Anati 1971: Fig. 19: 7), Abu Habil (de Contenson 1960: Figs 25: 8; 26: 9), Abu Hamid (*Abu Hamid* 1988: Fig. 17 [?]), Teleilat Ghassul (Hennessy 1969: Fig. 9a: 1 [?]; 1982: Fig. 2: 4, 5), Horvat Beter (Dothan 1959a: Figs 8: 22 = TUH141: 6, 7; 14: 9), and Sinai (Oren and Gilead 1981: Fig. 8: 18 [?]).

EB I A examples are known at Beth Shan (Fitzgerald 1935: Pl. I: 10), Tell Shuneh North (Gustavson-Gaube 1985: Fig. 9: 23, 27; 1986: Figs 10: 28a-29b; 15: 56e-56f), En Shadud (Braun 1985: Fig. 15: 10 [?]) Ruweiha (Fig. 256: 1), and Kataret es-Samra (Leonard 1983: Fig. 9: 11) - the latter two sites lie within a few kilometres of Um Hammad. Some crude holemouth jars at Jawa may be related to genre 1 (Betts [ed.] 1991: Fig. 120: 129, 130).

These vessels are probably too simple and crude to yield up any meaningful parallels beyond Palestine. However, similar simple shapes do occur at Habuba Kabira (Sürenhagen 1978: Tab. 24: 7 [?]).

Genre 1-2: holemouth jars (Figs 137; 237: 1; Pl. 4: 3)

Only two examples of this 'genre' (a hybrid: i.e. features from genre 1 and genre 2) have been found, of which only one is sufficiently complete to allow reconstruction (Fig. 53: c). The reconstruction is based on characteristics of genres 1 and 2 (Figs 53 and 56; Betts [ed.] 1991: genre/type AA). Genre 1-2 shares attributes from both of these genres: it is slightly 'bowed' in the neck, slurred or finely grooved on, along, and below the rim, its external surface is 'finger streaked', and it is painted with the red 'trickle-' or 'splash paint' style like genre 1. On the other hand, the rim form (Fig. 55) and the four pushed up rounded lug handles above the shoulder are directly parallelled in genre 2 (e.g. Figs 57: c; 143-6). One of the handles was stamped before being fired (see 'Special features').

The only parallels - not close ones - come from Arad (Amiran 1978: Pl. 3: 1, 2 [Str. V]).

Genre 2: holemouth jars (Figs 143 - 6; cf. Pl. 5: 2 [Jawa])

These holemouth jars may be reconstructed in two basic shapes and sizes: a tall form (Fig. 56: a); and a shorter one (Fig. 56: b). The genre finds its closest parallel - a precise one - at early Jawa (Betts [ed.] 1991: Figs 110-16) where the same size-shape distinction was found (*idem*: Fig. 101). The vessels are all made of the same fabric, and most - if not all - have four rounded or slightly pointed, pushed up lug handles at, or near, the rim. Most vessels also have a band of incised, impressed or slashed decoration near the rim, usually on the line of the handles. All vessels probably had flat bases. Rim forms (Fig. 57) vary from plain rounded (a), to in rolled (g), with variants of bulbous rims which can be pointed (b), plain (c), pronounced (d), recessed (e), or bevelled (f). Many of these vessels show signs of having been in, or near, fires suggesting that they may have been used as cooking pots. Closely related genres appear later in the ceramic sequence (e.g. Fig. 151: genres 5 and Fig. 154: genre 9, and perhaps also Fig. 154: 11).

The characteristic lug handles near the rim of holemouth jars appears to be a feature of Palestinian pottery that can be traced back to the Late Neolithic: e.g. Abu Zureiq (Anati 1971: Fig. 35: 19); Ghrubba (Mellaart 1956: Fig. 4: 36); Afula (Sukenik 1948: Pl. III: 3 [?], 15a, 16a); Arad (Amiran 1978; Pls 3: 1, 11 [Str. V]); and Jericho (Kenyon and Holland 1983: Figs 2: 16; 7: 1-7; 34: 11; 35: 4; 40: 25; 42: 19, 20; 77: 3, 4; 120: 15; 124: 7; 125: 29). Farther afield the type can be recognized at Byblos (Dunand 1973: Figs 23: 26165; 24: 23686 ['néol. anc.' = examples from Chalcolithic/EB I {A} Afula]).

Precise parallels in EB I A contexts, apart from genre/type AA at Jawa (see above), come from Kataret es-Samra (Leonard 1983: Fig. 9: 7-8), Tell Handaquq North (Mabry 1989), and the wadi Zerqa/Jerash region (Hanbury-Tenison 1987), including Jebel Mutawwaq (see also Glueck 1951: Pl. 163: 9 [Meghaniyeh = Mutawwaq]). A developed form of the genre is known in EB I B contexts in the Jordan Valley (see genres 5 and 9 below). A parallel for the developed forms comes from a Chalcolithic context in Sinai (Oren and Gilead 1981: Fig. 7: 2).

Genre 3: holemouth jars (Fig. 147)

These holemouth jars are characterised by their distinctive decoration along the rim: i.e. a band of impressed patterns which might be described as 'reed' impressed (see similar decoration below; see also 'Special features'). Reconstruction suggests forms similar to most holemouth jars at the site (Fig. 58: a), including the common flat bases. Rim forms vary a great deal (Fig. 59): most are variants of bulbous rims (a-c), plain (a), slightly recessed (b), or bevelled. No handles could be associated with genre 3.

Apart from the parallels with regard to the 'reed' impressed decoration at Tell el-Far'ah and Megiddo (see below), similar forms occur at Tell Shuneh North (Gustavson-Gaube 1985: Figs 10: 30; 12: 43; 1986: Figs 12: 38, 39a; 13: 45 [?]).

Genre 4: holemouth jars (Figs 148 - 50)

Relatively high shouldered, these holemouth jars are related to genre 3 through their impressed decorative bands on some variants (e.g. Figs 148: 1, 2; 149: 1; 150: 8), but characterized by their rim form and stance. Most vessels have very high shouldered profiles; rims are often scalloped or internally recessed. Many examples have impressed 'wavy' patterns along the lip, varying from low regularly spaced indentations (e.g. Fig. 148: 3, 4) to pronounced 'wavy' rims (e.g. Figs 149: 9; 150: 2, 4, 7). Reconstruction is uncertain on the basis of the internal evidence from the site. Two possible variants are, therefore, presented (Fig. 58: b): a low, squat bowl like form, and/or a taller one which is closer to the 'normal' holemouth jars at the site, and elsewhere. But for one variant (Fig. 60: a), which is plain and rounded, rims consist of variants of externally recessed forms: (b) internally bevelled with a lip, (c) rilled and recessed, (d) rilled and bevelled, (e) plain recessed, (f) recessed with an upper lip, (g) recessed-bevelled, slightly bulbous with a low vertical lip, and (h) bevelled bulbous with a low everted 'wavy' lip.

The wavy lip in some examples may be related to similar features in Chalcolithic vessels at Tell Fara South (Macdonald 1932: Pl. XL: 68) and Afula (Sukenik 1948: Pl. III: 2). The form occurs at Ghrubba (Mellaart 1956: Fig. 4: 31-33), Jericho (Kenyon and Holland 1983: Fig.

147: 11 - 'unstratified'), N.T. Jericho (Pritchard 1958: Pl. 56: 11, 13, 20 [EB I A]), Ai (Callaway 1972: Fig. 15: 9 [though in EB I B context]), En Shadud (Braun 1985: Figs 16: 4-14 [especially no. 14]; 15: 5, 9), Tell Shuneh North (Gustavson-Gaube 1985: Fig. 11: 38 [?]), and Tell el-Far'ah (de Vaux and Steve 1947: Fig. 7: 14 [?]; 1948, Figs 5: 8, 9; 6: 4).

Genre 5: holemouth jars (Fig. 151: 1 - 8)

This genre, as was noted above, is a development of genre 2 and can be reconstructed in much the same way as its parent genre (Fig. 58: c, d) in a smaller and a larger shape. Rim forms (Fig. 61) vary from plain bulbous (a) to bulbous, slightly externally recessed (c), with elongated bulbous forms between the two. All examples have pushed up rounded lug handles near, or at, the rim, the form of the handle being more rounded than in genre 2. It is likely that, as in genre 2, there were four of these small, almost vestigial handles. For slightly later parallels see genre 9 below.

Genre 6: holemouth jars (Figs 151: 9 - 10; 152: 1 - 7; 220: 3 - 7)

As was the case with genre 4, these vessels could be classified as either holemouth jars, or as bowls; they have relatively wide mouths and reconstruction is not certain: i.e. they could be low forms (Fig. 62: a). Most vessels are decorated with a band of incised or impressed patterns on the shoulder or below the rim. Rim forms (Figs 63, 64) are all everted on an in sloping neck, varying from rounded-bevelled (a, c), rilled or recessed (b), to bulbous (e), or ridged (d). No bases could be associated with this genre, although it is likely that these would be flat.

Genre 6 can be recognized in Palestinian Chalcolithic repertoires: e.g. Abu Matar (Commenge-Pellerin 1987: Figs 47: 8 [?]; 25: 72; 23: 3); Shiqmim (Levy [ed.] 1987: Fig. 12.7: 3); Teleilat Ghassul (Hennessy 1969: Fig. 6: 9 [?]; Mallon *et al.* 1934: Fig. 45 [?]); Abu Habil (de Contenson 1960: Figs 23: 10 [?]; 25: 7); and Rasm Harbush in the Jawlan (Epstein 1978: Fig. 12: top centre).

EB I (A) examples come from Jawa (Betts [ed.] 1991: Fig. 117: 94), Tell el-Far'ah (de Vaux and Steve 1947: Fig. 2: 4 [?]), Jericho (Kenyon and Holland 1983: Fig. 133: 25 [?]), N.T. Jericho (Pritchard 1958: Pl. 56: 8 [?]), Kataret es-Samra (Leonard 1983: Fig. 9: 22 [?]), and Arqub edh-Dhahr (Parr 1956: Fig. 14: 123).

Genre 7: holemouth jars (Fig. 153: 1 - 8)

Holemouth jars with high shoulders (Fig. 62: b), probably flat bases, no decoration, apparently no handles, and rolled or down turned rims. Rim forms (Fig. 65) are rolled (a, b) and slightly internally recessed or bevelled, or bevelled with a rounded, down pointing internal lip (c).

There appear to be no Chalcolithic fore-runners for this genre in the Chalcolithic period of Palestine. EB I (A) examples are known at Jawa (Betts [ed.] 1991: genre/type AF, Figs 117: 88 [form]; 120: 137-40), N.T. Jericho (Pritchard 1958: Pls 56: 1, 2, 4, 21; 57: 2 [the last related to genre 4?], Tell el-Far'ah (de Vaux and Steve 1947: Fig. 7: 13 [?]; de Vaux 1955: Figs 4: 9 [?]; 5: 18 [?]; 13: 8 [?], 37, 42 [? into EB II]; 14: 18 [?], 34), Tell Handaquq North (Mabry 1989), En Shadud (Braun 1985: Fig. 17: 1-5), and in the Jerash region (Hanbury-Tenison 1987: *passim*).

Genre 8: holemouth jars (Fig. 154: 1 - 6)

The genre is related to genres 3 and 4 through the distinctive bands of impressed decoration at the rim, some of which is 'reed' impressed (e.g. Fig. 154: 4). These holemouth jars have high shoulders, rolled rims, apparently no handles, and probably flat bases (Fig. 62: c). Rim forms (Fig. 66) are mostly in rolled (a, c), some are plain and slightly bulbous (a), some are bevelled and a combination of rolled and bulbous forms (e.g., Fig. 154: 3). The rolled rim form also occurs at Jawa (Betts [ed.] 1991: Fig 114: 56, 58: genre/type AA = TUH genre 2).

Parallels can be found at Tell el-Far'ah (de Vaux and Steve 1947: Fig. 5: 15 [?]; 1948: Fig. 6: 6; de Vaux 1961: Fig. 2: 3 [?]), Afula (Sukenik 1948: Pl. III: 2, 3, 19), Meser (Dothan 1959b: Fig. 5: 3 [?]), and Beth Shan XIV (Fitzgerald 1935: Pl. IV: 5).

Genre 9: holemouth jars (Fig. 154: 7 - 10 [11])

This genre of holemouth jars is also related to genre 2 (and 3); it is a later development (predominantly in stage 3: i.e. in EB I B). The form of these vessels must be closer to its proto-types, although the few available profiles make reconstruction uncertain (Fig. 62: d). Rim forms (Fig. 67) are rounded or slightly rilled with the neck profile being slightly bulbous. The pushed up lug handles appear in the same positions, near the rim. Their form is less rounded and some examples show signs of 'finger' or 'thumb' impressions. A related variant (Fig. 154: 11) has a vestigial version of this characteristic handle form. The rim shape in this case is bulbous, externally slightly recessed, and internally bevelled.

Palestinian parallels occur in EB I B contexts at Jericho (Kenyon and Holland 1983: Figs 13: 29 [?]; 16: 19; 33: 15; 63: 6; 85: 12, 14; 88: 13 [cf. TUH154: 7, 10] a hybrid form combining the developed TUH genres 2/5/9 and genre 11; 95: 6; 133: 33 [a hybrid]; 140: 3), and Arad (Amiran 1978: Pl. 8: 15 [Str. IV]).

Genre 10: holemouth jars (Figs 155 - 7)

This genre includes a variety of vessel sizes, although these, once again, divide into a smaller and larger group (Fig. 62: e, d). The larger forms (Figs 155-6) have thicker, more bulbous rims; the smaller forms (Fig. 157) parallel internal-external profiles. With the exception of two examples (Fig. 157: 11, 12), which have traces of impressed and incised decorative bands below the rim, there are no traces of decoration nor, apparently, any handles. Rim forms (Fig. 68) are all in turned and internally recessed, the larger forms - as was noted above - tending to be more bulbous, or splayed (a-c) with more pronounced internal recessing, while the smaller forms (d, e) are less recessed, some showing a slightly everted lip (e).

Genre 10 can be found in predominantly EB I B contexts at Kataret es-Samra (Leonard 1983: Fig. 9: 5 [?], Tel Rosh ha-'Ayin (Eitan 1969: Fig. 2: 3), Afula (Sukenik 1948: Pl. III: 5, 10), Tell el-Far'ah (de Vaux and Steve 1947: Fig. 2: 10; 1948: Fig. 6: 4; de Vaux 1955: Fig. 13: 24 [EB II?], 36, 41, 42 [EB II?]; 1955: Fig. 14: 13, 30, 31, 34 [EB II?]), Jericho (Garstang 1936: Pl. XXXVIII: 16; Kenyon and Holland 1983: Figs 12: 23 [less the applied decoration]; 18: 4; 49: 14; 50: 5 [a hybrid including elements of genres 5 and 9]; 53: 7, 21, 22; 54: 27-29; 57: 24; 60: 27; 126: 26, 28; 130: 1; 136: 17; 139: 11; 140; 15; 143: 14, 32, 34; 144: 13; 146: 29 [some forms may be related to genre 14 which is probably a development from genre 10]), Tell Handaquq North (Mabry 1989), Tell Shuneh North (Gustavson-Gaube 1985: Fig. 11: 40 [?]), Arad (Amiran 1978: Pl. 8: 12, 27 [Str. IV: = TUH 157: 11]), and in the Jerash region (Hanbury-Tenison 1987: *passim*).

Genre 11: holemouth jars (Figs 158 - 61)

Genre 11 is a very distinctive group of holemouth jars whose general forms - as in many other genres - can be reconstructed in two versions: a tall form (Fig. 69: c) and a shorter one (Fig. 69: b). These vessels have flat bases (e.g. Fig. 251: 3 - 10 [genre 93]). There appear to have been no handles, unless some of the 'grain-washed' ledge handles belong to this genre (Fig. 241: 1, 2 [genre 74]), in which case they would be attached just above the waist of the vessel. All of these vessels are slipped and their surfaces treated in the same way, in a form of slurred reserve slip which is known as 'grain-wash' or 'band-slip painting' in early Palestinian ceramic typology (Amiran 1969: 41ff.; see also Fig. 244: 8 [genre 83]). This surface treatment is applied to the entire external area of the vessel. Rim forms (Fig. 70) are all variations of bulbous profiles with a pronounced external ridge or lip. Details vary a great deal: e.g. rolled with a raised ridge at the lip and neck (a); rolled with internal bevelling, a recessed upper profile, and a rounded lip or ridge (b); rolled (or internally folded), recessed on top with a rounded lip (c); rolled-bulbous with a groove beneath the external lip (d); rolled, slightly bevelled with a slightly rounded lip (e); bulbous, slightly recessed on top with an everted, rounded lip (f); a plain version of (f, g); bulbous-rolled with an external ridge (h);

bulbous with rilled top (i); bulbous with a pronounced external ledge (j); and an elongated bulbous rim with externally recessed profile and a slight raised ridge to the neck (k). It is extraordinary that Mellaart (Leonard n.d.) appears not to have found even one sherd of this quite common genre; neither, apparently, did Glueck (1951). This lacuna may be the result of a bias against holemouth forms which have, until recently, been considered virtually undiagnostic: compare, in this regard, the preponderance of illustrated examples of the so-called 'Umm Hamad esh-Sherqi Ware' in both Mellaart and Glueck's reports (see 'Correlation with previous work' below).

Very close parallels exist in EB I B (and later) contexts: e.g. at Tell Handaquq North (Mabry 1989); Jericho (Garstang 1936: Pls XXXVII: 8; XXXVIII: 8, 11; Kenyon and Holland 1982: Figs 40: 25; 65 ff., especially no. 69; 1983: *passim*, mostly 'EB' - i.e. EB I-II); N.T. Jericho (Pritchard 1958: Pl. 57: 2 [?]); Ai (Callaway 1972: Figs 19: 7-24, 26; 20: 1-15, particularly no. 4; the type continues in later phases: e.g. Fig. 29: 7-15, 17, 18, etc.); Tell el-Far'ah (de Vaux and Steve 1947: Figs 2: 6, 8, 9, 11; 5: 8; 1948: Fig. 5: 2, 3; de Vaux 1955: Figs 5: 20, 21; 13: 25; 1961: Fig. 2: 19); Afula (Sukenik 1936; Pl. I: 15 [?]; 1948: Pl. III: 32-33, 38-39); Tel Rosh ha-`Ayin (Eitan 1969: Fig. 2: 2, 5); Megiddo XIX (Loud 1948: Pls 3: 3 [?]; 97: 16 [?]); En Shadud (Braun 1985: Figs 21: 19-22; 22: 1-7); Beth Shan XIV (Fitzgerald 1935: Pl. IV: 2, including an impression]); and Kataret es-Samra (Leonard 1983: Fig. 9: 4 [?]).

Genre 12: holemouth jars (Fig. 162: 1 - 11, 268: 1)

Heavy holemouth jars with internally recessed rims, these vessels are part of the distinctive ceramic repertoire first called 'Umm Hamad esh-Sherqi Ware' by Mellaart (1962; see also Leonard n.d.; Fig. 268: 1 here) and classed as 'pré-urbaine D' by Miroschedji (1971). This repertoire includes genres 17, 18, 27, 50, 73, 84 and 92 (see 'Repertoires': R6). No complete forms have been found, but the preserved profiles suggest a globular shape which might have had a rounded base (but cf. Fig. 268: 1, from Mellaart's collection [Leonard n.d.]). These vessels may also have had horizontal ledge handles at the waist (e.g. Fig. 240: 14 [genre 73]). A common characteristic of genre 12 - as is the case with the other forms in this repertoire - is the application of a single (?) heavy moulded, incised or impressed band of decoration along the rim. Rim forms (Fig. 71) are all internally recessed with rounded transitions to the neck. The larger examples tend to be splayed (a-c), some with small rounded lips (b). Comparison may be made with the complete vessel (?) in Figure 268: 1.

Similar heavy holemouth jars are also found at Shiqmim (Levy [ed.] 1987: Fig. 12.5: 7 = TUH162: 10), Arad (Amiran 1978: Pl. 8: 13, 16-20 [Str. IV; decoration is similar, although not the shape]), Horvat Usa

((Ben-Tor 1966: Fig. 3: 10), Beth Shan XIV (Fitzgerald 1935: Pl. IV: 1), Meser (Dothan 1957: Fig. 3: 2 [?]), Tel Rosh ha-`Ayin (Eitan 1969: Fig. 2: 3 = TUH162: 8 [?]), Afula (Sukenik 1948: Pls III: 40 [decoration?]; IX: 11, 12 [?]), Tell el-Far'ah (de Vaux and Steve 1947: Figs 1: 6; 2: 5; 5: 7; 7: 15; 1948: Fig. 6: 7; de Vaux 1955: Figs 4: 9 ['chalc. moy.']; 5: 14, 16, 22, 29; 1961: Figs 1: 9, 12 ['chalc. moy.']; 2: 20, 21, 37' 3: 14, 15), Ai (Callaway 1972: Fig. 34: 7, 14 [? from Marquet-Krause]), and Jericho (Garstang 1936: Pl. XXXIV: 17; Kenyon and Holland 1982: Fig. 39: 25).

Genre 13: holemouth jars (Fig. 163: 1 - 9; see also Fig. 233: 1 - 5)

These high shouldered holemouth jars are decorated with 'grain-wash' on their exterior surfaces. No complete forms were found and, as was the case with genre 12, both flat and rounded bases can be reconstructed (Fig. 72a). Up turned ledge handles may have been attached at the waist (see also Leonard n.d. and the parallels at Afula). Rim forms (Fig. 73) are varied: plain, rounded (a); bevelled (b); bevelled with internal lip (c); slightly splayed and bevelled (D); rolled (e); and pointed, slightly recessed on top (f).

Close parallels exist at Jericho (Garstang 1936: Pls XXXII: 25A, 25B [shape?]; XXXVIII: 16), Ai (Callaway 1972: Fig. 15: 10), Tell el-Far'ah (de Vaux and Steve 1948: Fig. 6: 6 [shape?]; de Vaux 1961: Fig. 1: 8 [shape?]), Afula (Sukenik 1948: Pl. VI: 1-10; a possible Chalcolithic proto-type might be seen in Pl. I: 3), Tel Rosh ha-`Ayin (Eitan 1969: Fig. 2: 3 [shape?]), Ghrubba (Mellaart 1956: Fig. 4: 31-33 [shape?]), Beth Shan XIV (Fitzgerald 1935: Pl. VI: 13), En Shadud (Braun 1985: Figs 14: 4-14 [especially no. 14]; 15: 5 [?]), Horvat Usa (Ben-Tor 1966: Fig. 3: 11, 12 [form]), and Arqub edh-Dhahr (Parr 1956: Fig. 17: 206, 207 [variants]).

Genre 14: holemouth jars (Figs 164 - 6)

High-shouldered holemouth jars with flat bases. There is no surface decoration but for slurring or fine grooving at the rim in some cases (e.g. Fig. 165: 8, a feature reminiscent of the earlier genre 1). Many of these vessels are incised with isolated slashed patterns near the rim (see 'Special features'). Reconstruction is based on one complete vessel (Fig. 164: 1), suggesting that the lower walls of these jars were nearly straight. There appears to be a size gradation (Fig. 72: b, c). Rim forms (Fig. 74) consist of variations of rilled or internally slightly recessed profiles (e.g. d, e), some of which are almost plain (a), some slightly 'bowed' (b), or bevelled (c), and some recessed internally (f), or slightly rolled and recessed on top (g).

Genre 14 is probably related to genre 15. Parallels are found at Horvat Usa (Ben-Tor 1966: Fig. 3: 11), Tell Handaquq North (Mabry 1989), Jericho (Kenyon and Holland 1982: Figs 65-8), and Ai

(Callaway 1972: Fig. 30: 7-9 [Phase III]). The parallels appear to begin in EB I B and become common in EB II.

Genre 15: holemouth jars (Figs 167, 168, 169: 1 - 6)

This genre of holemouth jars is related to genre 14. It is also undecorated but for a few vessels which have incised lines at the shoulder, slurring or fine grooving at the lip and rim, and external 'finger streaking', recalling surface decoration in other genres (e.g. genre 1; see also genre 16 below). Like genre 14, slashed isolated patterns (in one case accompanied by a boss) were made near the lip (see 'Special features'). Bases were flat, the lower walls of these vessels slightly rounded, curving out to the base (Fig. 72: d). There is also a size gradation. Rim forms (Fig. 75) are all based on a bulbous form, ranging from simple, rounded (a), slightly pointed and bevelled (b), to rounded and internally slightly recessed (c).

Parallels in EB I-II are common in Palestinian repertoires (see Amiran 1969: *passim*; examples at Jericho were noted under genre 14 above; Arad, Amiran 1978: Pls 18, 19 [especially nos 6, 12], *passim* [Str. II: EB II]; Ai, Callaway 1972: *passim* - common from Phase III onward).

Unclassified: holemouth jars (Figs 169: 7-9; 170 - 173)

These include single or unique examples, some of which can be linked with genres, as follows:

Fig. 169: 7, bulbous rim with external ledge, ledge decorated with impressed band. Parallels come from Jericho (Garstang 1936: Pl. XXV: 23), N.T. Jericho (Pritchard 1958: Pl. 56: 10 [EB I A]), Tell el-Far'ah (de Vaux and Steve 1947: Fig. 1: 7 [?]; de Vaux 1955: Figs 5: 9; 14: 18), Afula (Sukenik 1936: Pls I: 11, 12 [?]; II: 35; 1948: Pl. III: 19-28, 31), and Beth Shan XVI (Fitzgerald 1935: Pl. I: 2). Similar forms also occur at Jawa (Betts [ed.] 1991: Fig. 115: 60-67). *Fig. 169: 8*, rolled in turned rim and (?4) rounded lugs near the rim = genres 2, 5, and 9. A similar forms was found at Jawa (Betts [ed.] 1991: Fig. 120: 136). *Fig. 169: 9*, bevelled, internally slightly recessed rim with raised lip and slightly rolled = genres 4, 6, 10, and 13 (see also Jawa, Betts [ed.] 1991: Fig. 117: 92 [?]).

Fig. 170: 1-2, rolled rims, one of them finely grooved at the rim = genres 7 and 8. Parallels exists at Jawa (Betts [ed.] 1991: Figs 114: 56, 58; 120: 137-140 [?]). *Fig. 170: 3-7*, rounded, pointed, bevelled in turned rims, some with fine grooving at the rim and 'finger streaked' exterior surfaces, some painted (red 'splash paint') = genres 1 (decoration) and 14 (recessing). A parallel for TUH170: 7 comes from Ein Gedi (Ushishkin 1980: Fig. 10: 1). Other parallels occur at Jawa (Betts [ed.] 1991: Fig. 121: 152-54 [?]). *Fig. 170: 8*, high indented shoulder. Comparable forms appear at Jawa (Betts [ed.] 1991: Fig.

121: 143 [?]), Horvat Usa (Ben-Tor 1966: Fig. 3: 6 [?]), Megiddo XX (Loud 1948: Pl. I: 2 [?]), Beth Shan (Fitzgerald 1935: Pl. II: 18 [?]), Meser (Dothan 1959b: Fig. 6: 6), and Kataret es-Samra (Leonard 1983: Fig. 9: 19, 20).

Fig. 171: 1-6, out rolled rims. Parallels exist at Tell Handaquq North (Mabry 1989), Tell el-Far'ah (de Vaux and Steve 1948: Fig. 5: 6), N.T. Jericho (Pritchard 1958: Pl. 56: 9), Afula (Sukenik 1936: Pl. I: 14 [?]; 1948: Pls IV: 45; V: 21), Megiddo XX (Loud 1948: Pl. I: 7), Kataret es-Samra (Leonard 1983: Fig. 11: 5-7 [?]), Tell ed Duweir (Tufnell 1958: Pl. 57: 62), Meser (Dothan 1957: Fig. 3: 4), and Beth Shan XIV (Fitzgerald 1935: Pl. IV: 18, 20). *Fig. 171: 7-12*, externally recessed on top (cf. Fig. 170: 3-7?). TUH171: 7-10 can be compared with vessels from Jawa (Betts [ed.] 1991: Figs 115: 70-72; 120: 134); TUH171: 11, 12 are also similar to forms from the same site (*idem*: Fig. 121: 152, 154 [?].

Fig. 172: 1, rolled and recessed (EBIV); *2*, bulbous rim = genre 1 (paint); *3-4*, splayed, bevelled = genre 14 (cf. Fig. 166: 5, etc.); *5-10*, plain.

Fig. 173: 1, 3-9, rilled or externally recessed = genres 4 and 10. *Fig. 173: 2*, bulbous. *Fig. 173: 10*, bevelled bulbous with band of incised patterns on the rim = genres 3, 4, and 8. *Fig. 173: 11*, plain, incised or impressed band along the rim = genre 4. *Fig. 173: 12*, recessed. *Fig. 173: 13*, bulbous, 'pie-crust' decoration along the rim (common in EB III-IV). For some parallels see Afula (Sukenik 1948: Pl. IX: 12) and Jericho (Garstang 1935: Pl. XLII: 5).

Genre 16: jars (Figs 174 - 86; Pl. 4: 2)

Genre 16 is a broad category of large, often heavy jars with everted rims (Fig. 76) ranging from bag-shaped to more globular forms. Apart from related rim forms, they share various decorative and technical attributes such as slurring or fine grooving at the external rim, 'finger-streaked' external surfaces, 'thumb-impressed' flat bases, rows of impressed or incised decoration at the shoulder (Pl. 4: 4), and red 'splash- or 'trickle paint' on exterior surfaces applied in random patterns as well as more regular vertical and horizontal stripes. A number of handle forms seems to be associated with this genre (e.g. Figs 231-3: 1-4, 9, 10; 240: 1-4). If this is so, they would have been attached at the waist (e.g. Fig. 76: a). Rim shapes (Figs 77-8) include the following: (Fig. 77: a) plain rounded; (Fig. 77: b, c) rounded, bulbous with external groove (b) or a ridge (c); (Fig. 77: d) splayed; (Fig. 77: e, f) everted pointed; (Fig. 77: g) rounded, slightly 'bowed'; (Fig. 77: h - m) ranging from rounded, in sloping (h) to sharply everted (m); (Fig. 77: n, o) bevelled or slightly recessed, bulbous with rounded lip; (Fig. 77: p-t) everted rounded on in sloping, occasionally splayed, neck; (Fig. 78: a-d) rounded, sometimes recessed everted;

(Fig. 78: e) bevelled everted; (Fig. 78: f) out rolled; (Fig. 78: g) pointed everted on a tall neck from a sharp carination at the shoulder (cf. also Fig. 77: k); and (Fig. 78: h, i) out rolled, rilled on a low neck.

Most, if not all, of the variants in this genre can be traced back to Chalcolithic proto-types: e.g. forms at Abu Matar and Zoumeili (Commenge-Pellerin 1987: Figs 23: 3, 7; 29: 1; 30; 33: 1, 3, 5-7; 47: 5, 6, 8, 9, 11; 50: 1-10, 13; 51: 1-3); Horvat Beter (Dothan 1959a: Figs 9: 7; 15: 7, 8, 11, 18; *passim*); Neve Ur (Perrot *et al.* 1967: Figs 16: 1; 17: 1, 3); Sinai (Oren and Gilead 1981: Figs 7: 5, 13; 8: 20 [=TUH178: 6, etc.]), Tel Esdar (Kochavi 1969: Fig. 17: 30, 31); Shiqmim (Levy [ed.] 1987: Figs 12.8: 1; 12.10: 3-7; 12.15: 5); Nahal Mishmar (Bar-Adon 1980: Ills 3: 1-5; 4: 3, 5-7, 9; for body sherds [genre 79, 81] see Ill. 13: 3, 10), Teleilat Ghassul (Hennessy 1969: Fig. 7b: 3 [= TUH178: 3-5]; 1982: Fig. 2: 10, 11; Mallon *et al.* 1934: Figs 37: 6 [= TUH178: 5; 39: 1 = TUH183: 1], 5 - both top row, bottom row: 4, 5 [=TUH175: 1, TUH181: 5-9]; 50: 5 [form, less handles and moulded decoration]; 52: 4 [form], 6 [form]); Ghrubba (Mellaart 1956: Figs 5: 99, 101-106; 6: 107-118, 122); Tell al-Sa'idiya al-Tahta (de Contenson 1960: Fig. 33: 3-14); Abu Habil (*idem*: Figs 23: 10; 24: 3, 4; 25: 7-11); Tell Shuneh North (*idem*: Figs 4: 2-11; 12: 1-6; Gustavson-Gaube 1985: Fig. 24a-24d; 1986: Figs 14: 48e-51f; 15: 56a-56g; 16: 57a-58h); Abu Hamid (*Abu Hamid* 1988: Figs 28; 83; Dollfus and Kafafi n.d.: Figs 8: 9; 9: 8-10); Pella (McNicoll *et al.* 1982: Pl. 104: 2); Yiftahel (Braun 1989b: Figs 1; 2 - in comparison with vessels from Teleilat Ghassul); Azor (Perrot 1961: Figs 40: 3, 8, 16; 41: 3, 9); Abu Zureiq (Anati 1971: Fig. 19: 11); Tell Turmus (Dayan 1969: Fig. 5: 1-5); Majami' (Epstein 1978: Fig. 6a, lower left); and Rasm Harbush (*idem*: Fig. 12, top left).

EB I (A) parallels occur at Meser (Dothan 1957: Fig. 2: 4), Tell Handaquq North (Mabry 1989), Jericho (Garstang 1935: Pls XLII: 10-12; XLIII: 3, 5, 8, 9, 14 ['Chalcolithic']; 1936: Pls XXXIII: 4 [VIII]l; XXXIV: 12 [EB I {B}]; Kenyon and Holland 1982: Fig. 19: 9 = TUH186: 11; 1983: Fig. 113: 5, among others, with vertical red painted stripes on a white slip, common in EB I B: i.e. a developed, later form from the TUH genre), N.T. Jericho (Pritchard 1958: Pl. 57: 4, 7, 8), Afula (Sukenik 1936: Pl. I: 20, 21; 1948: PL. v: 1, 5, 11-20), En Shadud (Braun 1985: Fig. 23: 13 = TUH182: 1ff.), Arqub edh-Dhahr (Parr 1956: Fig. 17: 211, 212 [shape?], Kataret es-Samra (Leonard 1983: Figs 9: 20; 11: 4-8), Ruweiha (Figs 256: 7-10; 257), Tell ed-Duweir (Tufnell 1958: Pls 56: 26; 57: 39, 48, 68, 72), Tell Fara South (Macdonald 1932: Pl. XL: 32, 63, 64), Meser (Dothan 1957: Fig. 3: 10-12; 1959b: Fig. 7: 8, 16), and Beth Shan (Fitzgerald 1935: Pl. I: 10; *passim*, though not the moulded decoration). Although there is nothing obviously similar among the major genres at Jawa, especially with regard to decoration (although a few body sherds with 'finger streaking' have been observed at the site), some forms such as TUH175: 3-6 can be compared with the larger forms in Jawa's genre B (Betts [ed.] 1991: Figs 123-27; cf. also TUH180: 3-5 and Jawa, *idem*: Figs 136: 342; 136: 338-40).

Parallels from contemporary, although more distant, sites come from Byblos (Dunand 1973: Fig. 169: 23581 [rim shape only = TUH175: 1]; apart from this there is nothing comparable except for Neolithic types which, however, are too simple to be considered proto-types), Hama (Fugman 1958: Fig. 30: 5E566 [= TUH175, etc. for shape, TUH178: 5 for painted stripes]), and Habuba Kabira (Sürenhagen 1978: Tab. 24: 6 [?], 16 [?] perhaps too crude).

Genre 17: jars (Figs 187, 188, 189: 1 - 5; Pl. 6: 1)

This genre is part of the same repertoire as genre 12 (see 'Repertoires': R6) and consists of large heavy bag-shaped jars (pithoi). No complete forms have been recovered, but the type is known in Chalcolithic repertoires throughout Palestine and southern Syria (e.g. Abu Hamid, *Abu Hamid* 1988, *passim*) and can be reconstructed with a flat base (e.g. Figs 250: 10-12; 251: 1-2) and a low centre of gravity (Fig. 74: a). All of these jars are decorated with heavy impressed, incised or slashed multiple bands all over the body. In most cases the lip of the rim is similarly treated. Rim forms (Fig. 80) are all splayed, some 'hammer-rimmed' (a-c), some more in turned (c), or everted (d-f), some are recessed on top (g). If the vessels had handles (e.g. Fig. 240: 15, genre 73) these would probably have been attached at the widest point of the body. Chalcolithic vessels (including related jars and bowls) often have handles in such positions; the difference between Um Hammad's pottery and that of the Chalcolithic period lies in the form of the handles: the earlier ones are usually pierced and vertical; those at Um Hammad are solid ledge handles, horizontally applied to the body of the vessel.

The closest parallels in form and decoration come from the north of Palestine/Transjordan; they are sometimes attributed to the 'northern Chalcolithic', separating this repertoire from the 'southern' Chalcolithic typified by the sites about Beersheba. However, it is clear that this northern repertoire is closely related to the southern ones. The northern 'style' is represented at Tell Turmus in the Huleh Basin (Dayan 1969: Fig. 4: 1-4) and related sites in the Jawlan (Epstein 1978: *passim*). Similar, or related, forms are found at Abu Matar/Zoumeili (Commenge-Pellerin 1987: Figs 23: 5; 24: 2-4; 25: 2-6; 47: 1, 2), Horvat Beter (Dothan 1959a: Figs 9: 8-10, 13; 14: 8, 10, 20), Neve Ur (Perrot *et al.* 1967: Fig. 17: 6), `Ein el-Jarba (Kaplan 1969: Fig. 7: 2), Shiqmim (Levy [ed.] 1987: Fig. 12.7: 1 [?]), Teleilat Ghassul (Mallon *et al.* 1934: Figs 39: 7 [though with vertical handles; 41: 14; 52: 9; 53 [form]), North 1960: Fig. 15: 8485), Abu Hamid (*Abu Hamid* 1988: Fig. 74), Pella (McNicoll *et al.* 1982: Pl. 104: 1; Smith 1973: Pl. 34: 717), wadi

Rabah (Kaplan 1958: Fig. 5: 1-3), near Beth Shan (Tzori 1958: Pl. IVC), Azor (Perrot 196: Figs 40: 16; 41: 3, 6, 16), and Abu Zureiq (Anati 1971: Fig. 19: 4, 5).

EB I (B) parallels come from Beth Shan (Fitzgerald 1935: Pl. I: 3), Meser (Dothan 1957: Fig. 3: 6), Kataret es-Samra (Leonard 1983: Figs 8: 25, 26; 10), Afula (Sukenik 1948: Pl. IX: 7), Tell el-Far'ah (all direct parallels: e.g. de Vaux and Steve 1947: Fig. 2: 2; 1948: Figs 5: 12, 13; 6: 7; de Vaux 1955: Fig. 5: 27; 1961: Figs 2: 9, 10, 38; 3: 16, 17), Jericho (Garstang 1935: Pls XLI: 2-4; XLIII: 12 ['Chalcolithic']; 1936: Pl. XXXII: 24A, 24B [VIII]; Kenyon and Holland 1983: Fig. 57: 19, a precise parallel), Horvat Usa (Ben-Tor 1966: Fig. 3: 10 [?]), and Arad (Amiran 1978: Pl. 6: 4, 6 [Str. {IV}V, {III}V respectively: presumably Chalcolithic]).

Other parallels can be recognized at Byblos (Dunand 1973: Figs 125-27), Habuba Kabira (Sürenhagen 1978: Tab. 4: 51 [?]), and Hama (Fugman 1958: Fig. 49: 7B815 [shape and decoration]).

Genre 18: jars (Figs 189: 6, 7; 190)

Genre 18 is also part of the same repertoire as genres 12 and 17 (see 'Repertoires': R6). Some examples are almost undistinguishable from genre 17. The reconstructed form (Fig. 79: a, b) tends to be rounder and wider than genre 17. Bases were probably flat (see genre 17). Rim forms (Fig. 81) are all everted, ranging from straight bevelled-rounded forms (a) to slightly recessed (b), and recessed with an up turned, pointed rim (c). Surface decoration is the same as that of genre 17. If at all, ledge handles would have been attached in the same position as was suggested for genre 17 above.

There seem to be no direct parallels in the 'northern Chalcolithic' repertoires in so far as these have been published. Parallels might be seen in a vessel from Abu Matar (Commenge-Pellerin 1987: Fig. 25: 5 [?]) and another from Pella (Smith 1973: Pl. 34: 730). Close parallels have been found in EB I (B) contexts at Tell el Far'ah (de Vaux and Steve 1947: Fig. 5: 17; 1948: Fig. 5: 9; de Vaux 1955: Fig. 5: 17 ['chalc. sup.']; 1961: Fig. 2: 10 ['chalc. sup.']), Jericho (see genre 17 above), Afula (Sukenik 1948: Pls V: 14, 15 [?]; VI: 36 [?]), En Shadud (Braun 1985: Fig. 23: 1 [?]), and Beth Shan (Fitzgerald 1935: Pls I: 3; IV: 26).

Genre 19: jars (Figs 191-3)

Like genre 16, this classification is a broad one. All forms tend to be bag-shaped below a low everted rim on an elongated neck (Fig. 82), ranging in size from medium jars with rounded bodies (a), and more bag-shaped ones (b), to smaller jars with 'bowed' necks and rounded bodies (c, d). Base forms are uncertain, although they are most likely rounded or, in the case of the smaller versions of the genre, omphaloid. Rim forms are varied (Fig. 83): (a) recessed; (b) plain or pointed; (c) internally recessed neck ('bowed') and bevelled; (d) rounded on 'bowed' neck; (e) recessed; (f) sharply everted on a straight in sloping neck; (g-i) everted, pointed, some with a sharp carination at the junction of neck and shoulder; (j, k) everted pointed; (l) plain, in sloping; (m-q) rounded or pointed everted rims on a 'bowed' neck, or internally carinated, slightly recessed neck. Two unclassified forms (Fig. 194: 1-2) may be related to this genres at the larger end of the size range.

The smaller range of s-shaped jars and 'bowed' neck/rim profiles can be traced back to Chalcolithic proto-types; the larger range apparently not, but for recessed rims as in TUH191: 1-4. Chalcolithic parallels are found at the following sites, among others: in Sinai (Oren and Gilead 1981: Fig. 8: 3, 5, 19); Abu Matar and Zoumeili (Commenge-Pellerin 1987, Fig. 30: 1 = smaller vessels in Figure 193; some have 'bowed' profiles [e.g TUH193: 21] Fig. 49: 11, etc.; cf. also Fig. 51: 1-5); Horvat Beter (Dothan 1959a: Figs 17-26 = smaller jars; 15: 2, 3; 16: 2-5); Tel Esdar (Kochavi 1969: Fig. 17: 33); Shiqmim (Levy [ed.] 1987: Figs 12.10: 5 [shape/stance = TUH192: *passim*]; 12.13: *passim*; 12.15: 2); Ein Gedi (Ushishkin 1980: Fig. 10: 5, 7 [?], 10); Ghrubba (Mellaart 1956: Fig. 4: 38 [?], 44, 46); Tell es-Sa'idiyeh al-Tahta (de Contenson 1960: Fig. 33: 11, 15 [the latter is 'bow'-rimmed]); Abu Habil (*idem*: Figs 23: 10; 26: 12, 13); Tell Shuneh North (*idem*: Fig. 14: 10 [?]); Abu Hamid (Dollfus and Kafafi n.d.: Fig. 8: 3, 7); Azor (Perrot 1961: Fig. 40: 15); Tell Turmus (Dayan 1969: Fig. 5: 3, 6); and Rasm Harbush (Epstein 1978: Fig. 12: top right). The larger form might be recognized at Teleilat Ghassul (Hennessy 1969: Figs 5: 8 [= TUH192: 1; 9a: 3; 9b: 7 [?]; Mallon *et al.* 1934: Figs 38: 6 [?]; 51: 1 [form]).

Parallels in the EB I (A) range come from Beth Shan (Fitzgerald 1935: Pl. I: 22, 23 for recessed rims = TUH191: 1-4), Meser (Dothan 1957: Fig. 4: 3; 1959b: Figs 5: 5, 6; 6: 8; 7: 8 for 'bowed' rim/neck), Tell Fara South (Macdonald 1932: Pls XXXIX: 25; XL: 44, 45, 57, 60 'bowed' rim/neck), Tell ed-Duweir (Tufnell 1958: Pl. 56: 4, 8, 19, 20, 27, including 'bowed' profiles), Arad (Amiran 1978: Pl. 9: 5 [Str. {III}IV]), Kataret es-Samra (Leonard 1983: Fig. 11: 7, 9-13), Bab edh-Dhra' (Saller 1964/5: Fig. 15: 5 = TUH192: 12, 13, etc.; Schaub p.c.: small size range), Azor (Ben-Tor 1975: stone vessel [Egyptian?] with bowed rim/shoulder profile = TUH193: 21), Afula (Sukenik 1948: Pls IV: 15, recessed rim = TUH192: 1-4; no. 17 = TUH192: 12ff.; V: 3 ['bowed'], 9, 16; VI: 37 [stance]), Jericho (Garstang 1936: Pl. XXXII: 23A [VIII]; Kenyon 1960: Figs 15: Tomb A94 [no. 7 Chalcolithic?]; 18: *passim*; Kenyon and Holland 1982: Fig. 38; 1983: Figs 11: 8, 21, 25; 48: 14 [?]; 113: 22; 114: 24; 115: 13; 116: 23; 126: 25; 132: 30; 134: 36 [?]; 136: 10 [?] - none direct parallels [i.e. they are later forms] and these limited to the larger size range), N.T. Jericho (Pritchard 1958: Pl. 57: 5-11), Tell el-Far'ah (de Vaux and Steve 1947: Fig. 1: 1-3 ['én. moy.']; 1948: Fig. 5: 4 ['en. sup.']; 1949: Figs 1: 27; 6: 19; 8: 8, 9, 13; 13: 13, 16, 18, 19; de Vaux 1951: Figs 1: 6; 4: 4-6; 6: 10-1, 15; 11: 21, 24-27; 12: 7; 1952: Figs 10: 14, 15, 24; 12: 16; 1955: Fig. 1: 8, 9; 1961: Fig. 2: 1, 2), Tell Handaquq North (Mabry 1989), and Horvat Usa (Ben-Tor 1966: Fig. 3: 2, 3, 6). A possible parallel occurs at Jawa (Betts [ed.] 1991: Fig. 131: 280).

A related form appears at Byblos (Dunand 1973: Fig. 155: 21207 [?]). Other parallels can perhaps be observed at Habuba Kabira (Sürenhagen 1978: Tabn 24: 8 [?]; 25: 32 [?]), Hama (Fugman 1958: Figs 37: 7A632No. 15; 46: 7A612-4B872), and in the Amuq region (Braidwood and Braidwood 1960: Figs 178: 2 [?], 5; 179: 18 [?] - Amuq F).

Unclassified: jars (Fig. 194: 1-2)

Everted rim jars with wide mouths and a characteristic sharply indented shoulder. Parallels may be found at Abu Matar (Commenge-Pellerin 1987: Fig. 24: 5).

Genre 20: jars (Figs 194-5)

The genre consists of medium sized jars with low, slightly everted and bevelled rims on an in sloping neck. The form is high shouldered (Fig. 82: e) on a globular body with a shallow curve to the flat base. Surface decoration consists of red slip (Fig. 195: 2, 3) and, occasionally, a band of red paint on the rim and external surface of the neck (Fig. 195: 6). Some variants have small pushed up, rounded lugs on the shoulder (Figs 194: 6; 195: 3) which are similar to those in genre 2; some variants have a single (?) broad loop handle from the rim to the shoulder (Fig. 195: 2). Rim forms (Fig. 84) are either bevelled on top (a, b, e), rounded and internally recessed (c), or recessed on top (d).

The rim shape of TUH194: 1-2 is similar to forms at Abu Matar (Commenge-Pellerin 1987: Figs 24: 5; 33: 9). Similar forms can be found in Sinai (Oren and Gilead 1981: Fig. 8: 11 [?]), and at Shiqmim (Levy [ed.] 1987: Fig. 12.10: 3), Tell es-Sa'idiyah al-Tahta (de Contenson 1960: Fig. 33: 14), Yiftahel (Braun 1989: Figs 1; 2 [?]), Azor (Perrot 1961: Fig. 41: 12 - rim shape = TUH194: 6, 9, TUH195: 2), Abu Zureiq (Anati 1971: Fig. 36: 10 [general shape], and perhaps Tel Turmus (Dayan 1969: Fig. 5: 1).

EB I (A) parallels exist at Jawa (Betts [ed.] 1991: Fig. 37), Tell Handaquq North (Mabry 1989), Jericho (Garstang 1935: Pl. XLIII: 8 [Chalcolithic?]; Kenyon and Holland 1983: Fig. 114: 25 [rim and shoulder form = TUH194: 1, 2]), Tell el-Far'ah (de Vaux and Steve 1947: Fig. 5: 14 [?]), Afula (Sukenik 1948: Pl. V: 18, 19 [?]), Megiddo

XX/XIX (Loud 1948: Pls I: 3 [?]; 3: 1), Tell ed Duweir (Tufnell 1958: Pl. 56: 26) and Meser (Dothan 1957: Fig. 3: 5 [rim form?]).

A similar form is known in the Amuq region (Braidwood and Braidwood 1960: Fig. 179: 21 [Amuq F]).

Genre 21: jars (Figs 196-7; 268: 4)

This genre is probably related to genre 20 (cf. Fig. 197: 4), sharing many attributes. There appears, however, to be a greater size range, from small jars similar to genre 20, to large vessels with high necks (Fig. 196). In general, the form of this genre (Fig. 82) consists of a high neck on a high shouldered body. In some cases the neck-shoulder junction is sharply indented (g, h; cf. also Figs 196: 5; 197: 1, 5). Some vessels may have had rounded bases (g, h), but this is not certain (e.g. one vessel from Mellaart's collection [Leonard n.d.]: see Fig. 268: 4, it is reconstructed with a round or rounded base). Two types of handles appear on various parts of these vessels: small pushed up rounded lugs (like those of genres 2 and 20) are placed on the shoulders of the smaller size range (f, g), while pairs of up turned ledge handles with incised decoration (Figs 197: 4; 238: 5-8 [genre 68]) appear on the waist. Various other ledge handle forms (e.g. Fig. 238: 1-4, etc.) can be associated with this genre, including one handle with a distinctive stamp seal impression (Fig. 238: 4; see also chapter 5). Rim forms (Fig. 85) are plain (b, e), or - mostly - recessed on top (a, d, d, f). (See also Figure 273 for the closely related genre [B] at Jawa.)

Chalcolithic parallels (proto-types) are known at Neve Ur (Perrot *et al.* 1967: Fig. 16: 1, 4, 7 [?]), Shiqmim (Levy [ed.] 1987: Fig. 12.13: 12 = TUH197: 6 [?]), Ghrubba (Mellaart 1956: Fig. 4: 49 [rim/lip shape = TUH196: 6]), Tell es-Sa'idiyah al-Tahta (de Contenson 1960: Fig. 33: 14), Abu Hamid (*Abu Hamid* 1988: Fig. 28), Teleilat Ghassul and Yiftahel (Mallon *et al.* 1934: Fig. 38: 8 [+TUH196: 1, 5-7 [?]; Braun 1989: Figs 1; 2; cf. Amiran 1969: Pl. 2: 18; Elliott 1978: Fig. 2: 12), and Tell Fara South (Macdonald 1932: Pl. XL: 67 = TUH197: 1, 5 [?]).

EB I (A) parallels appear at Kataret es-Samra (Leonard 1983: Fig. 9: 18 [?]), Bab edh-Dhra' (Saller 1964/5: Figs 15: 39; 25: 7, etc.; Lapp 1968: Fig. 9: 19, etc. - these are all plausible parallels, though only distantly related), Jebel Mutawwaq (Hanbury-Tenison 1987: Fig. 6: 11; 1989), Afula (Sukenik 1936: Pl. I: 20 [?]; 1948: Pl. V: 1, 6, 7 [?]), Tell Turmus (Dayan 1969: Fig. 5: 9 [rim/lip shape]), Tell el-Far'ah (de Vaux 1952: Fig. 10: 23; 1955: Fig. 5: 6 [?]), and Jericho (Garstang 1932: Pl. XII: 10 [?]; 1935: Pl. XLIII: 14 [Chalcolithic]). The closest parallels appear in genre B of the Jawa assemblage (Betts [ed.] 1991: Figs 122-27; and for the associated handles [genres 67, 68, 71] *idem*: Fig. 128; for decoration, *idem*: Fig. 129) with some distantly related forms at Bab edh-Dhra' (see also Helms 1987a).

Genre 22: jars (Figs 198, 199, 200: 1-14)

Genre 22 consists of medium sized jars with sharply everted rims. Three basic shapes can be reconstructed (Fig. 86): a globular jar (a); an elongated jar with ridged shoulders (b); and a high shouldered jar (c). Bases are flat in most cases, although the high shouldered jars could have had rounded ones. Surface treatment varies and includes 'finger-streaking' (Fig. 198: 1), red slip and burnishing (Fig. 200: 4), pattern slip (Fig. 199: 1), and slurring of the rims (e.g. Figs 198: 9; 200: 5). No handles have been found. Rim forms (Fig. 87) are all sharply everted, including rounded simple forms (a, d, e, etc.), recessed forms (b, c, e), bevelled (f, g, h), slightly bulbous (f, g, m, n), and various elaborations at the neck: i.e. in sloping neck (b), sharp carinations (b, d, e, etc.), external ridges (d), and internal lips (h).

The genre can be recognized in Chalcolithic repertoires of Palestine: e.g. at Abu Matar and Zoumeili (Commenge-Pellerin 1987: Figs 23: 3 [?]; 34; 47: 8; 50: 1-7); Horvat Beter (Dothan 1959a: Figs 9: 14, 27-9; 15, 8, 9, 16, 17, 20); Neve Ur (Perrot *et al.* 196: Figs 15: 13; 17: 3); Shiqmim (Levy [ed.] 1987: Fig. 12.13: 5, 8); Nahal Mishmar (Bar-Adon 1980: Ills 3: 8; 14: 1); Azor (Perrot 1961 Fig. 41: 10, 11); Teleilat Ghassul (Mallon *et al.* 1934: Fig. 39: 7 [top row]); and Tell Turmus in the Huleh Basin (Dayan 1969: Fig. 4: 5 [?]).

There are close parallels at Jawa (Betts [ed.] 1991: genre E, especially Fig. 139: 389) and in other EB I (A) repertoires: e.g. at Jericho (Kenyon 1960: Fig. 21: 6 [?]; Kenyon and Holland 1982: Figs 37, 38 [perhaps derived forms]; 1983: Fig. 13: 10 = TUH198: 9 [?]); Tell Handaquq North (Mabry 1989); Tell Shuneh North (Gustavson-Gaube 1985: Fig. 29: 46a [?]); Tell el-Far'ah (de Vaux and Steve 1947: Fig. 2: 4 [?]); En Shadud (Braun 1985: Fig. 20: 9 [?]); Afula (Sukenik 1948; Pls IV: 15-17, 19-24, 26, 30-37; V: 16); Arad (Amiran 1978: Pl. 12: 12 [Str. IV]); Bab edh-Dhra' (Saller 1964/5: Fig. 15: 3 [?]); Megiddo XX/XIX (Loud 1948: Pls 1: 5, 6, 29; 3: 2); Kataret es-Samra (Leonard 1983: Fig. 11: 1-3, 7, 8); Tell Fara South (Macdonald 1932: Pl. XL: 63, 64 [?]); Meser (Dothan 1957: Fig. 3: 10 [?], 11); and Beth Shan (Fitzgerald 1935: Pl. IV: 13 [?]).

Possible parallels, though by no means suggesting actual contact between regions in this case, can be seen at Habuba Kabira (Sürenhagen 1978: Tab. 25: 31, 33, 36, 40 [?]), Hama (Fugman 1958: Fig. 46: 4C301 No. 27 [rim/shoulder profile], 4B758 No. 8), and in the Amuq region (Braidwood and Braidwood 1960: Fig. 171: 21 [?]).

Genre 23: jars (Fig. 200: 15-19)

This genre is close to genre 22 in shape (Fig. 86: d) and rim form; it is distinguished by impressed (some of them 'reed' impressed) decorative bands on the inner side of the rim (see also 'Special features'). Rim forms (Fig. 88) are all everted, including simple rounded (a), more pointed and slightly recessed (b), and bevelled, slightly recessed on top (c).

The decoration is the same as in genres 4, 8, 39, 82 (bs), and the vessels in TUH207: 2, 3 (see 'Repertoires': R3). The closest, and apparently only, parallel comes from Tell el-Far'ah (de Vaux 1955: Fig. 5: 8 ['chalc. sup.'] in an EB I B context. Precise parallels in terms of style are known at Megiddo XX/XIX (Loud 1948: Pls 94: 29; 99: 26-29). At Jawa parallels belong to genre E (i.e. the same as for genre 22; Betts [ed.] 1991: *passim*), though without the characteristic 'reed' impressions.

Genre 24 (Fig. 201)

These rounded everted rim jars may be loosely related to genre 34 (Fig. 209: 1-11). The shape (Fig. 86: e) is globular. Bases could be either flat, omphaloid, or rounded: none was found complete (but see Fig. 268: 5-7, from Mellaart's collection [Leonard n.d.]: one pedestal base; one flat). Many examples have a loop handle (or handles?), either from the lip to the shoulder (Fig. 201: 1-3, 8), or on the shoulder (Fig. 201: 5, 7). Exterior surfaces are 'finger streaked' (Fig. 201: 1), rims are sometimes finely grooved (Fig. 201: 4), and some variants are painted in the red 'splash paint' style (Fig. 201: 6-8). Rim forms (Fig. 89) are all simple and s-shaped, varying from rounded, in turned (a), rounded everted (c, d), to pointed, internally slightly recessed (b).

But for one example at Teleilat Ghassul (Mallon *et al.* 1934: Fig. 37: 7) there is nothing strikingly close in Chalcolithic repertoires (but see Commenge-Pellerin 1987: Figs 23: 6 [too big]; 30: *passim* [for the general shape, less handles]).

EB I (A) parallels come from Jericho (Kenyon 1960: Figs 14: 9, 12, 13; 18: 14; 1965: Fig. 4: 34; Kenyon and Holland 1983: Fig 116: 8 [a derived form: paint/slip is similar to that on parallels for genre 16]; see also *idem*: Fig. 148: 2), N.T. Jericho (Pritchard 1958: Pl. 57: 9, 10 [shape only], 26 [?]), Horvat Usa (Ben-Tor 1966: Fig. 5: 3), Tell el-Far'ah (de Vaux and Steve 1948: Fig. 5: 16; 1949: Figs 1: 19 [but for mouth shape], 22; 8: 30 [but for mouth shape]; 13: 18 [but for mouth shape]; de Vaux 1951: Figs 4: 1, 3; 6: 15 [but for mouth shape]; 11: 24, 27 [but for mouth shape]; 1952: Figs 10: 15; 12: 16; 1955: Fig. 5: 25), Afula (Sukenik 1948: Pls V: 9 [shape]; VIII: 26 [?]), Tell ed-Duweir (Tufnell 1958: Pl. 60: 218, 219 [EB II/III?]), Bab edh-Dhra' (Saller 1964/5: Fig. 18: 7; Lapp 1968: Fig. 11: 15 [as with other parallels, distantly related]), Kataret es-Samra (Leonard 1983: Fig. 11: 9 [shape]), Meser (Dothan 1959b: Fig. 6: 10, 12 [?]), and Beth Shan (Fitzgerald 1935: Pls I: 18 [shape]; II: 18 [?], *passim*; IV: 13, 21). One possible parallel form might be seen at Jawa (Betts [ed.] 1991: Fig. 136: 341 [?]).

Genre 25 (Fig. 202: 1, 2)

No complete rims have been found: only the characteristically sharply indented shoulder to neck junction. The forms can be reconstructed as a low everted rim on a globular, 'finger streaked' body (Figs 86: f; 90; Fig. 268: 8, from Mellaart's collection [Leonard n.d.]; but, this form could also be related to genre 22: i.e. TUH198: 9 and its slightly indented shoulder).

Jawa's genre D may be related to this form (Betts [ed.] 1991: Fig. 135); genre D can be compared with forms in northern Syria, at Hama and Habuba Kabira (see below; see also Helms 1987a). There are vessels with indented shoulders in Chalcolithic repertoires, such as those at Abu Matar (Commenge-Pellerin 1987: Figs 25: 11; 33: 9), Horvat Beter (Dothan 1959a: Figs 8: 13 [hmj]; 9: 11, 18), Neve Ur (Perrot *et al.* 1967: Fig. 17: 3), Shiqmim (Levy [ed.] 1987: Figs 12.11: 1, 2 [hmjs]; 12.13: 16 [relatively close parallel]), and Ghrubba (Mellaart 1956: Fig. 4: 47 [?]).

Some parallels might be sought in EB I (A) assemblages, as follows: at Azor (Ben-Tor 1975); Horvat Usa (Ben-Tor 1966; Fig. 5: 2); Arad (Amiran 1978: Pl. 12: 9 [Str. IV]); Jericho (Kenyon 1960: Fig. 15: 7 [?]); and Megiddo XX (Loud 1948: Pl. 1: 10).

Other parallels exist at Hama (Fugman 1958: Figs 37: 5B849, 5E565; 46: 4A892), and Habuba Kabira (Sürenhagen 1978: Tab. 12: 78); the form becomes common in Syria and Mesopotamia during the 3rd millennium BC (Helms 1987a: Fig. 20; Mathias and Parr 1989: Fig. 11: 60).

Genre 26: jars (Fig. 202: 3-8)

The jar form is close to that of genres 22 to 24. It is globular or slightly elongated (Fig. 86: g) and has rounded everted rims. Several examples have rounded, pushed up lug handles (4?) on the shoulders. These handles link genre 26 with genre 2, and others with similar handles in similar positions (see 'Repertoires': R2). External decoration consists of a red painted stripe along the rim and reddish slip (Fig. 202: 3) and, occasionally, slurring along the neck (Fig. 202: 7). Rim forms (Fig. 91) are simple, one variant being slightly recessed internally (a).

For parallels in terms of the general shape reference should be made to genres 22 and 23. There are close parallels at Jawa (Betts [ed.] 1991: genre E, Figs 138, 139, and the rounded, pushed up lug handles generally: i.e. 'Repertoires': R2).

Genre 27: jars (Figs 202: 9-12; 203)

Genre 27 belongs to the repertoire which includes genres 12, 17, and 18 (see 'Repertoires': R6). All rims are everted. There are two main divisions: (i) thin, everted rim, medium sized (Fig. 92: a); and (ii) heavy rimmed large jars (Fig. 92: b). Surface decoration is the same as in the rest of the repertoire: i.e. heavy, mostly horizontal, bands of impressed, moulded, incised or slashed patterns. Base form is not known, although the smaller size range could have been rounded; the larger was probably flat (e.g. Figs 250: 10-12; 251: 1, 2; 268: 9, Mellaart's collection [Leonard n.d.]: a flat base is reconstructed; there is also a handle similar to the one in genre 76 [Fig. 240: 14]). Rim forms (Fig. 93) are as follows: (a) plain everted rounded rims showing a scar at the neck-shoulder junction; (b) splayed everted rounded; (c) splayed and recessed on top with an out rolled lip; (d) splayed and recessed on top with an out rolled lip; (e) splayed and everted with a down pointing lip, internally recessed at the neck; and (f) rounded with an internally recessed neck and an out rolled lip.

As we have noted, genres of the so-called 'Umm Hamad esh-Sherqi Ware' have close stylistic parallels in Palestinian Chalcolithic repertoires, despite their appearance in EB I B contexts at Um Hammad. Parallels occur at Teleilat Ghassul (Mallon *et al.* 1934: Figs 39: 6[?]; 54; North 1960: Fig. 15: 8026; see also Braun 1989b: Fig. 1: A, B [?]), Abu Habil (de Contenson 1960: Fig. 26: 4 [?]), Abu Matar (Commenge-Pellerin 1987: Figs 25: 4-6 [?]; 29: 2; 33: 8), Shiqmim (Levy [ed.] 1987: Fig. 12.10: 7), and in the Jawlan (Epstein 1978: Fig. 2d, 2e). Somewhat similar forms appear at Byblos (Dunand 1973: Figs 173-77 ['én. réc'.]).

EB I (B) parallels in Palestine come from Megiddo XX (Loud 1948: Pl. 2: 47), Jericho (Garstang 1936: Pl. XXXIV: 19 [VII]), Tell el-Far'ah (de Vaux 1955: Fig. 5: 11 ['chalc. sup.']), Afula (Sukenik 1948: Pl. V: 13, 14 [?]), and Beth Shan (Fitzgerald 1935: Pl. I: 11-14, 20, 21).

Genre 28: jars (Fig. 204: 1-8)

The genre consists of globular, miniature, spouted jars (Fig. 92: c) whose bases are probably rounded and/or omphaloid. The spouts are vertical and either false (i.e. partly pierced) or hollow. One example is shaped as a face, the eyes stabbed, the mouth slashed before firing (Fig. 204: 1). One nearly complete example (Fig. 204: 2) was made in two halves, the join visible as a continuous scar. Surfaces were red slipped and highly burnished. The nearly complete vessel has two rounded, up turned ledge handles at the waist and two rounded knobs on the shoulder. Rim forms (Fig. 94) are all everted and pointed, some very thin (a), others slightly bulbous and recessed on top of the lip (b), or bulbous and recessed with a down turned internal lip at the junction of the neck and shoulder (c). (See also genre 33 and references to spouts there.)

These miniature versions of a well-known EB I B genre are not common (see Amiran 1969: Photos 20, 33, 34, 45; Pls 9: 28; 11: 25 - from Ai, Tell el-Far'ah, and Ghor es-Safi). Similar vessels are known

at Arad (Amiran and Cohen 1977: Pl. 36D [from an EB I tomb]), Azor
(Ben-Tor 1975: Figs 8: 1-13 [precise parallels, including the
construction method in two halves]; 9: 5, 7, 8), Bab edh-Dhra' (Saller
1964/5: Fig. 32: 23), Arqub edh-Dhahr (Parr 1956: Fig. 16: 202, 204),
Tell el-Far'ah (de Vaux and Steve 1949: Figs 6: 16, 19 [also similar
construction method]; 8: 29, 31; 1955: Fig. 1: 6, 17), and Jericho
(Garstang 1935: Pl. XXXVI: 14; 1936: Pl. XXXV: 15; Kenyon 1965: Fig.
9: 2-4). One vessel at Jawa may be related to this genre (Betts [ed.]
1991: Fig. 143: 450 [knobs]).

Similar forms are known in the Amuq Plain of northwestern Syria
(Braidwood and Braidwood 1960: Fig. 171: 34 [Amuq F]).

Genre 29: jars (Fig. 204: 9-17)

Genre 29 consists of globular jars (Fig. 92: d) with vertical, or nearly
vertical, rims. Surface decoration includes grooving of the external
rim (Fig. 204: 9), red painted bands along the lip (Fig. 204: 17), and
'pattern slip' or 'grain-wash' on the exterior surfaces, including the
neck and rim. Rim forms (Fig. 95) are simple and include rounded (a),
slightly pointed (b), and out rolled (c) variants.

But for the characteristic 'grain wash' slip (see below), the genre
can be related to Chalcolithic proto-types: e.g. at Zoumeili
(Commenge-Pellerin 1987: Fig. 50: 7 = TUH204: 11 [?]); Horvat Beter
(Dothan 1959a: Figs 15: 6; 16); Ghrubba (Mellaart 1956: Fig. 4: 39 [?],
45); Tell es-Sa'idiya al-Tahta (de Contenson 1960: Fig. 32: 3); Abu
Habil (idem: Fig. 26: 4 [form only]); and Shuneh North (idem: Figs 5: 1;
9: 4).

Closer parallels in EB I (B) contexts come from Megiddo (Loud
1948: Pl. 1: 1, 2, 11), Arad (Amiran 1978: Pl. 12: 10 [Str. IV]), Jericho
(Kenyon 1965: Fig. 8: 18; Kenyon and Holland 1982: Fig. 38: 21, 23),
Tell el-Far'ah (de Vaux and Steve 1949: Fig. 8: 23 [?]), Afula (Sukenik
1936: Pl. I: 21; 1948: Pl. IV: 5, 9-12), and Meser (Dothan 1957: Fig. 3: 12
[?]; 1959b: Fig. 6: 10 [?]).

Unclassified: jars (Fig. 205: 1, 2)

These represent a rare form of jar (unclassified) at Um Hammad,
which has a pointed, everted rim on a 'bowed' vertical neck making a
sharp carination at the shoulder junction. One example has a rounded
vertical handle (or handles?) at the neck-shoulder join and is red
polished (cf. genre 36, Figs 211, 212: 1-7, for similar surface
treatment); there are traces of 'trickle paint'. The lip of the rim is finely
grooved. The shape of these jars can be reconstructed as globular
(Fig. 92: g). No bases can be associated with these jars: flat or rounded
ones are possible.

The shape of the rim/neck with its handle can be seen in
Chalcolithic assemblages. Parallels may be sought at Neve Ur (Perrot

et al. 1967: Fig. 16: 7), Shiqmim (Levy [ed.] 1987: Fig. 12.9: 1 [?]), Nahal Mishmar (Bar-Adon 1980: ill. 3: 3 [form, no handles]), Ghrubba (Mellaart 1956: Fig. 4: 47 [?]), Teleilat Ghassul (Elliott 1978: Fig. 2: 12), Tell es-Sa'idiyah al-Tahta (de Contenson 1960: Fig. 33: 16 [shape only, not stance]), Abu Hamid (*Abu Hamid* 1988: Fig. 83 [rim-neck profile?]), Abu Habil (de Contenson 1960: Fig. 26: 2 [shape, not stance]), and Yiftahel (Braun 1989b: Figs 1; 2).

EB I (A) parallels come from Beth Shan (Fitzgerald 1935: Pl. I: 19, 25 [shape]), Meser (Dothan 1959b: Fig. 7: 8 [shape, not stance), Tell Fara South (Macdonald 1932: Pls XXXIX: 19 [shape, not stance]; XL: 67 [shape]), Bab edh-Dhra' (Saller 1964/5: Figs 15: 39; 18: 6 [distantly related]; Lapp 1968: Figs 8: 9; 9: 19), Afula (Sukenik 1948: Pl. VIII: 22), and Jericho (Garstang 1935: Pls XLII: 16; XLIII: 14 [shape]; Kenyon 1965: Fig. 8: 22 [rim/neck shape]). The form - without handle(s) - also occurs at Jawa (Betts [ed.] 1991: Fig. 136: 338).

The shape of the neck/rim can also be found at Habuba Kabira (Sürenhagen 1978: Tab. 30: 18 [without handles]).

Genre 30: jars (Fig. 205: 3-17)

Only rims and necks have been found. The genre represents high necked jars (Fig. 92: e) which are decorated with red slip (externally), occasionally pattern burnished in narrow vertical stripes (Fig. 205: 5). Rim forms (Fig. 96) are simple, everted and rounded. Some have an external groove at the shoulder-neck junction (a; cf. also genre 21, Figs 196-7), a slight indentation outside the lip (b), and plain (c, d).

These jar rims are not very diagnostic (see also genre 31, and Fig. 208). However, some similar forms are known in Chalcolithic assemblages: e.g. at Abu Matar and Zoumeli (Commenge-Pellerin 1987: Figs 30: 4 = TUH205: 14, *passim*; 50: 7 = TUH205: 8); Horvat Beter (Dothan 1959a: , Figs 9: 7, 22, 25; 1;: 4, 5); Neve Ur (Perrot *et al.* 1967: Figs 16: 6; 17: 2); Shiqmim (Levy [ed.] 1987: Figs 12.13: 7, 12; 12.15: 6; 15.19: 1, 4); Ghrubba (Mellaart 1956: Fig. 4: 38, 43); and Azor (Perrot 1961: Fig. 39: 4-6 [?]).

Similar shapes occur in EB I contexts at Jawa (Betts [ed.] 1991: Fig. 144: 464-66), Jericho (Kenyon 1960: Figs 14: 7; 18: 9; 22: 12, 13; 1965: Figs 7: 6, 6; 8: 15; 10: 4), Tell el-Far'ah (de Vaux and Steve 1947: Figs 2: 28, 30; 3: 3, 4, 9, 11; 7: 20; 1948: Fig. 5: 29), Afula (Sukenik 1936: Pl. I: 19; 1948: Pls I: 1; IV: 4; V: 2), Arqub edh-Dhahr (Parr 1956: Figs 15: *passim*; 16: *passim*), Tel Rosh ha-`Ayin (Eitan 1969: Fig. 2: 19), Bab edh-Dhra' (Saller 1964/5: *passim*), and Meser (Dothan 1959b: Fig. 7: 2).

Genre 31: jars (Fig. 206: 1-11)

High necked jars. The forms of this genre, like genre 30, are preserved only as necks and rims (Fig. 92: f), although the body can be reconstructed as globular. Surface decoration includes external and internal slurring of the neck and some examples have red 'trickle-' or 'splash paint' on the outside (e.g. Fig. 206: 10). Rim forms (Fig. 97) are bevelled (a), pointed and out folded (b), rounded and bulbous (c), pointed and tucked with a sharp carination at the neck-shoulder junction (d), and rounded with an external ridge below the lip and a sharp 'scarred' junction at the neck and shoulder (e).

Chalcolithic parallels may exist at Abu Matar and Zoumeli (Commenge-Pellerin 1987: Figs 30: 5, 8, 10, 12; 32: 1-7; 33: 2 [jarres à col curt]; 50: 1-6, 8-10, 13), Horvat Beter (Dothan 1959a: Figs 9: 14; 15: 11), in Sinai (Oren and Gilead 1981: Fig. 8: 2), and in the Jawlan region at Tell Turmus (Fig. 5: 5 [?]).

EB I (A) parallels have been found at Jawa (Betts [ed.] 1991: Fig. 139: 390, 391), Meser (Dothan 1957: Fig. 3: 10), Afula (Sukenik 1936: Pl. I: 18; 1948: Pls IV: 16, 26, 27; V: 20), Jericho (Garstang 1932: Pl. VIII: 17; 1935: Pl. XLII: 13; Kenyon 1965: Fig. 9: 4, 5 [?]), N.T. Jericho (Pritchard 1958: Pl. 57: 30, 31 [?; shape only] - in EB I A contexts), and Megiddo XX (Loud 1948: Pl. 1: 11).

Genre 32: jars (Fig. 206: 12-22)

The genre consists of high, vertical necked jars (Fig. 92: h) which have a characteristic 'bowed' shape. Surface decoration includes red slip and burnishing (Fig. 206: 19), internal slurring (Fig. 206: 14), and internal and external red slip with narrow vertical red painted stripes (Fig. 206: 17, 18). One example (Fig. 206: 17) also has the remains of a flat (strap) high loop handle at the rim-shoulder junction. Rim forms (Fig. 98) are all rounded, some plain (a, c, d), some slightly recessed on top (b).

The 'bowed' rim is reminiscent of some Chalcolithic churn rims (e.g. Commenge-Pellerin 1987: Fig. 38: 1-10); the same form can be seen in hollow pedestal bases (e.g. Neve Ur, Perrot *et al.* 1967: Fig. 15: 15). Parallels occur at Tel Esdar (Kochavi 1969: Fig 17: 29 = TUH206: 12, 15 [?]), Nahal Mishmar (Bar-Adon 1980: Ill. 3: 7), Tell es-Sa'idiya al-Tahta (de Contenson 1960: Fig. 33: 8, 15 [?]), Abu Habil (*idem*: Fig. 26: 2), Tell Shuneh North (*idem*: Fig. 5: 3), Yiftahel (Braun 1989b: Figs 1; 2), Abu Zureiq (Anati 1971: Fig. 36: 11), and Horvat Beter (Dothan 1959a: Fig. 15: 10 [?]).

EB I parallels have been found at Jericho (Garstang 1932: Pl. XII: 15; Kenyon 1960: Fig. 13: 12, 27-30 [high loop-handled juglets]; 1965: Fig. 89: 22), Tell el-Far'ah (de Vaux and Steve 1947: Fig. 2: 28 [vert. painted stripes = TUH206: 17, 18]; de Vaux 1955: Figs 3: 14 [?]; 5: 6), Arqub edh-Dhahr (Parr 1956: Fig. 15: *passim* [including vertical painted stripes]), Tell ed-Duweir (Tufnell 1958: Pl. 57: 44 [juglet], 61 [wavy lip]), and Bab edh-Dhra' (Saller 1964/5: Figs 18: 1; 23: 9, 15).

Some parallels might be seen at Hama (Fugman 1958: Fig. 30: 7A865 No.24).

Unclassified: jars (Fig. 207: 1-3)

Only three examples of this type were found at Um Hammad, of which one is complete (Figs 92: i; 207: 1); body sherds of genre 82 (Fig. 244: 1-6; Pl. 8: 3) may belong to this category. Necks are high and near vertical making a sharp transition to the shoulder. Rims are everted. The one preserved base is flat. All three examples have moulded, or impressed, bands of decoration at, or just above, the shoulder-neck junction. The complete variant has a heavily moulded band; the others have 'reed' impressed bands. One variant (Fig. 207: 2) also has a 'reed' impressed band on top of the lip (see also 'Special features'). Rim forms are everted and pointed.

There seem to be no Chalcolithic parallels or proto-types for this group of vessels (but cf. a vessel from Tel Esdar, Kochavi 1969: Fig. 17: 31 [?]). However, several close parallels are known in EB I (A) assemblages: e.g. at Tell el-Far'ah (see Amiran 1969: Pl. 9: 14); Tell ed-Duweir (Tufnell 1958: Pl. 56: 21 [almost a precise parallel]); Jericho (Kenyon 1960: Fig. 14: 14, 15 [close parallel; see also genre 63]); Beth Shan (Fitzgerald 1935: Pl. I: 14, 21); Bab edh-Dhra' (Saller 1964/5: Fig. 18: 4; Lapp 1968: Fig. 11: 17 [a distant parallel; a related form and decoration, as is the case with other parallels from this site]; Schaub p.c.); Megiddo (Loud 1948: Pl. 96: 23 [a close parallel with two raised and impressed bands on the neck?]; for decoration [TUH207: 2, 3] see *idem*: Pl. 99: 26-29); and Assawir (Amiran 1969: Photos 24, 25; Pl. 9: 15).

Genre 33: jars (Fig. 207: 4-10)

No rims are preserved, but they were probably everted and pointed on an out sloping neck (Fig. 92: j). One related form (decoration) was found by Mellaart (Fig. 268: 11): it has a vertical spout, relating it to genre 28). The body sherds suggest a globular shape. One flat base was recovered. The genre is mainly distinguished by its surface decoration which consists of pattern burnishing on a light red slip. This takes the form of a net pattern from the neck-shoulder junction down to near the base where a register of horizontal burnishing begins and continues down to the bottom of the vessel.

The characteristic surface decoration is attested in EB I B contexts (cf. Amiran 1969: Photo 21 [Afula], and Loud 1948: Pl. 99: 11-14, among others). The style might be regarded as a regional variant of the 'line group-painting' and 'net-painting' (e.g. Amiran 1969: Photos 44 [Ghor es-Safi]; Pl. 13: 9 [Jericho]). Other parallels come from Jericho (Garstang 1935: Pl. XXXVI: 19; 1936: Pl. XXXVI: 1), Tell el-Far'ah (de Vaux and Steve 1949: Fig. 8: 51; de Vaux 1951: Fig. 12: 5), and Arqub edh-Dhahr (Parr 1956: Figs 15: 143; 16: 184, 186, 200, 204).

Unclassified: jars (Fig. 208: 1-7)

These are everted rim jars, or bottles, which are related to the typical 'Syrian bottles', jugs and juglets of the EB II-III period of Palestine (see Amiran 1969: *passim*). Surfaces are red slipped and highly polished, or burnished. Bases are flat. The larger, complete example has two vertical strap handles at the waist and a slurred rim. Three of the others have remains of high loop handles at the rim.

For the larger size range (TUH208: 1; see also genre 78, especially Fig. 242: 5), the following parallels can be cited, among others: Beth Shan (Fitzgerald 1935: Pl. IV: 27); Bab edh-Dhra' (Saller 1964/5: Fig. 28: 1); Arqub edh-Dhahr (Parr 1956: Fig. 16: 190); Afula (Sukenik 1948: Pl. V: 2); Jericho (Garstang 1932: Pl. VI: 15-17; Kenyon and Holland 1983: Figs 33: 3; 130: 30); and Megiddo (Loud 1948: Pls 5: 7; 6: 5 [with painted stripes]).

Parallels for the smaller vessels occur at Megiddo (Loud 1948: Pl. 4: 1), Jericho (Garstang 1932: Pls VIII: 16; XII: 22), Tell el-Far'ah (de Vaux and Steve 1947: Fig. 7: 29; 1949: Fig. 6: 34; de Vaux 1952: Fig. 12: 19; 1955: Figs 1: 15; 14: 23, 29; 1961: Fig. 4: 2, 16), Arqub edh-Dhahr (Parr 1956; Figs 14: 125, 128-131; 15: 151-154), Arad (Amiran 1978: Pls 25-30, etc. - mostly from Str. II]), Bab edh-Dhra' (Saller 1964/5: Fig. 28: 2-5, 11, 14, 15), Giv`atayim (Sussman and Ben-Ariel 1966: Fig. 9: 24), and Beth Shan (Fitzgerald 1935: Pl. V: 12). (See also Amiran 1969: Photos 54-56 and Plate 17: 1.) The 'time' range for these vessels at Um Hammad is EB I B - EB II.

Genre 34: jars (Fig. 209: 1-11)

This genre consists of high loop-handled juglets and is formally (or stylistically) related to genre 35. There are two basic forms (Fig. 92): a plain juglet with loop handle (double or single coil) and an everted pointed-rounded rim, probably with an omphaloid base (l); and (m) a juglet, or small jar (handle?), with a pointed, everted, slightly recessed rim on an in sloping 'bowed' neck which makes a sharp angle with its globular body. Surface decoration consists of stabbed or punctate bands (Fig. 209: 2, a plain, otherwise undecorated variant), cream slip and red painted vertical strips in 'trickle-' or 'splash paint', and red slip which is highly polished. Rim forms (Fig. 99) are everted, pointed-rounded, occasionally, slightly recessed.

Palestinian parallels of the Chalcolithic period occur at Tell es-Sa'idiyeh al-Tahta (de Contenson 1960: Fig. 33: 15 = TUH209: 10), and Abu Habil (*idem*: Fig. 26: 2; Leonard n.d. [see Helms 1987a: Fig. 18: 1] - both = TUH209: 10, though perhaps without the loop-handle).

EB I (A) parallels come from Kataret es-Samra (Leonard 1983: Fig. 12), Tell ed-Duweir (Tufnell 1958: Pls 56: 27 [shape = TUH209: 10]; 57: 44 = TUH209: 4-7, 9 and, particularly, 10), Arqub edh-Dhahr (Parr

1956: Fig. 15: 146, 164, 167, though these juglets probably belong to EB I B), Afula (Sukenik 1948: Pl. V: 3 = shape of TUH209: 10), Tell el-Far'ah (possible parallels, although mostly EB I B, i.e. see genre 35 below), Jericho (Kenyon 1960: Figs 13: 12, 27-30; 14: 1, 6 [shape close to genres 34, particularly TUH209: 9-11]; 1965: Fig. 4: 18, 23, 24 = TUH209: 1; Kenyon and Holland 1983: *passim*), and Khirbet Kerak/Beth Yerah (Esse 1984). A few handles, including double-coil handles, at Jawa may be related to genre 34 (Betts [ed.] 1991: Figs 142: 444, 448, the latter with red painted patterns).

'Foreign' parallels may be found at Byblos (Dunand 1973: Fig. 164: 25335, 34732, etc. for the form of these vessels, including the form of genre 35), Habuba Kabira (Sürenhagen 1978: Tab. 5: 58 [?]), Tarsus (Goldman 1956: Figs 231-33, 343: 25, 27, 30 [?], 33), Mersin, in a later version at Arslantepe (Palmieri 1981: Fig. 7: 2 [shape of body and low loop handle = TUH209: 9-11]), and Gerzeh (see Helms 1987a: Fig. 19: 4; cf. also Hennessy 1967 and de Miroschedji 1971).

The shape of these vessels, therefore, may be derived from Chalcolithic proto-types; the high loop handles and the general form, however, might stem from foreign repertoires (see 'Repertoires': R4).

Genre 35: jars (Figs 209: 12-22; 210; 253; 268: 12, 13; 269: 5)

The general form - high loop-handled juglets - is similar to that of genre 34. The loop handles (single or, rarely, double coil) are very high and steep, often reaching down to the base. Bases are both flat and omphaloid (cf. also Fig. 248 [genre 88]). Surface treatment consists of red slip which is either highly polished or burnished. Some variants are left red slipped. Rim forms (Fig. 100) are simple everted, pointed-rounded with some variants slightly recessed. The genre consists of a great variety of vessels sizes, from very small ones to heavy, large forms with bands of 'rope-moulded' decoration somewhat similar to the surface decoration in repertoire R6 (see 'Repertoires'). Other complete forms are shown in figures 268 (12, 13) and 269 (5), from Mellaart's collection (Leonard n.d.) and Tubb's excavations (1990).

Parallels are found at Megiddo (Loud 1948: Pls 5: 4; 6: 1, 2 [EB II?]), Jericho (Kenyon 1960: Figs 12: 5-34; 13: *passim*; 14: 1-6; 18: 1-7; 21: 5; 1965: Figs 4: 12-24; 8: 16-21; 10: 3; Kenyon and Holland 1983: *passim*), N.T. Jericho (Pritchard 1958: Pl. 57: 26 [?]), Tell el-Far'ah (de Vaux and Steve 1949: Figs 3: 11-14, 18; 6: 11-13, 17; 5: 17-21; 13: 9-14, 17; de Vaux 1951: Figs 4: 8, 9; 6: 11-13, 14; 11: 14, 15, 17, 18, 20; 1952: Figs 10: 16, 20, 21, 26; 11: 1-3, 5-7; 1955: Figs 1: 3, 4, 16; 3: 10, 12), Tell Shuneh North (Gustavson-Gaube 1985: Fig. 20: 97), Arqub edh-Dhahr (Parr 1956: Fig. 15: 139, 144-153. 155, etc.), Tell ed-Duweir (Tufnell 1958: Pls 11: 24, 25; 57: 41), Bab edh-Dhra' (Saller 1964/5: Figs 14: 7; 16: 12-16; 21: 18 [pointed handle a regional variant]; 23: *passim*; 14: 1-8,

10; Lapp 1968: Figs 8: 1, 4-6, 10; 9: 15, 18; 10: 4, 7, 10; 11: 12, 14; 12: right; Schaub p.c.), Azor (Ben-Tor 1975: Figs 6: 10-18-; 11: 5-12), Kataret es-Samra (Leonard 1983: Fig. 12), Giv`atayim (Sussman and Ben-Arieh 1966: Fig. 9: 19-21), Arad (Amiran 1978: Pls 1: 19, 20 [Str. V]; 7 [Str. IV]; 13 [Str. III] - including developed forms; see also *idem*, Pl. 22 [Str. II]), Tell Fara South (Macdonald 1932: Pl. XXXI: H), and Beth Shan (Fitzgerald 1935: Pl. V: 13, 26 [EB II: a developed form?]). (See also Hennessy [1967] and de Miroschedji [1971] for foreign parallels, some more convincing than others: de Miroschedji, for example, includes some Mesopotamian examples which are probably not related at all to what went on in Palestine; if there was a relationship, it was most likely indirect, via northern Syria.)

Genre 36: bowls (Figs 211, 212: 1-7)

There are two main forms of these small finely made shallow bowls: a fuller form (Fig. 101: a); and a flatter, shallower one (Fig. 101: b). They all have thin walls, thickening to rounded, flat and, in one case, shallow disc bases. Surfaces are slipped, polished or burnished inside and out. Profiles are rounded in most cases with only a few examples of slight external carinations (e.g. Fig. 211: 17, 28, 30, and 31). Rim forms (Fig. 102) range from in turned (a-c, e) to open (d, f-i), with in rolled lips (a, b), rounded lips (c, f), out rolled lips (g), and pointed lips (d, e, i).

A few parallels can be recognized in Chalcolithic assemblages: e.g. at Horvat Beter (Dothan 1959a: Figs 11: 43 [similar shape]; 18: 18, 19 [similar shape but larger]); `Ein el-Jarba (Kaplan 1969: Fig. 7: 3 [though deeper]); Tell es-Sa'idiyah al-Tahta (de Contenson 1960: Fig. 32: 11, 12, 21); Azor (Perrot 1961: Fig. 41: 15 = TUH211: 6, 7); and Abu Zureiq (Anati 1971: Fig. 35: 6). The form is rare in Chalcolithic assemblages, the most common bowl being the 'bol conique' (cf. Commenge-Pellerin 1987: *passim*).

EB I (A) examples come from Tel Esdar (Kochavi 1969: Fig. 17: 14 [similar shape, but larger]), Meser (Dothan 1957: Fig. 2: 8 [or = genre 37?]; 1959b: Figs 6: 7 [or = genre 37?; occurs with 'Esdraelon' ware]; 7: 18, 20 [?]), Giv`atayim (Sussman and Ben-Arieh 1966: Fig. 9: 4), Tel Rosh ha-`Ayin (Eitan 1969: Fig. 2: 7), Azor (Ben-Tor 1975: Figs 5: 1-5 [?] - later forms; 11: 1), Arqub edh-Dhahr (Parr 1956: Fig. 13: 58 [?], 62), Afula (Sukenik 1948: Pl. VI: 14, 18), Jericho (Garstang 1935: Pls XVII: 24 [Chalco.]; XXXVI: 13 [EB I B?]; 1936: Pl. XXXVI: 8, 13, 14; Kenyon 1960: Figs 9-11, with some exceptions; 17: 3, 4, etc.; 1965: Figs 4: 4; 8: 9; 10: 1; 12: 1, 2; Kenyon and Holland 1983; *passim*), N.T. Jericho (Pritchard 1958: Pl. 57: 21, 22 [?]), Ai (Callaway 1972: Figs 15: 1 [Phase I]; 16: 4, 7, 9, 10, 12 [Phase II] - related forms), Tell el-Far'ah (de Vaux and Steve 1947: Fig. 1: 29 ['én. moy.']; 1949: Figs 1: 1, 2, 3 [omphalos based]; 6: 1; de Vaux 1951: Fig. 11: 4, 7 [omphalos based],

8; 1952: Fig. 10: 5; 1955: Fig. 1: 11 [omphalos based], 12), Arad (Amiran 1978: [shallow bowls which could also be related to genre 37] Pls 1: 19, 20 [Str. V]; 7 [Str. IV]; 13 [Str. III] - a later, developed form in EB II; also *idem* Pl. 22 [Str. II]), and Megiddo (Loud 1948: Pl. 2: 7 [?]). A few small fine bowl fragments were found at Jawa (Betts [ed.] 1991: Figs 145: 488, 489; 146: 494, 495 [form only]).

The form of the vessel can also be found at Byblos (Dunand 1973: Fig. 119: 33799 ['én. réc.'], Hama (Fugman 1958: Fig. 37: 4B595), Tarsus (Goldman 1956: Figs 343: 24, 26, 28, 29, 31, 32; 231; 232, 233 [together with vessels close to genres 34 and 35]), in the Amuq region (Braidwood and Braidwood 1960: Fig. 234 [Amuq G: red-black burnished]), Habuba Kabira (Sürenhagen 1978: Tabn 2: 25 [raised interior base similar to examples from Tell el-Far'ah]; 3: 41 [form]; 20: 1). With other genres (i.e. 34/35) it may be a 'foreign' import in EB I A/B (see 'Repertoires': R4; cf. also Helms 1987a: Fig. 19: 11, 13, 14, 16, 17, from Tarsus).

Genre 37: bowls (Fig. 212: 8-16)

These shallow, open bowls are similar to those of genre 36; they are, however, thicker and heavier (Fig. 101: c). Bases are rounded and, in one case, slightly omphaloid (Fig. 212: 16). All bowls are red slipped and heavily burnished. Rim forms (Fig. 103) are pointed (a), out rolled (b, d), rounded (c), pointed and slightly recessed on the inside of the lip (e), and rounded, slightly in turned (f).

Similar simple bowls are found at Tell Shuneh North (de Contenson 1960: Fig. 10: 9 [?]), Jericho (Kenyon 1960: [see also genre 36 above] Figs 10: 14; 11: 12; 1965: Figs 8: 3; 12: 3), Tell el-Far'ah (de Vaux and Steve 1948: Fig. 5: 22 [?]), Afula (Sukenik 1948: Pl. II: 23 ['Esdraelon' ware, close to genre 37: one vessel in genre 37 is made in the same ware: Vaillant p.c.), and Meser (Dothan 1959b: Fig. 6: 7 [?]). A similar shape is known at Teleilat Ghassul (Mallon *et al.* 1934: Fig. 5 [?]).

Genre 38: bowls (Fig. 212: 17-24)

Heavy bowls with rounded profiles. They occur in two forms: a deep version (Fig. 101: d); and a shallow, almost platter like one (Fig. 101: e). Surfaces are 'finger streaked', plain and, in one case, red slipped and burnished or polished. The main attribute, which distinguishes these forms from other crude bowls, is the treatment of the lip which, in all cases, appears to have been smoothed on the upper and outer surfaces while the curve of the inner wall comes to a sharp carination, as if the vessel had been made in a mould and was cut free when 'leather dry'. (The other possibly form-made vessels at Um Hammad belong to genre 54: see below.) Rim forms (Fig. 104) are uniform, but for the stance.

There are a few shallow bowls with wavy rims at Abu Hamid (Dollfus and Kafafi n.d.: Fig. 7: 16, 17 = TUH212: 23, 24). Somewhat similar forms occur at Ein Gedi (Ushishkin 1980: Fig. 8: 12 [form of vessel; not rim]), Tell Shuneh North (de Contenson 1960: Fig. 10: 8 [?] = TUH212: 19), Kataret es-Samra (Leonard 1983: Fig. 8: 15 [?]), and Jericho (Garstang 1935: Pl. XLI: 18 [?; Chalco.]).

Genre 39: bowls (Figs 213, 214: 1-14)

This genre includes a variety of forms. There are two basic shapes (Fig. 101): deep bowls with vertical to slightly in turned rims, in some cases slightly bulbous below the lip (f); and more open forms (g). Bases are flat and, occasionally, of disc form (e.g. Fig. 213: 20). Surface treatment is plain, red slipped, and red slipped and burnished. One example (Fig. 214: 7) is decorated with a band of 'reed' impressed patterns below the rim (see 'Repertoires': R3). Another example (Fig. 213: 19) has a drilled mendhole. Rim forms (Fig. 105) are rounded (a), pointed, internally slightly recessed (b, f, h), pointed and in turned (c), rounded and in rolled (d), rounded bulbous (e), and pointed, in turned and bulbous (g).

These relatively undistinguished bowls might have Chalcolithic parallels: e.g. at Neve Ur (Perrot *et al*. 1967: Fig. 15: 5 = TUH214: 8-13); Ein Gedi (Ushishkin 1980: Fig. 8: 9); `Ein el-Jarba (Kaplan 1969: Fig. 7: 3 [?]); Ghrubba (Mellaart 1956: Figs 4: 13, 23 [?]; 5: 83, 85, 96, 97 [?; without the painted decoration]); Azor (Perrot 1961: Fig. 41: 14 [shape of lip?]); and Tel Turmus (Dayan 1969: Fig. 6: 3 [?; without the decoration]).

EB I parallels occur at Jawa (Betts [ed.] 1991: Fig. 146: 496-503 [?form]), Megiddo (Loud 1948: Pls 2: 10; 6: 10 = TUH213: 30 [base shape]), Jericho (Garstang 1932: Pls IV: 10 = TUH214: 8-13; VIII: 12, 14 = TUH 213: 20 [base shape]; 1936: Pl. XXXIV: 13 [rim]; Kenyon 1960: Figs 9: 13, 19 = TUH214: 8-14, etc.; 12: 3, 4 = TUH214: 20; 17: 4, etc. = TUH213: 5, etc.; 1965: Figs 4: 4; 8: 5, 9, 11 [later forms; but for hollow base = TUH213: 20]; 13: 1, 3), N.T. Jericho (Pritchard 1958: Pl. 57: 15, 18), Ai (Callaway 1972: Fig. 16: 14 = TUH213: 20 [form]), Tell el-Far'ah (de Vaux 1947: Figs 1: 28, 29; 4: 16-18; 1948: Fig. 5: 28; 1949: Figs 3: 4; 6: 1; de Vaux 1951: Fig. 4: 7 [but for the hollow base = TUH214: 8-14]; 1955: Figs 1: 14; 3: 3-6 [rim/body shape]; 1961: Fig. 61: 27), Azor (Ben-Tor 1975: Figs 5: 8-13 [?]; 6: 1), Afula (Sukenik 1948: Pl. VI: 14 [?], 44), Arqub edh-Dhahr (Parr 1956: Figs 13 and 14, *passim*), Tel Rosh ha-`Ayin (Eitan 1969: Fig. 2: 15 [?]), Tell ed-Duweir (Tufnell 1958: Pl. 57: 56, 58), Bab edh-Dhra' (Saller 1964/5: Fig. 28: 13 [but for the hollow base; cf. also parallels at Tell el-Far'ah above]; Schaub p.c.: 0569.11.22), Kataret es-Samra (Leonard 1983: Fig. 8: 12), Giv`atayim (Sussman and Ben-Arieh 1966: Fig. 9: 2-5 [hollow bases]), and Tell Fara South (Macdonald 1932: Pl. XL: 39 = TUH213: 20).

Genre 40: bowls (Fig. 214: 15-17)

Small deep bowls with rounded profiles (Fig. 101: h). No bases were found. The external and internal surfaces are decorated with vertical red painted stripes pendent from a horizontal red painted stripe along the lip. Rim forms (Fig. 106) are rounded (a), pointed and externally slightly recessed (b), and rounded in rolled (c).

Parallels may be found at Ghrubba (Mellaart 1956: Fig. 5: 80), Meser (Dothan 1959b: Fig. 7: 22), Bab edh-Dhra' (Saller 1964/5: Fig. 21: 13 [?]), Arqub edh-Dhahr (Parr 1956: Figs 13: 59, 75, 78; 14: 83, 84, 111, 113, 114), Tell el-Far'ah (de Vaux 1951: Fig. 1: 4; 1952: Fig. 12: 7 [?]), and Jericho (Garstang 1932: Pl. VIII: 14; 1936: Pl. XXXVI: 7; Kenyon 1960: Fig. 11: 18; 1965: Figs 4: 7; 8: 14 [decoration]).

Genre 41: bowls (Figs 214: 18-26, 215: 1-6)

Small deep flat-based bowls with slightly in turned rims and high shoulders (Fig. 96: i). External and internal surfaces are slurred. Surface treatment is plain, red slipped, and red slipped and burnished. One example (Fig. 215: 5) has a horizontally pierced vertical lug handle on the shoulder. Rim forms (Fig. 102) are rounded (a), rounded-pointed (b, d), out rolled or externally grooved below the rim (c), and rounded and in rolled (e).

Some of the small bowls in Chalcolithic assemblages might served as proto-types: e.g. at Abu Matar and Zoumeli (Commenge-Pellerin 1987: Figs 17: 1, et.; 22: 2; 45: etc. [?]); Horvat Beter (Dothan 1959a: Figs 7: 1-16; 12: *passim*); Shiqmim (Levy [ed.] 1987: Figs 12.2: 1-13; 13.15; 13.16: 1, 4-6 [?]); Ein Gedi (Ushishkin 1980: Fig. 8: 10 [form]); Ghrubba (Mellaart 1956: Figs 4: 13-17; 5: 75, 82, 96, etc.); and Azor (Perrot 1961: Fig. 42: 10, 12 = TUH214: 23, TUH215: 4, etc.?).

Later parallels come from Jericho (Garstang 1932: Pl. IV: 8, 9 [?]; 1935: Pl. XLIII: 6 [Chalco.]), Tell el-Far'ah (de Vaux and Steve 1949: Figs 6: 20 = TUH215: 5 [?]; 13: 1; de Vaux 1952: Fig. 12: 2; 1955: Fig. 1: 14), Arqub edh-Dhahr (Parr 1956: Fig. 14: 93, 97 [?]), and Meser (Dothan 1959b: Fig. 8: 7 = TUH214: 23).

Similar forms occur at énéolithique récent Byblos (Dunand 1973: Fig. 154: 21199 [= TUH214: 23]) and at Habuba Kabira (Sürenhagen 1978: Tabn 1: 7 [form; 22: 68].

Genre 42: bowls (Fig. 215: 7, 8)

Small open bowls with round profiles (Fig. 101: j). The walls are thick. Surface treatment includes external vertical 'finger streaking' and red 'splash paint'. No bases were found. Rim forms (Fig. 108) are rounded (a), and rounded with a slight internal recessing.

For parallels in general see genre 40; the painted pattern is more random (cf. also genres 79, 81 and related forms).

Genre 43: bowls (Fig. 215: 9-12)

Shallow in turned bowls with soft carination at the shoulder or waist (Fig. 101: k). No bases or handles were encountered. Surface treatment is plain, red slipped and burnished. Rim forms (Fig. 109) are pointed (a), pointed and externally slightly recessed (b), rounded with an internal recessing (c), and rounded, slightly everted with an internal recessing (d).

This early version of the common carinated platter/bowls (see the composite genre 59 below) can be seen at Tell Handaquq North (Mabry 1989), Tell el-Far'ah (de Vaux and Steve 1948: Figs 1: 5 ['én. moy.']; 6: 17), and Jericho (Garstang 1935: Pl. XLII: 23 [Chalco.]; Kenyon 1960: [where some of the shallow bowls have slight carinations] Figs 9: 16, 19; 10: 12, 13; [and even double carinations] Figs 11: 6; 17: 12, 13; 1965: Fig. 8: 7 = TUH215: 12 [but see also genres 58 and 60 below]).

The source region(s) for carinated platters or shallow bowls is probably in the north, in northern Syria, Cilicia, and Anatolia. Parallels for genre 41 can be found at Habuba Kabira (Sürenhagen 1978: Tabn 3: 33-5; 20: 3-7, 9, etc.), and Hama (Fugman 1958: Figs 37: 4B631, 4B624; 46: 7A608 No.5).

Genre 44: bowls (Fig. 215: 13-17)

Small open bowls with slightly everted, near vertical sides and flat or rounded bases (Fig. 96: l). Internal surfaces are heavily slurred; external ones red-brown slipped and highly burnished. Rim forms (Fig. 105) are rounded (a) and rounded and slightly recessed inside and out (b).

Some parallels may be found at the following sites: Azor (Perrot 1961: Fig. 42: 13 [?]); Jericho (Garstang 1932: Pl. III: 2 [?]; 1935: Pls XXXVI: 10 [?]; XXXVIII: 22 [?]; Kenyon 1960: Fig. 17: 13 [?]); Horvat Usa (Ben-Tor 1966: Fig. 4: 13 [?]); Tell el-Far'ah (de Vaux and Steve 1949: Fig. 8: 5 [?]; de Vaux 1955: Fig. 3: 6, 7; 1961: Fig. 2: 30); Arqub edh-Dhahr (Parr 1956: Fig. 14: 95 [?]); and Beth Shan (Fitzgerald 1935: Pl. V: 16).

Genre 45: bowls (Figs 215: 18, 19; 216)

'Esdraelon' ware. There are two main forms: an open bowl with an everted, often down-turned rim (Fig. 101: m); and an open bowl with an in turned rounded-pointed rim (Fig. 216: 9). Bases are flat (Fig. 216: 8, 10, 11). Most vessels have distinctive raised knobs along the waist. All vessels are highly burnished, colours ranging from black, through dark violet, to grey and red. Rim forms (Fig. 111) are pointed and everted (a), rounded and everted (b), rounded, slightly pointed and everted, with a sharp internal carination (c), rounded and everted and down turned (d), pointed and everted, down turned with a sharp lip (e), and rounded, slightly in turned (f).

For the distribution (and relative frequency of occurrence) Hennessy's summary (1967) is still valid (see also de Miroschedji 1971: *passim*; Hanbury-Tenison 1986: *passim*). Close parallels occur at Beth Shan (Fitzgerald 1935: Pl. III: 1-5), Meser (Dothan 1957: Fig. 2: 2, 3; 1959b: Figs 6: 1-4; 8: 1-3), Arqub edh-Dhahr (Parr 1956: Fig. 13: 24), Tell Shuneh North (Gustavson-Gaube 1985: Fig. 15: 71-75c; 1986: Fig. 21: 115a-118; Leonard n.d.), En Shadud (Braun 1985: Fig. 19: 1-10), Afula (Sukenik 1948: Pl. II), N.T. Jericho (Pritchard 1958: Pl. 57: 28-35), and Tell el-Far'ah (de Vaux and Steve; de Vaux: references *passim*: mostly in the tombs).

Genre 46: bowls (Fig. 217: 1-3)

Deep conical and rounded bowls (Fig. 101: n). No bases or handles were found. Surfaces are red-orange slipped and highly burnished and decorated with bands of small round knobs or, in one case, three slightly larger ones in a row. Rim forms (Fig. 112) are rounded, slightly everted or recessed (a), pointed and internally bevelled (b), and pointed, externally slightly recessed (c).

Some similar forms occur at Tell Handaquq North (Mabry 1989: tomb NE. 1 [= EB I]), Afula (Sukenik 1948: Pl. VI: 15 [?]), Tell ed-Duweir (Tufnell 1958: Pl. 56: 13 [?]), Bab edh-Dhra' (Saller 1964/5: Figs 20 [particularly no. 4 = TUG217: 1]; 21: 5, 10, 11, 17; 22: 7, 14, 16 [similar decorative bands]; 26 [stone bowls with similar decorative bands]; 27 [basalt mug]; 34: 19, 20; Lapp 1968: Fig. 9: 12, etc.), and Meser (Dothan 1959b: Fig. 6: 5 ['Esdraelon' ware, but with a similar decorative band, as well as the same general form]).

Genre 47: bowls (Fig. 217: 4-7)

Medium sized open bowls with in turned rims and rounded sides (Fig. 101: o). No bases were found. All examples have at least one raised knob, or vestigial ledge handle, on the shoulder. (Mellaart [Leonard n.d.] found several, more complete, versions: Fig. 268: 14; see also 'Correlation with previous work'.) Surface treatment is plain, red slipped or, in one case, internally red slipped with burnishing (Fig. 217: 4). Rim forms (Fig. 113) are rounded, in-turned and externally bevelled making a sharp carination at the shoulder (a), rounded and bevelled on the inside (b), and rounded, bulbous (c). The form may be loosely related to the bowl in genre 45 (Fig. 216: 9).

Parallels come from the following sites: Meser (Dothan 1957: Fig. 2: 12 [?]; Afula (Sukenik 1936: Pl. I: 7, 8); Jericho (Garstang 1935: Pl. XLI: 8-12 [Chalco.]; 1936: Pls XXX: 9, 10 [Middle Neo.: IX]; XXXII: 28, 29 [Late Neo.: VIII]; XXXIV: 13 [EB I]; Kenyon 1965: Fig. 7: 8 [multiple knobs: EB I B]); N.T. Jericho (Pritchard 1958: Pl. 57: 15, 16 [shallower bowls]); and Tell el-Far'ah (de Vaux and Steve 1947: Fig. 4: 17 [shallow]; 1948: Fig. 5: 8, 10, 11 [rim shape slightly different: cf. genre 3, Fig. 150: 2]; de Vaux 1952: Fig. 12: 10).

Genre 48: bowls (Figs 217: 8-10; 218-19)

Large deep bowls with everted rims. There are several possible reconstructions (no bases can be associated), all of which could favour round, or rounded, shapes (Fig. 101: p, q). There is also a great variety of rim shapes (see below), as well as surface treatment, all of which is reminiscent of genre 16. Surface treatment includes diagonal, horizontal and random 'finger streaking', slurred or finely grooved rims and necks, red slip and high polish (not found in genre 16: but see one body sherd in genre 80, Fig. 243: 9), and red 'splash-' or 'trickle paint'. One variant (Fig. 219: 2) has horizontal bands of incised or punctate decoration on the shoulder: both this attribute, and the form of the vessel might make it more comfortable in genre 6 (Fig. 220: 3-7), or related to jars in figure 194 (1, 2). No handles can be associated. Rim forms (Fig. 114) include the following (all are everted): (a) rounded; (b) rounded with a sharp internal carination; (c) down pointed; (d) down pointed with a sharp internal carination; (e) bulbous and pointed; (f) pointed, slightly bevelled with a sharp internal carination; (g) rounded with a sharp internal carination and a sharp indentation at the neck-shoulder junction; (h) short everted, rounded rim with a sharp indentation at the shoulder; (i) rounded-rolled with shallow external scalloping; (j) rounded, internally recessed with a sharp internal carination; and (k) pointed-rounded, internally slightly bevelled. The form of some variants (e.g. Figs 217; 8-10; 218: 7; 219: 3) is similar to that of the 'Esdraelon' ware bowls of genre 45 (see also Fig. 268: 16, 16, the larger bowl with raised, applied [?] squares, from Mellaart's collection [Leonard n.d.]). The 'floruit' of genre 48 is in about phases 2/3, while genre 45 appears to decrease in frequency of occurrence at this time (Fig. 129). Genre 48, therefore, could be regarded as a local imitation of genre 45, gradually replacing it in the overall pottery assemblage at the site (see also 'Relative distribution of genres' below).

Chalcolithic proto-types occur at Abu Matar and Zoumeili (Commenge-Pellerin 1987: Figs 22: 1 [see also genre 49]; 24: 5 = TUH219: 2 [grande vase à bord inflechi], perhaps better in the larger versions of genre 6; 46: 6 [see also genre 49]), Teleilat Ghassul (Mallon et al. 1934: Fig. 43: 8), Tell es-Sa'idiyeh al-Tahta (de Contenson 1960: Fig. 32: 19), and wadi Rabah (Kaplan 1958: Fig. 5: 18 [?]).

EB I parallels come from Horvat Usa (Ben-Tor 196: Fig. 4: 7 [?]), En Shadud (Braun 1985: Fig. 19: 11-13 [?]), Afula (Sukenik 1948: Pl. VI: 24-28 [though recessed]), Tell ed-Duweir (Tufnell 1958: Pl. 56: 30 [but see also genre 49]), Tell Fara South (Macdonald 1932: Pl. XL: 69, 70 [but see also genre 49]), and Tell el-Far'ah (de Vaux 1952: Fig. 12: 20 ['Esdraelon' ware?]).

Parallels might also be recognized at Habuba Kabira (Sürenhagen 1978: Tab. 3: 32 [?]).

Genre 49: bowls (Fig. 220: 1, 2)

Open bowls with everted rims and rounded sides (Fig. 101: r). As was the case with genre 48, no bases can be associated: however, close parallels (see below; Helms 1987a: Fig. 17: 15, 16) have flat, or slightly pedestalled, bases; some have fenestrated pedestal bases. Surface decoration includes a horizontal band of impressed patterns below the rim. Rim forms (Fig. 115: a, b) are everted with an external groove below the lip.

Some Chalcolithic proto-types might be recognized at Abu Matar and Zoumeili (Commenge-Pellerin 1987: Figs 19: 3, 7-11 [?]; 22: 1; 46: 6), Horvat Beter (Dothan 1959a: Fig. 13: 17), Shiqmim (Levy [ed.] 1987: Fig. 12.3: 9), and Tell Turmus (Dayan 1969: Fig. 6: 10 [?], 15 [?]).

EB I comparisons can be made with forms at Tell el-Far'ah (de Vaux and Steve 1949: Fig. 8: 32 [minus the fenestrated pedestal base: see also Bab edh-Dhra']), Afula (Sukenik 1948: Pl. VI: 21 [?]), Tell ed-Duweir (Tufnell 1958: Pl. 56: 30 [?]), Bab edh-Dhra' (Saller 1964/5: Fig, 30: 4; Lapp 1968: Figs 9: 12, 13; 10: 1, 2, 5, 6, 11; 11: 16), Meser (Dothan 1959b: Fig. 6: 11 [?]), and Tell Fara South (Macdonald 1932: Pl. XL: 69, 70 [?]).

Genre 6: bowls (Fig. 220: 3-7; see also Fig. 151 and 152 for smaller range)

Parallels appear at Zoumeili (Commenge-Pellerin 1987: Fig. 46: 15 [bassins]), Horvat Beter (Dothan 1959b: Figs 7: 24; 13: 6 [stance?]), and Tell Turmus (Dayan 1969: Fig. 4: 7).

Similar vessel forms exist at Habuba Kabira (Sürenhagen 1978: Tab. 21: 54 [?]).

Genre 50: bowls (Figs 221, 222, 223: 1-6; 268: 17, 18; 269: 1; Pl. 6: 2)

Genre 50 belongs to the same repertoire as genres 12, 17, 18, and 27 (see 'Repertoires': R6). It consists of heavy deep bowls which could have either rounded (as suggested for genres 12 and some variants in genre 27), or flat bases (Fig. 116: a, b; cf. also Figs 250: 10-12; 251: 1, 2). Handles may have been attached at the waist, although no complete forms were recovered. (See, however, Leonard n.d., and Figs 268: 17, 18; 269: 1 - the former from Um Hammad, the latter from Tell Mafluq.) All examples are decorated with heavy horizontal and, occasionally, also 'wavy' or diagonal bands of impressed, incised, or slashed, patterns. Most variants have impressed external lips. Rim forms (Fig. 117) are vertical and bevelled (a), slightly in turned, splayed and bevelled (b), splayed and recessed on top (c), splayed and recessed on top with raised, rounded lips (d, f, g), and in turned and rounded, and splayed (e).

Close parallels exist in Chalcolithic assemblages of Palestine: e.g. at Zoumeili (Commenge-Pellerin 1987: Fig. 46: 11, 12 [?]); Ein Gedi (Ushishkin 1980: Fig. 9: 2, 7, 8); Teleilat Ghassul (Mallon *et al*. 1934: Figs 38: 4th from left; 41: 14; North 1961: Fig. 15: 8635, 8485; Elliott 1978: Fig. 2: 10); wadi Rabah (Kaplan 1958: Fig. 5: 1, 2); Abu Zureiq (Anati 1971: Fig. 19: 4, 5); Tell Turmus (Dayan 1969: Fig. 4: 8); and in the Jawlan (Epstein 1978: Fig. 9: a-d).

Close parallels also occur in EB I (B) contexts at Jericho (Garstang 1935: Pls XLI: 4, 5 [Chalco.]; XLIII: 12 [Chalco.]; 1936: Pl. XXXII: 24A [Late Neo.: VIII]), Tell el-Far'ah (de Vaux and Steve 1947: Fig. 2: 1; 1948: Fig. 5: 12; de Vaux 1955: Fig. 5: 1 [?]; 1961: Figs 2: 38; 3: 16, 17), Afula (Sukenik 1948: Pl. IX: 10, 12), and Kataret es-Samra (Leonard 1983: Figs 8: 24; 10 [bs]).

Genre 51: bowls (Fig. 223: 7-12)

This genre of mostly open, almost conical, heavy bowls may be related to the 'Umm Hamad esh-Sherqi ware/pré-urbaine D' repertoire. The bowls all have splayed rims and one heavy band of impressed decoration at the shoulder or just below the rim; Mellaart (Leonard n.d.) found similar vessels with flat bases. No bases were found (Fig. 116: c). Rim forms (Fig. 118) are recessed on top with a low internal lip (a), bevelled and in rolled (b), bevelled with a rounded outer lip (c), recessed on top with a rounded, grooved internal lip (d), bevelled with a low external lip (e), and recessed on top with rounded internal and external lips (f).

Parallels occur at Shiqmim (Levy [ed.] 1987: Fig. 12.7: 5 [similar rim form]) and N.T. Jericho (Pritchard 1958: Pl. 56: 19 [?]).

Genre 52: bowls (Fig. 224: 1-6)

Small thin walled open bowls, possibly with rounded bases (Fig. 116: d). Most profiles are rounded but for a few variants which have a slight carination at the waist (e.g. Fig. 224: 1). The carinated form also has internal reddish slip. Rim forms (Fig. 119) are flat topped, or slightly recessed on top, with internal and external grooves (a), recessed on top with a more pronounced internal groove (b), everted and internally slightly recessed (c), and out rolled with an external groove under the lip (d).

Some parallels may be found at Nahal Mishmar (Bar-Adon 1980: ill. 8: 10 [?]), Ein Gedi (Ushishkin 1980: Fig. 8: 11 [?= TUH224: 2]), Ghrubba (Mellaart 1956: Fig. 4: 6, 15 [?]), and Horvat Beter (Dothan 1959a: Fig. 7: 24 [?]).

Genre 53: bowls (Fig. 224: 7-12)

Small deep rounded open bowls which may have rounded bases (Fig. 116: e; cf. also the related genre, 54, which has rounded bases). Two variants have a high loop handle (double coil) preserved at one side (there may have been two; Fig. 224: 8, 10). External surfaces are plain; internal ones are sometimes red slipped along the lip. All examples have 'crazed' interiors, a feature which may have something to do with either the manufacturing technique (i.e. form-made) or, perhaps, their original contents (see genre 54). Tufnell (1958) called similar vessels (i.e. = genre 54) from Tell ed-Duweir 'crucibles'.

A similar shallow bowl with a single high loop handle is known in Mersin XVI (Garstang 1953: Fig. 93: 3; see also Helms 1987a: Fig. 18: 16). Palestinian Chalcolithic parallels (or proto-types) might be recognized at Zoumeili (Commenge-Pellerin 1987: Fig. 46: 1 = TUH224: 7?), Shiqmim (Levy [ed.] 1987: Fig. 12.2: 11, 12 [painted band along rim]; 15.20: 3 [paint on rim]), and Ghrubba (Mellaart 1956: Fig. 5: 70, 72, etc. [similar shape]).

EB I (A) examples come from Tel Esdar (Kochavi 1969: Fig. 17: 5, 8 [paint/slip along lip]), Jericho (Kenyon 1960: Fig. 19: 3 [a single handled cup]; 1965: Fig. 4: 11 [single lug just below the rim, possibly a later development]), Tell el-Far'ah (de Vaux and Steve 1949: Figs 6: 9, 10 [pierced lug]; 13: 6; de Vaux 1952: Fig. 10: 3 [high loop handle = TUH224: 8, 10], 6), Afula (Sukenik 1948: Pl. VIII: 33 [bowl with high loop handle]), Arqub edh-Dhahr (Parr 1956: Fig. 14: 102-114 [single pierced lugs below rim, similar to the examples from Jericho and Tell el-Far'ah]), Tell ed-Duweir (Tufnell 1958: Pl. 57: 66 [single small pierced lug handle on rim]), Bab edh-Dhra' (Saller 1964/5: Figs 31: 5 [cup with single high loop handle on rim]; 34: 22, 25 [single {?} lugs below rim]), and Giv'atayim (Sussman and Ben Arieh 1966: Fig. 9: 5 [single pierced lug below rim]).

Genre 54: bowls (Figs 224: 13-25; 225; Pl. 6: 3)

This genre of small deep open bowls is related to genre 53 (perhaps as a development from that genre, or a variant; see also 'Relative distribution of genres' and 'Repertoires'). There are two basic shapes (Fig. 116): a deep bowl, often with slightly in turned rim and rounded or omphaloid base (f); and a shallower version with a flat base (g). Almost all examples have recessed rims which have been heavily scored (not slurred), leaving an irregularly shaped rim (e.g. TUH224: 13); almost all examples have 'crazed' interiors. (The scoring might have been caused by the construction technique [cut from a form], or by whatever may have been the contents, as was noted with regard to genre 53: see also Chapter 3 and 'Construction methods' with regard to storage bins.) Rim forms (Fig. 121) are very similar: but for a few (k, l), all are everted and most are also internally recessed; some are on parallel sided shoulders (a, c, e, etc.); others on bulbous ones (b, d, h, etc.). There is a great variety of body width (e.g. compare g and j).

There are some recessed rimmed bowls in Chalcolithic assemblages which might serve as proto-types for this genre: e.g. at Abu Matar (Commenge-Pellerin 1987: Figs 19: 2-11; 22: 1 [?]); Shiqmim (Levy [ed.] 1987: Fig. 13.2: 9 [?]); and Abu Zureiq (Anati 1971: Fig. 36: 4 [?]).

The closest parallels, however, come from EB I (A) contexts, from Jericho (Kenyon 1960: Figs 11: 1, 22, 23; 21: 2; 1965: Fig. 13: 2, 5; there are some derived forms in the tell assemblage: e.g. Kenyon and Holland 1982: Figs 34-6), N.T. Jericho (Pritchard 1958: Pl. 57: 14), Azor (Ben-Tor 1975: Figs 5: 14-16; 11: 2), Afula (Sukenik 1948; Pl.VI: 35 [?]), Arqub edh-Dhahr (Parr 1956: Fig. 14: 53), Tell ed-Duweir (Tufnell 1958: Pls 56: 1, 12, 14, 31; 57: 45, 46, 65), Bab edh-Dhra' (Saller 1964/5: Figs 21: 15 [?]; 25: 8, 9 [?]), and Tell Fara South (Macdonald 1932: Pl. XL: 48-50).

Similar vessel forms, particularly the rim shape, occur at Byblos (Dunand 1973: Figs 119: 27138 ['en. anc.']; 150: 21663 ['én. réc.'] - see also genre 56), Habuba Kabira (Sürenhagen 1978: Tab. 18: 107 [?], Hama (Fugman 1958: Figs 37: 4B607 [?]; 46: 4B753, 4B998), and in the Amuq region (Braidwood and Braidwood 1960: Fig. 172: 31, 32).

Genre 55: bowls (Fig. 226: 1-8; Pl. 6: 4, 5)

Genre 55 is related to genre 54 in terms of forms (cf. Fig. 116: h and f); none, however, has the characteristic internal 'crazing'. Bases are rounded (Fig. 226: 2, 3, 5) and profiles round, but for a few examples which can be reconstructed with a flattened waist (Fig. 226: 2). All examples are painted with red stripes, in some cases pendent from a horizontal red painted band along the internal and external sides of the rim; the paint is similar to 'trickle paint' in other genres at Um Hammad (see 'Repertoires': R1). In some cases the painted lines form an irregular net pattern (e.g. Fig. 226: 2, 5; Pl. 6: 4) which is not to be confused with 'group-line' painting of the 'EB I B/'Proto-Urban B' classification (e.g. Schaub 1982; see also earlier reports on Um Hammad [Helms 1984a] where this mistake was made). Rim forms (Fig. 122) are pointed and externally recessed (a, b), rounded and externally recessed (c), 'beaded', or out rolled, on a bulbous neck (d), rounded and internally recessed (e), pointed, slightly recessed, or grooved, externally (f), and rounded, internally recessed, with a slight external carination at the waist (g).

Good parallels occur at Jericho (Garstang 1936: Pl. XXXVI: 7; Kenyon 1960: Figs 11: 18; 22: 6; 1965: Figs 4: 3; 13: 4 - almost precise parallels, although those at Tell Um Hammad belong to EB I A and not, as at Jericho, to EB I B), Tell el-Far'ah (de Vaux 1951: Fig. 1: 4 [?];

1952: Fig. 12: 7 [?] - although genre 54, related in form, appears to be completely absent at Tell el-Far'ah), Azor (Ben-Tor 1975: Fig. 5: 6, 7 [though not the rim form]), and Arqub edh-Dhahr (Parr 1956: Fig, 13: 7, 8, 27, 28, 31-44, etc.).

Genre 56: bowls (Fig. 226: 9-27)

Genre 56 may be regarded as a development (see 'Relative distribution of genres') of genre 54 in terms of forms and rim shape; once again, as with genre 55, there is no internal 'crazing'. Profiles are rounded and bases probably also rounded (Fig. 116: i). Surface treatment consists of red slip and red slip with burnishing. Rim shapes (Fig. 123) are varied, although all examples are variations of recessed, everted forms.

Some of the parallels cited for genre 55 might also apply to this genre. The best parallels come from Jawa (Betts [ed.] 1991: Fig. 145: 470-83). Similar forms occur at Jericho (Kenyon 1965: Fig. 12: 4 [?]), Horvat Usa (Ben-Tor 1966: Fig. 4: 13), Tell el-Far'ah (de Vaux and Steve 1949: Fig. 6: 6 [?]; de Vaux 1951: Fig. 11: 3), and Afula (Sukenik 1948: Pl. VI: 21 [?]).

Comparable forms exist at énéolithique récent Byblos (Dunand 1973: Fig. 150: 21663) and, perhaps, in the Amuq region (Braidwood and Braidwood 1960: Amuq F and G).

Genre 57: bowls (Fig. 227: 1, 2)

Small shallow bowls. No bases were found: these could be flat or rounded (Fig. 116: j). Surface treatment is either red slipped or red slipped and burnished. Rim forms (Fig. 124) are uniform: rounded, with a sharp external indentation just below the lip.

Some possible parallels might be seen at Jericho (Kenyon 1965: Fig. 8: 4 [?]), Tell el-Far'ah (de Vaux 1955: Fig. 1: 10), Arad (Amiran 1978: Pl. 22: 56), and Arqub edh-Dhahr (Parr 1956: Fig. 13: 70 [?]).

It may be possible to trace this form to vessels at énéolithique récent Byblos (Dunand 1973: Fig. 119: 21229), and even Habuba Kabira (Sürenhagen 1978: Tab. 20: 8).

Genre 58: bowls (Fig. 227: 3-10)

Shallow open bowls (or platters), some with double carination (Fig. 116: k). Surfaces are red slipped and, most commonly, red slipped and burnished. Bases could be rounded or flat (cf. Fig. 227: 5). Rim forms (Fig. 125) are rounded (a) and slightly everted (b).

Parallels are found at the following sites: Jericho (Garstang 1936: Pl. XXXVIII: 2, 3; see also Kenyon and Holland 1982, 1983: *passim*); Tell el-Far'ah (de Vaux and Steve 1947: Figs 2: 25; 4; 7: 35, 36, 38; 1948: Figs 5: 20, 21; 6: 10, 11; 8: 4-6; 1949: Fig. 6: 23-26; de Vaux 1961: Fig. 3: 27, 35-38); Tell Handaquq North (Mabry 1989); Tel Rosh ha-`Ayin

(Eitan 1969: Fig. 2: 10); Giv`atayim (Sussman and Ben Arieh 1966: Fig. 9: 6, 7); and Beth Shan (Fitzgerald 1935: Pl. V: 18, 21).

Genre 59: bowls (Figs 227: 11-17; 228-29)

This is a broad category of platters which could be subdivided into a number of genres (Fig. 116: l-n) whose parallels in Palestinian pottery typology range from 'EB I B' to 'EB II' (some possibly 'EB III'). They are grouped together here since they come from a limited set of stratified contexts at the site (see 'Repertoires': R9). This is due to deflation and erosion of the upper occupation layers (see Chapter 2). Bases are mostly flat (cf. examples in Amiran 1969). Most variants are red slipped and burnished; some of them are radially pattern burnished on the inside (e.g. Figs 227: 14; 228: 6, 11; 229: 3). Rim shapes are summarised in Figure 126. (For specific stratified contexts, see 'Catalogue' and 'Relative distribution of genres'.)

The simpler forms (e.g. TUH228: 2-13) first appear in EB I B. For parallels see Amiran's summary (1969: Pls 11: 3, 4; 13: 2-15; 15: 1-6; 9).

With reference to genre 43, similar shapes can be found at Habuba Kabira (see genre 43 and references), and at Hama (Fugman 1958: Figs 37: 4B615 No.37; 46: 7A609 No.10; 49: S.; 54: 4B816, 6B948 [i.e. into EB III: with Khirbet Kerak ware, cf. Figs 46: 4C50; 49: 4C46 {?}]).

Genre 60: bowls (Fig. 230: 1-7)

Small deep bowls with round profiles and high, indented shoulders and, perhaps, rounded (or omphaloid) bases (Fig. 116: o). Surfaces are red slipped, and red slipped and burnished. Rim forms (Fig. 127: a-d) are all similar, varying only in stance from in turned to everted.

One precise parallel comes from Tel Rosh ha-`Ayin (Eitan 1969: Fig. 2: 16). Similar, and possibly related, forms occur at Tell ed-Duweir (Tufnell 1958: Pl. 56: 37), Jericho (Kenyon and Holland 1983: Fig. 13: 22), and Tell el-Far'ah (de Vaux and Steve 1947: Fig. 7: 19, 31), the latter perhaps representing an earlier, simpler version.

Possible inspirations for these vessels may be noted at Habuba Kabira (Sürenhagen 1978: Tabn 1: 10; 21: 63).

Genre 61: bowls (Fig. 233: 8, 9)

Small closed bowls with s-shaped rims and, perhaps, rounded bases (Fig. 116: p). Surfaces are red slipped or red slipped and burnished. Rim shapes are summarised in figure 128 (a, b).

Parallels are found at Shiqmim (Levy [ed.] 1987: Fig. 12.13: 16 [?]), Jericho (Garstang 1932: Pl. III: 11 [?]), and N.T. Jericho (Pritchard 1958: Pl. 57: 13).

Unclassified: bowls (Fig. 230: 8-13)

Deep open bowls with rounded sides. No bases were found. Surfaces are reddish slipped and, in some cases, highly burnished. Rim forms are generally splayed, some approaching the 'hammer rim' type (e.g. Fig. 229: 10, 11), others are slightly recessed on top.

Similar vessels may be found at Megiddo (Loud 1948: Pl. 1: 27, 28 = TUH230: 11, though shallower), Jericho (Garstang 1936: Pls XXXV: 5; XXXVIII: 4, 13), Tell el-Far'ah (de Vaux and Steve 1947: Fig. 2: 3; 1948: Figs 1: 1 ['én. moy.']; 5: 5 ['én. sup.']), and Arqub edh-Dhahr (Parr 1956: Fig. 14: 112, 115-118, 120 [rim forms]).

Unclassified: bowls (Fig. 231: 1-7)

Deep conical bowls. No bases were found. Surfaces are plain, reddish slipped and one example is red slipped and burnished on the outside. Rim shapes are either everted and slightly bevelled, or plain and round.

These vessels could be derived from conical bowls and basins of the Chalcolithic period (e.g. Commenge-Pellerin 1987: *passim*; Hennessy 1969: Fig. 9a: 2 [?]). Other parallels, in EB I (A) contexts, come from Jericho (Kenyon 1960: Figs 12: 2; 17: 21, 22; 19: 4; 22: 1, 3; 1965: Figs 4: 10; 8: 12-14; 10: 2; 13: 6), Horvat Usa (Ben-Tor 1966: Fig. 4: 7-9), Tell el-Far'ah (de Vaux and Steve 1949: Fig. 8: 6; de Vaux 1952: Fig. 12: 11; 1955: Fig. 3: 2; 1957: Fig. 1: 4, 4 [Chalco.]), Afula (Sukenik 1948: Pl. VI: 49, 50), Arqub edh-Dhahr (Parr 1956: Fig. 13: 11-14), Tell ed-Duweir (Tufnell 1958: Pl 56: 35), Bab edh-Dhra' (Saller 1964/5: Fig. 34: 17; Schaub p.c.: 0560.11), Kataret es-Samra (Leonard 1983: Fig. 8: 6-8), Tell Fara South (Macdonald 1932: Pl. XXXIX: 14-16), and Meser (Dothan 1959b: Figs 5: 1, 2; 6: 9; 8: 4-6).

Unclassified: bowls (Fig. 231: 8-13)

Medium depth open bowls. Several examples have moulded decoration along the rim (e.g. nos 9, 11), three have raised knobs (nos 10, 12, 13; see also genre 47). Rim forms, but for one rounded shape (no 8), are all splayed or in rolled and recessed on top. The group is somewhat similar to genres 47 (knobs) and 51 (rim form).

Unclassified: bowls (Fig. 231: 14-16)

Heavy deep open bowls. Two have thick loop handles at and below the rim.

Similar forms occur at Jericho (Garstang 1936: Pl. XXV: 4 [?]), Afula (Sukenik 1948: Pl. VI: 11 [?]), Arqub edh-Dhahr (Parr 1956: Fig. 14: 120 [?]), Bab edh-Dhra' (Schaub p.c.: 059.11.22 [handle form only]), and Beth Shan (Fitzgerald 1935: Pls VI: 3; VIII: 17).

Unclassified: bowls (Fig. 232: 1-3)

Deep open bowls. Surfaces are red slipped and burnished (no. 1), or plain. One example (no. 2) has a band of 'reed' impressed patterns along the exterior of the rim (see, generally, genres 3, 4, 8, 23, 39, and Fig. 207: 2, 3; see also 'Repertoires': R3). Rim forms are bevelled and rounded, rounded with a sharp interior lip (cf. genre 38), and simple and rounded.

Unclassified: bowls (Fig. 232: 4-11)

Various open, mostly shallow, carinated bowls. No bases were found. Surface treatment includes red slip, red slip and burnishing and, on one occasion (no. 12), a band of impressed decoration along the carination. This loose group may be distantly related to genres 43, 57, 58, and 59.

Unclassified: bowls (Fig. 233: 1-5)

Deep bowls with in turned lips and high shoulders. No bases were found. Surfaces are plain, red slipped and (no. 1) 'grain-washed'. Fig. 233: 1, particularly, is related to holemouth jars in genre 13 (cf. especially Fig. 163: 4).

Some Chalcolithic parallels may be recogized at Ein Gedi (Ushishkin 1980: Fig. 9: 9 [a proto-type?]) and at sites in Sinai (Oren and Gilead 1981: Fig. 7: 10 [a proto-type?]).

Parallels from EB I contexts are found at Tell el-Far'ah (de Vaux and Steve 1947: Fig. 5: 4 [?]), N.T. Jericho (Pritchard 1958: Pl. 56: 17 [shape of rim, form: an earlier prototype?]), Afula (Sukenik 1936: Pl. I: 16; 1948: Pl. VI: 1-10 [very close parallels]), and Arqub edh-Dhahr (Parr 1956: Figs 14: 99, 101 [very close parallels]; 17: 207).

Unclassified: bowls (Fig. 233: 6-7)

Simple, open bowls with thick, rounded rim and bodies.

Unclassified: bowls (Fig. 233: 10-13)

Small open bowls with everted rims. Surfaces are red slipped and burnished. Rim forms are everted, some tending to be internally recessed. Their form can be compared with variants in genres 54, 55, and 56.

A Chalcolithic proto-type might be seen in vessels from Ein Gedi (Ushishkin 1980: Figs 7: 17 [form]; 8: 16 [form]).

No. 13 has related forms in EB I assemblages: e.g. at Jericho (Kenyon 1960: Figs 15: 3; 17: 14; 22: 7); N.T. Jericho (Pritchard 1958: Pl. 57: 6); Tell el-Far'ah (de Vaux and Steve 1949: Figs 6: 5, 6; 8: 4; de Vaux 1951: Fig. 5: 5); and Azor (Ben-Tor 1975: Fig. 5: 22-26).

Unclassified: bowls (Fig. 234: 1-3)

Deep bowls or holemouth jars. Two have bands of moulded decoration on the shoulder. Rims are in-turned and recessed or bevelled. The group may be related to genre 4 or genre 12 (cf. Fig. 1632: 8) and/or genre 50 (cf. Fig. 222: 6), possibly also genre 51 (cf. Fig. 223: 12).

Unclassified: bowls (Fig. 234: 4-6)

Small deep closed bowls (or jars). No. 4 is plain and has an out rolled rim; no. 5 is painted in the red 'trickle paint' style and has an external, bevelled, slightly recessed rim (cf. genre 47: especially Fig. 217: 4); no. 6 is plain and has a pointed everted, rim above a sharp indentation at the shoulder. (For similar rims forms see genre 48 [particularly Fig. 219: 2] and genre 60, and Fig. 194: 1, 2.)

Genre 62: spouts (Fig. 235: 1-3)

Wide spouts. All examples are body sherds and, therefore, the position of the spout on the host vessel is uncertain. Surface decoration includes red pattern painting and red slip and burnishing.

Parallels exist at Arad (Amiran 1978: Pls 10: 7 = TUH235: 1; 11: 2, 5 [Str. IV]); see also Amiran's summary of types (1969: Pls 5: 6; 14: 6); similar forms occur at Jawa (Betts [ed.] 1991: Fig. 143: 452-54).

Genre 63: spouts (Fig. 235: 4-7)

Narrow tall spouts. Their position on the host vessel is uncertain, although parallels suggest that the spouts were attached on the shoulders of the vessels. Most examples are slightly curved; all are red slipped and highly burnished.

Parallels may be sought in Amiran's summary (1969: Photos 24-26, from Assawir and Tell el-Far'ah; Pls 9: 11-16; 12: 15-17, from Ras el-Ain, Tell el-Far'ah, Assawir, Beth Shan, and Jericho); see also figure 207 (1-3) for possible related vessel forms. Similar forms occur at Jericho (Kenyon and Holland 1983: Fig. 84: 10), and Azor (Ben-Tor 1975: Fig. 9: 18). Comparisons with Egyptian vessels have been discussed by Kroeper (1989). The type is also common in Syria and Mesopotamia (e.g. Habuba Kabira: Sürenhagen 1978: Tabn 4: 53-55; 5: 60; 9: 69.1; 12: 75, 76; *passim*).

The origin of high spouted vessels is probably to be sought in the north and east. Examples, among many others, occur at Habuba Kabira (Sürenhagen 1978: *passim*), Hama (Fugman 1958: Fig. 46: 4B608), and el-Kowm in a steppic location (Cauvin and Stordeur 1985: Fig. 7).

Unclassified: spouts (Fig. 235: 8-10 ; see also genre 62)

Miscellaneous spouts. No. 8 is a 'trumpet' spout on a heavy holemouth jar or deep bowl with a splayed, bevelled rim and surface decoration of red net pattern paint; no. 9 is a long spout on an open, red burnished bowl with an in turned, rounded, rim; no. 10 is a wide spout on a deep bowl with an in turned, rounded, rim.

Churns (Fig. 235: 11-14; Pl. 3: 1)

These are probably churns (cf. Amiran 1969: Pl. 7, 6 and 7, from Gezer and Jericho ['EB I']). Nos 11 and 12 have flat bases (or, rather, ends) and one thick, transverse, loop handle; nos 13 and 14 are grouped here because of the handle form, and because of the patched (pre-firing) opening partly under the handle no. 14.

Amiran has discussed the chronology and distribution of these essentially Chalcolithic forms (e.g. 1969: Pls 7: 7; 1981; see also Hennessy 1969: Fig. 5: 11; Mallon *et al.* 1934: Fig. 59: 3), noting that they were used as far away as Iran. (For a parallel at Habuba Kabira, see Sürenhagen 1978: Tab. 14: 8; for a parallel at Byblos see Dunand 1973: Fig. 170: 32258; a possible related from comes from the Amuq region, Braidwood and Braidwood 1960: Fig. 228: 2). Parallels for the form as it occurs at Um Hammad appear at nearby Ruweiha (see below), Meser (Dothan 1957: Fig. 4: 5, 12), and Jericho (Kenyon and Holland 1983: Figs 12: 22 [closer to Chalcolithic forms]; 113: 19 [very similar to the examples from Um Hammad]).

It may be assumed that the form is derived from Chalcolithic proto-types, but is obviously not as common during EB I A as it was before. This is not to say that people necessarily stopped making butter, cheese, or whatever they made in the 'churns' but, rather, that they used some other mechanism that we have not yet been able to identify, most likely something made from bio-degradable materials. The more distant foreign parallels (as cited by Amiran) probably have nothing to do with Palestine or Transjordan: they may be, simply, ceramic versions of a ubiquitous dairy processing mechanism which is normally made of animal skin. The depiction of a 'churn' on a seal impression from Choga-Mish is probably irrelevant (Amiran 1981: Fig. 3).

Genre 64: handles (Fig. 236)

Horizontal and slightly up turned ledge handles. Shapes vary from flat curves (Fig. 236: 6-9), parabolic (Fig. 236: 1, 2, 5), to 'duck-billed' (Fig. 236: 3). All are decorated with bands of incised or impressed patterns along the sharp edge of the handle, the bands stopping at the handle-body junction. Surfaces are plain.

Genre 65: handles (Fig. 237: 1-4)

Slim rounded ledge handles with sharp wavy edges. They are slightly up turned and concave beneath. Most are plain; one example (Fig. 237: 3) is decorated with red painted stripes which cover the top of the handle. The body of this vessel had similar, vertical, stripes.

A Chalcolithic (?) parallel comes form Nahal Mishmar (Bar-Adon 1980: Ill. 18: 1 [=TUH237: 3]).

Genre 66: handles (Fig. 237: 5-7)

Up turned rounded and 'duck-billed' ledge handles, convex beneath. All examples have slashed or punctate bands along the edges stopping at the handle-body junction; all have a crescent of punctate patterns above the handle. Most examples are painted (as are the host vessels) with red 'splash-' or 'trickle paint'; many of the host vessels are also 'finger-streaked'. These handles, therefore, can be attributed to genre 1 (if handles were applied), genre 16 (almost certainly), and genre 48 (again, if handles were applied). (See also 'Repertoires': R1.)

Genre 67: handles (Fig. 238: 1-4; Pl. 7: 3))

Rounded, up turned ledge handles, concave beneath. All have plain surfaces, without decoration. One example (Fig. 233: 4) is stamped, before firing, with a seal (see 'Special features'). Similar handles occur at Jawa (see genres 21 and 68; Betts [ed.] 1991: genre B).

Genre 68: handles (Fig. 238: 5-8)

Rounded, up turned ledge handles, concave beneath. Surfaces are plain; all are decorated with bands of impressed, or punctate, patterns along the leading edge, stopping at the handle-body junction; many examples also have a crescent-shaped band of punctate, or impressed, patterns above the handle. Parallels exist at Jawa (Betts [ed.] 1991: genre B; see also genre 21 here). On this basis these handles must belong to genre 21 (cf. particularly Fig. 197: 4; see 'Repertoires': R2).

Genre 69: handles (Figs 238: 9, 10; 239: 1-4)

Rounded, up turned, bulbous ledge handles, mostly concave beneath. One example (Fig. 239: 4) is 'duck-billed'. Surfaces are plain or 'finger streaked' with red 'splash-' or 'trickle paint'; some examples have a crescent-shaped band of impressed patterns above the handle. Just like genre 66, these handles must belong to genres 1, 6, and/or 48 (i.e. repertoire R1).

Genre 70: handles (Fig. 239: 5-9)

Shallow rounded, up turned, ledge handles, concave beneath, with a sharp leading edge. All examples have a row of deeply impressed ovals beneath; some examples have wavy leading edges (Fig. 239: 7); some have a band of punctate patterns along the leading edge which (the edge), in some cases, is not sharp but slightly bevelled. Some examples are painted with red stripes which also cover the body of the vessel.

Genre 71: handles (Fig. 239: 10)

'Lump' handles. Surfaces are plain. Precise parallels occur at Jawa (Betts [ed.] 1991: Fig. 128; see also genres 21, 67 and 68) and in the Jerash Region (Glueck 1951: Pl. 163: 1-3, 7; Hanbury-Tenison 1987).

Genre 72: handles (Fig. 240: 1-13)

Small (horizontal) pierced lug handles. All are body sherds and, thus, their position on the vessel is unknown, but for nos 1-3 which occur on the shoulders of the host vessels (jars). Surfaces are plain, red slipped, red slipped and highly burnished, and red slipped and pattern burnished. (For the last mentioned [Fig. 240: 8, 13] see also genre 33 [Figs 207: 4-10; 244: 7, 9].)

Genre 73: handles (Fig. 240: 14, 15)

Heavy horizontal and up turned, rounded, ledge handles. All have thick bands of impressed decoration along the leading edge continuing on to the body of the host vessel, in some cases (Fig. 240: 15), splitting into two or more such bands. These handles belong to the 'Umm Hamad esh-Sherqi ware/pré-urbaine D' repertoire (see 'Repertoires': R6) and are most likely to be associated with genres 12 and 50 (see also Figs 268: 9, 18; 269: 1 - from Mellaart's collection [Leonard n.d.]: Um Hammad and Tell Mafluq).

Genre 74: handles (Fig. 241: 1-4)

Medium sized, rounded horizontal and up turned ledge handles. Some have single, or multiple, rounded impressions either on the handles, or under it; some are concave beneath; some are red slipped and burnished; others are red painted. Most handles are 'grain-washed' and on that basis should best be related to genre 13 and vessels in Figure 233: 1-5 (cf. also Sukenik 1948: Pl. VI: 1, 2).

Genre 75: handles (Fig. 241: 6)

Up turned, rounded, wavy ledge handles. One example is attached at the waist of a vessel with a flat base.

Genre 76: handles (Fig. 241: 7-10)

Up turned, rounded, ledge handles, concave beneath. All have deeply impressed hollows on the leading edge.

Genre 77: handles (see also genre 1/2) (Fig. 242: 1, 2)

Pushed up, rounded, lug handles. Some are on host vessels which are decorated with 'finger streaking' and red 'splash-' or 'trickle paint'; others are plain. One example (Fig. 242: 2) has a row of punctate decoration on the pushed up surface. TUH242: 1 can be attributed to genre 1/2. The majority (listed as genre 95 in Fig. 129) consists of pushed up lugs or somewhat generalized ('pinched') versions of them which could be attributed to genres 2, 5, some of 19, 20, and 21 (see also 'Repertoires': R2).

Unclassified: handles (Fig. 242: 3, 4)

An undecorated, plain double-coil loop handle (?genre 35) and a double vertical lug.

Genre 78: handles (Fig. 242: 5-8)

Strap (loop) handles (cf. also Fig. 208: 1). They are attached to the waist of jars (or bottles), or on the shoulders up to the rim (jugs, juglets). All examples are red slipped and burnished (see 'Repertoires': R9).

Unclassified: handles (Fig. 242: 9-14)

Various rounded and impressed ledge handles. (Some, e.g. nos 12 and 13, probably belong to the late 'EB III' or 'EBIV' period.)

Genre 79: body sherds (Fig. 243: 1-7; Pl. 4: 4)

Surfaces are 'finger streaked' and decorated with red 'splash-' or 'trickle paint'. Most examples have bands of incised and/or impressed decoration; some of these decorative bands are heavy and were probably applied separately to the host vessel (e.g. Fig. 243: 5, 6).

Genre 80: body sherds (Fig. 243: 8-10)

Surfaces are plain or, in one case (Fig. 243: 9), dark slipped and burnished. All have band(s) of impressed decoration. Some of these bands are raised: they probably belong to genre 16.

Genre 81: body sherds (Fig. 243: 11-18)

Surfaces are 'finger streaked' and decorated with red 'trickle paint' in irregular stripes. These sherds are similar to genre 79, but no impressed or incised bands of decoration were preserved.

Genre 82: body sherds (Fig. 244: 1-6; Pl. 8: 3)

Surfaces are plain, or painted with vertical red stripes. All have single, or multiple, bands of 'reed' impressed decoration (cf. also genres 3, 4, 8, 23, 39, Fig. 207 [2, 3], 39, and Fig. 232 [1-3] and parallels cited there). They are grouped in repertoire R3 ('Repertoires': Fig. 263).

Genre 33: body sherds (Fig. 244: 7, 9)

Surfaces are red-orange slipped and decorated with a net pattern of burnish (cf. also Figs 207: 4-10; 240: 8, 13; 252: 6; 254: 1).

Genre 83: body sherds (Fig. 244: 8)

Surfaces are red-orange slipped and 'grain-washed': i.e. they are body sherds of repertoire R5 ('Repertoires': Fig. 264).

Genre 84: body sherds (Fig. 239: 10-16)

Surfaces are plain and decorated with heavy, often raised, bands of impressed patterns. They belong to the 'Umm Hamad esh-Sherqi Ware/pré-urbaine D' repertoire ('Repertoires': R6).

Unclassified: body sherds (Fig. 244: 17, 18)

Red painted net patterns and stripes pendent from a red painted register. The former is somewhat similar to painted sherds at Jawa (Betts [ed.] 1991: Fig. 149: 535), but see also TUH255: 11. The net pattern is probably the same as that of genre 94 (Fig. 252: 1-4).

Genre 85: bases (Figs 245-46)

Heavy pedestal bases. These range from pronounced, large, pedestals to small, low, ones. They are 'finger streaked', diagonally as well as vertically. Many examples are 'thumb impressed' along the pedestal; many are hollow based, in some cases being constructed in two section (e.g. Fig. 245: 1). Some bases are bevelled. Often red 'trickle-' or 'splash paint' is applied. The form (also of genre 86 below) is common in Chalcolithic repertoires of Palestine (Helms 1987a); it is also common at Jawa (Betts [ed.] 1991: Figs 150-51).

Genre 86: bases (Fig. 247: 1-9)

Splayed flat bases. Some are decorated with impressed or slashed bands. Many are vertically 'finger streaked'.

Genre 87: bases (Fig. 247: 10-18)

Splayed flat bases. Some have 'thumb' impressions; all are 'splash-' or 'trickle painted' in red.

Genre 88: bases (Fig. 248: 1-10)

Omphaloid bases. All are either red slipped, or red slipped and highly burnished. They can be related to genre 35, for the most part. Some of the highly polished ones may belong to genre 34 (cf. Fig. 209: 11).

Genre 89: bases (Figs 248: 11-18; 249: 1-4)

Flat bases, some splayed. Surfaces are plain. All are decorated with red 'trickle-' or 'splash paint'.

Genre 90: bases (Fig. 249: 5-8)

Small pedestal bases. Some are hollow; some are splayed. Decoration takes the form of grooving (Fig. 249: 5), red slip (Fig. 249: 6), and 'thumb' impressions (Fig. 249: 8). (For Chalcolithic parallels see Commenge-Pellerin 1987: Fig. 22: 6, 7 - southern region; Mallon *et al.* 1934: Fig. 56: 4, 7, 12, 15, 16, and Hennessy 1969: Fig. 6: 9 [=TUH249: 5] - central region.)

Genre 91: bases (Figs 249: 9-13; 250: 1-9)

Flat bases, some splayed. Surfaces are either plain (red buff) or red slipped and burnished. Many may be related to jars, jugs or bottles like the one in Fig. 208: 1 (cf. Fig. 250: 5, 6, 8, 9).

Genre 92: bases (Figs 250: 10-12; 251: 1, 2)

Heavy flat bases. All have single, or multiple, raised horizontal bands of impressed decoration. They belong to the 'Umm Hamad esh-Sherqi Ware/pré-urbaine D' repertoire ('Repertoires': R6).

Genre 93: bases (Fig. 251: 3-10)

Flat bases, some splayed. Vessel shapes are straight sided and curved. All examples are 'grain-washed' (cf. genres 11, 13, and perhaps 29, and Fig. 233: 1). They belong to repertoire R5 ('Repertoires': Fig. 264).

Genre 94: bases (Fig. 252: 1-4)

Flat bases, some splayed. Body shapes are straight sided and curved. All examples are slipped and decorated with a red painted net pattern in wide stripes. (Cf. Amiran 1969: Photo 53 [EB II].)

Unclassified: base (Fig. 252: 5; Pl. 3: 2)

One example of a flat, slightly splayed, plain base with 'mat' impressions. (Cf. Hennessy 1982: 57: 2: c on the relative position of such bases at Teleilat Ghassul.) A related base was found at Ruweiha (Pl. 3: 3; see also 'Ruweiha and other related sites' below) together with EB I A material.

Unclassified: base (Fig. 252: 6)

A round based vessel decorated with a burnished (red) net pattern (cf. genre 33 *passim*).

Unclassified: bases (Fig. 253)

Flat bases which may be linked with genre 35. Some are red slipped; most are red slipped and highly burnished: some may, therefore, belong to genre 34.

Miscellaneous forms (Fig. 254: 1)

A small holemouth jar with a bevelled, 'beaded', rim, red burnished and net pattern burnished (cf. genre 33 *passim*).

Parallels exist at Megiddo XIX (Loud 1948: Pl. 97: 46 [decoration]) and Jericho (Kenyon and Holland 1983: Fig. 116: 6, 7 [shape; not rim form]).

Miscellaneous forms (Fig. 254: 2-3)

Heavy deep bowls or holemouth jars with everted, bevelled, rims. No. 2 has a heavy raised band of impressed decoration along the exterior lip.

Miscellaneous forms (Fig. 254: 4-11)

Various everted rim jars. Nos 4 and 6 can be compared with variants in genre 16 (Figs 174-86: particularly Fig. 186: 11 for no. 6). No. 5, with its 'bowed' or bulbous neck, is close to variants in genre 32 (Fig. 206: 12-22). Nos 7 to 11 find parallels in the larger variants of genre 19 (Figs 191-92), 22 (Figs 198-200), 23 (Fig. 200), and perhaps genre 31 (Fig. 206).

Miscellaneous forms (Fig. 255: 1-3)

Everted rim jars. They are similar to those in Fig. 254: 4-11.

Miscellaneous forms (Fig. 255: 4-5)

Everted rim jars with 'wavy' impressed rims. They can be related to 'wavy' rimmed variants in genre 4 (cf. Figs 149: 9; 150: 4, 7, 9).

The type is a development from Chalcolithic vessels (e.g. Commenge-Pellerin 1987: Fig. 33: 6; Mallon *et al.* 1934: Fig. 52: 6 [though heavier]; Ushishkin 1980: Fig. 10: 3); it has also been found at al-Hibr in the eastern Jordanian steppe (Betts *et al.* 1991: Fig. 3; Betts in press).

Miscellaneous forms (Fig. 255: 6)

A large, heavy open bowl with an impressed, splayed and bevelled rim. It is similar to variants in genre 50 (Figs 221-23).

Miscellaneous forms (Fig. 255: 7)

A small bowl with a pointed base and a beaded rim. There is one flattened strap handle from rim to base.

Miscellaneous forms (Fig. 255: 8-11)

Miscellaneous decorated body sherds. TUH255: 11 is similar to painted patterns on body sherds at Jawa (Betts [ed.] 1991: Fig. 149: 531, 538).

Miscellaneous forms (Fig. 255: 12)

A 'pot stand' with rounded rims. The exterior lips are slurred or finely grooved.

A full discussion of this 'pot stand' has been published by Hanbury-Tenison (1988), citing a vessel from Pella (Chalcolithic) and parallels at Shuneh North, Abu Habil, and Jericho VI-VII, and also suggesting comparison with copper 'crowns' from Nahal Mishmar (Bar Adon 1980). Other parallels occur at Abu Matar (Commenge-Pellerin 1987: Fig. 31: 10-12), Jericho (Kenyon and Holland 1983: Fig. 113: 12 [PNA/PU: presumably EB I A/B]), and Shuneh North (Gustavson-Gaube 1986: Fig. 17: 76a, 76b).

RUWEIHA AND OTHER RELATED SITES

The sub-region

The surveys of Glueck (1951) and Mellaart (1962; Leonard n.d.) and the more recent Jordan Valley Survey (Ibrahim *et al.* 1976; Yassine *et al.* 1988) have reported on a number of sites (see Fig. 3) whose surface pottery can now be linked to the typology at Tell Um Hammad (see also Helms 1986: Fig. 1). Among these sites are a few which belong to the Chalcolithic period (i.e. Ghassul/Beersheba/Abu Hamid) and, therefore, should be contemporary with stage 1 at Um Hammad: i.e. the much disturbed small (?) open village represented by Tell Qa`adan just northeast of Tell Deir Alla (Ibrahim *et al.* 1976; Kafafi 1982); the open village at basal Kataret es-Samra (Leonard 1983; 1989); basal Tell Handaquq North (Mabry 1989); and the site of Jiftlik across the Jordan River to the west, on wadi Far'ah (Leonard n.d.).

EB I A open village sites contemporary with stage 2 at Tell Um Hammad, in some cases with precise pottery parallels, comprise the following: the small, now virtually destroyed, settlement at Ruweiha (Yassine *et al.* 1988; see also below and Figs 256-60); Kataret es-Samra (Leonard 1983); Tell Mafluq (Fig. 269: 1 [Leonard n.d.]; Glueck 1951: Pl. 163: 9); and Tell Handaquq North (Mabry 1989). The Damiya dolmen might belong to this stage (see now Yassine 1985). Ruweiha (see also below) appears to be the earliest of these EBA sites, its earliest occupation (but see Pl. 3: 3) corresponding to the early phases of stage 2 at Tell Um Hammad; the rest include among their pottery some of the distinctive styles known at Jawa (Betts [ed.] 1991) which are, signally, absent at Ruweiha. Tubb (1990: 47-50) uncovered one

shaft-chamber burial belonging to EB I A/B (Fig. 269: 5) at Tiwal esh-
Sharqi which served as the extensive cemetery for the EB IV period
(Tell Um Hammad stages 5 onwards; Betts and Helms in press).

EB I B sites include upper Ruweiha (see below), Kataret es-Samra
(Leonard 1983), Tell Mafluq (Fig. 269: 1; Leonard n.d.), Tell
Handaquq North (Mabry 1989), and Tell Abu Zighan, also called Tell
Handaquq South (Yassine 1988; Helms in press).

The following parallels with the assemblage at Um Hammad may
be cited for Kataret es-Samra: Chalcolithic (painted wares) perhaps
contemporary with stage 1 (Leonard 1989: *passim*); EB I: holemouth
jars: genre 1, repertoire R1 (Leonard 1983: Fig. 9: 11, 14-16), genre 2,
repertoire R2 (*idem*: Fig. 9: 7-8), genre 6 (*idem*: Fig. 9: 22), genre 11 [?],
repertoire R5 (*idem*: Fig. 9: 4); jars: genre 16, repertoire R1 (*idem*: Fig. 9:
10, 18-20), genre 17, repertoire R6 (*idem*: Fig. 8: 25, 26), genre 19,
repertoire R4 (*idem*: Fig. 11: 8-13, genre 22, repertoire R2 (*idem*: Fig. 11:
1-3, 5-7 [?]), genre 35, repertoire R4 (*idem*: Fig. 12); bowls: genre 37
[form only], repertoire R8 (*idem*: Fig. 8: 12), genre 49, repertoire R2 [?]
(*idem*: Fig. 9: 21, 23), genre 50, repertoire R6 (*idem*: Fig. 8: 23, 24);
handles: genre 68, repertoire R2 (*idem*: Fig. 13: 8), genre 70 [?] (*idem*:
Fig. 13: 5); and, generally, forms in stage 2 (*idem*: Fig. 13: 1-4) and EB
II forms (Fig. 13: 7, 8); the rest, but for bowls (*idem*: Fig. 8: 16-21)
which are similar to one bowl found at Um Hammad by Glueck (Fig.
269: 3; 1951), are undiagnostic. At this stage in the protohistory of the
sub-region (wadi Zerqa and wadi Far'ah flood plain) current data
from surveys suggests a major change in settlement strategy in
favour of more secure sites along the hill slopes on either side of the
Jordan Valley (Helms in press). EB II-III occupation at Tell Um
Hammad, though attested, is no longer as extensive as it was in EB I,
while sites like Tell Handaquq North, Tell Abu Zighan, and Khirbet
Mahruq (Yeivin [Z.] 1977) were probably fortified. These sites are
very large (e.g. Tell Abu Zighan about 30 hectares, or more) and
densely built up. Tell Abu Zighan continued to be occupied into the
EB IV period or, at any rate, into whatever is represented by stage 5 at
Tell Um Hammad (Betts and Helms in press). The changes in
settlement strategies and some notions regarding demographic
trends have been discussed elsewhere (Helms in press).

Ruweiha (Fig. 2: 29)

The remains at Ruweiha are sparse, most of the original sites having
be ploughed away over the last decade. What has remained is a
small, low ridge between the field fence and the modern track at the
west end of the site. Depth of occupation is no more than one metre.
No recognizable architectural remains can be discerned now,
although occupation surfaces are visible, as are many loose stones
which could have served as foundations for dwellings. On the basis

of the pottery (see below) two stages of settlement can be established: one - the major stage - early in EB I A; the other in EB I B. The site is located in the same general relation to wadi Zerqa as is Um Hammad. It must have been a relatively small open village surrounded by fields which could have been irrigated via canals (though there is no proof of this).

With reference to figures 256-60, it is clear that the majority of the recovered pottery types belong to stage 2 of Um Hammad. Genres 1, 16, and 48, the 'type fossils' of Um Hammad's EB I A period, are well-represented, as are the typical pushed up, decorated ledge handles and heavy pedestalled bases. 'Esdraelon' ware is present in some quantities. The small bowls with the characteristic 'crazing' on the interior surfaces support the notion of placing the occupation at Ruweiha early in TUH stage 2: their closest parallels at Um Hammad occur in genre 53 (the recessed rims may be later: at any rate, the related forms represented by genre 56 are the ones which also occur at Jawa). Finally, the two fragmentary 'churns' (Fig. 260: 7, 8) seem to be stylistically closer to Chalcolithic examples (the aspect of the handles) in comparison with the examples from Tell Um Hammad (cf. Fig. 235: 11, 12): i.e. Ruweiha may have been first occupied during the Chalcolithic period. One pattern impressed ('mat impressed'?) base (Pl. 3: 3) was also found at Ruweiha and can be compared with TUH252:5. Whether this means that the site was occupied before EB I A is uncertain, although, like Um Hammad's 'phantom' stage 1, this is not impossible.

It might be appropriate to suggest a micro pattern in the general trend to move from scattered small settlements of the Chalcolithic period toward larger, more numerous, settlements and greater settlement nucleation: i.e. a visible increase in settlement density throughout EB I A, the early phases of which did not yet have (or had not yet made) close contact with areas to the north and east (i.e. southern Syria): these early phases of EB I A could, therefore, be regarded as a regional continuation of Chalcolithic culture in the Jordan Valley typified here in repertoire R1 at Tell Um Hammad and Ruweiha (see 'Repertoires'). We might, furthermore, argue that the EB I A period saw a population increase in the region which cannot easily be explained away through natural propagation of an indigenous 'Chalcolithic' population (see Chapter 7; see also Helms in press).

DISTRIBUTION OF GENRES

Analysis of the data from the core squares 1, 2, 4, and 30-31 has been tabulated in the master matrix (squares 1, 2, 4; Chapter 2: Table 2), the structural matrix (Fig. 36), and Table 3, the latter presenting the relative frequency of occurrence of the genres for squares 1, 2, 4, 30-31. The calculations in Table 3 are summarized in three histograms (Figs 129-31) which are analyzed further with regard to repertoires (see below). Genres are arranged by form (i.e. hmjs, jars, bowls, and other forms, as is the catalogue [Figs 139-255]), and ranked according to first occurrence in time (phases). The histograms reveal at least five categories: (i) genres which begin in phase 1 of stage 1 (EB I A) and include the vessels displaying clear 'Chalcolithic' stylistic features (Fig. 129; see also 'Repertoires'); (ii) genres which are 'introduced' or appear at various times throughout stage 2 (EB I A) (Fig. 130); (iii) genres beginning in phase 11 and stage 3 (EB I B) (Fig. 131); (iv) genres which appear at various later times in stage 3 (EB I B) (? possibly a meaningless pattern owing to the small size of the sample); and (v) genres which begin in phase 14 and stage 4 (EB II). A correction is included in figures 129, 130, and 131 (per cent occurrence not filled in). Since bases and body sherds (bs) could not be easily related to specific vessels, or even to repertoires, their inclusion in the frequency of occurrence calculations could skew the histograms. However, this 'skewing' does not seriously alter the general trends. The 'corrected' histograms are used in the analysis of repertoires (Figs 133-38), where the trend (of relative frequency of occurrence) is schematized, blank phases being interpolated, or extrapolated, where the general trend appears to warrant this. Most 'occurrences' after stage 3 (i.e. phases 14 onwards) are unreliable (see also Chapter 2, 'Stratigraphy'); the same may apply, in some cases, to stage 3 itself.

It is clear from the patterns displayed in the histograms that some genres, such as the plain, polished, and burnished high loop-handled juglets, continue in use in stage 3, but were first 'introduced' at the very beginning of stage 2 (see 'Division of genres'). On the other hand, most of genre 16 probably went out of use (or fashion) by phase 10 of stage 2, its appearance in stage 3 simply being a matter of dredging up earlier material during excavation: unavoidable in the case of such a common genre. In one case a genre, which first appears early in stage 2 (genre 2), seems to be imitated or copied with some technical and formal variations (genre 5), still in stage 2, and was then made in a derived form (genre 9) exclusively in stage 3. We therefore have both continuity of some pristine forms from stage 2 into stage 3, and also formal or stylistic evolution across the stage interface (i.e. EB I A - EB I B).

Division of genres

Further examination of the histograms suggests that some genres, particularly the numerically very large ones such as genre 16, can be divided, and that these subsets or sub-genres have their own distribution pattern through time at Tell Um Hammad al-Sharqi. Many genres display a simple distribution (when the numbers are significantly large) as follows: introduction, gradual decrease, end; introduction, gradual increase, end; and introduction, 'floruit', decrease, end. Some genres must be examined more closely, and this is done below. Other genres are discussed further in the section dealing with the reconstruction of repertoires.

Genre 16 might be divided into five subsets (Figs 133, 261): the large bag-shaped jars (b: e.g. Figs 177: 6-8, 179, 180: 1-5) beginning in phase 1, decreasing in frequency, and ending in phase 6 or 7; everted rim forms (e: e.g. Fig. 186: 1-5) also beginning in phase 1, but increasing in frequency up to phase 5; everted rim jars with red painted patterns (d: e.g. Figs 183, 184, 185: 1-7), similarly beginning in phase 1, increasing in frequency more slowly ('floruit' in phase 6/7), and ending in phase 10; jars (a: e.g. Figs 171-76; and c: e.g. Figs 180: 6, 181, 182: 1-7) starting about phase 7 and continuing in use well into phase 3 (but see remarks above regarding accidental survival of common forms). (See also Fig. 133: repertoire R1 and remarks in 'Repertoires' below.)

Genre 19 (Figs 136, 263) can be divided as follows: (a: e.g. Fig. 191) bag-shaped jars with pushed up lugs (hybrids) start in phase 1 and decrease in frequency, ending in phase 7; (b: e.g. Fig. 192) polished and burnished jars beginning in phase 1, increasing in use, peaking in phase 9/10, and ending with phase 10; (c: e.g. Fig. 193) the 'bow'-shouldered (hybrids) and s-shaped jars also begin in phase 1, peak in frequency in phase 8/9, and end with phase 10; and (d: e.g. Fig. 191: 5) bag-shaped jars start in phase 7, decrease in frequency, and end with phase 9 or 10.

Genre 22 (Fig. 134) can be divided into three subsets: (a) plain everted rim jars (e.g. Figs 199: 8-18, 200: 1-14) beginning in phase 1, peaking (early?) in phase 2, and decreasing to end in phase 4/5; (b) internally recessed rim jars (e.g. Fig. 198: 1-8) starting in phase 6, decreasing to end in phase 7 or 8; and (c) jars with slightly bulbous rims (e.g. (Fig. 199: 1-6) which begin in phase 7, decrease in frequency, and end with phase 9 or 10.

Genres 34 and 35 (high loop-handled juglets) are obviously related in form and decoration. The distribution of genre 34 (painted and plain versions) is irregular, possibly suggesting continuous use throughout stage 2 following their 'introduction' at Um Hammad in phase 1 (Fig. 134). Genre 35, on the other hand (Fig. 136), could be divided into two subsets: (a) red polished juglets which start in phase 1 and slowly decrease in frequency up to about phase 5 (this subset could represent the unpainted variants of genre 34 which are regarded as hybrids in repertoire R1); and (b) the same form, but now

highly burnished, beginning in about phase 5, peaking in phase 10
(end of stage 2) and, apparently, continuing throughout stage 3,
decreasing slightly before ending with the stage in phase 13 (they
may even continue, in terms of some variants, into phase 14 of stage
4).

Genre 36 (Fig. 136), the small fine shallow bowls, also divides into
two subsets, like genre 35: (a) plain red bowls which begin in phase 1
and decrease in frequency to end in phase 4 or 5; and (b) the same
forms, but highly polished and (later?) burnished, appear to replace
subset (a) in phase 4 and increase in frequency, peaking and ending
with phase 10 and stage 2. A small number of variants (Fig. 136: 36c)
appear to continue in use in stage 3, decreasing in frequency, and
ending in phase 12 or 13: this, however, is not certain and may simply
be the result of dredging up earlier forms during excavation (see also
'Repertoires').

Genre 45, 'Esdraelon' ware, is problematical. The histogram (Fig.
129) indicates a division into two: (a) a subset starting in phase 1 and
decreasing to end in phase 3 or 4; and (b) a subset which is
'introduced' with phase 4, peaking in phase 5, and, more or less
gradually, decreasing to end with phase 10; the few 'survivals' in
stages 3 and 4 are probably accidental. However, unless there is a
technological change to explain this apparently significant pattern,
we cannot recognize a formal or stylistic separation within the genre.
This could be interpreted in a number of ways: e.g. as a 're-
introduction' of the ware in phase 4 through renewed or intensified
contact with the putative region of origin, the north of Palestine
(Yizre'el Valley, Tiberias, Galilee, etc.); gradual replacement by genre
48 (Figs 129, 133, 261: see also 'Repertoires'); or that the pattern might
simply be accidental, or reflect a change in local preferences. No
formal separation is possible on the basis of the bowl form (e.g. cf.
TUH216: 8 and TUH213: 9). In any event, this genre is almost unique
at Um Hammad because of its construction and firing techniques
which have produced an extremely friable ware which is rarely
preserved in recognizable form in occupational debris: the bulk of
genre identification rests on small, undistinguished body sherds.

The recessed rim, 'crazed' bowls of Genre 54 are obviously related
to the simpler form, genre 53 (Fig. 138; see 'Repertoires'). The
histogram suggests a division of genre 54 into one subset (a) which
starts in phase 1, decreases in use, ending in phase 2/3, and another
subset (b), which begins in phase 3, peaks and ends in phase 9 or 10.
Genre 53 begins in the same way as the former subset (a) of genre 54:
i.e. they may be the same. When they are combined (the early set of
genre 54 plus genre 53), the pattern could suggest the introduction of
the earlier form in phase 1, gradually decreasing and ending in about

phase 4-6, while the later subset of genre 54 becomes more popular, taking the place of the earlier form from phase 3 onwards (Fig. 138). Genre 55 is merely a painted version (a hybrid: see 'Repertoires') of genre 56 (Fig. 226: 9-27) which begins in phase 3 (Figs 129, 130, 133, 134), and appears to increase in frequency, ending with phase 10: i.e. it, genre 56, can perhaps be regarded as a derived form of genre 54.

The histograms can be used to link the necessarily 'floating' phases of the other sondages, notably those in squares 40 (see also Fig. 37) and 50. The latter (square 50) was the only one which produced numerically meaningful data. Figure 129 (top row) shows the frequency of genres for the entire sample: obviously this covers several phases, though within stage 2. When the time-ranges of the various genres are plotted in relation to the core squares (i.e. 1, 2, 3, 30-31) the mean phase correlation is phase 7 to 9 (Fig. 132). This phasing range is given in the catalogue, though some forms are clearly very early within stage 2.

REPERTOIRES

The assemblages of both EB I A and EB I B are not homogeneous (in contrast to those of EB II); it is evident that they consist of a variety of styles in both form and decoration. An attempt ought, therefore, to be made to separate out distinctive repertoires consisting of the three basic forms: holemouth jars (hmj), jars, and bowls and, further, to see whether some of these repertoires may not be localized in the greater region (although they were not necessarily made there [Vaillant p.c.]), beyond the central Jordan valley. Others were obviously made locally and could represent an indigenous, earlier ceramic tradition. Attribution to repertoires for unclassified material is summarized at the end of this section. An attempt is also made to identify hybrid forms (H) which may suggest a stylistic merging of separate repertoires at Tell Um Hammad itself, or in the greater region (the Jordan valley).

Repertoire 1 [EB I A] (Figs 129, 133, 261, 270)

This repertoire, among the earliest at the site in stage 2, can be regarded as essentially 'Chalcolithic' in form and decoration: i.e. as a development from the Palestinian Chalcolithic ceramic tradition, perhaps using a slightly different (improved?) technology. Virtually all genres in the repertoire can be 'paralleled' in the assemblages of 'Ghassul/Beersheba/Abu Hamid'. This is reiterated below with regard to the assemblages from Abu Matar/Zoumeili, the most comprehensive Chalcolithic pottery typology to hand in published form (Commenge-Pellerin 1987). Repertoire 1 may be summarized as follows:

Table 5. Repertoire R1

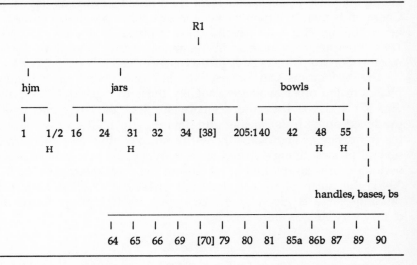

The criteria for selection included 'trickle paint', 'finger streaking', and finely grooved rims or lips, as well as formal relations to Chalcolithic 'proto-types' (see Abu Matar/Zoumeili below). On this basis, the jar with 'bowed' rim and traces of 'trickle paint' (TUH205: 1) is added to the repertoire (see also below). There are several 'hybrid' forms which combine decorative features of another repertoire: i.e. genre 1/2 (related to genre 2 of repertoire R2); genre 31 (cf. genre 22, R2); genre 34 is clearly related to the juglets of genre 35 (repertoire R4); TUH219: 2, a deep bowl or even a holemouth jar in genre 48, may be related to the large vessels in genre 6 (repertoire R2: see below); some forms in genre 48 (i.e. Figs 217: 8-10; 218: 5; 219: 3-5) could be regarded as hybrids, their form perhaps influenced by 'Esdraelon' ware (genre 45, R7); and genre 55 must be related to the plain, recessed rim and 'crazed' bowls of genre 54 ('repertoire' R8). The various ledge handles may be related to repertoire R2: in any event, these handles are a phenomenon of the EB I (A) period; the typical Chalcolithic handles (on large, heavy vessels) are applied vertically (see also repertoire R6 below).

In view of the close affinities with local Palestinian Chalcolithic ceramic traditions (see also 'Ruweiha' above), it is reasonable to suggest that repertoire R1 represents an indigenous ceramic tradition which is probably to be localized in the Jordan Valley and Palestine/Transjordan generally. The presence of recognizable hybrids suggests that pottery was made at the site, or nearby, and that there was some 'cross-breeding' of genres from different repertoires. It might even be suggested that separate workshops existed side by side at Um Hammad, or in the immediate region.

Repertoire 2 [EB I A] (Figs 134, 262, 270)

The criteria for selection are as follows: punctate bands of decoration near or on the rim, rounded pushed up lugs and ledge handles (including 'lump handles'), stamp 'seal' impressions on handles and the body of vessels; and the close formal parallels in the fourth millennium BC assemblage of Jawa (Betts [ed.] 1991).

Table 6. Repertoire R2

			R2										
hmj			jars			bowls			bs				
1/2 2	5	6	20 21	22 25 26	49 56	67 68 71	85b 86b 95						
H				H	H								
[9]													
H													

As before (i.e. in repertoire R1), there are hybrid forms: e.g. genre 1/2 (related to repertoire R1); genre 25 has the typical 'finger streaking' of repertoire R1; genre 56 is related to genre 54 ('repertoire' R8); and, at Jawa itself, a few examples of the plain high loop-handled juglets (= genres 34/35) have been found which are attributed to repertoire R4 here (Betts [ed.] 1991: Figs 142, 143: 441-446, 448). The painted sherd (TUH255: 11) can also be compared with similar decoration at Jawa (*idem*: Fig. 149: 535) and might be included in repertoire R2.

The repertoire can be localized in the Hawran (i.e. Jawa where, however, it represents only about 30-40 per cent of the assemblage: Betts [ed.] 1991) and probably southern Syria (although no examples have yet come to light, but for Jawa; Braemer p.c.), the Irbid/Ajlun/Jerash region, and along wadi Zerqa. The histogram depicting the distribution of genres through time suggests that the bulk of this repertoire appeared at Um Hammad (and also, perhaps, at Kataret es-Samra, etc.) after the beginning of stage 2, between phases 3 and 5 (Fig. 134). This is supported by the evidence from nearby Ruweiha (see above; Figs 256-60) where the predominant repertoire is R1, without any traces of R2. (On the other hand, it could be argued that the two sites are contemporary, though only some people availed themselves of repertoire R2 which, if it was transported down wadi Zerqa, would have passed by Ruweiha.) The characteristic combination and distribution of features such as lug handles and punctate bands of decoration (cf. particularly genre 21 and its parallels at Jawa: e.g. Fig. 273) is paralleled in the EB I (A) repertoire at Bab edh-Dhra'. The general connection, although distant, between Jawa's assemblage and that of Bab edh-Dhra' has bee noted before (Helms 1987a). We argued above that Bab edh-Dhra' (EB I A - EB IV) ought to be regarded as a marginal settlement and this might be borne out by the nature of the relationship between its pottery styles and those farther north: i.e. that EB I (A) Bab edh-Dhra' represents a regional (marginal) development, perhaps the result of a southward movement of people during the second half of the fourth millennium; the EB I (A) assemblage has little, if any, connection with the southwest of Palestine, or any area farther south. This is in almost total disagreement with Rast (1980) who states, categorically and without proof, that during '... EB I Palestinian [i.e. all of Palestine and, presumably, also Transjordan] assemblages and features suggest greater contacts with the Sinai and Egypt and less with Syria and Mesopotamia' (*idem*: 6). Mesopotamia may only be 'connected' indirectly (via northern Syria); Syria, particularly the Damascene and the Hawran/Jawlan, most certainly provided some of the ceramic types, in combination with material from other, northwestern, regions (see Figs 270, 271, and remarks regarding areas of origin below).

Repertoire 3 [EB I A - EB I B] (Figs 135, 263, 270)

The selection criteria are the very distinctive 'reed' impressed bands of decoration applied at or near the rim and neck of the vessels.

There is a number of possible hybrids: e.g. genre 8 may be related to repertoire R2 (cf. Jawa, Betts [ed.] 1991: Fig. 114: 56); genre 23 could be derived from genre 22, also of repertoire R2; and genre 39 is similar to genre 36 of repertoire R4.

So far as the limited parallels may be representative in geographical terms, repertoire R3 ought to be localized in the Jezre'el/Tiberias area (parallels at Megiddo: see 'Analysis of genres and comparative study'). The repertoire seems to appear at Um Hammad in part (i.e. holemouth jars and bowls: genres 3, 4, and 39) at the beginning of stage 2, with other forms being introduced from phase 5 onward. This distribution in stage 2 may of course be illusory, a function of the small sample.

Table 7. Repertoire R3

```
                            R3
                            I
        _____|_____
        I            I            I         I
       hmj          jars        bowls      bs
     _____     _____     _____     I
     I   I   I    I    I        I    I       I
     3   4   8    23  207:2    39  232:2    82
         H        H             H
```

Repertoires R1 to R3 all belong to stage 2 at Um Hammad (although some elements of R3 continue in use in stage 3), that is to say, to EB I A. To reiterate this 'Chalcolithic' connection the following comparisons with pottery repertoires at Abu Matar/Zoumeili (Commenge-Pellerin 1987) might be made, the majority of which refer to the early repertoires at Um Hammad (i.e. predominantly repertoire R1): R1, genre 1, TUH140: 4 = *idem*: Fig. 49: 8, TUH141: 2 = *idem*: Fig. 49: 6, 7, TUH141: 6, 7 = *idem*: Fig. 27: 5; TUH170: 7 = *idem*: Fig. 27: 6; R2, genre 6 (?) = *idem*: Fig. 46: 15; R1: genre 16, TUH175: 1 = *idem*: Fig. 50: 3, TUH176: 1 = *idem*: Fig. 50: 8, TUH177: 1-7 = *idem*: Fig. 51: 3, TUH181: 5 = *idem*: Fig. 33: 1, TUH182: 11, TUH184: 4 = *idem*: Fig. 33: 3, TUH185: 8 = *idem*: Fig. 47: 11; R4, genre 19, (hybrid <R2), TUH191: 1-4 = *idem*: Fig. 33: 3 (see also genre 16 above); R4, genre 19, TUH193: 14 = *idem*: Figs 26: 9, 30: 1, etc.; TUH194: 1-2 = *idem*: Fig. 24: 5 (see also genre 48, a hybrid, below); genre 22 = *idem*: Figs 47: 8, 9, 50: 1, 2; TUH255: 4 = *idem*: Fig. 47: 9; R1, genre 24 = *idem*: Fig. 33: 5, 7 [?]; R1, genre 32 = *idem*: Figs 37: 1, 2, 38: 1-10 (churn necks); genre 41 = *idem*: Fig. 22: 2, 3; R1; genre 48, TUH219: 2 = *idem*: Fig. 24: 5; genre 49 = *idem*: Fig. 22: 1; TUH231: 1 = *idem*: Fig. 19 (bassins); TUH233: 11 = *idem*: Fig. 18: 3, 6; TUH234: 6 = *idem*: Fig. 33: 9 (rim shape only); TUH235: 8-10 = *idem*: Fig. 26: 1-6; TUH255: 5 = *idem*: Fig. 21: 4, 6-8 [?]; genre 90 = *idem*: Fig. 22: 6, 7; TUH255: 12 = *idem*: Fig. 31: 10-12. A similar exercise will no doubt be possible in terms of the typologies from Teleilat Ghassul and Abu Hamid, once these are completely published.

Repertoire 4 [EB I A - EB I B] (Figs 136, 263, 270)

The repertoire is characterized by highly polished and/or burnished exterior, and sometimes also interior, surfaces, including pattern burnishing in vertical stripes. Vessel forms are alien to the indigenous Palestinian Chalcolithic ceramic traditions as these are defined in terms of Ghassul/Beersheba/Abu Hamid and, predominantly, repertoire R1. On the basis of the parallels cited in the comparative study above, the repertoire must have its origins beyond the Jordan valley, perhaps even beyond Palestine: some of the forms such as genres 35 and 36 have been traced as far north as Cilicia and, according to Hennessy (1967), as far south as Egypt. Minimally, we might regard the repertoire to stem from the coastal Levant. In this regard, genre 53 might be included here (but see repertoire R8 below) and its related genres (54, etc.) as local imitations or developments.

There is one subset of genre 19 (see also 'Distribution of genres' above) which can be regarded as a hybrid: the jars with pushed up lug handles (Fig. 191: 1-4), a feature which links them to repertoire R2. A second hybrid form can be seen in TUH193: 21 whose 'bowed' shoulder is reminiscent of Chalcolithic forms. A similar 'bowed' shoulder appears in genre 34 (Fig. 209: 10). Genre 28, introduced late in EB I A (?), is obviously related to genre 33 of repertoire R5 (see also Fig. 268: 11), at least in terms of its characteristic spouts. The surface treatment of genre 33 itself (see also below) could be regarded as a northern variant of 'line group-painting' (e.g Amiran 1969: 49ff.) No holemouth jars can be attributed to repertoire R4.

Table 8. Repertoire R4

				R4					
hmj		jars			bowls			bs/bases	
?	19	28	35	36	39	41	63	72a	88
	H								
		[33]							

Repertoire 5 [EB I B] (Figs 137, 264)

The criterion for selection is the unmistakable surface decoration of these vessels, the so-called 'grain-wash' technique, and also pattern burnishing in net patterns and horizontal registers. There are some hybrid forms: e.g. genre 33 (from genre 28 of repertoire R4); genre 72(c) might be derived from genre 72a/b of repertoire R4 (Fig. 137); and genre 74, the ledge handle, could be connected with repertoire R1 and, probably, with repertoire R2.

Table 9. Repertoire R5

			R5						
hmj				jars		bowls	handles, bs, bases		
11	13	254:1	29	33	72c	233:1	74	83	93
				H	H		H		

The sparse excavation and survey data suggest that this repertoire might be localized in the Ajlun/Irbid/southern Syria (Hawran) regions and perhaps also in the area of the Jezre'el Valley/Tiberias: more or less the same region (but for the Jezre'el/Tiberas area) which we have suggested for the earlier (EB I A) repertoire R1. It is possible to consider this repertoire as a regional variant contemporary with what is sometimes called the southern 'line group-painting' tradition, also generally regarded as EB I B (cf. Amiran 1969: 49ff.).

Repertoire 6 [EB I B] (Fig. 265)

This repertoire is the most easily identified at Um Hammad because of its heavy red fabric and thick, thumb-impressed and moulded bands of decoration: i.e. 'Umm Hamad esh-Sharqi Ware/pré-urbaine D'.

Repertoire 6, as has been noted above ('Analysis of genres and comparative study'), represents a conundrum because of its apparently anachronistic features (decoration and form, and virtually one to one correspondence in vessel types) which are almost precisely paralleled in the 'northern Chalcolithic', especially as it has been recognized in the Huleh Basin and the Jawlan of southwestern Syria (e.g. Dayan 1969; Epstein 1978). We have also noted a generic relationship with the Ghassul/Beersheba/Abu Hamid assemblages. This relationship exists with regard to the majority of genres in the repertoire. The area of origin, therefore, is most likely to be northern Palestine, Transjordan and southwestern Syria.

Table 10. Repertoire R6

		R6	
hmj	jars	bowls	handles, bs
12	17 18 27	50 51?	73 84 92
			H

The appearance of this starkly idiosyncratic repertoire at Tell Um Hammad is not easily explained, as was the case, for examples, with repertoire R1. In the latter case, the time gap between the late Ghassul/Beersheba/Abu Hamid Chalcolithic and EB I A is not so great: indeed, the two periods are virtually contiguous; they might, more plausibly, have been partly contemporary (cf. Chapter 1: 'Tell Um Hammad in EB I A/B - EB II'), at least in some areas of the region. However, as we argued above, repertoire R1 can be explained in direct evolutionary terms. Repertoire R6 is another matter. There we are almost forced to decide between two alternative explanations: (i) that the repertoire was a totally new and independent invention, down to the last detail of design and form; or (ii) that it represents a technically superior, later development, behind which (somewhere in the Levant, Transjordan, and/or southern Syria) lies a flourishing Chalcolithic tradition, surviving virtually unchanged for more than a quarter of a century before manifesting itself as a part of Um Hammad's (and also Tell el-Far'ah's, among others) plural ceramic assemblage in EB I B: that is to say, some 'Chalcolithic' folk lived in the region well into the second half of the fourth millennium BC. There is nothing wrong with the second choice; the first is improbable. This notion is supported by the apparent lack of hybrid forms, with one, possibly telling, exception: the handles (genre 73) are clearly derived from post-Chalcolithic repertoires, in contrast to the normal, vertically applied forms (e.g. Epstein 1978: Figs 2: b, c, d; 6: a [right]; 8 [lower]; 11: bottom row; etc.). This relationship with EB I (A and B) repertoires could be used to suggest that repertoire R6 was already in production during EB I A, though not at Um Hammad itself.

Repertoire 7 [EB I A] (Figs 129; 215: 18, 19; 216; 270)

The repertoire appears to divide into two at about phase 3/4, although neither stylistic nor formal seriation seem to be possible, as was noted above. 'Esdraelon' ware (genre 45) is most abundant in the north of Palestine (Hennessy 1967) and is normally thought to be a local, Palestinian production, in contrast to 'Khirbet Kerak' ware in EB III whose origins lie far beyond Palestine.

Other repertoires?

We have already separated out those genres which clearly refer to Chalcolithic assemblages of Palestine: i.e. genres 38, 90, and TUH231: 1-7 (see also repertoires R1-R3 and the discussion with regard to the assemblages from Abu Matar/Zoumeli). The rest can be divided into two main categories according to the cited parallels ('Analysis of genres and comparative study'): (i) vessels which belong exclusively to EB I A contexts at Um Hammad; and (ii) genres which begin in EB I B contexts but appear to continue in use well into EB II and EB III.

Table 11. Repertoire R8

```
                                    R8
                                    |
         _____
         |    |                    |
        hmj  jar              bowls handles?
         |    |         _____
         |    |    |    |    |    |    |    |    |    |    |
         7   30   37   38   46   47   52   53   54   57   61
         H         H         H
```

The former might be assembled as 'repertoire' R8 (without, however, any immediately obvious localization) to include the holemouth jars of genre 7 (a hybrid combining features from repertoires R1 and R2) , jar rims of genre 30, and a series of bowls: e.g. genre 37 (a hybrid), the shallow, highly burnished bowls, one of which appears to be made in the same fabric as genre 45 ('Esdraelon' ware, R7), and genre 47 whose decoration is similar to that of genre 45 (R7) and a form similar to that of genre 36 (R4), genres 52, 53, and 54, all of which may be related (see also repertoire R1 and genre 55, as well as repertoire 2 and genre 56; see also Fig. 138: the early variants of genre 54[a] could belong to genre 53, in which case the histogram would suggest an initial introduction of the latter and its gradual replacement by the former after about phase 3), genres 57 and 61 whose recessed or indented rims may be related to genre 54, and genre 46 (Fig. 266). Many of these vessels have parallels in the north, in Cilicia, northwestern Syria, and Anatolia: they could, therefore, be related to repertoire R4.

The latter grouping (EB I B - EB II/III) - 'repertoire' R9 - would consist of the plain rimmed and incised holemouth jars (genres 10, 14, 15), TUH208: 1, bowls (and platters) of genres 43, 44, 58, 59, and 60, the spouts in genre 62, handles (genres 75, 76, 78), and bases of genres 91 and 94 (fig. 267).

Table 12. Repertoire R9

					R9								
hmj		jar		bowls					spout	handles			bases
10	14	15	208:1	43	44	58	59	60	62	75	76	78	91	94
H	H	H	H	H	H		H	H	H	H	H			H

'Repertoire' R9 includes many forms which can be regarded as hybrids: e.g. the holemouth jars (genre 10, 14, and 15) are all derived or developed from EB I A forms; TUH208: 1, the typical EB I B/II 'bottle' jar, can be related to genre 35 of repertoire R4; genre 43 is related to genre 36 (R4); genre 44 is similar to genre 41 (R4); genre 59 is also related to genre 36 (R4: note the incipient carinations on some variants, e.g. Fig. 211: 17, 30), as well as to forms which have their origin in pottery repertoires of north Syria and Anatolia; genre 60 could be linked with genre 57 and 61 ('repertoire' R8); genre 62 is related to genre 28 and 33 of repertoires R4 and R5, respectively; the handles (genres 75, 76) come from EB I A proto-types; and genre 94 is connected with genre 33 (R5, etc.).

The unclassified vessels (see also 'Analysis of genres and comparative study') might be summarized as follows:

Table 13. Unclassified vessels and related genre/repertoires

Catalogue	Context	Related genre(s) or repertoire(s)
hmj		
169: 7	EB I A	?
169: 8	EB I A/B	gs 2, 5, 9: R2 [developed]
169: 9	EB I B	gs 4, 6, 10. 13; Rs 3, 5, 9
170: 1-2	EB I B/II	gs 7, 8; Rs 2 [developed], 3, 8
170: 3-7	EB I B	<R1 [decoration]

170: 8	EB I A	R2
171: 1-6	EB I B	?
171: 7-12	EB I A/II	?
172: 1	EB IV?	?
172: 2	?	R1
172: 3-4	EB II	g. 14; R9
172: 5-10	EB I B/II	?; R9
173: 1, 3-9	EB I A/B	gs 4, 10; Rs 3, 9
173: 2	EB II	R9
173: 10, 11	EB I B	gs 3, 4m 8; R3
173: 12	?	?
173: 13	EB I B	?

jars

194: 1-2	EB I A	g. 48 [hybrid]; R1
205: 1-2	EB I A	R1
207: 103	EB I A	R3
208: 1-7	EB I B/II	R9

bowls

230: 8-13	EB I B	R9
231: 1-7	EB I A	<Chalcolithic
231: 8-13	EB I B	gs 47, 51 [<'Esdraelon']; R6
231: 14-16	EB II	R9
232: 1-3	EB I A	R3
232: 4-11	EB I B/II	R9
233: 1-5	EB I B	R5
233: 6-7	EB I A	?
233: 10=13	EB I B	gs 54, 55, 56; Rs 2, 8
234: 1-3	EB I A	gs 4, 12, 50, 51; Rs 3, >6?
234: 4-6	EB I A/B	R1?

miscellaneous

235: 8-10	EB I A/B	<Chalcolithic
235: 11-14	EB I A	<Chalcolithic
242: 3	EB II	R9?
242: 4	EB I A	?
242: 9-14	EB II/IV	R9
244: 17, 18,	EB I B/II	R9
252: 5	Chalcolithic (Stage 1)	
254: 1	EB I A/B	R5
254: 2-3	EB I A	R1?
254: 4	EB I A	g. 16: R1
254: 5	EB I A	g. 32; R1
254: 6	EB I A?	g. 16; R1
254: 7-11	EB I B	gs 19, 22, 23; Rs 2, 3
255: 1-3	EB I A/B	Rs 2, 3
255: 4-5	EB I A	<Chalcolithic
255: 6	EB I A	>R3
255: 7	EB I B	R4?

255: 8	?	?
255: 9, 10	EB IV?	?
255: 11	EB I A R2	
255: 12	EB I A	<Chalcolithic

CORRELATION WITH GLUECK AND MELLAART

The two earlier explorations of Tell Um Hammad (Glueck 1951; Mellaart 1962 [and Leonard n.d.]) gathered up a large amount of surface pottery which should be correlated with the present typology. As we have noted above, Mellaart's collection includes a large number of whole vessels stemming not only from surface collection but also from sondages. While all of Glueck's material is represented in the present typology (though naturally lacking some of the smaller vessels), that of Mellaart is useful in the reconstruction of complete forms. It is clear from both collections, that the so-called 'Um Hammad esh-Sharqi Ware' or 'pré-urbaine D' ware (Mellaart 1962; de Miroschedji 1971; cf. Hanbury-Tenison 1986, who has now made this 'Proto Urban D') caught the attention of both surveyors and is, therefore, over-represented: the ware is distinctive, and certainly ubiquitous on the surface owing to its robustness. In statistical terms, based on the present excavations, the ware is only one part (repertoire R6) of a relatively secondary occupation stage (3) at the site in EB I B.

Glueck (1951)

Holemouth jars

Genre 2 (*idem*: Pl. 162: 7); genre 10 [?] (*idem*: Pl. 162: 5); genre 12 (*idem*: Pls 156: 10, 11; 159: 5; and other, unclassified, holemouth jars some belonging to EB I/II (*idem*: Pls 156: 1, 2; 157: 7; 162: 3, 5, 6, 11. One holemouth jar (*idem*: Pl. 157: 8) belongs to EB IV.

Jars

Genre 16 (*idem*: Pls 157: 6; 158: 1, 3; 162: 4, 8, 9); genre 17 (*idem*: Pls 157: 5; 158: 6-8; 159: 1, 2, 7); genre 18 (*idem*: Pls 158: 15; 159: 6); genre 27 (*idem*: Pls 156: 6; 158: 4; 159: 8; 160: 1); genre 19 [?] (*idem*: Pl. 162: 15); genre 21 (*idem*: Pl. 162: 10 [see also Fig. 269: 2]); genre 22 (*idem*: Pl. 162: 13, 14, 16, 17); and genre 31 [?] (*idem*: Pl. 162: 2).

Bowls

Genre 50 (*idem*: Pls 156: 4, 7, 8; 157: 1-4, 5 [?], 9; 158: 2); genre 49 (*idem*: Pl. 157: 49); one bowl (Fig. 269: 3), though decorated like the rest of genre 50, has a different rim form (*idem*: Pl. 156: 9) which is common in EB I contexts in northern Palestine (e.g. at Tell Shuneh North [Gustavson-Gaube 1985; 1986] and En Shadud [Braun 1985]).

Handles

Genre 64 (*idem*: Pl. 161: 1, 2, 4-8, 10); genre 67 (*idem*: Pl. 162: 2); genre 69 (*idem*: Pl. 161: 11); genre 70 (*idem*: Pl. 162: 1); genre 73 (*idem*: Pl. 161: 3, 9); and genre 78)*idem*: Pl. 162: 18).

Bases

Genre 85 [?] (*idem* Pl. 160: 4); genre 92 (*idem*: Pl. 160: 9, 10) - the latter (no. 10) is also decorated on the inside (Fig. 269: 4), a curiously 'Chalcolithic' feature also noted in a similar deep jar (i.e. TUH genres 17/92) one set into a pit at Abu Hamid (Dollfus and Kafafi n.d.: Fig. 6 [note the ledge attached on the inside near the base]; Abu Hamid 1988: Fig. 74); genre 94 (*idem*: Pl. :3). Various bases in Glueck (1951) are undiagnostic; three bases belong to EB IV (i.e. *idem*: Pl. 156: 16-18).

Mellaart (Leonard n.d.: number in brackets = number illustrated)

Holemouth jars

Genre 1(1); genre 2(2); genre 3(1); genre 4[?] (3); genre 8 (3); genre 10 (2); genre 12 (6: see Fig. 268:1); unclassified (6), including one shape which is similar to TUH233: 1-5, as well as genre 13; and two vessels of EB IV.

Jars

Genre 16 (5); genre 17 (4); genre 18 (4); genre 19 (10: see Fig. 268: 2, 3) including one 'hybrid' vessel (Fig. 268: 3) which includes the pushed up lugs of repertoire R2; genre 20 (2); genre 21 (3: see Fig. 268: 4); genre 23 (3: see Fig. 268: 5-7, 10); genre 24 (7), of which one (Fig. 268: 10) might better fit into genre 28 [?]; genre 25 (2: see Fig. 268: 8); genre 26 (2); genre 27 (6: see Fig. 268: 9); genre 31 (4); genre 33 (1), particularly the decoration (Fig. 268: 11); and genres 34/35 (7: see also Fig. 268: 12, 13).

Bowls

Genre 36 (6); genre 39 (5); genre 45 (4); genre 47 (4: see Fig. 268: 14); genre 48 (4: see Fig. 268: 15, 16), including a 'hybrid' form related to genre 45 (Fig. 268: 15); genre 50 (19: see Fig. 268: 17, 19); genre 51 (5); genre 54 (3); genre 56 [?] (2); genre 27 [?] (1); genre 60 [?] (2); unclassified (4); 4 vessels which can be compared with TUH234: 1-3; and 4 bowls of EB IV.

Spouts

Genre 62 (2); and genre 63 (1).

Handles

Genre 64 (1); genres 66/69 (6); genre 67 (2); genre 68 (8), some with stamp 'seal' impressions (see also 'Special features'); genre 69 (3);

genre 70 (2); genre 71 (1); and unclassified (10), including some EB II types.

Bases

Genre 88 [?] (1); genre 92 [or EB IV?] (1); and unclassified (3).

Miscellaneous

In addition there are two (basalt?) bowls (Fig. 268: 19) and some pierced stone rings (see Chapter 7), as well as chipped stone blades, including a tabular scraper and a polished ('Ghassulian') chisel.

SPECIAL FEATURES

Tell Um Hammad's early pottery assemblages include several categories of idiosyncratic features, some of which can be related to specific geographical regions in the southern Levant and southern Syria. These categories consist of the following: (i) stamp 'seal' impressions on the bodies and handles of vessels; (ii) characteristic 'reed' impressions on rims, on raised bands, and randomly distributed over the body of the host vessel; (iii) 'specialized' handles; and (iv) 'potter's marks'. The first three appear exclusively on jars (genres 2 and 21) in one repertoire ('Repertoires': R2); the fourth (with one exception) appears on holemouth jars in two related genres (14 and 15) which begin in EB I B and become almost 'canonical' in EB II.

Stamp 'seal' impressions

It is now certain that these impressions were made deliberately, using (at least on one occasion) a stone-cut seal (e.g. from Tell Handaquq North: Mabry 1989). This specific practice, down to fine details of design and the placement of impressions on the host vessels, is now attested in a specific region of Palestine and south Syria (Fig. 274) whose southern limit presently appears to be the line between Tell Um Hammad (the area of the Jordan/Zerqa confluence), along wadi Zerqa (cf. also Fig. 2), and Jawa to the southeast of Jebel Druze. Tell Handaquq North (Mabry 1989) seems to be the northern limit in the Jordan Valley (no such practice is adduced at Tell Shuneh North, for example, nor in the Jezre'el Valley at En Shadud, Megiddo [but see 'Reed impressions' below], or Yiftahel: cf. Gustavson-Gaube 1985, 1986; Braun 1984, 1985). It may, therefore, be suggested that this peculiar practice of marking a limited number of vessels within discrete genres (in a discrete repertoire) is to be localized in the uplands and steppic fringes of northern Transjordan and, probably, southern Syria (certainly in the Hawran and Jebel Druze area), possibly as far north as Damascus. The broader aspects of this have been discussed with regard to Jawa (Betts [ed.] 1991: e.g. Fig. 167).

The corpus of stamp 'seal' impressions from Um Hammad includes examples found by both Glueck (1951) and Mellaart (Leonard n.d.). The closest parallels appear at Kataret es-Samra, Tell Mafluq, Tell Handaquq North, and Jawa.

The corpus

1). Glueck (1951: Pl. 103:7) illustrated one sherd which was stamped with a row of impressions of which five are visible. The design is similar to that of other impressions on handles (e.g. Pl. 7:1-3). A similar, single, impression on a body sherd was found during the present excavations (see Chapter 6: catalogue No. 8). A precise parallel occurs at Kataret es-Samra (Fig. 272:2; Leonard p.c.). The position of the impression on the vessel is not known although, by analogy with Jawa's genre B (Betts [ed.] 1991; see also Fig. 273: lower left), it may have been about the shoulder.

2). Mellaart (Leonard n.d.) found three examples stamped on ledge handles of which two (Pl. 7: 1, 2) are parallelled in the present typology (Fig. 238: 4; Pl. 7: 3). A fourth impression, also on a ledge handle (Pl.7: 4), is related in style, although it is more complex in design. The first group - a vertical line crossed by shorter lines - also appears at Jawa, likewise on ledge handles (Betts [ed.] 1991). The more complex example finds a close parallel in the stone stamp seal from Tell Handaquq North (Mabry 1989). A related stamp impression was found at Kataret es-Samra (Fig. 272:3; Leonard p.c.). As was noted above, all of these stamp impressions, probably including those noted above (1), belong to genre 21 (= genre B at Jawa), within repertoire R2.

3). Mellaart (Leonard n.d.) also found a related ledge handle (genre 21/67) which was decorated with two rows of stabbed patterns (9 and 7) on the upper surface of the handle, in line with the curve of the host vessel.

4). Two related impressions - criss-cross or net patterns in a circle - were found on a holemouth jar of genre 2 (Fig. 143: 1; Pl. 8: 1), also of repertoire R2. The same pattern occurs at Tell Mafluq Pl. 7: 5; Leonard n.d.), stamped on the upper surface of a ledge handle in a curving row of four.

5). A quite different stamp impression (a set of two) appears on the pushed up lug handle on a holemouth jar (genre 1/2; Figs 142; 272:1; Pls 4: 3; 8: 2). The host vessel is a 'hybrid': the form belongs to genre 2 of repertoire R2; the characteristic surface treatment ('finger streaking' and 'trickle paint') is typical of repertoire R1. The design of the stamped impression (net pattern) has also been found at Tell Qurs (Glueck 1951: Pl. 84:10) and elsewhere in Palestine (Ben-Tor 1978): it probably represents a different region of origin in contrast to the impressions above (i.e. the Levant, rather than Transjordan and south Syria).

6). One vessel in genre 21 (Fig. 197: 1) has two rows of stabbed or punctate impressions (7 and 8) on the shoulder. A similar set of impressions was found at Tell Qurs (Glueck 1951: Pl. 84:7; see also Betts [ed.] 1991: Fig. 167:TQ1). It might be related to the stabbed impressions on number 3 above.

All of the stamp impressions, but for nos 5 and 6, are closely related since they all appear on host vessels from one discrete repertoire (Fig. 262: R2). A cautious case has been made with regard to Jawa's pottery repertoire (Betts [ed.] 1991: Figs 168, 169; genres A and B; see also Helms 1987b) that some genres represent a size-ranked series (e.g. Fig. 273). If so, this must necessarily also apply to genre 21 at Tell Um Hammad. Whether the stamp impressions can be interpreted in terms of numeration is debatable (but see Betts [ed.] 1991: e.g. Fig. 169); they do, however, indicate a trend toward special designation of property which, in turn, could suggest some form of social ranking in some regions of Transjordan and south Syria in the second half of the fourth millennium BC (see also Chapter 7).

'Reed' impressions

Bands made up of characteristically patterned impressions which look as if they were made with a reed-like object (hence 'reed' impressions: cf. de Vaux 1955) were first noted by Loud at Megiddo (1948: Pls 94: 29; 96: 23) and later by Nelson Glueck at Tell Um Hammad (1951: Pl. 103: 12) where they appear on a body sherd, on a raised band, and also more randomly. They do not seem to have anything to do with handles. Similar impressions on a vessel close to those in genre 23 (Fig. 200: 15-19) were next found at Tell el-Far'ah North (de Vaux 1955: Fig. 5: 8) in what appears to be an EB I B context (i.e. together with 'Umm Hamad esh-Sherqi Ware', among others). The present excavations at Um Hammad have expanded this repertoire ('Repertoires': R2; Fig. 263) to include not only everted rim jars, such as the one from Tell el-Far'ah, but also holemouth jars and bowls (see also Pl. 8: 3, 5). 'Reed' impressions appear as follows: genres 3 and 4 (Figs 142: 1, 2, 5, 6; 143: 2, 7; 150: 8 [blank: 142: 3, 4, 7, 12; 143: 1, 3-6]; Pl. 8: 5; including impressed 'wavy' lips); genre 8 (Fig. 154: 1, 4, 6 [blank: 154: 2, 3]); genre 23 (Fig. 200: 18; including blanks); Fig. 207: 2, 3, on raised bands about the neck of jars (cf. Loud 1948: Pl. 96: 23, a double band); genre 39 (Fig. 214: 7); and genre 82 [bs] (Fig. 244: 1-6; Pl. 8: 3).

Decorated handles

Handles in genres 66 (repertoire R1), 68 (repertoire R2), 69 (repertoire R1), and 21 (repertoire R2) are provided with special decoration in addition to the more common stabbed, slashed, or impressed bands along the leading edges (Figs 197: 4; 237: 5, 6; 238: 5, 6, 9). The decoration consists of an arc of stabbed or slashed patterns on the body of the host vessel, immediately above the handle. The same practice is known at Jawa where one example also has a stamped 'seal' impression (Betts [ed.] 1991: genre B). On the basis of the relationship with the stamped handles (including some in repertoire R1: i.e. influenced by repertoire R2 - cf. also genre 1/2 and remarks above) it might be suggested that this peculiarity is related to whatever lay behind the stamp 'seals'. Furthermore, the practice of stamping or otherwise enhancing handles on pottery vessels (mostly vessels which were probably used for storage of dry goods) becomes a particularly 'Syrian' practice which continues in use up to, and beyond, the Iron Age (e.g. the 'L MLK' stamps; see also Broshi and Tsafrir 1977: Fig. 4: 9, for a stamp impression very like those a Um Hammad and Tell Mafluq, on a late handle), in contrast to the use of roll seals and tokens in sealed clay containers, this latter practice originating in the fourth millennium and even earlier in southern Mesopotamia (Friberg 1984; Nissen 1985). In south Syria, Transjordan, and Palestine the fashion of treating handles in a special way can already be seen in the Chalcolithic period (e.g. Commenge-Pellerin 1987: Figs 24: 4; 29: 2; 33: 5, 7, 9 [?]; 35: 4, 5, 6; 48: 4); it reappears in what might be called a 'familiar' numbering system (cf. also Potts 1981) in EB IV (Helms 1987b; cf. also du Mesnil du Buisson 1935: Pl. XLIX, for 'potter's marks' on contemporary vessels, although without any hint of numerical or volumetric ranking).

'Potter's marks'

Whether these patterns were actually intended as manufacturer's identification or not is uncertain; 'potter's marks' represent common usage in describing anything that was cut or scratched into the surface of a pottery vessel, usually before firing. Such marks have been found on bowls, for example, in the Jericho tombs of the EB I period (Kenyon 1960: Figs 9: 1, 4, 6, 8, 12; *passim*; including one example in paint, recalling the Chalcolithic handles noted above). One similar example occurs in genre 37 at Tell Um Hammad (Fig. 212: 9). Similar practices are known in various Chalcolithic repertoire of Palestine (e.g. Elliott 1977, with an implausible religious interpretation); there they are equally enigmatic or, rather, unexplained.

The 'potter's marks' are most common at Um Hammad in two related genres of holemouth jars (genre 14 and 15; Figs 164-196: 1-6) where they occur near the rims (Fig. 275). Whether the number of 'strokes' or slashes in any one set might represent more than just a loose identification of manufacture (i.e. workshop/artisan) or ownership or, more remotely, primitive ('familiar') numeration, is uncertain. At any rate, the practice appears to take the place of the stamp 'seal' impressions from EB I B onward (cf. Tufnell 1958: Pl. 18), becoming common in EB II (see 'Analysis of genres and comparative study' [genre 14, 15] for parallels). At about the same time, roll seal impressions, mostly on storage jars, also appear in Palestinian pottery repertoires.

SUMMARY

To summarize the analyses presented here, we may state that Tell Um Hammad's pottery assemblage of the EB I period consists of a number of recognizable, distinct repertoires (there may, of course, be others) which could stem from various regions beyond the central Jordan Valley, as well as from an indigenous Chalcolithic ceramic tradition. The 'Chalcolithic' features can be summed up as follows: the presence of a few churns and one pot stand, trumpet spouts, 'mat' impressions on one base, thumb-impressed and slashed pedestal bases, wavy lipped vessels and, in particular, repertoire R1 which, as we have shown, is derived from the Chalcolithic ceramic tradition of Palestine. The repertoires can be 'periodized' and, to varying degrees also localized (Table 14, Fig. 270).

The pottery assemblages of EB I A and EB I B stand in stark contrast to those of the following periods (EB II - III) whose pottery becomes increasingly homogeneous in style, form, and technology throughout the region, including southern Syria (e.g. Leboué: al-Maqdissi 1984; Braemer p.c.). The same contrast pertains with regard to the preceding Chalcolithic period, when the pottery is likewise virtually homogeneous throughout Palestine, though there are obvious regional, and even sub-regional, variations (e.g. some assemblages appear to have more specialized vessels, such as 'cornets, than others, often in sub-regions very close to each other). The conclusion to be drawn from this is that the period between the Chalcolithic and EB II (or the so-called first 'urban' stage, 'walled town culture', etc.), i.e. EB I, which is also often regarded as a period of transition, is a plural one in ceramic terms (not, however, in lithic terms: see Chapter 5).

Table 14. Summary of repertoires

EB I A

Repertoire R1	derived from the Palestinian Chalcolithic of the late 5th and first half of the 4th millennium BC (i.e. Ghassul/Beersheba/Abu Hamid, etc.)

	Repertoire R2	north Transjordan/south Syria (part of Jawa's assemblage)
	Repertoire R7	north Palestine (i.e. Yizre'el Valley, Tiberias, Galilee, etc.)
Repertoire R8		north Syria/Anatolia [?]
EB I A - EB I B		
	Repertoire R3	north Palestine (the same as R7)
	Repertoire R4	coastal Levant (Cilicia, Syria, Lebanon, Palestine, Sinai, and Egypt)
EB I B		
	Repertoire R5	north Transjordan/south Syria - north Palestine
	Repertoire R6	north Palestine/southwest Syria (Jawlan and Transjordan [?])
EB I B - EB II (III)		
	Repertoire R9	Palestine/Transjordan/south Syria - north Syria, Anatolia

Within this plurality are included continuing, or developing, styles which stem from the Chalcolithic period, proving some cultural continuity, alongside new inventions and/or the introduction of 'foreign' traditions, accompanied by the occasional merging of forms and styles (hybrids), suggestive of local adaptation and, perhaps, peaceful coexistence of a number of initially different populations. The contrast of plurality in EB I and conservatism, or cultural uniformity, before and after, might, therefore, be interpreted in demographic terms. It is evident that settlement number, size, and density increased noticeably with EB I A, at least in the sub-region of Tell Um Hammad and, thus, it may be plausible to suggest population 'increments' (virtually 'increments', as first used by Lapp 1968) to an existing, indigenous Chalcolithic population. If the analysis of the origins of the various identifiable repertoires is at all valid, this might argue for a number of different groups appearing in the sub-region at various times throughout both EB I A and EB I B. However, other interpretations are possible, including the notion of initially separate, sub-regional pottery production areas whose populations increasingly made contact with each other, in some way or another (e.g. down-the-line [trade], and thereby produced plural assemblages as well as local production of hybrid forms throughout the EB I period, without significant demographic shifts. This, at least, is the picture that we can present on the basis of the evidence from

Um Hammad and some of the neighbouring sites in the 'Zerqa triangle'. A similar case can be made for the pottery assemblage of fourth millennium Jawa (Betts [ed.] 1991). The published pottery from Tell el-Far'ah near Nablus and Jericho indicate comparable trends; the currently available evidence from sites like En Shadud, Yiftael and Tell Shuneh North is similar: i.e. the pottery assemblages at these sites share some of the repertoires which we have reconstructed at Tell Um Hammad (although probably in different proportions) while others are not present. Further research may identify other sub-regions in the southern Levant in which a similar merging of distinctive sub-repertoires occurred. The now established connection between the Um Hammad-'Zerqa triangle' region and Jawa demonstrates the interlinking of sub-regions, a pattern which almost certainly holds true as far north as the Damascene in the east, and as far north as the southern Lebanon in the west. Jawa's 'ceramic' connection with northern Syria (cf. Figs 270 and 271) might extend this 'proto-urban' landscape of EB I, if only marginally, into the realm of real urbanism in terms of northern Syria. 'Urban' Byblos is arguable different from Syro/Mesopotamian towns and cities of the period, although it could easily be called an incipient thalassocracy, or even a maritime city state. Repertoire R4, for example, appears to have parallels as far north as Cilicia, and as far south as the Nile Delta.

More locally, within the 'Zerqa triangle', we have noted the occupational correspondence, as well as the difference, between Um Hammad and Ruweiha which are virtually within direct sight of each other. The EB I A repertoire at Ruweiha corresponds to the early phases of Stage 2 at Um Hammad. This may suggest a contemporary, sub-regional variability in which two almost adjacent settlements shared the same basic repertoire which represents a direct development from the Chalcolithic period (repertoire R1), but where one site (Um Hammad) appears to absorb more sub-regional repertoires than the other. (Um Hammad was, of course, a much larger settlement: i.e. more people and, therefore, a greater probability of a larger local 'ceramic' market which would attract a greater variety of products?) The fact that a part of the (apparently later) EB I B assemblage at Um Hammad also includes an almost pure Chalcolithic repertoire (R6) could not only be used to support the notion of long-surviving 'older' traditions, side by side with new or different ones, but also that the 'Chalcolithic' site of Tell Qa'adan, a few kilometres northwest of Ruweiha, could have been occupied at the same time: it may simply have been a matter of preference for one form of pottery or another. Behind this may lie other factors such as ethnic differences, socio-political differences, and so forth. Finally,

Um Hammad's pottery assemblage clearly shows the end-result of merging repertoires in repertoire R9 which becomes the standard for EB II and III in the southern Levant. This, and other possibilities, are discussed further in Chapter 7.

5. The Chipped Stone Assemblage

A.V.G. BETTS

The chipped stone from Um Hammad comes from excavated and surface contexts at both Tell Um Hammad al-Sharqi and Tell Um Hammad al-Gharbi. All chipped stone encountered during excavation was kept for analysis. The sample is based on visual recognition by the excavators as no soil was sieved, but it can be regarded as a reliable macro-sample since the lithic specialist was on hand during the excavations to encourage recovery. The analysis presented here covers two separate assemblages: the Early Bronze Age I/II assemblage from Tell Um Hammad al-Sharqi; and the Early Bronze Age IV collection from Tell Um Hammad al-Gharbi and some upper levels at Um Hammad al-Sharqi.

Both assemblages are typical of Early Bronze Age industries in Palestine as described in a number of analyses (see particularly Rosen 1983c; 1989). The early assemblage is dominated by sickle elements, with some tabular tools and miscellaneous pieces. The EB IV assemblage consists largely of sickle blades, with an admixture of retouched flakes and miscellaneous tools. Raw material used for both assemblages comes from several sources. Some of the small irregular tools are made on local cherts obtained as water-rolled cobbles in the bed of the Zerqa River. Tabular flakes in the EB I/II assemblage are of dark grey/brown fine-grained chert, presumably traded in to the site. Blades in both assemblages are struck from a variety of different types of chert, ranging from pale and coarse to darker, fined grained and banded. No blade cores were recovered, although a small number of crested blades was found.

THE EARLY BRONZE AGE I/II ASSEMBLAGE

Technology

The only knapping apparently carried out on site is the production of flakes used, when retouched, for a variety of tasks (see Table 16: miscellaneous tools). There is no evidence for on-site production of blades or tabular flakes, although fragments among the debris indicate some secondary working of blanks presumably traded in. Flake production is basic. Raw material is provided by cobbles from local river beds. Striking platforms are produced by removing one flake from the end of an elongated cobble, and using the resultant scar as the basis for blank removal. Several flakes have cortex or water-rolled facets on the dorsal surface. Size of blanks is limited to some degree by the size of available cobbles, although large chert lumps can be seen in the bed of the Zerqa River. Size may also have been limited by the need to carry the cobbles up to the site. There are no very large flakes. This suggests possibly that there was no use for them, or that knapping was not generally carried out away from the site. Working of local cherts was only carried out to a limited degree. Most tools are made on large blades or tabular flakes, and there is only a small amount of knapping waste (Table 15), although low numbers in the 'chip' category may be partly accounted for by recovery procedures. The low numbers of unretouched blades in comparison to the figures for retouched blades in the toolkit (Table 16), are a strong indication that blades were not only traded in, but regarded as a relatively valuable commodity which was not wasted. The presence of some crested blades may be explained by regarding them as blanks rather than waste products.

The blades used at the site are regular, parallel sided, trapezoidal in cross-section and struck from single platform cores. Only a few have a triangular cross-section. Where preserved, most have facetted striking platforms, although a small number had punctiform platforms. Blade width varies but most are between 1.3 and 1.7 centimetres. Figure 282 shows the distribution of blade widths for excavated and surface deposits at Tell Um Hammad al-Sharqi. There is a good fit between the two groups, with the higher range among the surface group explained by some mixing with artefacts from later periods.

Table 15. Chipped stone debitage (EB I/II)

	st. 2	st. 3	st. 4
flake core	6	4	1
primary flake	1	7	1
crested blade	2	0	0
flake	48	85	34
blade	1	2	3
chunk	11	24	5
chip	9	23	5
Total	78	145	49

The tabular flakes are broad or elongated, with large facetted platforms and marked bulbs of percussion. The cortex is smooth and creamy white in colour. Uniformity in raw material among the tabular pieces suggests a common source of raw material.

Retouched Pieces

For convenience of comparison, categories used in analysis of the Jawa chipped stone (Betts [ed.] 1991: Chapter 5) have been adopted here, although with the sample from Um Hammad a wider, and different, range of tool types can be recognised. Classification is based partly on Rosen's typology (1983a; 1989), but with a few adaptations. Tools have been divided into three broad categories: knives; scrapers; and other tools. The first category comprises all blade tools, including sickle elements.

Table 16. Chipped stone tools from stratified deposits (EB I/II)

	st. 2	st. 3	st. 4
Knives			
Sickle blades			
plain	3	2	4
denticulate	12	5	3
other retouch	8	3	1
Other blades			
misc. retouch	8	2	7
Scrapers			
Tabular scraper	3	2	3
Endscraper	0	0	1
Steep scraper	1	1	0
Misc. tools			
Denticulated flake	1	2	2
Notched piece	0	1	0
Retouched flake	1	2	0
Total	30	18	14

Only 62 chipped stone tools were found in stratified contexts. Retouched pieces found on the surface fitted broadly into the assemblage breakdown shown in Table 16 above.

Knives

The commonest tool in this class is the sickle blade. Most are snapped or, more rarely, truncated blade segments, designed as elements in a composite sickle (for a suggested reconstruction see Betts [ed.] 1991: Fig. 184). Over half the sickle blades from stratified contexts were denticulated (Fig. 277: 1, 2), and a small number had backing or thinning created by abrupt or inverse retouch along one edge (Fig. 276: 3, 5). One piece (Fig. 276: 4) had traces of bitumen along one side. About a third of the segments had gloss on both edges, suggesting that they had been turned in the haft and re-used. The blades varied in length from short, almost square, segments to largely complete blades. Medium length blade segments were most common. Complete blades with sickle gloss, Rosen's 'reaping knives' (1983a), are not represented in the stratified assemblage. In the typology above, the 'other retouch' category includes backing and truncation as well as miscellaneous working. There was also one mixed tool (Fig. 276: 2), an endscraper on a large blade with sickle gloss along one edge. The semi-abrupt working for the endscraper appears to be secondary to use of the blade as a harvesting/cutting tool.

A significant proportion of the blade tools did not have sickle gloss. These included snapped segments and nearly complete blades (Fig. 276: 1). All blades in this category had some retouch. Working included backing, denticulation, and irregular trimming. Rosen (1989) makes a distinction between Canaanean and non-Canaanean blades. This distinction is not clear at Um Hammad. Most of the blades are of Canaanean type, but some might be locally produced although there is no evidence of this in the debitage.

Scrapers

The tabular scrapers vary in form. Most are elongated and, where they are preserved, have facetted platforms (Fig. 277: 4, 5). Some are markedly elongated, with semi-steep bilateral retouch (Fig. 278: 1). The surface collection included one large sub-circular scraper (Fig. 279), similar to those from Jawa (Betts [ed.] 1991: Figs 175, 176). Unlike the Jawa pieces, the Um Hammad scraper has no traces of gloss.

There are only three other pieces in the 'scraper' class: one endscraper; and two irregular steep scrapers on pebble flakes.

Miscellaneous tools

Apart from those in the categories discussed above, there are few tools in stratified contexts at Tell Um Hammad al-Sharqi. There are five flakes with irregular denticulation, three retouched flakes and one notched piece. Surface collections produced a few more miscellaneous pieces, of which the most carefully worked was a thick, steep-sided perforator (Fig. 278: 2).

Stratigraphic variation

As Table 16 shows, there is little appreciable variation through time from Stage 2 to Stage 4. No flints were recovered in Stage 1 (but see Leonard n.d.). The lack of change in lithic technology through this period is reflected at other sites (e.g. Schick 1978 [Arad]).

THE EARLY BRONZE AGE IV ASSEMBLAGE

The EB IV assemblage has been treated as a single unit, since the excavated sample was small, and showed no signs of change or development through time.

Table 17. Chipped stone debitage (EB IV)

flake core	14
primary flake	12
crested blade	1
flake	154
blade	8
chunk	27
chip	56
Total	272

Technology

As in earlier periods, the only knapping carried out on site in the EB IV period was the production of small flakes from local wadi cobbles. Flaking techniques are similar to those of the EB I/II assemblage. Flakes have broad, plain platforms. Blades are more massive, and less regular, than those of the EBI/II assemblage. They have facetted platforms and a trapezoidal cross-section. No blades with triangular cross-section were found in EB IV levels. Blade widths are greater than in earlier periods. The excavated sample peaks around 2.0 to 2.1 centimetres, but the larger surface sample suggests that the normal size range is higher. Figure 282 might also suggest two clusters, one with a blade width range peaking around 2.0 centimetres and a second, less numerous, cluster peaking around 2.7 centimetres. In any event, it is clear that blades are consistently larger in the later periods of the Early Bronze Age.

Retouched Pieces

39 retouched pieces were recovered in excavation. Blades are commonest, but miscellaneous tools feature more strongly than in the earlier assemblage, while tabular scrapers are absent.

Table 18 . Chipped stone tools from stratified deposits (EB IV)

Knives	
Sickle blades	
plain	9
denticulate	6
other retouch	2
Other blades	
misc. retouch	8
Scrapers	
Endscraper	1
Steep scraper	1
Misc. tools	
Denticulated flake	1
Notched piece	3
Burin on break	1
Borer	1
Bilaterally backed piece	1
Retouched flake	5
Total	39

Knives

Blades are larger and somewhat more irregular than in the EB I/II assemblage (Figs 280, 281). Blade segments are longer and may have functioned as knives, rather than as part of composite tools. Backing and denticulation occur infrequently, although a few pieces are naturally backed. Two sickle blades are broken crested pieces.

A number of the blades had no gloss, but some irregular retouch and use damage (Fig. 281: 1). One such blade (Fig. 280: 3) came from the shaft of a burial chamber in the adjacent cemetery of Tiwal esh-Sharqi (Helms 1983). The chamber contained characteristic EB IV pottery.

Scrapers

Only two scrapers were found in stratified contexts. One was an endscraper on a flake and the other a steep scraper on a broken piece.

Miscellaneous tools

Miscellaneous tools form a slightly higher proportion of the assemblage than in the earlier periods. Tools include notched and retouched pieces, one denticulated flake, one simple burin and a crude flake borer (Fig. 281: 2, 3). The miscellaneous tools are all made from local raw materials.

DISCUSSION

The earliest occupation at Um Hammad falls close to the period of the Chalcolithic/Early Bronze Age 'transition', and it is necessary to look for evidence of some overlap in the Um Hammad assemblage. Chalcolithic assemblages in Palestine are characterised by blade industries, in combination with flake and core tools. Blade manufacture is at least sometimes carried out on site (e.g. Levy and Rosen 1987: 283). Blades are trapezoidal or triangular in cross-section. Canaanean blades occur occasionally in Late Chalcolithic contexts (Baird 1987; Hanbury-Tenison 1986: 147). Sickle blades are commonly finely denticulated, truncated and backed (cf. Levy and Rosen 1987; *Abu Hamid* 1988: 42). Bilateral gloss is uncommon. Some of these traits are carried over into Early Bronze Age flint assemblages. The Canaanean blade becomes the dominant blade form, and backing of sickle elements becomes a residual trait. Since blade segments are no longer backed, and presumably also because, as trade items, they are a valuable commodity, the elements are frequently turned in the haft and re-used. This results in bilateral gloss (Rosen 1989). At Tell Shuneh North, and possibly elsewhere, core tools continue on briefly into EB I (Baird 1987). Tabular tools continue but alter their shape, changing from short and wide to more narrow, elongated forms.

Bearing these points in mind, there appears to be some overlap in tool forms from the late Chalcolithic to EB I. These residual traits include backed and truncated sickle blades, and possibly some core tools. Backed sickle blades occur in Stage 2 at Tell Um Hammad and Mellaart found a chisel/adze tool in an unstratified context (Leonard n.d.). However, the early assemblage at Tell Um Hammad relates closely to the 'Canaanean' industry, typical of the Early Bronze Age in

Syria/Palestine. Both the EB I/II and the EB IV assemblages contain the hallmarks of the industry: Canaanean blades with facetted platforms and trapezoidal cross-section; sickle elements with bilateral lustre; ovoid or elongated tabular scrapers with facetted platforms and prominent bulbs; imported blades and tabular flakes found in conjunction with a local 'ad-hoc' flaking tradition (cf. Betts [ed.] 1991: Chapter 5 [Jawa]; Rosen 1985 [En Shadud]; Crowfoot Payne 1983 [Jericho]; Schick 1978 [Arad]; Crowfoot Payne 1948 [Afula]; Garrod 1934 [Megiddo]). The two Um Hammad assemblages are important because they offer a clear illustration of changes in the Canaanean industry through the Early Bronze Age, developments which have been masked in collections from more complex, multi-period tell sites. There is little evidence for change throughout the EBI/II sequence, but marked development between the EBI/II assemblage and that of the EB IV period. The local flake industry continues, and even appears to become more important in the EB IV assemblage, tabular scrapers disappear and blades get larger and somewhat more irregular. Finely denticulated sickle elements with careful backing and truncation also disappear, to be replaced by longer, minimally retouched segments. Rosen (1983b) suggests that there is no increase in blade width throughout the Early Bronze Age, a view contradicted by the evidence from Um Hammad (and also by Hanbury-Tenison [1986: 148]). The peak width range for Um Hammad of 1.3 to 2.0 centimetres in EBI/II (Fig. 282) fits with Rosen's data for EB I En Shadud (1983b: Fig. 6), while his higher width range for EB IV Sha'ar ha-Golan fits equally well with EB IV Um Hammad.

Lack of blade cores at Um Hammad reinforces the evidence for trade in Canaanean blades at this period. However, the extent of these trade networks is still unclear. Rosen (1983b), along with others (Hennessy 1967; Crowfoot Payne 1960; Waechter 1958) draws a parallel between regular parallel-sided blades occurring on fourth and third millennium sites in Mesopotamia (e.g. Kozlowski 1986; Valla 1978) and the Canaanean blade of Syria/Palestine. There are reasons for caution in making this connection (Betts [ed.] 1991: Chapter 5) as the technology of blade production is markedly different in each case. While Canaanean blades have wide facetted platforms, the Mesopotamian blades have trimming of the mid-rib spurs and punctiform platforms, thus suggesting a different method of blade removal. Lack of cores on Mesopotamian sites have led scholars to suggest trade networks (e.g. Kozlowski [1986] for the Ubaid period), but given the different technologies, it seems likely that Mesopotamian exchange systems operated separately from those in Syria/Palestine with regard to distribution of flint blades.

Rosen (1983b) also discusses the more local distribution of Canaanean blades. Here he uses width variation to imply local variety and so local centres of production. Unfortunately, on the basis of the Um Hammad evidence, his width variation may have a chronological explanation, rather than presenting evidence for 'individual cells' in the Canaanean blade trade network (but see Rosen 1989: 208). Canaanean blades occur on most Early Bronze Age sites in Palestine, but not on sites in the central and southern Negev (Rosen 1983b). They are found in the coastal Levant (Hours 1979) and into the Amuq plain in western Syria (Crowfoot Payne 1960). They also occur in the Hawran, notably at Jawa (Betts [ed.] 1991: Chapter 5), where the Canaanean industry at the site is distinct from contemporary local steppic flake assemblages. North of Syria, blades of Canaanean type are found into Turkey and Anatolia (Palmieri 1973: Figs 2, 5; Caneva 1973: 187, 189, Fig. 2: 6).

A second and different, trade pattern has been suggested for tabular scrapers (Rosen 1983c; 1989) where, in contrast to the supposed local blade exchange networks, tabular scrapers are traded over much greater distances. Rosen has suggested that the proportion of tabular scrapers in lithic assemblages increases the further south the site, and argues that this is because the scrapers originate in the steppe/desert regions of the Negev and Sinai and were traded into the Mediterranean climatic zone by groups living in, or beyond, the steppe border lands. He suggests that a similar trade may have been carried out by steppic groups in Transjordan.

Since data from Um Hammad calls into question Rosen's notion of local blade exchange 'cells', it is possible that scrapers and blades were passed on through the same networks. It should also be considered that greater numbers of tabular scrapers on sites in or near the steppe/desert regions of Sinai, the Negev and the *badiyat al-sham* may be due as much to economic factors as to distance from source. Jawa has high proportions of tabular scrapers in the flint assemblage, yet despite close local sources of tabular cherts, the scrapers are all of a fine olive/brown flint imported from beyond the *badiya*, and of markedly similar type to tabular flint in Canaanean assemblages in Palestine such as the tools from Jericho. Similarly, tabular flint is available in the vicinity of Arad, yet the tabular tools from the site are made from a better quality raw material traded in from further afield (Schick 1978: 62). Microwear analysis of tabular tools (McConaughy 1979) suggests their primary use may have been cutting and butchering. Large tabular tools from Jawa have marked blunting and silica gloss around the edges which may be caused by their use for cutting reeds (Unger-Hamilton 1991). Henry (p.c.) suggests that tabular flakes may have been used for shearing. Use of flint flakes for this purpose is a practice which continued sporadically into the recent past among the bedouin. Activities relating to sheep-rearing and butchery are likely to be more common on steppic sites than in the farming villages of the Levant, which may help to explain relatively high proportions of tabular tools in the assemblages of steppic sites just as well as proximity to sources of raw material.

However, Rosen's hypothesis of separate trade networks might be substantiated by evidence for high proportions of tabular scrapers on sites close to the steppe, whether the flint was traded from local sources or from farther afield. If relative proportions of blades and scrapers in an assemblage reflect the economy of the site where that assemblage occurs (blades = agriculture; scrapers = animal husbandry) then pastoral groups trading on the borders of the steppe might only deal in scrapers while the blades could perhaps be produced somewhere closer to agricultural regions. Certainly comparison between the lithic assemblages of Um Hammad and Jawa shows that Jawa (Betts [ed.] 1991: Chapter 5) has high proportions of tabular tools relative to blades. Um Hammad, on the other hand, has low proportions of tabular tools relative to blades in the EBI/II assemblage, while the EB IV assemblage consists to a large extent of sickle blades. The differences between the two sites must be largely related to economic activities, and particularly to agriculture. Jawa is a steppic site, in an area of limited agricultural potential, while Um Hammad lies in the heart of good farmland, and the relative proportions of sickle blades reflect this. Clearly, the markets for scrapers and blades varied from region to region, and may thus have been exchanged through differing networks.

6. OTHER FINDS

N. O' TOOL

The excavations at Tell Um Hammad (al-Sharqi) produced only a small number of 'special' finds, and among these are only a few which are of diagnostic use. Most do not require illustration (i.e. the copper alloy fragments and various partly worked stone objects). The diagnostic objects consist of pierced stone rings, one mace head, and heavy, flat-based, conical stone bowls with an external band of knobs. Various stone 'palettes' (Fig. 283: 6, 16) and pounders or pestles (Fig. 283: 26) need no further comment. There are also basalt 'saddle' querns which have a wide distribution in both space and time in the southern Levant (see Betts [ed.] 1991).

DIAGNOSTIC OBJECTS

Pierced stone rings (Fig. 283: 9, 10, 18)

These rings are bi-directionally drilled through, their exterior surfaces shaped and smoothed. Parallels exist in a broad range of contexts, from the Neolithic well into the Bronze Age. Chalcolithic and EB I parallels exist at Tell Handaquq North (Mabry 1989), Jericho (Kenyon and Holland 1983), Ghrubba (Mellaart 1956: Fig. 6: 135), Tell Turmus (Dayan 1969: Fig. 9: 2-6, some partially pierced), Nahal Mishmar (Bar Adon 1980: *passim*), Azor (Perrot *et al.* 1961: Fig. 41: 24), Horvat Beter (Dothan 1959a: Figs 10: 41-45, ceramic; 11: 7-10, 15-17; 18: 48 ff.; 19: 8, 10 ff.), Kataret es-Samra (Leonard 1983: Fig. 20), and Meser (Dothan 1959b: Fig. 5: 18). They are also common in contemporary contexts at Hama (Fugmann 1958: *passim*).

Mace heads (Fig. 283: 12)

The mace head is bi-directionally drilled through and externally polished. It is a type which is well attested in Chalcolithic and EB I contexts: e.g. at Abu Hamid (*Abu Hamid* 1988: Figs 48-50; Dollfus and Kafafi n.d.: Fig. 15: 5-8; Pl. VIII: 2-8); Nahal Mishmar (Bar Adon 1980: *passim*); Burqu' Site 27 (in the eastern steppe of Transjordan) (McCartney in press: Fig. 24, in late Neolithic and Chalcolithic contexts); at Jawa (Betts [ed.] 1991: Figs 194: 698, 699; 195), Jericho (Holland 1983); and in the eastern regions of the Hawran at Khirbet Umbachi and Hebariyeh (Dubertret and Dunand 1954 - 5: Pl. VII bis: 1). (Rast [1980: 7] attributes all mace heads at Bab edh-Dhra' to an Egyptian source [?].)

Conical basalt bowls (Fig. 283: 15, 23, [?], 38, 39; see also Glueck 1951: Pl. 163: 8; Leonard n.d.)

Braun (1990) has made an attempt to construct a typology of basalt bowls in EB I and the bowls from Tell Um Hammad fit into his Type I, although his illustrated examples (including, incorrectly, the reference to Jawa) share only the general form; they do not have the characteristic raised knob decoration which can be related to both Chalcolithic and EB I (A) prototypes. Chalcolithic examples come from Ain Shems (e.g. Braun 1990: Fig. 4: 3A); EB I (A) parallels exist at Jawa (Betts [ed.] 1991: Fig. 192: 687-689), Tell Handaquq North (Mabry 1989), Tell Mafluq (Mellaart: Leonard n.d.), and Jebel Mutawwaq (Hanbury-Tenison 1987: Fig. 6: 12, 14, 15; 1989b). The knobs can be related to ceramic vessels in 'Esdraelon' ware and thus perhaps represent a local Palestinian/Transjordanian 'invention' whose distribution, at present, appears to be limited to northern Transjordan (and southern Syria: the Hawran), wadi Zerqa, and the area about Tell Um Hammad, parallelling somewhat the distribution of pottery repertoire R2 (see Chapter 4: 'Repertoires'). In agreement with Braun (1990), we should consider these bowls as a 'continuation of an important Chalcolithic tradition', though changed in form and decoration according to sub-regional or local preferences, which indicates 'the existence of several workshops or centres of production ... during the EB I period' (*idem*: 94 - 95). Again, reflecting the ceramic evidence from Um Hammad, the notion of a continuing Chalcolithic tradition echoes the relationship of pottery repertoire R1 (developed from Chalcolithic traditions) and repertoire R2 (a regional, evolving, EB I A tradition).

Shells

Some shells and shell fragments were recovered from the excavations. Four of these were identified by D.S. Reese (Table 19: 1 - 4. Other shells and shell fragments have been classified on the basis of Reese's identification (Table 19: 5 - 28).

Table 19. Shells

No.	Prov.	St.	Description
1	4061	2	*Unio* (Freshwater bivalve): fragment of a large fresh-water bivalve. Max ht. 77 mm. A bit worn, but not modified.
2	4025	3	*Unio* (Fresh-water bivalve): left valve, ht. 24 mm., width 40+ mm. Hole at umbo made by grinding with ground-down area 12 mm. and hole 2.5 x 5.5 mm. The distal edge of the shell has thirteen cut marks present and others which have now been lost because the shell is broken here.
3	4018	3	*Glycymeris* (dog cockle - Mediterranean): water-worn, with broken umbo. Ht. 39+ mm., width 42 mm.
4	4018	3	*Glycymeris* (dog cockle - Mediterranean): water-worn, naturally holed at umbo (bivalve "beak"). Ht 38.5 mm., width 32 mm. Hole is 5 x 3 mm.
5	2088	2	*Unio* (Freshwater bivalve)
6	2148	2	*Unio* (Freshwater bivalve)
7	4109	2	*Unio* (Freshwater bivalve)
8	4125	2	*Unio* (Freshwater bivalve)
9	50001	2	*Unio* (Freshwater bivalve)
10	50002	2	*Unio* (Freshwater bivalve)
11	50003	2	*Unio* (Freshwater bivalve)
12	50005	2	*Unio* (Freshwater bivalve)
13	50006	2	*Unio* (Freshwater bivalve)
14	50007	2	*Unio* (Freshwater bivalve)
15	4088	3	*Unio* (freshwater bivalve)
16	1076	3	*Glycymeris* (dog cockle - Mediterranean)
17	4017	3	*Glycymeris* (dog cockle - Mediterranean)
18	4018	3	*Glycymeris* (dog cockle - Mediterranean)
19	40016	4	*Unio* (freshwater bivalve)
20	1002	EB IV	*Unio* (freshwater bivalve)
21	41013	EB IV	*Unio* (freshwater bivalve)
22	1047	I A	*Unio* (freshwater bivalve)
23	1003	+++	*Unio* (freshwater bivalve)
24	40001	+++	*Unio* (freshwater bivalve)
25	4103	+++	*Glycymeris* (dog cockle - Mediterranean)
26	-	+++	*Unio* (freshwater bivalve)
27	-	+++	*Unio* (freshwater bivalve)
28	-	+++	*Unio* (freshwater bivalve)

Table 20. Catalogue of small finds

No.	Prov.	St.	Ph.	Description
1	1048	-	20	small flat curved copper alloy fragments
2	1014	4	15	conical copper alloy fragment
3	++++	-	-	flat copper alloy fragments
4	2022	3	11	copper alloy fragment
5	1000	-	-	copper alloy fragment
6	1004	4+	16 - 18	stone (basalt) palette, red stains and scratch marks, shallow depression on one side
7	4018	3	11	pierced shell
8	++++	-	-	sherd with stamp seal impression (see Chapter 4)
9	1060	3	13	pierced stone ring
10	1060	3	13	pierced basalt ring
11	4025	3	11	pierced shell
12	++++	-	-	stone mace head
13	4029	3	11	stone with hole
14	2013	3	11	pierced stone ring fragment (cf. Fig. 283: 9, 10)
15	++++	-	-	basalt bowl fragment with two raised bosses
16	1034	4	14	rectangular stone palette, traces of red substance, regular scratches
17	Tomb 3 EB IV		-	copper alloy tanged weapon (Betts and Helms in press)
18	2070	2	9	stone ring
19	1014	4	15	limestone bowl fragment
20	3001	-	-	basalt quern fragment
21	4061	2	1	shell fragment
22	++++	-	-	basalt ring
23	++++	-	-	basalt bowl fragment
24	4008	4	15	worked fragment of haematite, with red ochre
25	1003	4+	16 - 18	worked fragment of haematite, with red ochre
26	++++	-	-	elongated limestone pebble, battered at one end
27	2057	2	7	limestone bowl fragments
28	2117	2	7	limestone bowl fragments (fit no. 27)
29	1021	-	-	flat rectangular basalt rubber
30	4072	3	11	rounded elongated pebble, scratches, signs of smoothing, traces of red ochre, battered at both ends
31	++++	-	-	copper alloy fragment
32	++++	-	-	copper alloy fragment
33	++++	-	-	worked white stone fragment
34	++++	-	-	scarab (Iron Age: see Betts and Helms in press)
35	++++	-	-	large pierced limestone pebble
36	++++	-	-	large pierced limestone pebble
37	++++	-	-	white elongated stone bead
38	++++	-	-	rim fragment of basalt bowl
39	++++	-	-	basalt bowl fragment, rim and raised boss
40	++++	-	-	ceramic figurine fragment (Iron Age: see Betts and Helms in press)
41	50000	-	-	pierced limestone ball

7. Conclusion

A. V. G. BETTS and S. W. HELMS

INTRODUCTION

Excavations at Tell Um Hammad have produced a comprehensive pottery assemblage for the problematical EB I period based on deep and reliable stratigraphy. In this lies the bulk of 'new' evidence which shows that significant changes in pottery production took place during this period, changes which have a bearing on the so-called transition from the preceding Chalcolithic period. Technological development apart, the main difference between the pottery assemblage of the Chalcolithic and that of EB I (A) is in terms of variety: the assemblage of EB I (A) is made up of a number of discrete repertoires, while that of the Chalcolithic period is essentially homogeneous. The difference between the two periods is further highlighted by stratigraphic evidence which confirms the findings from almost all earlier excavations in Palestine and Transjordan in that pure Chalcolithic pottery or other diagnostic artefacts have on no occasion been found together with EB I material in the same archaeological context. However, the new evidence from Um Hammad now demonstrates: (i) clear evidence that Chalcolithic ceramic traditions continue into EB I A, as part of the new pottery assemblage; and (ii) that almost pure Chalcolithic forms - a complete repertoire - seem to reappear in EB I B. The new evidence, therefore, contradicts much of what has become accepted concerning the so-called transition period between the Chalcolithic and the Early Bronze Age. In addition to this, the connection between Um Hammad and eastern Transjordan/southeastern Syria (Jawa) on the one hand, and links with both Palestinian sub-regions and the Mediterranean coast, suggest a new 'internationalism' in the land, again something that is quite different from the preceding period, something that cannot easily be explained away purely in terms of local development. Finally, the new evidence shows that the EB I period, particularly EB I A, was probably much longer than had been thought. It is possible that EB I generally (I A and I B) was as long as, or even longer than, the so-called 'urban' era of EB II and III which started to fall apart by 2500 BC or a little later (EB IV): that the 'transition' period may have been both more significant and perhaps more representative of a norm in the southern Levant than the 'full' Early Bronze Age.

Perhaps the main conclusion, given the new evidence presented here, is that we are more than ever reluctant to attempt an 'explanation' of what really happened in the fourth millennium BC, particularly with regard to the relation between the Chalcolithic period and the Early Bronze Age, and the perceived changes in settlement strategy and type in EB II/III. This hesitancy is highlighted when we reiterate the diametrically opposed notions expressed by Lapp and Kempinski (see 'Introduction'). The evidence from Tell Um Hammad, in conjunction with that from Jawa, could support both views, as well as other ideas that have been expressed by workers in this field. For example, we could make a plausible case for specific routes along which moved the often-cited impetus towards something new in EB I (A): e.g. the Zerqa Valley linking the uplands of Transjordan and southern Syria with the Jordan valley and, in the west, the Mediterranean littoral and the Yizre'el valley. On the other hand, the apparent material cultural plurality in EB I A (in some contrast to the Chalcolithic period) could also be explained in more local terms, as areas of local preference in village communities which were linked through mechanisms such as down-the-line trade, including the possibility of differential rates of stylistic development in pottery production which might result in the survival of apparently anachronistic forms.

To place our findings from Tell Um Hammad more clearly in context, it might be useful to summarise briefly the state of current approaches to problems which we first touched on in the 'Introduction'.

First of all, we might list a number of opposite, as well as composite notions, the latter representing a form of scholarly oecumenicity (e.g. Richard 1980: 'Towards a Concensus of Opinion on the End of the Early Bronze Age in Palestine - Transjordan'). One of the most fundamental separations of views has been the notion of sequential culture change (a form of strictly linear evolution) on the one hand, and substantially overlapping cultures on the other: a compromise in which both played a role might be the best resolution. Next, the change from one socio-economic system to the next (if indeed there was a real change) has been explained in terms of either totally indigenous development or completely foreign impetus by way of invasion and migration. The median position has been to speak of 'population increments' which are absorbed rapidly by the local population. And, once again, perhaps the more logical solution might be that all of these mechanisms are applicable in one combination or another. The various reconstructions based on state formation theory (e.g. independent nation state, client state of a foreign empire, secular or religious state, united kingdom, etc.)

appear to divide into similar opposed categories: a (city) state system either as a foreign imposition or in imitation of more sophisticated foreign structures, or a totally local development from a rural system to a form of statehood. The notion of secondary state formation would fit into the model of foreign impetus through the medium of trade and resultant prosperity. The compromise for the Early Bronze Age of Palestine might combine these views with, however, the suggestion that the titles of 'cities' and 'city states', even 'capitals of city states', are inappropriate to the land and to the social structure of the majority of the population there which, as has been argued (Helms 1990), was probably tribally organised. A much better socio-political parallel with regard to the new fortified settlements of EB II/III, and whatever caused them to be built in the first place, might be the *kasbahs* of Morocco which are the militarized seats of rival, though often related, sheikhs operating within commercial agreements with a central government, rather than parallels taken from classical and hellenistic Greece or the mega-economies of ancient Egypt and Mesopotamia. The suggestion that the typical walled settlement of EBA II/III Palestine might be regarded as a *megalopolis* is ridiculous: many of these settlements were pitifully small, squalid establishments, no more than villages crowded within a defensive perimeter which itself was primitive in terms of the military architecture of the 'civilised' parallels (e.g. Jericho, Bab edh-Dhra and Numeira, none of which is larger than four hectares in area).

A related set of opposites concerns the nature of the so-called new urban EBA era which is often regarded to be uniform throughout the land. To be sure, there appears to be greater uniformity in terms of pottery styles as well as in domestic architecture, but this should not mask environmental conditions which are remarkably varied for a landscape as small as that of the southern Levant: in other words, a case can be made that a variety of structural responses was made on the basis of where the new nucleated and 'militarized' settlements of the Early Bronze Age were located. Jericho, small though it was, was an oasis, and thus could attract settlement despite repeated disasters throughout almost all of the Early Bronze Age. Jericho represents a quite different environment from that in the area south of Hebron where the apparently short-lived EB II settlement of Arad took a quite different form, and probably also served somewhat different functions. In just such a way is modern Beersheba with its purpose-built bedouin market different from the oasis village of Ariha next to O.T. Jericho. Still on 'cities', so compelling has been the urge to see a formal expression of 'civilisation' in the Holy Land that simple, though slightly better built and larger than the norm, domestic architecture has almost invariably been interpreted as temples and palaces, encompassing some, if not all, of the civic amenities of a hellenistic *polis* for example, or the kind of architectural marvels perhaps best illustrated by German archaeologists in Mesopotamia (e.g. 'Das wiedererstandene Assur' [Andrae 1939]), when in fact very few of the currently excavated examples of architecture fit such titles convincingly, and when it is evident that only a few buildings could even distantly be compared with the urban architecture of neighbouring countries. This is particularly obvious when southern Palestinian architecture of the Early Bronze Age is compared with that of third millennium Egypt, particularly since so much has recently been made of the Egyptian impact on Early Bronze Age 'urbanism'. In any event, such comparisons can only be made towards the end of the 'urban' Early Bronze Age and then the connection is probably with Syria and not Egypt.

Another dichotomy concerns the often-cited fundamentally contrasting life patterns of agriculturalists and pastoralists (the notion of the conflict between 'desert and sown') which lies at the core of misunderstanding the nature of the indigenous populations of the Near East. The fact of the matter is that, where two separate groups can be distinguished, agriculturalists and pastoralists live largely in symbiosis. Both 'patterns' are an inextricable part of the same socio-economic system, probably back to the Late Neolithic period (see Helms 1990). Finally, most reconstructions or 'explanations' have included speculations about population size, again with two opposing stances: either a population explosion in between EB I and EB III, followed by a drastic reduction in EB IV, or the view of an essentially static number of people throughout the whole of the Early Bronze Age. Here the main problem has been the nature of the available empirical evidence (site area calculated on the basis of diagnostic sherd scatter, topography, limited excavations, and so forth) and the unreliability of all population estimates, particularly when mobile populations are discounted. The truth may lie, as usual, in a compromise. Absolute numbers will never be achieved.

Most of the apparently unresolvable differences noted above are the result of misconceptions regarding the social structure of the populations in the southern Levant and the adjacent steppic zones (i.e. north and central Arabia). Some of these misconceptions can be summarised as follows.

There has, first of all, been a signal failure to understand the economic disparity between the southern Levant on the one hand, and Syria-Mesopotamia and Egypt on the other: that is to say, the lands which served as models in the interpretation of EBA Palestine, Transjordan and southern Syria. Unlike these parts of the Middle

East, the southern Levant is a dissected landscape with, as we have already noted, a remarkable variety of environmental sub-regions separated by mountain ranges and the Jordan Rift valley, bounded on one side by the Mediterranean sea and on the other by the steppic lands of southern Syria, Transjordan and north Arabia. A land such as this could never (and never did) give rise to empire; it could never be completely dominated by one economic or political system, either from within or without. Historically it has always been the bone of contention between Syria and Egypt and, occasionally, Iran and Mesopotamia and the West. A corollary of this is the failure to recognise sub-regional differences within the land, as we have also noted above. Palestine is more like Greece than the geographically nearer, open landscape of Mesopotamia; the people, however, are different: the Greeks produced city states, thalassocracies, philosophy, democracy, and our current classical western bias with regard to the semitic speaking Middle East; the southern Levant produced that which we are trying here to reconstruct, a socio-economic structure which has been the bane of all foreign conquerors, west or east.

Secondly, there has been a failure to understand the socio-political nature of the majority of the populations in the southern Levant, particularly their tribal organisation and the proximity of north Arabia. This misconception has been exacerbated by scholars interpreting Near Eastern history (and protohistory) from an almost entirely western classical point of view: hence the grafting on of western notions of statehood to an oriental setting in the same manner as we have been trying to impose either western democracy or central European communism in the region today.

A third misconception, one to which we have often referred, concerns the application of linear evolutionary theories of cultural development which, moreover, have been built on a form of ceramic typological absolutism which is based on a horror of sustained cultural plurality in a small landscape.

Fourthly, there has been a perhaps understandable, though hardly useful, passion among scholars to discover the existence of organised religion before Judaism in the Holy Land, expressed in formal architectural terms (temples as one of the pillars of civilization and, therefore, urbanism). While it is likely that these early populations had religious beliefs, this is virtually impossible to prove on architectural grounds before about 2000 BC.

These are some of the constraints under which we have long struggled to make sense of the ever-increasing body of archaeological data for EBA Palestine. To these limitations may be added the problems of the 'discipline' of archaeology itself, where there is so little concensus on methodology and terminology, and where interpretation of data may long precede full publication of the evidence. To avoid the pitfalls of others, then, we are reluctant to take the evidence from Um Hammad (and Jawa) much beyond the empirical stage.

The evidence from Um Hammad, including reference to Jawa (Betts [ed.] 1991), is summarised here in terms of stratigraphy and architecture (Chapters 2 and 3), pottery (Chapter 4), and lithics (Chapter 5), followed by a general concluding statement.

STRATIGRAPHY AND ARCHITECTURE

It cannot be stressed enough that the material presented here represents an internal sequence of events whose apparent lengths, contiguity, continuity, and discontinuity need not necessarily be applicable to the landscape as a whole: not even in inter-site terms. That is to say, whatever periodization may be attached to stages, the relative lengths of these at the site may easily be different elsewhere; the stages may plausibly overlap elsewhere. At Um Hammad, as at most excavated sites of similar periods, there appears to be a break in occupation between the Chalcolithic and the Early Bronze Age (EB I A): however, this does not *prove* that essentially 'Chalcolithic' villages did not exist during EB I (A and/or B). Neither do the relative lengths of EB I A and B occupation at Um Hammad prove that the former was much longer. The only important evidence is that EB I A is now demonstrably longer, as we have said before, than had been thought; and that it represents a discrete stage at Um Hammad which saw continuous reuse of existing structures, their alteration, and the construction of new buildings and other installations. In contrast, the occupation of EB I B at Um Hammad consists of only one main structural event: i.e. EB I B occupation, varied though it seems to be (see 'Pottery' below), was a short episode at the site. In terms of architectural style (or tradition), the evidence suggests that EB I A was the anomaly. The architecture of the Chalcolithic period, of EB I B, EB II/III, and even EB IV, may be regarded as one and the same tradition, an indigenous Palestinian/Transjordanian/southern Syrian one which probably goes back to the Late Neolithic (as does much of the Chalcolithic pottery) and comes to an end, or at least is much changed, after about 2000 BC (MB II A). In other words, the 'architecture' of EB I A is intrusive: it is 'foreign'. In this sense, then, EB I A could be regarded as the first appearance of a form of internationalism in the southern Levant (apart from the remarkably international uniformity of the Pre Pottery Neolithic [B] period).

The evidence from Um Hammad suggests that settlement strategies in both EB I A and B were similar to those of the

Chalcolithic period in the sub-region of the Zerqa 'triangle'. This pattern probably applies to most of the Jordan valley and stands in stark contrast to the strategies of the EB II/III period when settlements were increasingly built on defensible sites, in most cases some distance from, though generally within sight of, the agricultural land. The EB I pattern of settling on the open land was repeated in EB IV (see Betts and Helms in press). In terms of settlement patterns, therefore, the Chalcolithic, EB I A and B, and EB IV appear to be the norm, while 'urban' EB II/III is the anomaly. However, this must be qualified on the basis of sub-regional environmental variability. More marginal zones elicited different structural responses: some Chalcolithic settlements or establishments such as Ein Gedi and other, more recently surveyed, sites in southern Jordan (Braemer p.c.) may have been fortified; Jawa, on the edge of the dry steppe, was heavily fortified in EB I A (Helms 1981; Betts [ed.] 1991). Similarly, recent discoveries in Transjordan have shown that some EB IV settlements in the more remote sub-regions were fortified (e.g. Khirbet Iskander [Richard 1987] south of Amman, and at least one other site near Zerqa [Palumbo p.c.]).

Although only one burial of the EB I period was found at Tiwal esh-Sharqi to the south of Tell Um Hammad (Tubb 1990), we can point out a clear change in funerary practices between the Chalcolithic and EB I. The use of shaft and chamber tombs begins in EB I, perhaps concomitantly with the use of cairns and dolmen (see now Yassine 1985), and continued, in one variation or another, well into the Persian period. Many recently explored sites of the EB I A category (e.g. Tell Mutawwaq: Hanbury-Tenison 1989b) have near them dolmen fields. Jawa's cairn cemetery has been tentatively identified (Betts [ed.] 1991: passim; Fig. 3: B1, B2); there is also one dolmen nearby. Perhaps we can suggest that dolmens preceded shaft and chamber graves, being gradually replaced by the latter. It is quite conceivable (in view of our other evidence) that Chalcolithic burial practices continued, probably well into EB I (see especially the conclusions regarding EB I B pottery and repertoire R6 below).

Finally, the evidence from Um Hammad, and its sub-region, proves that settlement number, size, and density increased dramatically with EB I A which, in turn, suggests a marked increase in population within the sub-region. Whether this measurable trend can be shown to be globally applicable to all of the southern Levant remains to be demonstrated: it is, however, likely. It is, moreover, a trend that is also becoming obvious in the hitherto unexplored regions of northeastern Transjordan and southern Syria. Jawa, of course, shows an almost monumental rise in the settlement of a marginal zone during EB I A. EB I B material has been found at both

Leboué and Khirbet Umbachi (Braemer p.c.), both of which were also occupied, perhaps more substantially, in EB II/III and EB IV, respectively. The tentative conclusion here must be (i) population increase (not necessarily growth) in zones which had been more sparsely settled during the Chalcolithic period, and (ii) perhaps an extension of settlement into more marginal sub-regions. Both notions imply some form of demographic, and possibly also socio-economic, change, during the second half of the fourth millennium BC.

POTTERY

The most striking evidence with regard to pottery is the great variety of ceramic forms and their decoration which appear in EB I A, apparently quite suddenly. In contrast to the Chalcolithic assemblages, which are almost completely homogeneous (see especially Commenge-Pellerin 1987), those of EB I (A and B) must be regarded as heterogeneous, or plural. If our seriation of genres into discrete repertoires is valid, the notion of cultural plurality in the southern Levant becomes inescapable. Therefore, something new happened towards the end of the Chalcolithic period: something that we may be able to map in terms of pottery production (repertoires), both in terms of sub-regional production areas (i.e. essentially indigenous, southern Levantine) and, most significantly, in terms of inter-regional, if not international, relations. In this regard, the EB I period, or rather the plural ceramic culture, must, minimally, represent separate, though inter-related, sub-regions in the land where such heterogeneity was much less visible during the Chalcolithic. How these sub-regions might be interpreted in social and demographic terms is an open question: we could be dealing with indigenous tribal or sub-tribal divisions and aggregations, representing micro-economies which combined agriculture, pastoralism, industry, and down-the-line trade in a variety of ways in response to local resources and opportunities. However, with strong evidence to suggest a form of internationalism in EB I, we cannot rule out other, less static, models which must include demographic shifts. The ceramic evidence of EB I at Um Hammad does not, however, support the idea of long-range, organized trade at international level.

Side by side with this remarkable plurality in EB I, we have now to face the implications of two key pieces of evidence: (i) the continuity of Chalcolithic pottery tradition as this is represented by repertoire R1 at Um Hammad; and (ii) the more tricky questions raised by the appearance of a complete Chalcolithic repertoire (R6) in an EB I B context, after the long occupation of EB I A at the site. To this should be added the appearance of hybrid forms in the repertoires of both the EB I A and B assemblages, suggesting merging pottery styles, and perhaps also merging traditions in terms of some cultural components. The juxtaposition of developed or (directly) derived Chalcolithic forms (repertoire R1) in use at the same time, probably by much the same people and in the same place, as totally new repertoires suggests that the two 'cultures' were in meaningful contact. This, in turn, lends some serious weight to the notion of overlapping 'cultures', something that is substantiated by the second piece of evidence, repertoire R6. As we have noted (Chapter 4), the repertoire is purely Chalcolithic in form and decoration; only the production technique is different: it is better. With collateral evidence of the introduction of new technology in EB I (e.g. in mining and, particularly, metallurgy), it is not far fetched, nor inappropriate, to hypothesize that repertoire R6 represents a living Chalcolithic tradition which must have existed somewhere in the land, at the same time as the so-called EB I culture. Whoever continued to make such pottery was influenced by the 'new' in the land only in terms of superior technology: whoever made this pottery clung to an 'earlier' tradition and only succumbed to the transformed, the 'new', in about EB II. And, once we can at least entertain such a hypothesis, it is much easier to regard with suspicion the strictly sequential array of EB I A followed everywhere by EB I B. They too, as many scholars have thought (e.g. Kenyon, Hennessy, *inter alia*), may be largely contemporary, though gradually merging over time (e.g. hybrid forms) until, by EB II, pottery assemblages at sites throughout the land became almost indistinguishable from each other.

A final piece of ceramic evidence concerns the increase in the use of stamp seals on pottery vessels in EB I A. Here the connection between the central Jordan valley and Jawa is important, although what precisely is implied by the practice is uncertain. The stamp seals serve, in the first place, to link unquestionably the two quite disparate sub-regions of the land: the semi-arid eastern flank of Jebel Druze in southern Syria and the verdant Jordan valley. What this link may have been is debatable. Secondly, the use of seals can imply a form of economic control and thus perhaps also social control (see now Betts [ed.] 1991: Chapter 4). It is tempting to see in this an early trend towards more formally structured society in the southern Levant, a trend whose outcome may have been nucleation and militarisation a little later, in EB II. The apparently limited distribution of these characteristic seal impressions (Fig. 274) may indicate the existence of a series of economically linked sub-regions, perhaps in terms of limited trade networks, transhumance, or even migration.

LITHICS

Conclusions which can be drawn from the lithic assemblage fit well with the evidence discussed above relating to architecture and ceramics. There is limited evidence for Chalcolithic traits in the early levels at Um Hammad, possibly up to stage 2, indicating at least some continuity of lithic technology into the Early Bronze Age. However, the most significant result of the analysis concerns the appearance of Canaanean 'technology' in EB I. The Canaanean industry is 'international', widespread throughout the Levant and supported by trade/exchange networks extending from Sinai and the Negev up into Lebanon, Syria, and possibly beyond. Evidence from Jawa shows that these networks reached out eastwards to the edge of the steppe. Given the architectural and ceramic evidence for external influences in EB I A, it is tempting to link the appearance of the Canaanean industry to other 'international' cultural traits introduced into Palestine at the beginning of the Early Bronze Age: i.e. to associate the introduction of Canaanean technology with EB I A at Um Hammad. If this was the case then the continuing trade in Canaanean blades and scrapers indicates that the incomers maintained contact beyond their immediate sub-region. The extent of this contact is not clear although the trade in lithics could, and most probably did, function as down-the-line exchange systems rather than as 'international' networks.

SUMMARY

In the end, it is evident to us that no all-encompassing explanation can be presented for the events that caused the perceived changes in the archaeological evidence pertaining to the fourth millennium BC: no model based on subsequent history can completely accommodate the evidence. One conclusion, however, is possible. Periodization, as it stands now, is flawed (most scholars will agree); it is, however, also misleading. The broad divisions into Chalcolithic, Early Bronze Age, and Middle Bronze Age are not the problem; the internal divisions within them are. In general, 'Chalcolithic' describes a long-lived indigenous culture which has its origins in the Late Neolithic; Early Bronze Age represents something that is clearly different, a period in which new technology, new architecture, even new or different aesthetic responses prevailed; the Middle Bronze Age may be regarded as the first era in which the southern Levant entered into the ambit of international events and became an albeit small part of Middle Eastern macro-economy and politics. The internal divisions, as we have said, do not make sense. In the Chalcolithic no one has ever demonstrated the difference between 'Early', 'Middle', and 'Late'. Similarly, there has been no plausible case for dividing the 'urban'

Early Bronze Age into two (EB II and EB III): not in terms of ceramics (regardless of Khirbet Kerak ware); not in terms of settlement patterns; not in terms of architecture. There is, rather, a development throughout 'EB II/III' which is not marked by any cultural, or other, watershed. Therefore, it seems that the evidence could only support a tripartite division of the Early Bronze Age: (i) a complex 'transition', relatively rapid cultural change, basically whatever is not purely 'Chalcolithic' (= EB I); (ii) a trend towards aggregation, nucleation, centralization, militarisation, and perhaps even a form of industrialization (= EB II + EB III); and (iii) the 'collapse' of whatever held (ii) together and a return to an economy (at the very least) which was very similar to what had gone on before (= EB IV/EB - MB/MB I, etc.). The internal divisions (e.g. EB I A, B, C [?], as well as 'D' [= repertoire R6 at Tell Um Hammad]) are almost exclusively based on *pottery typology* and should, therefore, never have been presented as chronological entities (see now Helms 1989 on EB IV); they reflect preferences which need not imply a linear typological evolution. In other words, all that the evidence can show (including that from Um Hammad and Jawa) is that a great variety of pottery styles came into use sometime near the end of the Chalcolithic period and - this is based on Um Hammad and Jawa - that the 'Chalcolithic' styles simply became a part of this plurality which eventually was rendered uniform, in some way, later on during the second major division of the period (EB II/III), only to re-emerge, somewhat changed, during the third period (EB IV). The absolute chronology of these events is non-existent. It may be guessed, however, that the second division, the 'first urban age of Palestine' was shorter than the rest, even shorter than EB I, and that, therefore, what we are seeing more clearly now is a long-lived cultural plurality which expressed itself in a village economy which included symbiosis with more mobile populations and that this is the norm for the southern Levant and its eastern steppic lands.

The question remains: what caused the different 'cultural' responses in the various sub-regions of the land, as we have proposed them to have been? Why did all of this happen, and why so suddenly in about the middle of the fourth millennium BC? In the first place, we can rule out an evolution out of the Chalcolithic, as we know it, since we have proved that a substantial repertoire of 'EB I' pottery, directly derived from earlier, Chalcolithic, prototypes co-existing with totally new forms, since we have thereby demonstrated the possibility that 'Chalcolithic' populations existed side by side with those that we call 'EB I'. We have also demonstrated in a measurable way that some, if not all, verdant and even sub-steppic, sub-regions of the land were more intensely settled during 'EB I' and that this indicates, without question, a steep rise in the total population. We have, further, shown that some of the new pottery types have a much wider distribution in terms of prototypes than was the case during the Chalcolithic period. Jawa, now irrevocably connected with Um Hammad and EB I (A), demonstrates these foreign connections which reach as far as Hama, perhaps even up to the Euphrates (e.g. Habuba Kabira). It is, therefore, not unreasonable finally to settle on the probability that people moved from one place to another during the fourth millennium BC, and that they did this over much longer distances than before. This is certainly the case throughout the history of the Middle East, up to the present; this is probably also the best demographic parallel that can be brought to bear on the problems of the early Early Bronze Age. The notion of internationally causative events has, therefore, to be included in whatever model we strive to construct.

Whatever happened in the southern Levant in about the middle of the fourth millennium BC, the developing mega-economies of Egypt, northern Syria, and Mesopotamia did not directly affect development; even a little later, there is very little evidence that the various dynastic entities had any pressing interests in Palestine: this did not happen until much later, in the Middle Bronze Age. These foreign powers were far too occupied with maintaining their dynastic suzerainty and wealth to be bothered with a difficult and essentially poor land like the southern Levant. The effect that this economic and military growth did have on Palestine was probably indirect, the result of rendering many more people mobile because of conflict and periodic economic collapse. Again, ancient and modern history is an evocative guide. This increased mobility, in addition to existing mobile populations must have had an effect far beyond the immediate areas of conflict, particularly with regard to Syria and Mesopotamia: precisely the regions (e.g. Syria) in which we find some of the typological parallels which distinguish EB I from the Chalcolithic. The same holds for new mining and metallurgical technology, lithics, and even the characteristic architecture of EB I (A). And since, as we have noted, there is no case to be made for organized bilateral trade in EB I, the only way in which these things and ideas could have come to the southern Levant is through migration (*not* invasion) of substantial numbers of people from a variety of backgrounds. This, more than anything else, can explain the remarkable cultural plurality of EB I and abrupt population increase which, as we have suggested, expressed itself in terms of autonomous or autochthonous sub-regions.

Fig. 1. The Levantine Near East: (1) *Mersin;* (2) *Tarsus;* (3) *Habuba Kabira;*(4) *Hama;* (5) *al-Kowm;* (6) *Palmyra;* (7) *Tell Nebi Mend;* (8) *Byblos;* (9) *Mumasakhin;* (10) *Saida;* (11) *Tyre;* (12) *Tell Turmus;* (13) *Rosh ha-Niqra;* (14) *Horvat Usa;* (15) *Kinneret;* (16) *Rasm Harbush;* (17) *al-Majami`;* (18) *el-Leboué;* (19) *Khirbet Umbashi;* (20) *Hebariyeh;* (21) *Khirbet Kerak (Beth Yerah);* (22) *Arqub edh-Dhahr;* (23) *Pithat ha-Yarmuk;* (24) *Baqura;* (25) *Neve Ur;* (26) *En Shadud;* (27) *Yiftahel;* (28) *Afula;* (29) *Hazorea;* (30) `*Ain Jarba;* (31) *Megiddo;* (32) *Asawir;* (33) *Meser;* (34) *Beth Shan;* (35) *Tell Shuneh North;* (36) *Pella;* (37) *Tell el-Far'ah North;* (38) *Abu Habil;* (39) *Ajlun;* (40) *Jerash;* (41) *Jawa;* (42) *Qasr Burqu';* (43) *Abu Hamid;* (44) *Kataret es-Samra;* (45) *Ruweiha;* (46) *Tell Abu Zighan;* (47) *Jebel Mutawwaq;* (48) *Mafluq;* (49) *Damiyah;* (50) *Khirbet Mahruq;* (51) *Jiftlik;* (52) *Fazael;* (53) *Wadi Rabah;* (54) *Ras el-Ain;* (55) *Giv'atayim;* (56) *Azor;* (57) *Gezer;* (58) *Ai (et-Tell);* (59) *O.T. Jericho;* (60) *Ghrubba;* (61) *N.T. Jericho;* (62) *Teleilat Ghassul;* (63) *Batashi;* (64) *Sahab;* (65) *al-Hibr;* (66) *Khirbet Iskander;* (67) *Lehun;* (68) *Bab edh-Dhra';* (69) `*Areyni;* (70) *Tell Hesi;* (71) *Tell ed-Duweir;* (72) *Tell Halif;* (73) *En Gedi;* (74) *Nahal Mishmar;* (75) *Arad;* (76) *Zoumeili;* (77) *Beersheba;* (78) *Abu Matar/Safadi;* (79) *Shiqmim;* (80) *Tell Esdar*

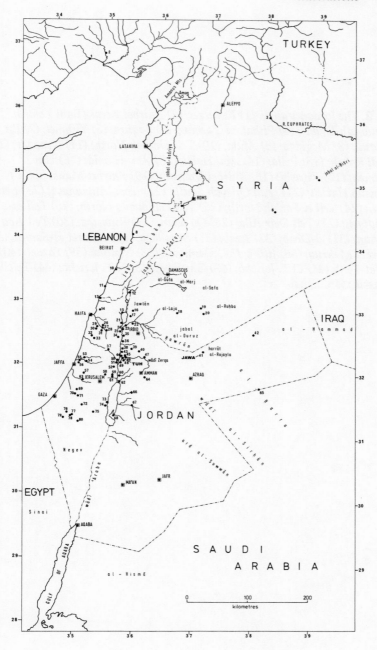

Fig. 2. The Jordan Valley: (1) Kinneret; (2) Khirbet Kerak (Beth Yerah); (3) Arqub edh-Dhahr; (4) Pithat ha-Yarmuk; (5) Baqura; (6) Yiftahel; (7) En Shadud; (8) Megiddo; (9) Afula; (10) Tell Shuneh North; (11) Neve Ur; (12) Wadi Rabah; (13) Pella; (14) Abu Habil; (15) Abu Hamid; (16) Um Bteimeh; (17) Riyashi; (18) Khirbet Mansub; (19) Khirbet Mansub; (20) Mansub Hazieh; (21) `Ain Qneyah South; (22) Jebel Mutawwaq; (23) Beth Shan; (24) Tell el-Far'ah North; (25) Tell Handaquq North; (26) Tell es-Sa'idiyeh; (27) Tell Deir Alla; (28) Qa`adan; (29) Ruweiha; (30) Tell Abu Zighan; (31) el-Dbab; (32) Azab; (33) Muallaqa; (34) Kataret es-Samra; (35) Khirbet Mahruq; (36) Jiftlik; (37) Damiyah; (38) Mafluq; (39) Fazael; (40) Ai (et-Tell); (41) O.T. Jericho; (42) Ghrubba; (43) N.T. Jericho; (44) Teleilat Ghassul; (45) Sahab

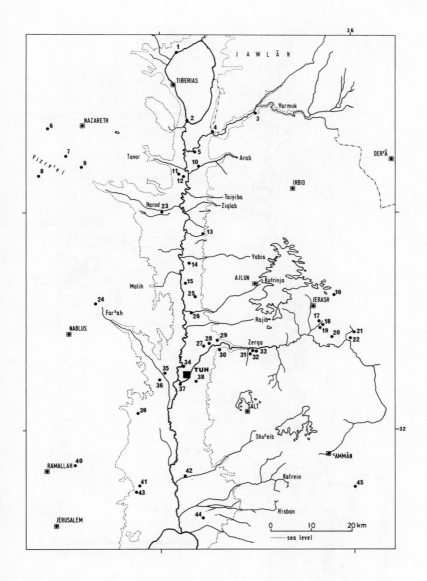

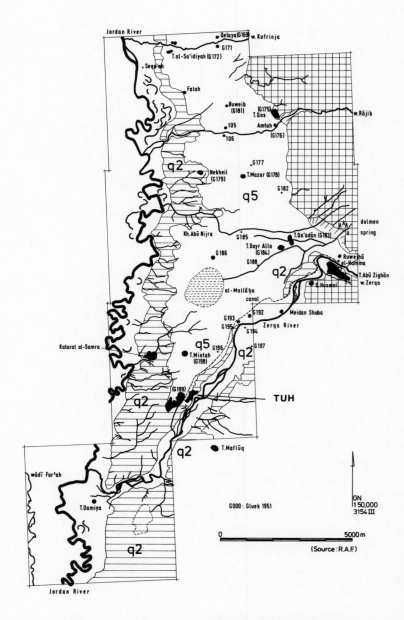

Fig. 3. The 'Zerqa Triangle' (q2, 'Lisan marls'; q5, fluvial deposits)

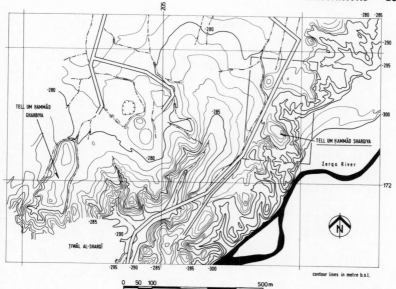

Fig. 4. Tell Um Hammad (al-Gharbi/al-Sharqi) and Tiwal esh-Sharqi

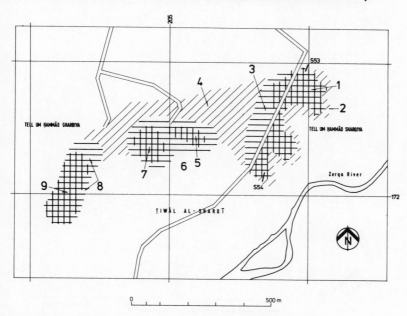

Fig. 5. Tell Um Hammad: extent of occupation (stages 1-9+): 1 (vertical hatching) presently (1984) preserved occupation of stages [1], 2, and 3; 2 (diagonal hatching) estimated loss to erosion; (horizontal hatching) estimated loss to recent ploughing; 4 light sherd scatter (EB IV), loss to recent ploughing; 5, 7, 9, EB IV occupation; 6, 8 (horizontal hatching) disturbed occcupation (EB IV)

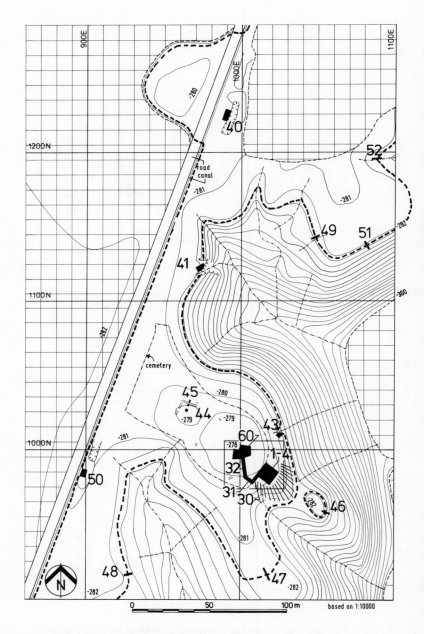

Fig. 6. Tell Um Hammad al-Sharqi: squares

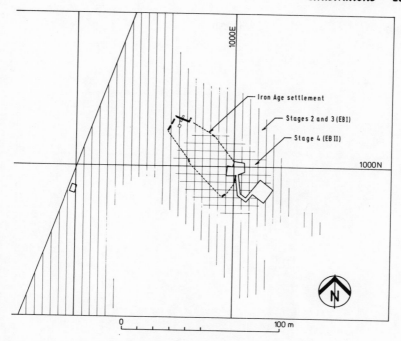

Fig. 7. The main tell: limits of preserved occupation

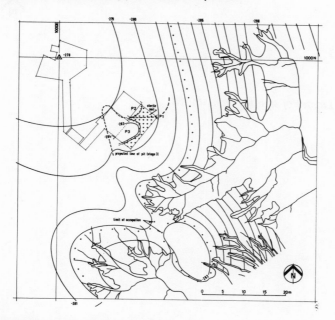

Fig. 8. The main tell: erosion patterns

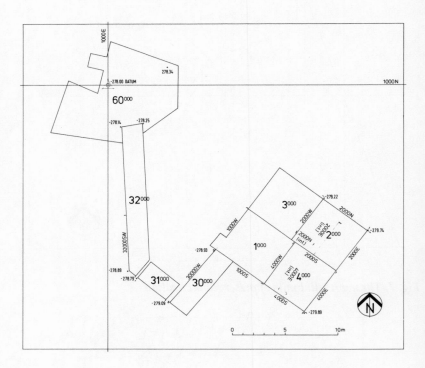

Fig. 9. Layout of squares on main tell

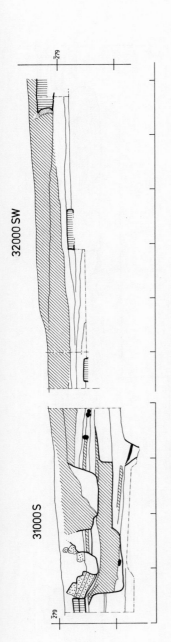

32000 SW

31000 S

Fig. 10. Section: 31000S/32000SW

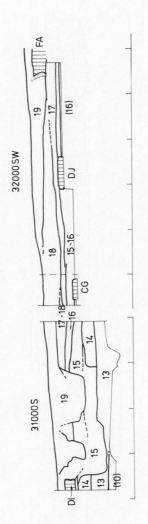

32000 SW

31000 S

Fig. 11. Section key for figure 10

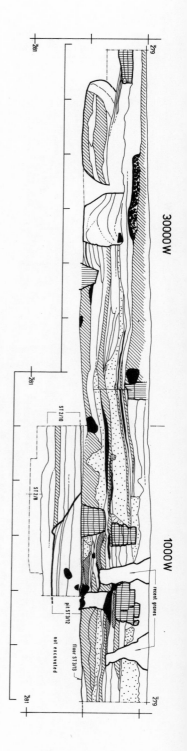

Fig. 12. Section: 30000W/1000W

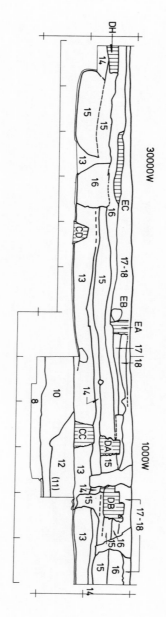

Fig. 13. Section key for figure 12

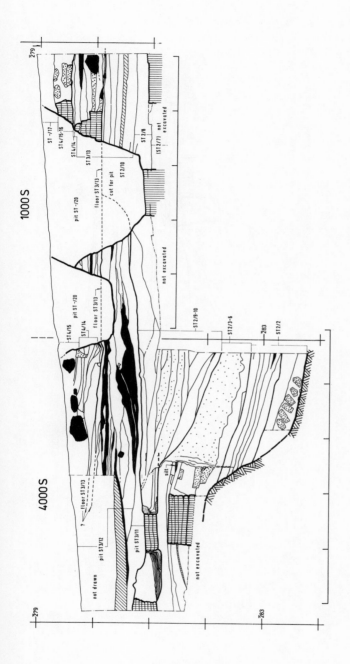

Fig. 14. Section: 4000S/1000S

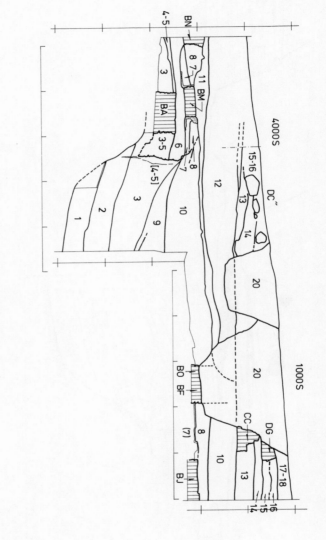

Fig. 15. Section key for figure 14

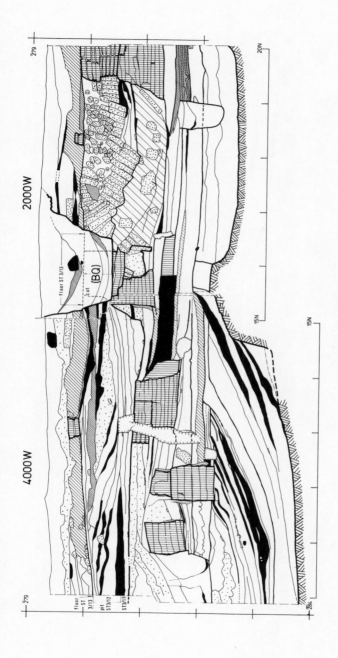

Fig. 16. Section: 4000W/2000W

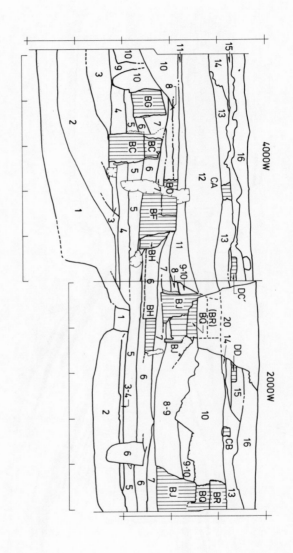

Fig. 17. Section key for figure 16

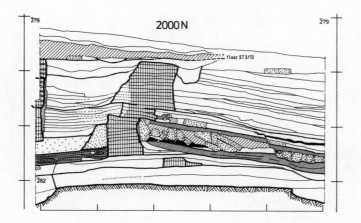

Fig. 18. Section: 2000N

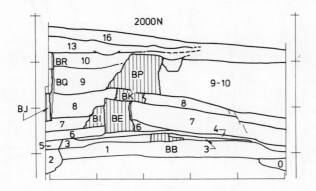

Fig. 19. Section key for figure 18

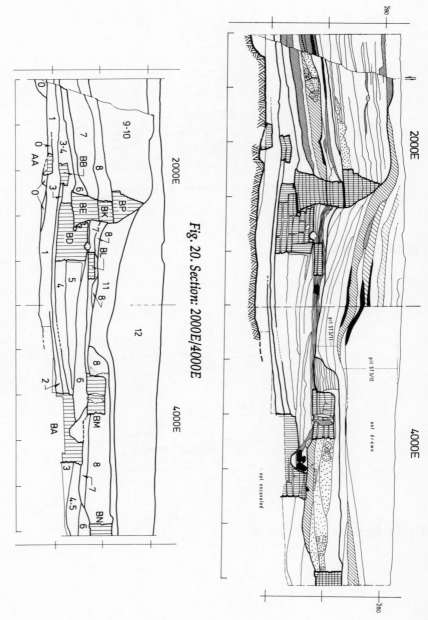

Fig. 20. Section: 2000E/4000E

Fig. 21. Section key for figure 20

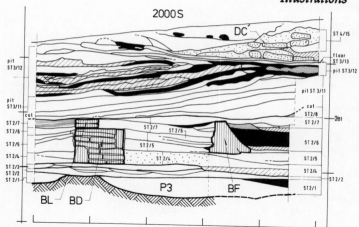

Fig. 22. Section: 2000S

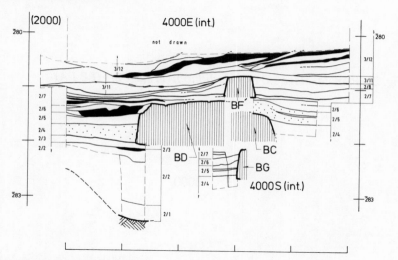

Fig. 23. Section: 4000E (int.)

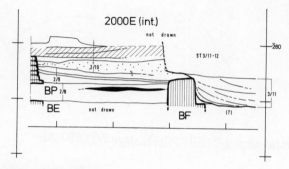

Fig. 24. Section: 2000E (int.)

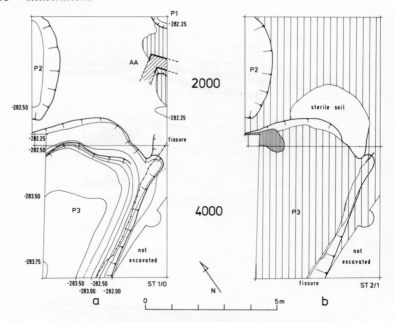

Fig. 25. Plan: (a) stage 1/0 ('Chalcolithic'); (b) stage 2/1 (EB I A)

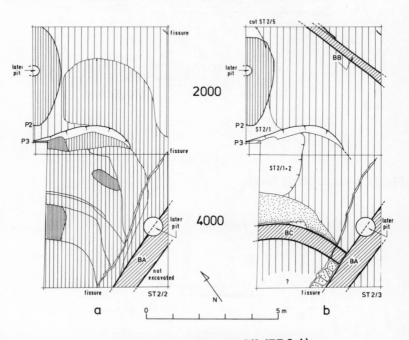

Fig. 26. Plan: (a) stage 2/2 (EB I A); (b) stage 2/3 (EB I A)

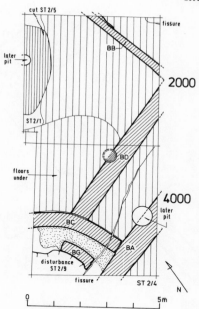

Fig. 27. Plan: stage 2/4 (EB I A)

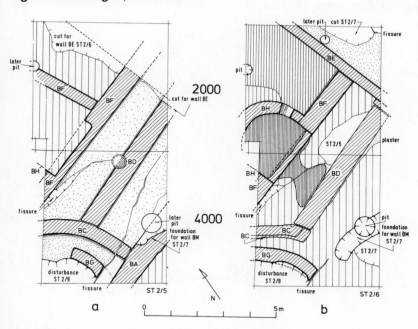

Fig. 28. Plan: (a) stage 2/5 (EB I A); (b) stage 2/6 (EB I A)

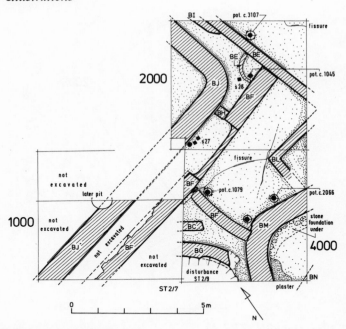

Fig. 29. Plan: stage 2/7 (EB I A)

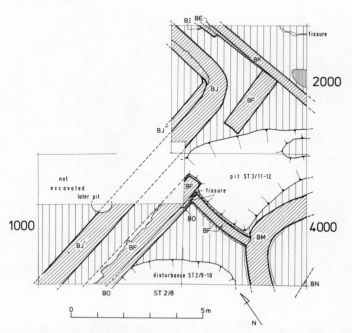

Fig. 30. Plan: stage 2/8 (EB I A)

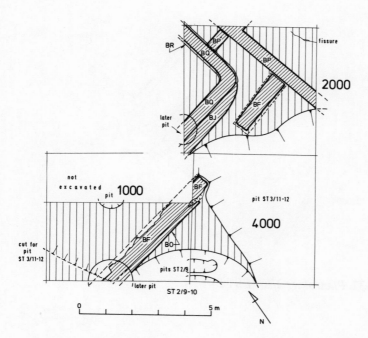

Fig. 31. Plan: stage 2/9-10 (EB I A)

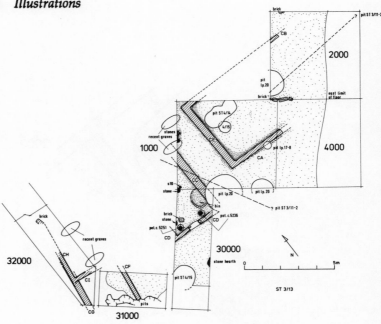

Fig. 32. Plan: stage 3/13 (EB I B)

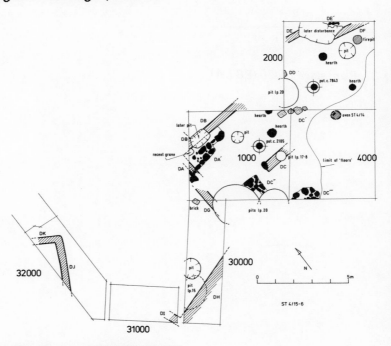

Fig. 33. Plan: stage 4/15-16 (EB II)

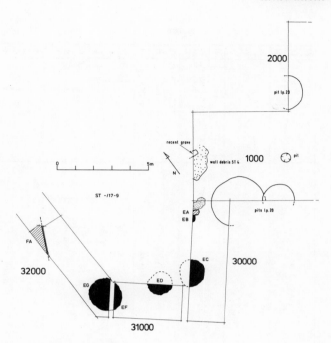

Fig. 34. Plan: stage ?/17-19 (EB IV)

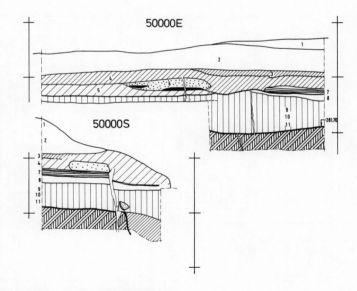

Fig. 35. Section: square 50 (5000E/S)

l p	1000	2000	4000	l p	ST	Period
0		AA		0	1	"Chalcolithic"
1		pit + occupation	BA	1		
2		pit fill	BC	2		
3			BG BD	3		
4	BB			4		
5		BD	BF BH´	5	2	EBIA
6	BF	BF BF˝	BC´	6		
7	BJ´	BH	BF´ BM BN BL	7		
8	BO	BE	BO	8		
9		BE´ BI´ BJ´ BJ BL		9		
10		BJ˝ BK		10		
11	pit + fill	pit + fill	pit + fill	11		
12	pit fill (ashy)	BO BP BP´	pit fill (ashy)	12	3	EBIB
13	CA CB CC CE	CB BR	CA	13		
14				14		
15	DA DA´ DB DC DC´ DC˝ DG	DC´ DA DE DE´ DF		15	4	EBII
16		[DH] DK]		16		
17		[EA] EC]		17		EBIV
18		[FA]		18		
19				19		
20	pits	pit	pit	20		Iron Age (II)
21		[structures]		21		
22				22		

Fig. 36. Structural matrix

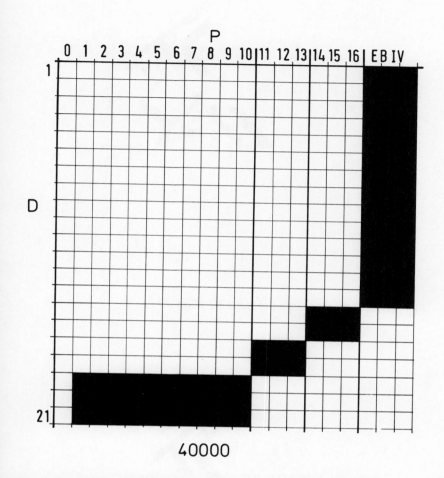

Fig. 37. Square 40: distribution of pottery: P, relative phase based on typology; D, soil depositions (layers, etc.)

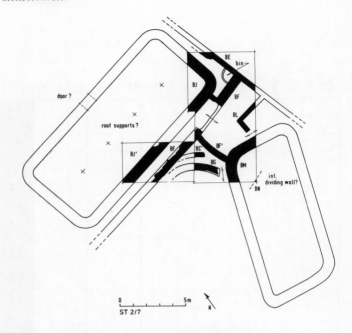

Fig. 38. Plan: reconstruction of stage 2/7 (EB I A)

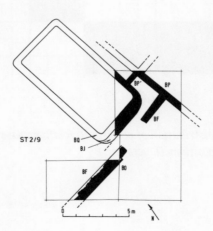

Fig. 39. Plan: reconstruction of stage 2/9 (EB I A)

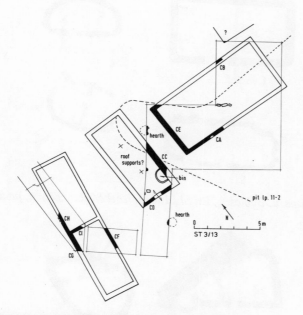

Fig. 40. Plan: reconstruction of stage 3/13 (EB I B)

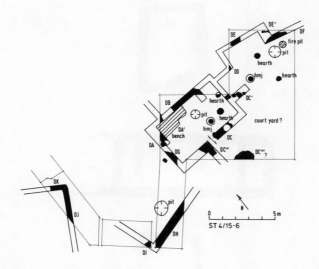

Fig. 41. Plan: reconstruction of stage 4/15-16 (EB II)

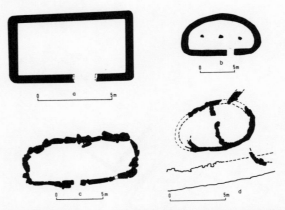

Fig. 42. Plans: *a, Byblos; b, En Shadud; c, Jebel Mutawwaq; d, Jawa*

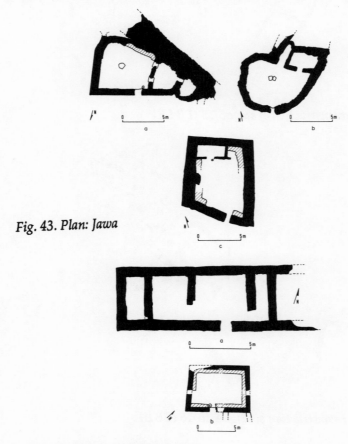

Fig. 43. Plan: *Jawa*

Fig. 44. Plans: *a, Jawlan; b, Arad*

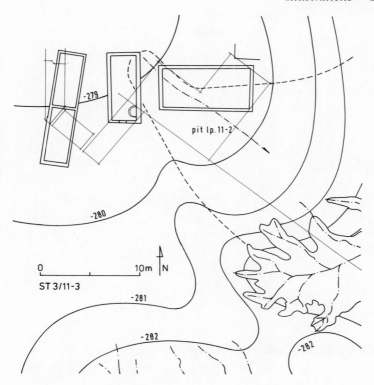

Fig. 45. Location of stage 3/13 (11-12)

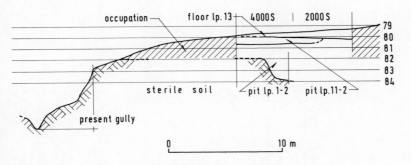

Fig. 46. Schematic section through site

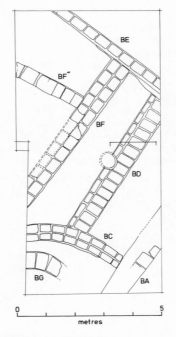

Fig. 47. Brickwork: walls BA-D, BF/F'/G

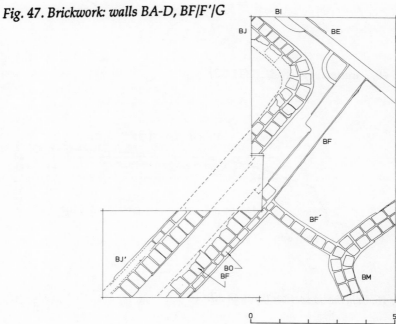

Fig. 48. Brickwork: walls BE, BF, BF', BI, BJ, BJ', BM, BO

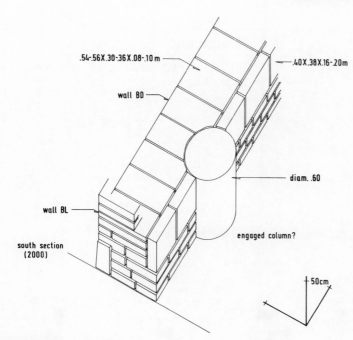

.54-.56X.30-36X.08-.10 m

.40X.38X.16-.20m

wall BD

diam. .60

wall BL

engaged column?

south section
(2000)

50cm

Fig. 49. Brickwork: wall BD

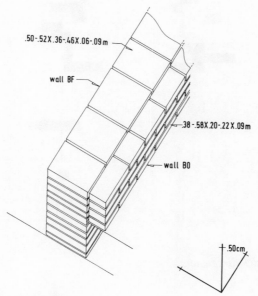

.50-.52X.36-.46X.06-.09m

wall BF

.38-.58X.20-.22X.09m

wall BO

.50cm

Fig. 50. Brickwork: walls BF/O

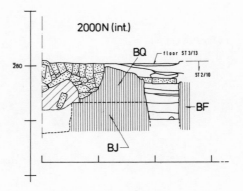

Fig. 51. Section: 2000N (int.) collapse of wall BJ/Q/(R)

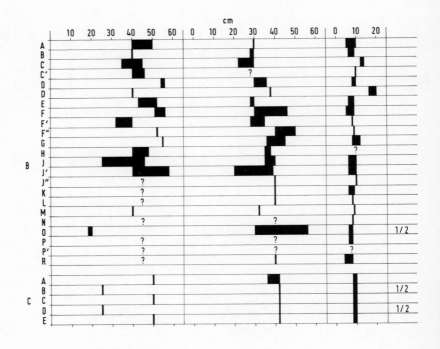

Fig. 52. Brick dimensions

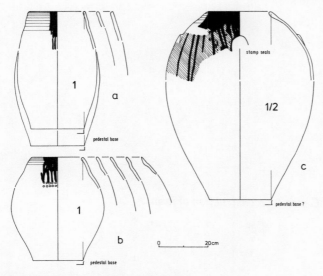

Fig. 53. Genre 1/(1/2): reconstruction of form

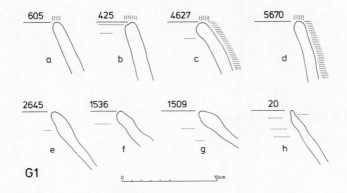

Fig. 54. Genre 1: rim forms

Fig. 55. Genre 1/2: rim form

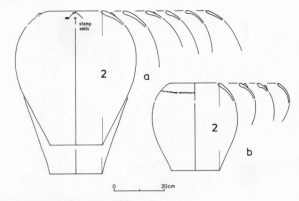

Fig. 56. Genre 2: reconstruction of form

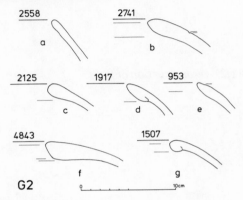

Fig. 57. Genre 2: rim forms

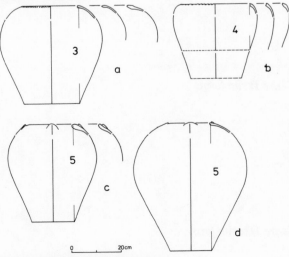

Fig. 58. Genres 3-5: reconstruction of form

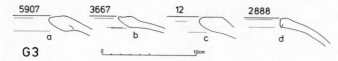

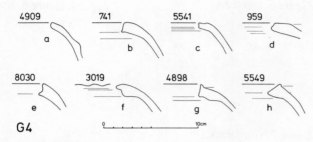

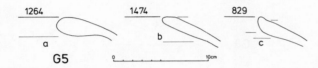

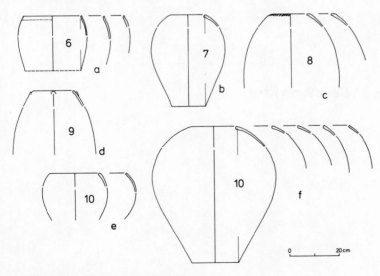

Fig. 59. Genre 3: rim forms

Fig. 60. Genre 4: rim forms

Fig. 61. Genre 5: rim forms

Fig. 62. Genres 6-10: reconstruction of form

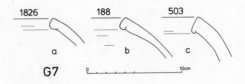

Fig. 63. Genre 6: rim forms   *Fig. 64. Genre 6: rim forms*

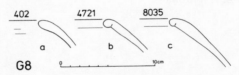

Fig. 65. Genre 7: rim forms

Fig. 66. Genre 8: rim forms

Fig. 67. Genre 9: rim forms

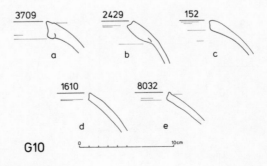

Fig. 68. Genre 10: rim forms

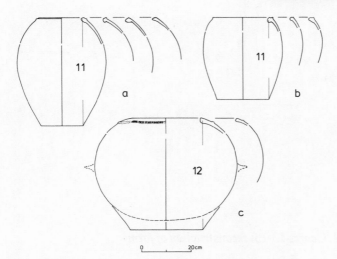

Fig. 69. Genres 11-12: reconstruction of form

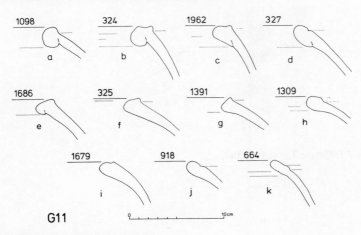

Fig. 70. Genre 11: rim forms

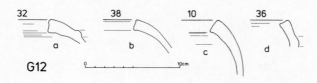

Fig. 71. Genre 12: rim forms

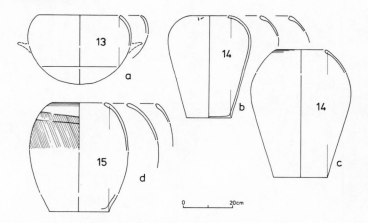

Fig. 72. Genres 13-15: reconstruction of form

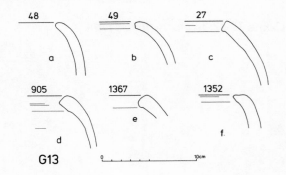

Fig. 73. Genre 13: rim forms

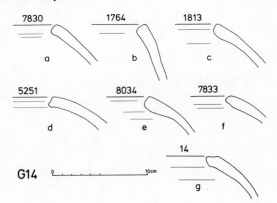

Fig. 74. Genre 14: rim forms

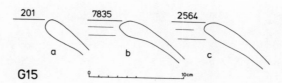

Fig. 75. Genre 15: rim forms

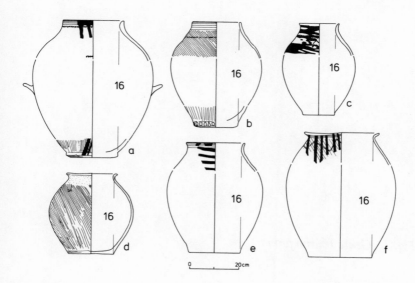

Fig. 76. Genre 16: reconstruction of form

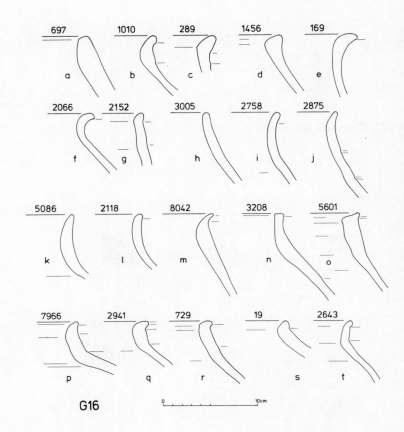

Fig. 77. Genre 16: rim forms

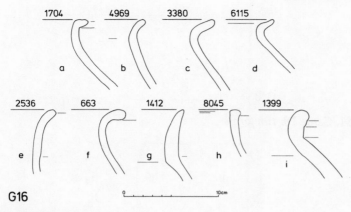

G16

Fig. 78. Genre 16: rim forms

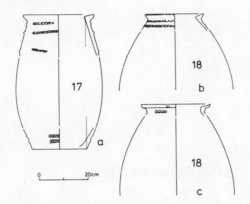

Fig. 79. Genres 17-18: reconstruction of form

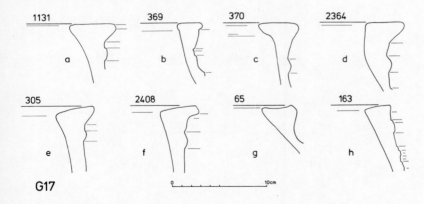

G17

Fig. 80. Genre 17: rim forms

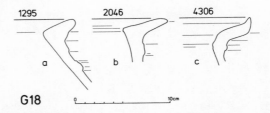

Fig. 81. Genre 18: rim forms

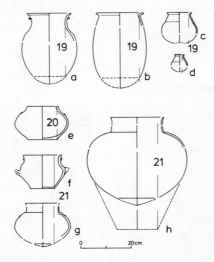

Fig. 82. Genres 19-21: reconstruction of form

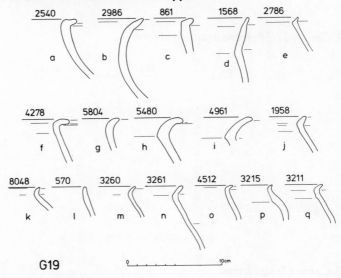

Fig. 83. Genre 19: rim forms

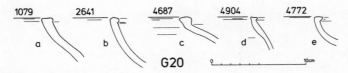

Fig. 84. Genre 20: rim forms

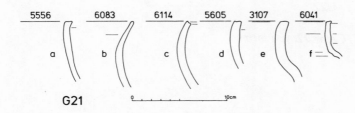

Fig. 85. Genre 21: rim forms

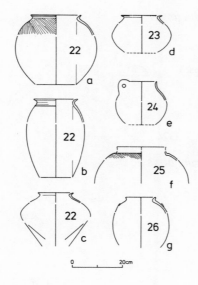

Fig. 86. Genres 22-26: reconstruction of form

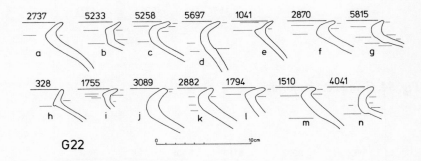

G22

Fig. 87. Genre 22: rim forms

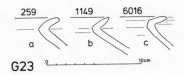

G23

Fig. 88. Genre 23: rim forms

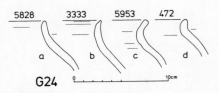

G24

Fig. 89. Genre 24: rim forms

Fig. 90. Genre 25: rim form

Fig. 91. Genre 26: rim forms

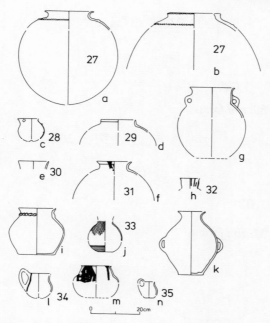

Fig. 92. Genres 27-35: reconstruction of form

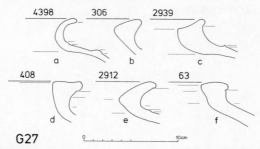

G27

Fig. 93. Genre 27: rim forms

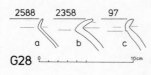

G28

Fig. 94. Genre 28: rim forms

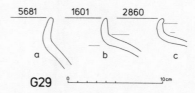

G29

Fig. 95. Genre 29: rim forms

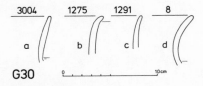

G30

Fig. 96. Genre 30: rim forms

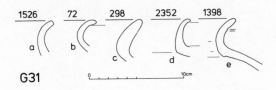

G31

Fig. 97. Genre 31: rim forms

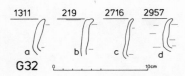

G32

Fig. 98. Genre 32: rim forms

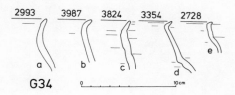

G34

Fig. 99. Genre 34: rim forms

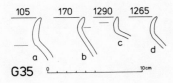

G35

Fig. 100. Genre 35: rim forms

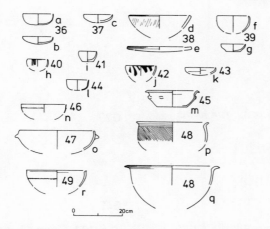

Fig. 101. Genres 36-49: reconstruction of form

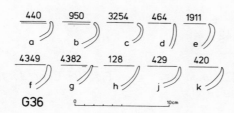

Fig. 102. Genre 36: rim forms

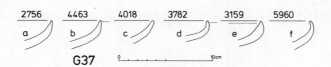

Fig. 103. Genre 37: rim forms

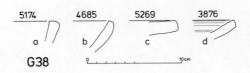

Fig. 104. Genre 38: rim forms

Fig. 105. Genre 39: rim forms

Fig. 106. Genre 40: rim forms

Fig. 107. Genre 41: rim forms

Fig. 108. Genre 42: rim forms

Fig. 109. Genre 43: rim forms

Fig. 110. Genre 44: rim forms

Fig. 111. Genre 45: rim forms

G45

G46

Fig. 112. Genre 46: rim forms

Fig. 113. Genre 47: rim forms

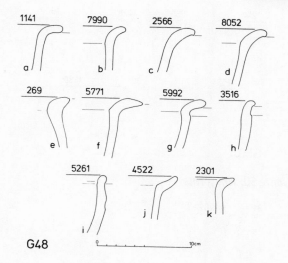

G48

Fig. 114. Genre 48: rim forms

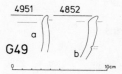

G49

Fig. 115. Genre 49: rim forms

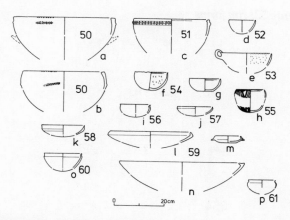

Fig. 116. Genres 50-61: reconstruction of form

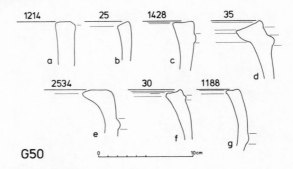

G50

Fig. 117. Genre 50: rim forms

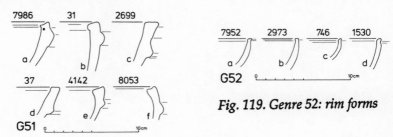

G51

G52

Fig. 119. Genre 52: rim forms

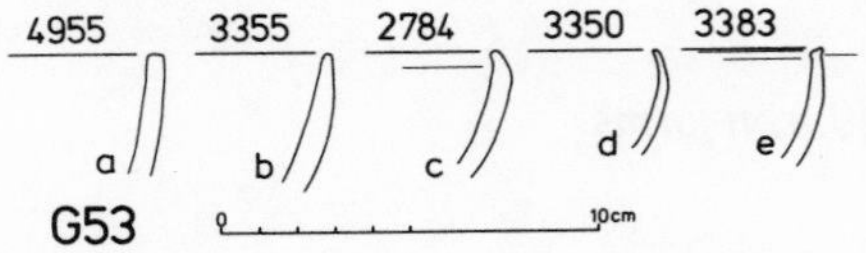

Fig. 118. Genre 51: rim forms

G53

Fig. 120. Genre 53: rim forms

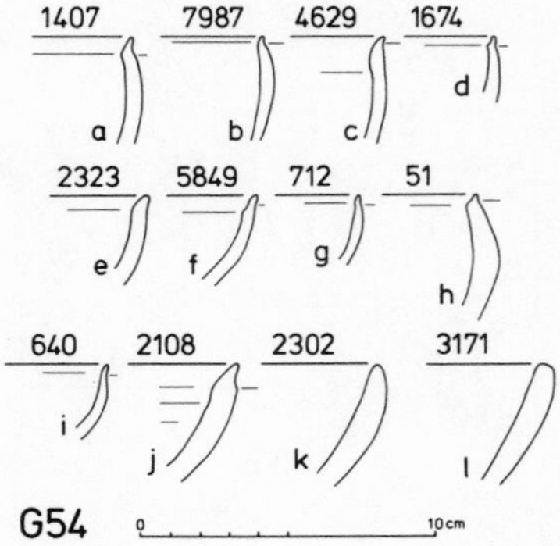

G54

Fig. 121. Genre 54: rim forms

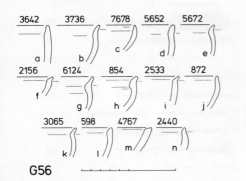

Fig. 122. Genre 55: rim forms

Fig. 124. Genre 57: rim form

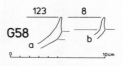

Fig. 123. Genre 56: rim forms

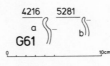

Fig. 125. Genre 58: rim forms

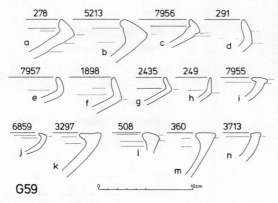

Fig. 126. Genre 59: rim forms

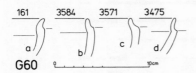

Fig. 127. Genre 60: rim forms

Fig. 128. Genre 61: rim forms

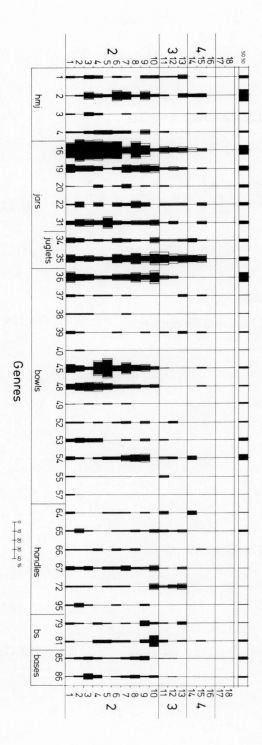

Fig. 129. Frequency of genres: beginning in stage 2/phase 1

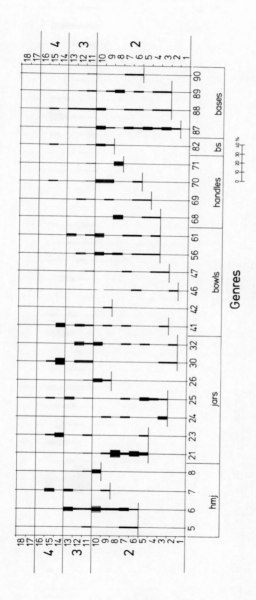

Fig. 130. Frequency of genres: stage 2 (beginning after phase 1?)

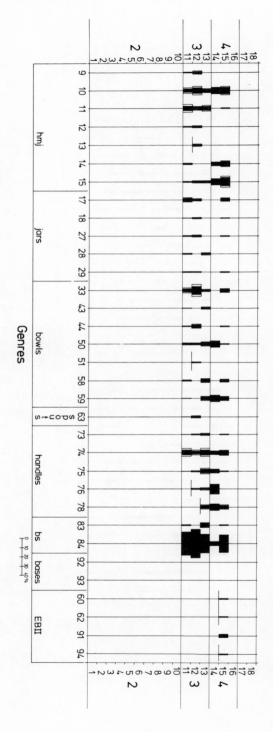

Fig. 131. Frequency of genres: stage 3 and 4

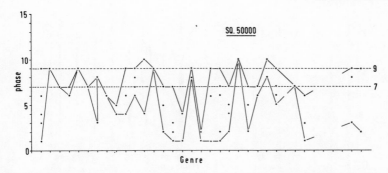

Fig. 132. Genres represented in square 50: mean stage 2/phases 7-9 (cf. Fig. 129, top)

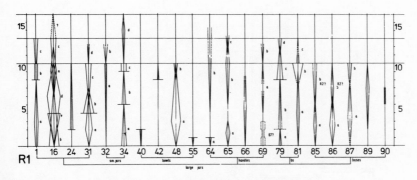

Fig. 133. Repertoire 1: frequency and possible subdivision

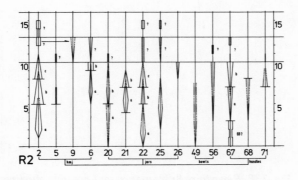

Fig. 134. Repertoire 2: frequency and possible subdivision

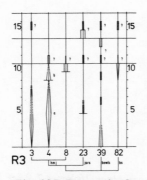

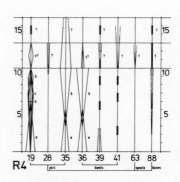

Fig. 135. Repertoire 3:
frequency and possible subdivision

Fig. 136. Repertoire 4:
frequency and possible subdivision

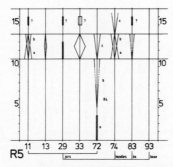

Fig. 137. Repertoire 5: frequency and possible subdivision

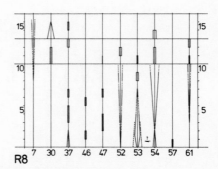

Fig. 138. Repertoire 8: frequency and possible subdivision

Pottery Catalogue

The illustrated material in the pottery catalogue is arranged in order of genres. The figure number is followed by the field catalogue number (C), the provenance (Prov.), stage and consecutively numbered phases (St./ph.), and the genre (G) (see Chapter 4).

No. C   Prov. St/ph G   Description

Fig. 139. Large heavy holemouth jars (hmj) (genre 1>)

1	5670	2153	2/4	1	hmj, rounded rim, shoulder 'bowed', finely grooved below rim, red paint below rim and trickling down body
2	4627	50006	2/7-9	1	hmj, rounded slightly in turned rim, shoulder 'bowed', slurred below rim on ext., top and ext. of rim painted red, paint trickling down over body, two bands of impressed decoration on shoulder
3	3221	4128	2/1	1	hmj, rounded rim, 'bowed' profile, slurred on and below rim ext., red paint on and below rim, paint trickling down on upper shoulder
4	1641	2062	2/9	1	hmj, rounded slightly flattened rim, shoulder slightly 'bowed', light wash of red paint or slip on rim and ext. body
5	3376	50006	2/7-9	1	hmj, rounded rim, 'bowed' shoulder, slurred rim and shoulder, ext. body diagonally finger streaked
6	790	2099	2/9	1	hmj, rounded in-turned rim, light red paint on rim and ext.

Fig. 140. Large heavy holemouth jars (hmj) (genre <1>)

1	1211	4037	3/11	1	hmj, rounded rim, patches of light red paint at rim, ext. body streaked horizontally
2	1213	4037	3/11	1	hmj, rounded rim, 'bowed' shoulder, patchy red paint ext., horizontal streaking, band of lightly impressed decoration on shoulder
3	2880	50000	2/7-9	1	hmj, rounded rim, 'bowed' shoulder, raised band with slashed/impressed decoration on shoulder
4	2645	50003	2/7-9	1	hmj, rounded int. recessed rim, 'bowed' shoulder, band of impressed decoration on shoulder
5	425	4066	2/1	1	hmj, rounded rim rilled on top, straight shoulder
6	600	2083	2/9	1	hmj, rounded slightly pointed rim, 'bowed' shoulder, rim slurred, body diagonally finger streaked

Fig. 141. Large heavy holemouth jars (hmj) (genre <1)

| 1 | 1536 | 4045 | 2/4 | 1 | hmj, rounded slightly pointed rim, 'bowed' shoulder, rim and shoulder slurred |
| 2 | 1509 | 4028 | 4/15 | 1 | hmj, rounded/pointed rim, 'bowed' shoulder, rim slurred |

3	605	2045	3/13	1	hmj, rounded rim, straight shoulder, slurred at rim and upper body
4	855	2115	2/6	1	hmj, rounded rim, slightly 'bowed' shoulder, slurred rim
5	2295	2049	3/11	1	hmj, rounded rim, 'bowed' shoulder, slurred rim
6	20	0000	0000	1	hmj, rounded/pointed slightly everted rim, 'bowed' shoulder, diagonal streaking int.
7	4950	4128	2/1	1	hmj, pointed/rounded rim, 'bowed' shoulder, rim slurred, two bands of impressed decoration below rim and on shoulder

Fig. 142. Large holemouth jar (hmj) (genre 1/2: 'hybrid')

1	5346	40017	2/-	1/2	hmj, rounded bulbous rim, slightly 'bowed' shoulder, rim and upper body slurred, red paint on rim and shoulder, paint trickling down over body, diagonal finger streaking on ext., 4 up-turned rounded lug handles on shoulder (cf. genre 2), one handle with two pre-firing stamp seal impressions (cf. Fig. 272: 1, Pls 4: 3; 8: 2)

Fig. 143. Holemouth jars (hmj) with [4] pushed up lugs (genre 2>)

1	4729	50005	2/7-9	2	hmj, pointed/rounded bulbous rim, pushed up rounded lugs below rim, band of incised decoration below rim, stamp seal impression on lug and ext. of rim (cf. Pl. 8: 1)
2	2741	50003	2/7-9	2	hmj, pointed bulbous rim, double band of incised/impressed decoration below rim
3	2445	2042	3/11	2	hmj, rounded rim, band of impressed decoration below rim
4	283	2025	4/15	2	hmj, rounded slightly bevelled bulbous rim, pushed up rounded lugs below rim, band of incised decoration below rim
5	280	1025	4/15	2	hmj, rounded slightly rilled bulbous rim, band of incised/impressed decoration below rim
6	2483	4077	2/11	2	hmj, rounded/pointed bulbous rim, band of incised/impressed decoration below rim
7	2125	2059	2/9	2	hmj, rounded bulbous rim, band of incised decoration below rim
8	150	1003	0000	2	hmj, rounded bulbous rim, band of stabbed ('punctate') decoration below rim
9	2069	4076	3/11	2	hmj, rounded bulbous rim, pushed up rounded lugs below rim, band of incised/impressed decoration below rim
10	2101	2098	2/7	2	hmj, rounded/pointed slightly bevelled bulbous rim, pushed up rounded lugs below rim, band of impressed/slashed decoration below rim

Fig. 144. Holemouth jars (hmj) with [4] pushed up lugs (genre <2>)

1	4843	50006	2/7-9	2	hmj, bevelled bulbous rim, band of slashed decoration below rim
2	4777	50001	2/7-9	2	hmj, rounded/bevelled bulbous rim, band of stabbed decoration below rim
3	1782	4039	3/13	2	hmj, rounded slightly bulbous rim, band of 'punctate' decoration on shoulder
4	2524	2116	2/4	2	hmj, rounded slightly bulbous rim, band of slashed decoration below rim
5	193	0000	0000	2	hmj, rounded/bevelled bulbous rim, pushed up rounded lugs below rim, band of slashed/impressed decoration below rim
6	475	2051	2/9	2	hmj, rounded bulbous rim, band of slashed decoration at rim
7	1917	2065	2/7	2	hmj, rounded slightly pointed bulbous rim, pushed up rounded lugs below rim, band of 'punctate' decoration below rim
8	2548	2090	2/10	2	hmj, rounded/bevelled bulbous rim, pushed up rounded lugs below rim, band of impressed decoration below rim
9	573	2074	2/9	2	hmj, rounded/bevelled bulbous rim, band of 'punctate' decoration below rim

Fig. 145. Holemouth jars (hmj) with [4] pushed up lugs (genre <2>)

1	2025	4002	4/15	2	hmj, bevelled bulbous rim
2	1912	2080	2/9	2	hmj, bevelled/rounded bulbous int. rilled rim, band of 'punctate' decoration below rim
3	1218	4037	3/11	2	hmj, rounded slightly bevelled bulbous rim, band of impressed decoration below rim
4	13	0000	0000	2	hmj, rounded/bevelled bulbous rim, pushed up rounded lugs below rim, band of impressed decoration below rim
5	1639	2062	2/9	2	hmj, rounded rilled bulbous rim, band of 'punctate' decoration below rim
6	267	0000	0000	2	hmj, rounded slightly pointed bulbous rim, band of slashed/impressed decoration below rim
7	1668	2064	2/9	2	hmj, rounded slightly rolled bulbous rim, pushed up rounded lugs below rim, band of impressed decoration below rim
8	2477	4077	2/11	2	hmj, rounded slightly rolled rim, pushed up rounded/pointed lugs below rim, band of incised/impressed decoration below rim
9	1507	4038	2/11	2	hmj, rounded slightly bevelled rolled rim, band of impressed decoration below rim
10	1918	2065	2/7	2	hmj, rounded int. rilled rim, pushed up rounded lugs below rim, band of impressed decoration below rim

11	789	209	2/9	2	hmj, rounded/pointed rim, band of impressed decoration below rim

Fig. 146. Holemouth jars (hmj) with [4] pushed up lugs (genre <2)

1	850	2115	2/6	2	hmj, bevelled/rounded bulbous rim
2	1529	4045	2/4	2	hmj, rounded int. recessed elongated bulbous rim, pushed up rounded lugs below rim, band of incised decoration below rim
3	1532	4045	2/4	2	hmj, rounded/ bevelled/int. recessed slightly bulbous rim, band of slashed/incised decoration below rim
4	653	4079	2/7	2	hmj, rounded rim, band of 'punctate' decoration below rim
5	953	4043	2/10	2	hmj, rounded int. and ext. recessed bulbous rim, pushed up rounded lugs below rim, band of impressed decoration below rim
6	2490	4085	2/6	2	hmj, rounded bulbous rim
7	2558	50000	2/7-9	2	hmj, rounded rim, band of slashed decoration below rim
8	2110	4081	2/6	2	hmj, rounded rim, band of impressed decoration below rim
9	4802	4114	2/5	2	hmj, rounded rim, pushed up lugs below rim, incised groove below rim
10	5028	50019	2/7-9	2	hmj, rounded slightly everted/pointed rim, band of slashed decoration below rim

Fig. 147. Holemouth jars (hmj) with impressed decoration on rim (genre 3)

1	4639	50006	2/7-9	3	hmj, rounded bulbous ridged rim, band of 'reed' impressed decoration on rim, finely grooved on lip
2	5907	2131	2/7	3	hmj, rounded bulbous rim, band of 'reed' impressed decoration on rim, top of lip slurred
3	3400	4117	2/4	3	hmj, rounded/pointed bulbous ridged rim, band of impressed decoration on rim
4	3667	4128	2/1	3	hmj, pointed recessed bulbous ridged rim, band of impressed decoration on rim
5	2567	0000	0000	3	hmj, pointed/rounded bevelled bulbous rim, band of 'reed' impressed decoration below rim
6	5520	4124	2/3	3	hmj, pointed/rounded bulbous rim, band of 'reed' impressed decoration on rim, top of lip slurred
7	5912	4103	2/3	3	hmj, rounded/pointed bulbous ridged rim, band of impressed decoration on rim, top of lip slurred
8	2568	0000	0000	3	hmj, rounded/pointed bulbous ridged rim, band of impressed decoration on ridge
9	12	0000	0000	3	hmj, rounded bevelled ridged bulbous rim, band of 'reed' impressed decoration on ridge, ext. reddish slipped

10	1930	2020	4/15	3	hmj, pointed/rounded bevelled rim, band of impressed decoration below rim
11	2888	50000	2/7-9	3	hmj, bevelled bulbous rim, band of impressed decoration at rim
12	2568	0000	0000	3	hmj, rounded slightly recessed rim, band of impressed decoration at rim

Fig. 148. Holemouth jars (hmj) with recessed rims (genre 4>)

1	5541	2130	2/7	4	hmj, doubly recessed rim, band of impressed decoration on rim
2	2794	50001	2/7-9	4	hmj, recessed bevelled (bulbous) rim, band of 'reed' impressed decoration at shoulder carination
3	5189	50009	2/7-9	4	hmj, recessed (bulbous) rim, band of impressed 'wavy' decoration on lip of rim
4	5582	2136	2/6	4	hmj, recessed rim with int. recessed bulbous profile, band of impressed 'wavy' pattern on lip of rim
5	2559	50000	2/7-9	4	hmj, recessed bulbous rim with groove, band of impressed decoration on rim
6	959	4043	2/10	4	hmj, recessed bevelled (bulbous) rim, band of impressed decoration on rim
7	810	2105	2/9	4	hmj, (recessed) bevelled bulbous rim, band of 'reed' impressed decoration on rim
8	4713	50007	2/7-9	4	hmj, (recessed) bevelled rim
9	741	2112	2/7	4	hmj, recessed bulbous rim
10	46	0000	0000	4	hmj, recessed rim with bulbous profile
11	6	0000	0000	4	hmj, recessed bulbous rim

Fig. 149. Holemouth jars (hmj) with recessed rims (genre <4>)

1	4770	50001	2/7-9	4	hmj, recessed (bulbous) rim, band of impressed decoration on rim
2	2089	2111	2/7	4	hmj, recessed rim
3	8030	0000	0000	4	hmj, recessed rim, band of impressed decoration on rim
4	3395	4117	2/4	4	hmj, recessed rim
5	5577	2136	2/6	4	hmj, recessed rim, band of impressed 'wavy' pattern on rim
6	2793	50001	2/7-9	4	hmj, recessed bulbous rim, band of impressed 'wavy' pattern on rim
7	3811	4115	2/7	4	hmj, (doubly) recessed rim, band of impressed 'wavy' pattern on rim
8	3663	4128	2/1	4	hmj, recessed rim
9	4898	50011	2/7-9	4	hmj, doubly recessed slightly everted (int. recessed) bulbous rim, impressed 'wavy' pattern on lip of rim
10	688	2093	2/9	4	hmj, recessed int. rolled rim
11	3653	40020	2/-	4	hmj, recessed rim (stance?)

Fig. 150. Holemouth jars (hmj) with recessed rims (genre <4)

1	4569	1083	2/7	4	hmj, (recessed) int. rolled rim, band of impressed 'wavy' pattern on rim
2	1381	2107	3/11	4	hmj, recessed bulbous rim, impressed 'wavy' pattern on rim, small rounded lug(s) on shoulder
3	1524	4052	2/5	4	hmj, recessed rim
4	3019	4125	2/2	4	hmj, recessed bulbous rim, band of impressed 'wavy' pattern on lip of rim
5	3066	2153	2/4	4	hmj, recessed bulbous rim, band of impressed 'wavy' pattern on rim
6	4578	1083	2/7	4	hmj, (recessed) bulbous rim, band of impressed 'wavy' pattern on rim
7	5549	2145	2/6	4	hmj, recessed slightly everted bulbous rim, band of impressed 'wavy' pattern on rim
8	4909	50011	2/7-9	4	hmj, rounded rim, raised band with band of 'reed' -impressed decoration on shoulder
9	4848	2148	2/5	4	hmj, (recessed/bevelled?) slightly everted rim, band of impressed 'wavy' pattern on lip of rim

Fig. 151. Holemouth jars (hmj) with [4] pushed up lugs (genre 5) and holemouth jars (hmj) with low everted rim (genre 6>)

1	1264	2033	3/11	5	hmj, rounded bulbous rim, pushed up rounded lugs at rim
2	1210	4037	3/11	5	hmj, rounded bulbous rim, pushed up rounded lugs at rim
3	1042	4022	3/11	5	hmj, rounded int. grooved rim, pushed up rounded lugs at rim
4	396	4077	3/11	5	hmj, rounded bulbous rim, pushed up rounded lugs at rim
5	829	4085	2/6	5	hmj, rounded ext. recessed bulbous rim, pushed up rounded lugs at rim
6	2485	4085	2/6	5	hmj, rounded ext. recessed bulbous rim, pushed up rounded lugs at rim
7	2329	4024	3/11	5.	rounded/bevelled bulbous rim, pushed up rounded lugs at rim
8	1474	4020	3/11	5	hmj, rounded/bevelled (bulbous) rim, rounded lugs below rim
9	975	4043	2/10	6	hmj, low everted bulbous rim, band of 'punctate' decoration on shoulder
10	1558	4047	2/10	6	hmj, low everted int. bevelled rim, band of 'punctate' decoration below rim

Fig. 152. Holemouth jars (hmj) with low everted rim (genre <6)

1	1652	2108	2/6	6	hmj, everted slightly recessed rim, band of impressed decoration on shoulder

2	6126	0000	0000	6	hmj, everted recessed rim, band of incised decoration below rim
3	820	2089	2/9	6	hmj, everted bevelled rim
4	981	4050	2/7	6	hmj, everted rim, incised groove below rim
5	2777	1075	3/12	6	hmj, everted bevelled rim
6	2157	2054	2/10	6	hmj, everted bevelled rim
7	2090	2111	2/7	6	hmj, everted int. grooved rim

Fig. 153. Holemouth jars (hmj) (genre 7)

1	784	2104	2/9	7	hmj, bevelled (rolled) rim
2	503	1052	3/13	7	hmj, bevelled down-lipped rim
3	1934	2020	4/15	7	hmj, bevelled rolled rim
4	7593	41022	-/-	7	hmj, bevelled (recessed) down-lipped rim
5	188	1004	0000	7	hmj, bevelled rolled rim
6	1976	1003	0000	7	hmj, bevelled rolled rim
7	1826	1023	4/15	7	hmj, bevelled rolled rim
8	197	1017	4/15	7	hmj, bevelled down-lipped rim

Fig. 154. Holemouth jars (hmj) with rolled rims and 'reed'-impressed bands (genre 8) and holemouth jars with 'developed' pushed up lugs (genre 9)

1	4721	50007	2/7-9	8	hmj, rolled rim, and of 'reed' impressed decoration below rim, finely grooved at ext. lip
2	8035	4043	2/10	8	hmj, rolled bulbous rim, band of 'reed' impressed decoration on rim
3	952	4043	3/10	8	hmj, rolled bevelled ridged bulbous rim, band of 'reed' impressed decoration on ridge
4	5181	50009	2/7-9	8	hmj, rolled rim, band of 'reed' impressed decoration below rim, top of lip slurred
5	7884	2123	2/9	8	hmj, rolled (down turned) rim
6	402	4077	3/11	8	hmj, rounded rim, band of 'reed' impressed decoration at rim
7	2866	1075	3/12	9	hmj, bevelled rim, pushed up lugs at rim
8	2776	1075	3/12	9	hmj, bevelled int. recessed (bulbous) rim, pushed up lugs below rim
9	1467	4020	3/11	9	hmj, rounded (bevelled) rim, pushed up lugs
10	1471	4020	3/11	9	hmj, rounded slightly int. recessed rim, pushed up lugs below rim
11	4674	50007	2/7-9	9	hmj, bevelled ext. recessed bulbous rim, vestigial pushed up lugs on shoulder

Fig. 155. Holemouth jars (hmj) with recessed rims (genre 10>)

1	3709	31014	3/14	10	hmj, doubly recessed down-lipped rim
2	1900	2000	0000	10	hmj, doubly recessed bulbous rim
3	1301	4019	3/11	10	hmj, doubly recessed (bulbous) rim

4	1947	4003	4/15	10	hmj, recessed bulbous rim
5	1727	1034	4/14	10	hmj, recessed bulbous rim
6	2429	1053	0000	10	hmj, recessed bulbous rim
7	1270	4017	3/11	10	hmj, doubly recessed bulbous rim
8	2052	4000	4/15	10	hmj, recessed rolled elongated bulbous rim
9	23	0000	0000	10	hmj, doubly (ext.) recessed rim
10	11	0000	0000	10	hmj, doubly recessed bulbous rim
11	230	4000	4/15	10	hmj, recessed rim
12	243	2018	4/15	10	hmj, recessed bulbous rim
13	1458	4020	3/11	10	hmj, recessed rim

Fig. 156. Holemouth jars (hmj) with recessed rims (genre <10>)

1	213	2011	0000	10	hmj, recessed bulbous rim
2	2424	1053	0000	10	hmj, recessed bulbous rim
3	9	0000	0000	10	hmj, recessed bulbous rim
4	1664	2077	3/11	10	hmj, recessed bulbous rim
5	1253	2036	3/13	10	hmj, recessed (bulbous) rim
6	1941	2019	4/15	10	hmj, recessed (bulbous) rim
7	152	1003	0000	10	hmj, recessed bulbous rim
8	1817	2018	4/15	10	hmj, recessed (bulbous) rim
9	5	0000	0000	10	hmj, recessed rim
10	1	0000	0000	10	hmj, recessed rim
11	7858	2021	3/13	10	hmj, recessed bulbous rim
12	171	0000	0000	10	hmj, recessed bulbous rim

Fig. 157. Holemouth jars (hmj) with recessed rims (genre <10)

1	8031	4020	3/11	10	hmj, recessed rim
2	1413	4074	3/11	10	hmj, recessed down lipped rim
3	1610	4072	3/11	10	hmj, recessed rim
4	2862	1075	3/12	10	hmj, recessed rim
5	288	4013	3/11	10	hmj, recessed rim
6	2772	1075	3/12	10	hmj, recessed (bevelled) rim
7	2938	1075	3/12	10	hmj, recessed rim
8	8032	0000	0000	10	hmj, recessed slightly everted rim
9	7974	4073	3/11	10	hmj, recessed rim
10	1605	4072	3/11	10	hmj, recessed rim
11	675	4068	3/11	10	hmj, doubly recessed rim, band of impressed decoration on shoulder
12	7862	1075	3/12	10	hmj, doubly recessed rim, diagonal finger streaked ext.

Fig. 158. Holemouth jars (hmj) with elaborately rolled rims and 'grain-washed' surfaces (genre 11>)

1	1047	4021	3/11	11	hmj, rolled ext. ridged rim, 'grain-wash' ext.
2	324	4016	3/11	11	hmj, rolled ext. ridged recessed rim
3	310	2022	3/11	11	hmj, rolled ext. ridged slightly bevelled rim

4   671   4068   3/11   11   hmj, rolled ext. ridged bevelled rim, 'grain-wash' ext.
5   1098   4025   3/11   11   hmj, rolled rim with raised lip
6   677   4068   3/11   11   hmj, rolled elongated rim with ridge, 'grain-wash' ext.
                                and inside rim
7   1956   4016   3/11   11   hmj, rolled ext. ridged rim, 'grain-wash' ext. and inside
                                rim
8   1686   4071   3/11   11   hmj, rolled rim with raised slurred lip
9   1350   4019   3/11   11   hmj, rolled ext. ridged slightly bevelled rim, 'grain-wash'
                                ext. and inside rim

Fig. 159. Holemouth jars (hmj) with elaborately rolled rims and 'grain-washed' surfaces (genre <11>)

1   2343   2047   3/11   11   hmj, rolled down turned rim with flattened int. recessed
                                ridge, 'grain- wash' ext. and inside rim
2   1962   4016   3/11   11   hmj, rolled ext. ridged rim, 'grain-wash' ext. and inside
                                rim
3   1035   4022   3/11   11   hmj, rolled ext. ridged rim, 'grain- wash' ext.
4   327   4016   3/11   11   hmj, rolled ext. grooved rim, 'grain- wash' ext.
5   2340   2047   3/11   11   hmj, rolled ext. ridged down turned rim, 'grain-wash'
                                ext. and inside rim
6   326   4016   3/11   11   hmj, rolled ext. ridged bevelled rim
7   2386   2043   3/12   11   hmj, rolled ext. ridged bevelled rim, 'grain-wash' ext. and
                                inside rim
8   639   4069   3/11   11   hmj, rolled ext. ridged down turned rim, 'grain-wash'
                                ext. and inside rim
9   1615   4072   3/11   11   hmj, rolled ext. ridged rim, 'grain-wash' ext. and inside
                                rim
10   1676   0000   0000   11   hmj, rolled ext. ridged slightly bevelled rim, 'grain-wash'
                                ext. and inside rim

Fig. 160. Holemouth jars (hmj) with elaborately rolled rims and 'grain-washed' surfaces (genre <11>)

1   2366   2047   3/11   11   hmj, rolled ext. ridged rim, 'grain-wash' ext. and inside
                                rim
2   325   4016   3/11   11   hmj, rounded slightly recessed rim with raised lip,
                                'grain-wash' ext. and inside rim
3   1679   4071   3/11   11   hmj, rounded ext. ridged rim, 'grain-wash' ext. and
                                inside rim
4   320   4015   3/11   11   hmj, rounded rim with raised lip, 'grain-wash' ext. and
                                inside rim
5   7972   0000   0000   11   hmj, rounded slightly bevelled rim with ext. ridge,
                                'grain-wash' ext. and inside rim
6   1687   4071   3/11   11   hmj, rolled slightly bevelled ext. ridge rim, 'grain-wash'
                                ext. and inside rim
7   2506   4023   3/11   11   hmj, rounded ext. ridged rim

8	321	4015	3/11	11	hmj, rolled ext. ridged rim, 'grain-wash' ext. and inside rim
9	1039	4022	3/11	11	hmj, rounded bevelled ext. ridged rim, 'grain-wash' ext.
10	3	0000	0000	11	hmj, rounded bevelled ext. ridged rim
11	7837	4001	4/15	11	hmj, rounded/rolled ext. ridged rim
12	918	4072	3/11	11	hmj, rounded ext. recessed/grooved/ridged rim, 'grain-wash' ext. and inside rim

Fig. 161. Holemouth jars (hmj) with elaborately rolled rims and 'grain-washed' surfaces (genre <11)

1	837	4067	3/11	11	hmj, rolled/folded ext. ridged rim, 'grain-wash' ext. and inside rim
2	266	4005	4/15	11	hmj, rolled/folded bevelled ext. ridged rim, 'grain-wash' ext. and inside rim
3	664	4068	3/11	11	hmj, rolled/folded ext. ridged rim, 'grain-wash' ext. and inside rim
4	1266	2033	3/11	11	hmj, rounded rim, 'grain-wash' ext. and inside rim
5	2443	2042	3/11	11	hmj, rounded down turned rilled and ext. ridged rim, 'grain-wash' ext. and inside rim
6	1309	4019	3/11	11	hmj, rolled slightly bevelled rim with ridge, 'grain-wash' ext. and inside rim
7	220	2013	3/11	11	hmj, rounded bevelled int. recessed rim, 'grain-wash' ext. and inside rim
8	319	4015	3/11	11	hmj, rounded/rolled rim with ridge
9	1391	4018	3/11	11	hmj, rolled/rounded bevelled rim, 'grain-wash' ext.
10	2075	4076	3/11	11	hmj, rolled rounded slightly bevelled rim with raised lip, 'grain-wash' ext.

Fig. 162. Heavy holemouth jars (hmj) with moulded bands (genre 12)

1	2560	50000	2/7-9	12	hmj, rounded recessed rim, band of impressed decoration on shoulder
2	1097	4025	3/11	12	hmj, recessed rim, band of impressed decoration below rim
3	38	0000	0000	12	hmj, recessed down pointing rim, band of 'wavy' pattern on lip
4	32	0000	0000	12	hmj, recessed rim, 'wavy' pattern on lip, band of impressed decoration below rim
5	2385	2043	3/12	12	hmj, recessed rim, band of impressed decoration below rim
6	1414	4074	3/11	12	hmj, recessed rim, band of impressed decoration below rim
7	1422	4073	3/11	12	hmj, recessed rim, band of impressed decoration below rim

8	10	0000	0000	12	hmj, recessed down pointed rim, impressed 'wavy' pattern on lip
9	8033	0000	0000	12	hmj, recessed rim, band of impressed decoration below rim
10	36	0000	0000	12	hjm, recessed rim, band of impressed decoration below rim
11	838	4067	3/11	12	hmj, recessed rim, impressed 'wavy' pattern on lip

Fig. 163. Holemouth jars (hmj) with 'grain-wash' slip (genre 13)

1	27	0000	0000	13	hmj, recessed rim, 'grain-wash ext.
2	49	0000	0000	13	hmj, recessed rim, 'grain-wash ext. and int.
3	1046	4021	3/11	13	hmj, rounded/pointed rim, 'grain-wash' ext.
4	48	0000	0000	13	hmj, rounded rim, 'grain-wash' ext. and int.
5	1352	4019	3/11	13	hmj, pointed recessed rim, 'grain-wash' int. and ext.
6	2330	4024	3/11	13	hmj, rounded slightly bevelled rim, 'grain-wash' ext. and inside rim
7	905	4070	3/11	13	hmj, rounded pointed int. recessed rim 'grain-wash' ext.
8	933	4072	3/11	13	hmj, rounded pointed int. recessed rim, 'grain-wash' ext.
9	1367	4074	3/11	13	hmj, rounded/rolled rim, 'grain-wash' ext.

Fig. 164. Holemouth jars (hmj) with recessed rims (genre 14>)

1	5251	30019	3/13	14	hmj, recessed rim, flat base, incised pattern on shoulder (on floor: cf. TUH165:2)
2	7834	4001	4/15	14	hmj, recessed rim, incised pattern below rim
3	8034	0000	0000	14	hmj, recessed bulbous rim, incised pattern below rim
4	207	2010	0000	14	hmj, recessed bulbous rim

Fig. 165. Holemouth jars (hmj) with recessed rims (genre <14>)

1	1819	2018	4/15	14	hmj, recessed bulbous rim
2	5236	30018	3/13	14	hmj, slightly recessed bulbous rim, incised pattern below rim (cf. TUH154:1)
3	277	1022	0000	14	hmj, recessed bulbous rim
4	1875	1032	4/14	14	hmj, slightly recessed bulbous rim
5	1419	4074	3/11	14	hmj, recessed bulbous rim
6	1945	4003	4/15	14	hmj, recessed bulbous rim
7	7982	1007	0000	14	hmj, recessed bulbous rim
8	1813	1021	4/15	14	hmj, slightly recessed bulbous rim, ext. lip slurred
9	7830	4001	4/15	14	hmj, rounded rim

Fig. 166. Holemouth jars (hmj) with recessed rims (genre <14)

1	225	2015	4/15	14	hmj, rounded/bevelled rim
2	214	2011	0000	14	hmj, rounded/recessed rim
3	1882	1004	0000	14	hmj, rounded/recessed rim
4	7833	4001	4/15	14	hmj, rounded recessed rim
5	1764	1025	4/15	14	hmj, rounded rim

6   14   0000 0000 14 hmj, rounded recessed rim, incised pattern below rim
7   2442 4031 3/11 14 hmj, rounded rim, ext. lip slurred

Fig. 167. Holemouth jars (hmj) with rounded bulbous rims (genre 15>)

1   7843 4001 4/15 15 hmj, rounded/pointed bulbous rim, flat base, ext. lip
                            finely grooved, body diagonally finger streaked, two
                            parallel incised grooves at shoulder (set in pit)
2   7835 4001 4/15 15 hmj, rounded/pointed (bevelled) bulbous rim
3   7836 4001 4/15 15 hmj, rounded bulbous rim
4   201   1019 0000 15 hmj, rounded bulbous rim
5   2043 4000 4/15 15 hmj, rounded bulbous rim
6   2421 1053 0000 15 hmj, rounded bulbous rim

Fig. 168. Holemouth jars (hmj) with rounded bulbous rims (genre <15>)

1   2565 0000 0000 15 hmj, rounded bulbous rim, incised pattern below rim
2   2564 4001 4/15 15 hmj, rounded int. recessed bulbous rim, round lug
                            surrounded by incised patterns below rim
3   2497 4033 3/11 15 hmj, rounded bulbous rim
4   7831 4001 4/15 15 hmj, rounded bulbous rim
5   2702 1076 3/12 15 hmj, rounded/pointed bulbous rim, incised patterns
                            below rim
6   190   1007 0000 15 hmj, rounded bulbous rim, incised patterns below rim
7   2105 1043 4/15 15 hmj, rounded/pointed bulbous rim, flat base (set in pit;
                            cf. TUH167:1)

Fig. 169. Holemouth jars (hmj) with rounded bulbous rims (genre <15) and miscellaneous jars

1   1831 1029 4/15 15 hmj, rounded slightly pointed bulbous rim
2   2420 1053 3/11 15 hmj, rounded bulbous rim
3   2124 2068 4/15 15 hmj, rounded bulbous rim, incised pattern below rim
4   7829 4001 4/15 15 hmj, rounded bulbous rim
5   2427 1053 0000 15 hmj, rounded/pointed bulbous rim
6   2430 1053 0000 15 hmj, rounded/pointed int. recessed rim
7   5202 50009 2/7-9   hmj, rounded bulbous rim with ext. ledge, impressed
                            decoration along ledge
8   2695 1076 3/12   hmj, rounded in turned rim, oval lug(s?) below rim
9   2436 1063 3/13   hmj, slightly recessed/rolled rim with raised lip

Fig. 170. Holemouth jars (hmj)

1   1988 2013 3/11   hmj, rounded rolled rim
2   279   1025 4/15   hmj, rounded/bevelled rolled rim, ext. of lip slurred
3   755   2101 3/13   hmj, rounded down turned rim, ext. of rim finely
                            grooved, body diagonally finger streaked

4	1417	4074	3/11	hmj, rounded down turned rim
5	497	2040	3/13	hmj, recessed elongated bulbous rim
6	6023	4087	3/11	hmj, pointed/bevelled in turned rim, red paint int. rim and along ext. rim and shoulder, paint trickling down over body
7	3795	30004	-/17	hmj, pointed/bevelled in turned rim
8	1521	4052	2/5	hmj, pointed up turned rim, indented shoulder

Fig. 171. Holemouth jars (hmj)

1	4549	1077	3/12	hmj, out rolled rounded rim
2	2690	1076	3/12	hmj, out rolled rounded rim, reddish slip ext., traces of burnishing
3	1024	4022	3/11	hmj, rounded rim with low raised lip
4	1083	4025	3/11	hmj, rolled rounded rim
5	2864	1075	3/12	hmj, rolled rounded/bevelled rim
6	1689	4071	3/11	hmj, rounded rolled int. recessed rim
7	1611	4072	3/11	hmj, up pointed rounded rim
8	281	1025	4/15	hmj, pointed recessed bulbous rim
9	18	0000	0000	hmj, pointed recessed bulbous rim, impressed decoration along ext. ridge
10	2091	2111	2/7	hmj, rounded/pointed recessed bulbous rim, band of impressed decoration along ext. ridge
11	7900	31005	-/18	hmj, pointed/bevelled recessed rim [EB IV?]
12	7	0000	0000	hmj, pointed/rounded ext. grooved rim, body scored with incised lines [EB III/IV?]

Fig. 172. Holemouth jars (hmj)

1	7954	0000	0000	hmj, rolled recessed rim, impressed/ incised pattern below rim [EB IV?]
2	5869	0000	0000	hmj, pointed/rounded rolled bulbous rim, red paint along lip, paint trickling down over body
3	1763	1025	4/15	hmj, rounded bevelled rim, vertical stance
4	130	1001	0000	hmj, rounded bevelled/recessed rim, vertical stance
5	268	4009	4/15	hmj, rounded slightly up turned rim
6	1321	2032	3/11	hmj, rounded rim
7	7873	41022		hmj, rounded/bevelled rim
8	15	0000	0000	hmj, rounded rim
9	2381	2043	3/12	hmj, rounded rim
10	7859	4026	0000	hmj, rounded rim

Fig. 173. Holemouth jars (hmj)

1	5332	50009	2/7-9	hmj, recessed slightly bulbous rim, ext. groove below rim
2	239	2018	4/15	hmj, rounded/pointed bulbous rim
3	569	2074	2/9	hmj, rounded/bevelled bulbous rim
4	8036	0000	0000	hmj, recessed bulbous rim

5	0037	0000	0000		hmj, recessed bulbous rim
6	8038	0000	0000		hmj, recessed bulbous rim
7	1402	4018	3/11		hmj, recessed int. grooved rim, near vertical stance
8	8039	0000	0000		hmj, recessed bulbous rim
9	8040	0000	0000		hmj, recessed bulbous rim
10	2559	50000			hmj, rounded/bevelled bulbous rim, band of incised pattern along lip
11	1347	4019	3/11		hmj, rounded rim, band of impressed decoration along lip, near vertical stance
12	7	0000	0000		hmj, rounded/pointed slightly up turned rim
13	3704	31014	3/14		hmj, pointed bulbous (folded) rim, raised band of moulded decoration below rim

Fig. 174. Heavy bag-shaped jars (genre 16>)

1	2884	50000	2/7-9	16	jar, rounded slightly bevelled everted rim, band of stabbed decoration at neck/ body junction
2	697	2093	2/9	16	jar, rounded/bevelled rim, band of stabbed decoration below rim
3	2425	1053	0000	16	jar, everted rounded rim, band of incised/ impressed decoration at neck/shoulder junction
4	1366	4074	3/11	16	jar, rounded bulbous rim, double band of stabbed decoration below rim
5	2561	50000	2/7-9	16	jar, everted rounded/pointed rim, band of stabbed decoration below rim
6	7869	4089	2/8	16	jar, everted pointed rim, band of stabbed decoration below rim
7	3540	50006	2/7-9	16	jar, everted pointed/rounded bulbous rim, ext. lip slurred, band of stabbed decoration below lip, second similar band below shoulder, red paint along lip and trickling down in bands over body
8	636	4069	3/11	16	jar, everted rounded bulbous rim, body diagonally finger streaked

Fig. 175. Bag-shaped jars (genre <16>)

1	1010	4022	3/11	16	jar, everted rounded slightly rolled bulbous rim, ext. lip slurred, body diagonally finger streaked
2	1058	4021	3/11	16	jar, everted rounded rim, red paint/slip in band ext./int. lip and trickling down over body
3	273	0000	0000	16	jar, everted rounded bulbous rim
4	289	4013	3/11	16	jar, everted rounded bulbous rim with int. carination, band of impressed and incised decoration below lip
5	7971	0000	0000	16	jar, everted rounded bulbous rim with int. carination, sharp ridge below rim
6	1456	4020	3/11	16	jar, everted rounded bulbous rim with slight int. carination

7   1276   2030   3/11   16   jar, everted pointed bulbous rim, ext. body diagonally finger streaked
8   79   0000   0000   16   jar, everted rounded rim, band of impressed decoration below rim
9   169   0000   0000   16   jar, everted rounded slightly out rolled rim, band of slashed decoration at neck/ shoulder junction

Fig. 176. Bag-shaped jars (genre <16>)

1   2066   4080   2/7   16   jar, everted down pointed rim, flat base, ext. neck beige slipped band, body diagonally finger streaked
2   709   2095   3/11   16   jar, everted rounded/pointed rim
3   1418   4074   3/11   16   jar, everted rounded slightly out rolled rim
4   5501   2118   2/9   16   jar, everted pointed bevelled rim
5   2300   2049   3/11   16   jar, everted rounded bulbous rim
6   1457   4020   3/11   16   jar, up turned rounded bulbous rim

Fig. 177. Bag-shaped jars (genre <16>)

1   89   0000   0000   16   jar, everted rounded rim, ext. tucks
2   3394   4117   2/4   16   jar, vertical pointed/rounded rim, ext. lip slurred, body diagonally finger streaked
3   428   4066   2/1   16   jar, everted rounded/pointed rim, band of impressed decoration below rim
4   2152   4048   2/4   16   jar, everted rounded rim on slightly 'bowed' neck
5   1580   4056   2/1   16   jar, everted pointed/rounded rim, band of red paint along int. lip with vertical painted bands appended, ext. broad vertical painted bands
6   3005   4125   2/2   16   jar, rounded rim, band of slurring along ext. lip, band of stabbed ('punctate') decoration above neck/shoulder junction, body diagonally finger streaked
7   4853   2148   2/5   16   jar, rounded/pointed rim, ext. lip and body red painted streaks
8   857   2091   2/7   16   jar, everted rounded rim

Fig. 178. Bag-shaped jars (genre <16>)

1   4583   2142   2/6   16   jar, up turned pointed bulbous rim
2   7951   0000   0000   16   jar, up turned pointed/rounded bulbous rim, band of impressed decoration below rim
3   156   0000   0000   16   jar, everted rounded rim
4   2547   4065   2/1   16   jar, everted rounded rim, three bands of impressed and incised decoration between neck and shoulder
5   2758   4125   2/2   16   jar, everted rounded rim, ext. lip slurred, red painted horizontal bands on body
6   2875   50000   2/7-9   16   jar, everted rounded slightly int. recessed rim, double band of stabbed decoration between neck and shoulder

Fig. 179. Bag-shaped jars (genre <16>)

1   2981   4125   2/2   16   jar, everted rounded/pointed rim, ext. lip slurred, body diagonally finger streaked

2   4600   4128   2/1   16   jar, everted rounded/pointed rim, red painted band on lip, paint trickling down int., ext. near vertical painted or trickled bands

3   2553   50000 2/7-9 16   jar, everted rounded rim, band of impressed decoration above shoulder

4   5086   32002 -/19 16   jar, everted pointed/rounded rim, bulbous neck, band of incised/ impressed decoration below rim

5   2118   2065   2/7   16   jar, everted rounded slightly out rolled rim

6   4736   4125   2/2   16   jar, everted rounded rim, ext. broad vertical bands of red paint from lip

7   2692   1076   3/12 16   jar, everted pointed rim, ext. lip slurred

Fig. 180. Bag-shaped jars (genre <16>)

1   2494   4085   2/6   16   jar, everted pointed rim on bulbous neck, inverse carination at neck/shoulder, band of impressed decoration on neck

2   2610   4125   2/2   16   jar, everted pointed rim on bulbous neck, band of impressed decoration below rim

3   5348   2134   2/6   16   jar, everted pointed rim, band of impressed decoration below rim

4   8042   4125   2/2   16   jar, everted pointed rim on bulbous neck, ext. lip slurred, band of impressed decoration below rim, body diagonally finger streaked

5   5431   4124   2/3   16   jar, everted pointed rim, band of impressed decoration on neck, horizontal irregular bands of red paint on body

6   3208   50005 2/7-9 16   jar, rounded slightly int./ext. rolled vertical rim on bulbous neck/shoulder, two bands of 'punctate' decoration on neck and neck/shoulder junction

Fig. 181. Bag-shaped jars (genre <16>)

1   2722   1076   3/11 16   jar, bevelled vertical rim, two bands of impressed/stabbed decoration below rim and at neck/shoulder junction

2   5601   2137   2/6   16   jar, slightly recessed ext./int. rolled rim on bulbous neck

3   7966   2127   2/8   16   jar, everted pointed/rounded rim on in sloping neck making sharp angle with shoulder

4   311   2022   3/11 16   jar, everted pointed rim, convex ridged neck, body diagonally finger streaked

5   2941   1075   3/12 16   jar, everted rounded rim, convex neck making sharp angle with shoulder

6   1011   4022   3/11 16   jar, everted rounded rolled rim on short bulbous neck

7   331   4016   3/11 16   jar, everted pointed ext. recessed rim

| 8 | 8043 | 4020 | 3/11 | 16 | jar, everted pointed/rounded rim on short bulbous neck |
| 9 | 8044 | 4074 | 3/11 | 16 | jar, everted pointed/rounded rim on short bulbous neck |

Fig. 182. Bag-shaped jars (genre <16>)

1	1673	2086	3/7	16	jar, everted pointed rim on short bulbous neck
2	1712	4013	3/11	16	jar, everted pointed rim on bulbous vertical neck, ext. lip slurred, body diagonally finger streaked
3	1671	2071	2/9	16	jar, everted pointed rim on in sloping bulbous neck, band of impressed decoration on neck
4	1752	2050	2/9	16	jar, everted pointed rim, ext. groove below rim
5	729	2113	2/7	16	jar, everted down pointed rim on in sloping bulbous neck, band of impressed decoration on neck
6	19	0000	0000	16	jar, everted rounded rim on bulbous in sloping neck, band of impressed decoration on neck
7	2121	2071	2/9	16	jar, everted pointed (?) rim, band of 'punctate' decoration on neck/shoulder junction
8	2643	2153	2/4	16	jar, everted rounded out rolled rim on near vertical neck, ext. neck horizontally finger streaked, raised (applied?) band of impressed/moulded decoration at neck/shoulder junction, body diagonally finger streaked
9	3079	2156	2/2	16	jar, everted rounded/rolled rim on near vertical neck, ext. neck horizontally finger streaked, raised (applied?) band of impressed/ moulded decoration at neck/shoulder junction, body diagonally finger streaked
10	2934	4125	2/2	16	jar, everted rounded rim on near vertical neck, ext. neck horizontally finger streaked
11	1704	2053	2/7	16	jar, everted rounded recessed rim on near vertical neck

Fig. 183. Bag-shaped jars (genre <16>)

1	4969	4128	2/1	16	jar, everted rounded neck on long in sloping neck, ext. red painted vertical bands or streaks
2	3380	50006	2/7-9	16	jar, everted rounded slightly recessed rim, ext. neck/shoulder junction slurred, vertical red/brown painted bands from below rim, ext. body diagonally finger streaked, int. vertically finger streaked
3	1144	4063	2/7	16	jar, everted rounded rim, int./ext. splashed of red paint
4	3525	2153	2/4	16	jar, everted rounded rim, ext. neck/ shoulder junction slurred
5	2656	4125	2/2	16	jar, everted rounded rim, ext. rim/neck junction slurred, ext. body diagonally finger streaked
6	1516	4052	2/5	16	jar, everted rounded rim, band of red paint along int./ext. lip, red paint splashed on ext. body
7	1139	4046	2/4	16	jar, everted slightly down turned rim, traces of red paint int./ext.

8   2529 2116 2/4   16 jar, everted rounded rim, ext. near vertical narrow bands
                           of red paint

Fig. 184. Bag-shaped jars (genre <16>)

1   3878 50007 2/7-9 16 jar, everted rounded rim, ext. neck slurred
2   90   0000 0000 16 jar, everted rounded rim, band of red paint along
                           int./ext. lip, near vertical bands of red paint ext. body
3   92   0000 0000 16 jar, everted rounded rim, bands and streaks of red paint
                           along int./ext. lip
4   6115 2129 2/7   16 jar, everted recessed pointed/rounded rim on short
                           vertical neck, finely grooved on lip, thick band of red
                           paint on neck and shoulder appended by thick vertical
                           stripes of red paint on ext. body
5   818   2089 2/9   16 jar, everted bevelled slightly down pointed rim, splashed
                           of red paint ext.
6   1595 4082 2/6   16 jar, everted rounded rim, band of red paint along
                           int./ext. lip, near vertical stripes of red paint on ext. body
7   172   0000 0000 16 jar, everted rounded rim
8   487   2051 2/9   16 jar, everted rounded rim on near vertical neck, ext.
                           splashes of red paint
9   852   2115 2/6   16 jar, everted rounded rim on in sloping neck, band of red
                           paint along ext. lip, splashes of red paint on ext. body
10 826   4085 2/6   16 jar, everted rounded slightly recessed rim, near vertical
                           narrow stripes of red paint from below lip on ext. body
11 890   4070 3/11 16 jar, everted rounded rilled rim
12 2536 0000 0000 16 jar, everted rounded rilled rim on near vertical slightly
                           bulbous neck, lattice pattern of red paint on ext. body

Fig. 185. Bag-shaped jars (genre <16>)

1   2461 1066 3/13 1   jar, everted rounded rim, red paint int., red pain on lip
                           and in irregular stripes on ext.
2   5878 0000 0000 16 jar, everted rounded rim
3   1553 4047 2/10 16 jar, everted rounded slightly rilled rim, red splashed
                           paint int. and ext.
4   650   4079 2/7   16 jar, everted rounded rim, red splashed paint ext.
5   1795 4039 3/13 16 jar, everted rilled rim
6   91   0000 0000 16 jar, everted rounded rim, splashed paint int./ext.
7   1237 1044 4/14 16 jar, everted rounded rim
8   663   4086 2/4   16 jar, everted rolled or bulbous down turned rim, red
                           painted band on lip, neck slurred under lip, traces of red
                           paint splashed over ext. body, band of shallow
                           impressed decoration on shoulder
9   2552 50000 2/7-9 16 jar, everted rounded rim, bands of splashed paint ext.

Fig. 186. Bag-shaped jars (genre <16>)

1   1619 4061 2/1   16 jar, everted pointed bulbous rim from sharp inverse
                           carination at neck/shoulder junction, band of impressed
                           decoration at neck/shoulder (stance? cf. TUH186:2)

2	1412	4074	3/11	16	jar, everted pointed bulbous rim from sharp inverse carination at neck/shoulder junction, bands of slashed decoration on neck and shoulder
3	5478	4123	2/4	16	jar, everted rounded/bevelled rim with sharp int. carination, impressed 'wavy' pattern on lip, band of slashed decoration on neck
4	1540	4045	2/4	16	jar, everted rounded rim, band of impressed 'wavy' decoration on lip
5	5062	32001	-/20	16	jar, everted rounded rim, band of impressed 'wavy' decoration on lip
6	1355	4019	3/11	16	jar, everted rilled rim, traces of impressed decoration on shoulder
7	1259	1046	4/15	16	jar, everted bulbous rim
8	8045	0000	0000	16	jar, rounded/rolled rim on in sloping neck, broad vertical band of red paint on ext. body
9	794	2099	2/9	16	jar, out rolled rim on in sloping neck, band of slashed decoration on neck
10	1541	4045	2/4	16	jar, everted rounded rim on in sloping neck
11	1399	4018	3/11	16	jar, everted rounded rim on short bulbous neck making sharp inverse carination with shoulder

Fig. 187. Large heavy bag-shaped jars (genre 17>)

1	305	1026	4/15	17	jar, everted rounded/bevelled splayed rim, raised band of impressed decoration below rim
2	1070	4021	3/11	17	jar, everted rounded/bevelled splayed rim, bands of impressed decoration along ext. lip and on neck below rim
3	199	1019	0000	17	jar, everted rounded recessed splayed rim, bands of impressed decoration along ext. lip and on neck/shoulder
4	1131	4025	3/11	17	jar, everted bevelled/rounded splayed rim, bands of impressed decoration along ext. lip and neck
5	6015	4087	3/11	17	jar, everted rounded recessed and out rolled splayed rim, band of impressed decoration along ext. lip, raised vertical and horizontal bands of impressed decoration on shoulder and body
6	2535	0000	0000	17	jar, everted rounded slightly recessed splayed rim, raised slightly diagonal impressed bands of decoration on neck and body

Fig. 188. Large heavy bag-shaped jars (genre <17>)

1	2076	4076	3/11	17	jar, everted slightly recessed splayed rim, bands of impressed decoration on ext. lip and neck/shoulder
2	2364	2047	3/11	17	jar, everted rounded bevelled splayed rim on bulbous neck, bands of impressed decoration on ext. lip and neck/shoulder
3	1125	4025	3/11	17	jar, everted rounded splayed rim, bands of impressed decoration on ext. lip and neck
4	66	0000	0000	17	jar, everted rounded splayed rim, band of impressed decoration on lip
5	369	2096	3/11	17	jar, everted bevelled rolled splayed rim, band of impressed decoration on ext. lip, horizontal bands of slashed and impressed decoration on neck and shoulder

6   1274 2030 3/11 17 jar, everted bevelled slightly recessed splayed rim, band
                          of impressed decoration on ext. lip
7   2408 4036 3/11 17 jar, everted rounded/bevelled splayed rim, bands of
                          impressed decoration on lip and neck

Fig. 189. Large heavy bag-shaped jars (genre <17) and jars with everted recessed rims (genre 18>)

1   887   4070 3/11 17 jar, everted rounded recessed splayed rim, band of
                          impressed decoration on ext. lip
2   1168 4032 3/11 17 jar, everted rounded recessed splayed rim
3   163   1004 0000 17 jar, everted bevelled rim, band of impressed decoration
                          on ext. lip, horizontal and diagonal bands of impressed
                          decoration on neck, shoulder, and body
4   65   0000 0000 17 jar, everted rounded recessed splayed rim, band of
                          impressed decoration on ext. lip
5   370   2096 3/11 17 jar, rounded splayed 'hammer' rim, band of impressed
                          decoration on neck
6   1295 4019 3/11 18 jar, everted rounded splayed rim, bands of impressed
                          decoration on ext. lip and neck/shoulder
7   2046 4000 4/15 18 jar, everted pointed recessed splayed rim, bands
                          of impressed decoration on ext. lip and neck

Fig. 190. Bag-shaped jars with everted recessed rims (genre <18)

1   4306 1079 3/12 18 jar, everted up turned pointed recessed splayed rim,
                          band of impressed decoration on neck
2   8026 [TUG] -/-   18 jar, everted up turned pointed recessed splayed rim,
                          bands of impressed decoration on ext. lip and neck
3   8027 [TUG] -/-   18 jar, everted pointed recessed splayed rim with int.
                          carination at neck and shoulder, band of impressed
                          decoration on neck

Fig. 191. Bag-shaped jars (genre 19>)

1   2540 0000 0000 19 jar, everted rounded recessed rim, in sloping neck,
                          pushed up rounded lugs on neck
2   764   4064 2/1   19 jar, everted rounded recessed rim
3   5304 4121 2/3   19 jar, everted rounded recessed rim, in sloping neck
4   2986 4125 2/2   19 jar, everted pointed recessed rim, in sloping neck,
                          pushed up rounded lugs below rim
5   861   2091 2/7   19 jar, everted slightly recessed rounded rim, in sloping
                          neck
6   5285 2139 2/6   19 jar, everted rounded recessed rim
7   1568 4056 2/1   19 jar, everted recessed pointed rim
8   2786 50001 2/7-9 19 jar, everted pointed recessed rim, pushed up rounded
                          lugs on straight in sloping shoulder
9   4913 50011 2/7-9 19 jar, everted pointed recessed rim

Fig. 192. Bag-shaped jars (genre <19>)

1   212   2011 0000 19 jar, everted rounded rim
2   3519 2153 2/4   19 jar, everted pointed rim, int. carination
3   2886 50000 2/7-9 19 jar, everted pointed rim, ext. and int. red burnished
4   8046 0000 0000 19 jar, everted pointed rim, int. carination, ext. red
                          burnished, int. red slipped

5	???	2080	2/9	19	jar, everted rounded down turned rim, ext. body and int. lip red burnished, int. red slipped
6	2151	4048	2/10	19	jar, everted rounded rim, ext./int. red burnished
7	8047	0000	0000	19	jar, everted rounded rim, ext./int. red burnished
8	4278	50004	-/-	19	jar, everted rounded slightly bevelled rim, ext. slurred under lip, ext. red slipped, traces of burnishing
9	5804	2135	2/8	19	jar, everted pointed rim, ext. body and int. lip red burnished
10	2145	4048	2/10	19	jar, everted rounded down turned rim, ext./int. red burnished
11	481	2051	2/9	19	jar, everted rounded rim
12	725	4084	2/6	19	jar, everted rounded rim, sharp int. carination, ext. body and int. lip red burnished
13	5480	4123	2/4	19	jar, everted rounded down turned rim, sharp int. carination at neck/shoulder, ext. neck/shoulder slurred, ext. body red burnished, vertical stripes of pattern burnish from neck/shoulder
14	399	4077	3/11	19	jar, everted pointed/rounded rim
15	4961	4128	2/1	19	jar, everted rounded rim, sharp int. carination at neck/shoulder
16	2135	4045	2/4	19	everted rounded/pointed down turned rim, ext./int. red burnished
17	563	1065	2/7	19	jar, everted rounded rim, int. carination at neck/shoulder, ext. body and int. lip red burnished
18	1958	4016	3/11	19	jar, everted pointed rim, sharp int. carination at neck/shoulder, slightly recessed below junction
19	2344	2047	3/11	19	jar, everted rounded rim, sharp int. carination at neck/shoulder, slightly recessed below junction
20	7973	4000	4/15	19	jar, everted pointed rim, sharp int. carination at neck/shoulder, irregular red slip ext.

Fig. 193. Bag-shaped jars (genre <19)

1	8048	0000	0000	19	jar, everted pointed rim
2	94	0000	0000	19	jar, everted rounded rim
3	316	4015	3/11	19	jar, everted rounded down turned rim
4	1380	2107	3/11	19	jar, everted bevelled rim, red slipped ext.
5	530	2061	2/8	19	jar, rounded in sloping rim and neck
6	570	2074	2/9	19	jar, slightly everted pointed/bevelled rim, ext. body and int. lip red burnished
7	3531	50006	2/7-9	19	jar, rounded/pointed in sloping rim, ext. red burnished, int. red slipped
8	270	4009	4/15	19	jar, rounded 'bowed' rim and neck, lumpy lugs on shoulder, ext. red burnished
9	2115	2065	2/7	19	jar, everted pointed rim, int./ext. red burnished
10	2642	2153	2/4	19	jar, everted rounded rim, ext. body and int. lip red slipped
11	3260	1086	2/7	19	jar, everted rounded rim, ext. body and int. lip red slipped
12	978	4055	2/6	19	jar, everted pointed rim, ext. body and int. lip red burnished, int. red slipped below lip
13	146	1003	0000	19	jar, everted rounded rim, ext. and int. irregularly red slipped

14	95	0000	0000	19	jar, everted rounded rim, ext. body and int. lip red slipped
15	2394	2043	3/12	19	jar, everted pointed rim, ext. body and int. lip red slipped
16	2544	0000	0000	19	jar, everted rounded rim, ext. red slipped
17	1138	4046	2/4	19	jar, everted rounded rim,
18	4499	4128	2/1	19	jar, vertical rounded rim
19	1128	4025	3/11	19	jar, everted rounded rim, int./ext. red slipped
20	984	4050	2/7	19	jar, everted rounded rim
21	3261	1086	2/7	19	jar, everted rounded rim from slightly 'bowed' neck, sharp int. carination at rim/neck junction, ext. red burnished, ext. vertical stripes of red pattern burnishing
22	4512	2154	2/3	19	jar, everted rounded rim, ext. body and int. lip red burnished, ext. horizontal band at neck/rim with vertical stripes appended in pattern burnish
23	2148	4048	2/10	19	jar, everted rounded rim, ext. body and int. lip red burnished
24	96	0000	0000	19	jar, everted rounded rim, traces of red slip int.
25	1650	2087	2/9	19	jar, everted rounded slightly out rolled rim, ext. red burnished, int. lip red slipped
26	4461	4128	2/1	19	jar, everted rounded rim, int./ext. red burnished
27	738	2090	2/9	19	jar, everted rounded rim, ext. body and int. lip red burnished
28	823	2089	2/9	19	jar, everted rounded rim, ext. body and int. lip red burnished, int red slipped
29	3215	1084	2/7	19	jar, everted pointed rim, in sloping neck, ext. red burnished, ext. vertical stripes of pattern burnish, int. trickle of red slip
30	98	0000	0000	19	jar, everted rounded slightly out rolled rim, ext./int. red slipped
31	1289	4019	3/11	19	jar, everted rounded rim, ext. body and int. lip red burnished
32	3211	50005	2/7-9	19	jar, everted rounded rim on slightly 'bowed' neck, ext. rim/neck slurred, ext. red slipped

Fig. 194. High-shouldered jars (genre 20>)

1	4728	50005	2/7-9		jar, everted pointed rim, sharply indented shoulder, ext. rim slurred
2	8028	0000	0000		jar. everted pointed rim, indented shoulder
3	4687	50007	2/7-9	20	jar, rounded int. recessed rim
4	1445	4075	3/11	20	jar, bevelled out pointing rim, slight int. recessing below lip
5	1146	4034	3/11	20	jar, rounded rolled 'hammer' rim, ext. groove below rim
6	4904	50011	2/7-9	20	rolled doubly recessed rim on bulbous in sloping neck
7	2354	2047	3/11	20	jar, rounded/bevelled 'hammer' rim, in sloping bulbous neck
8	4987	50011	2/7-9	20	jar, everted doubly recessed rounded rim
9	3314	50006	2/7-9	20	jar, rolled doubly recessed 'hammer' rim, in sloping slightly bulbous neck
10	4772	50001	2/7-9	20	jar, bevelled out pointing 'hammer' rim, in sloping neck

Fig. 195. High-shouldered jars (genre <20)

1	7970	1003	0000	20	jar, rounded out rolled rim, in sloping neck

2	5477	4123	2/4	20	jar, rolled doubly recessed 'hammer' rim, near vertical bulbous neck, thick loop handle at rim, int./ext. red slipped, traces of red painted diagonal narrow stripes at handle
3	1079	4040	2/7	20	jar, rolled/bevelled doubly recessed 'hammer' rim, in sloping slightly bulbous neck, high-shouldered rounded body, flat base, 4 pushed up lugs on shoulder, band of red slip about neck and rim, traces of horizontal and vertical finger streaking, (on floor)
4	378	2096	3/11	20	jar, rounded/rolled int. recessed 'hammer' rim, in sloping neck, sharp ridge on neck
5	2641	2153	2/4	20	jar, bevelled/ recessed rounded 'hammer' rim, in sloping slightly bulbous neck
6	4731	50004	2/7-9	20	jar, rolled 'hammer' rim, near vertical neck, band of light red paint about neck and rim, reddish slip on ext. body
7	1915	2080	2/9	20	jar, doubly recessed 'hammer' rim, in sloping slightly bulbous neck

Fig. 196. Large high-necked, high-shouldered jars (genre 21>)

1	5556	1245	2/6	21	jar, everted pointed recessed rim, in sloping slightly bulbous neck
2	7983	4052	2/5	21	jar, everted bevelled pointed rim, bulbous near vertical neck
3	1225	4037	3/11	21	jar, everted bevelled down pointing rim, everted neck
4	6083	2132	2/7	21	jar, long rounded recessed rim, ext. groove below rim
5	5695	2127	2/8	21	jar, rounded bevelled 'hammer' rim, out sloping neck, ext. wavy groove at neck/shoulder junction, ext. brown/violet slipped
6	6114	2129	2/7	21	jar, rounded recessed rim
7	4277	50004		21	jar, rounded recessed rim, in sloping long neck
8	4451	4128	2/1	21	jar, everted rounded rim, slightly 'bowed' neck

Fig. 197. High-shouldered jars (genre <21)

1	3381	50006	2/7-9	21	jar, no rim, in sloping neck from sharp inverse carination at shoulder, incised pattern below shoulder
2	5605	2137	2/6	21	jar, rounded recessed rim, near vertical slightly 'bowed' neck
3	2543	0000	0000	21	jar, rounded recessed rim, vertical slightly 'bowed' neck, sharp carination at shoulder
4	3107	2140	2/2	21	jar, bevelled out pointing rim, vertical neck, high shoulder, flat slightly hollow base, ext. rim slurred, two pushed up rounded lugs on upper neck above two rounded ledge handles (cf. genre 68) surrounded by punctate decoration
5	731	2090	2/9	21	jar, no rim, vertical neck from indented high shoulder, pushed up rounded lugs below shoulder
6	6041	2122	2/8	21	jar, rounded everted recessed rim, slightly bulbous vertical neck, sharp transition to shoulder

Fig. 198. Sharply everted rim jars (genre 22>)

| 1 | 2737 | 50003 | 2/7-9 | 22 | jar, everted rounded rim, sharp int. carination at neck/shoulder, ext. lip finely grooved, body diagonally finger streaked |

2   1050   4021   3/11   22   jar, everted pointed rim, slightly bulbous neck with inverse carination to lip, internal carination at neck/shoulder

3   5233   50009   2/7-9   22   jar, everted recessed pointed/rounded rim, in sloping straight neck with sharp inverse carinations to rim and shoulder, sharp int. carinations, ext. red slipped

4   3385   4117   2/4   22   jar, everted rounded recessed rim, int. carinations, neck/shoulder int. recessed

5   2088   2111   2/7   22   jar, everted rounded rim, slightly bulbous neck making sharp carination with lip and shoulder, ext. irregular red slip

6   2501   4033   3/11   22   jar, everted pointed rim, sharp int. carination at neck/shoulder, ext. lip slurred

7   1877   4017   3/11   22   jar, everted rounded/pointed rim, sharp int. carination at neck/shoulder

8   5258   2145   2/6   22   jar, everted recessed down pointing rim, int. carination and recess at neck/shoulder

9   5697   2127   2/8   22   jar, everted rounded rim, curved neck from small ext. indentation at shoulder, ext. neck slurred

10   2542   0000   0000   22   jar, everted rounded rim, sharp int. carination at lip/neck, ext. lip slurred

11   8049   4033   3/11   22   jar, everted rounded/pointed rim, sharp int. carination at neck/shoulder, indented ext. shoulder, ext. neck/lip slurred

12   1041   4022   3/11   22   jar, everted pointed recessed rim, int, carination at neck/shoulder

13   2870   50000   2/7-9   22   jar, everted rounded rim, int. carinations at lip/neck and neck/shoulder

Fig. 199. Sharply everted rim jars (genre <22>)

1   2652   50003   2/7-9   22   jar, everted rounded rim, int. carination at neck/shoulder, ext. body reddish slipped patterned

2   747   2112   2/7   22   jar, everted rounded recessed rim, int. carination at neck/shoulder

3   1018   4022   3/11   22   jar, everted rounded slightly recessed rim

4   74   0000   0000   22   jar, everted rounded rim, slightly bulbous neck with sharp inverse carination to lip

5   5815   2153   2/4   22   jar, everted rounded slightly recessed rim, int. carination at neck/shoulder, join of neck/shoulder scarred

6   328   4016   3/11   22   jar, everted rounded slightly recessed rim, sharp carination at neck/shoulder, scar at join, red slipped int./ext.

7   1755   2050   2/9   22   jar, everted rounded rim, sharp int. carination at lip/neck, slight int. recess at neck

8   3089   4125   2/2   22   jar, everted rounded rim, bulbous neck section

9   2882   50000   2/7-9   22   jar, everted rounded rim, carinations at lip/neck and neck/shoulder

10   3084   4125   2/2   22   jar, everted rounded rim, slight int. scar at neck/shoulder

11	2892	50001	2/7-9	22	jar, everted slightly recessed pointed rim from bulbous neck
12	71	0000	0000	22	jar, everted rounded rim
13	75	0000	0000	22	jar, everted rounded rim
14	6048	2122	2/8	22	jar, everted slightly recessed rim, carination at lip/neck, bulbous neck at shoulder junction
15	1542	4045	2/4	22	jar, everted rounded rim, sharp carination at neck/shoulder junction
16	1543	4045	2/4	22	jar, everted rounded/pointed rim
17	1632	4061	2/1	22	jar, everted pointed rim
18	77	0000	0000	22	jar, everted rounded rim

Fig. 200. Sharply everted rim jars (genres <22 and 23)

1	749	2112	2/7	22	jar, everted rounded rim, int. carination at neck/shoulder
2	297	1024	4/15	22	jar, everted slightly recessed rim, int. carination at neck/shoulder
3	73	0000	0000	22	jar, everted rounded rim, int. carination at neck/shoulder
4	1794	4039	3/13	22	jar, everted rounded rim, sharp int. carination at neck/shoulder, ext. body and int. lip red burnished
5	4130	50002	2/7-9	22	jar everted rounded rim, int. carination at neck/shoulder, ext. rim/neck/shoulder slurred
6	825	4085	2/6	22	jar, everted pointed rim, sharp int. carination at neck/shoulder, int./ext. rim/neck slurred
7	821	2089	2/9	22	jar, everted pointed rim, int. carination at neck/shoulder
8	1649	2087	2/9	22	jar, everted rounded/pointed rim, int. carination at neck/shoulder, bulbous shoulder profile
9	1510	4028	4/15	22	jar, everted rounded rim, sharp carination at int. lip/neck
10	1799	2052	2/9	22	jar, everted rounded rim, int. carination at neck/shoulder
11	1349	4019	3/11	22	jar, everted rounded rim
12	4041	4001	4	22	jar, everted rounded rim, bulbous neck, scar at neck/shoulder junction
13	1297	4019	3/11	22	jar, everted rounded rim, scar at neck/shoulder junction
14	317	4015	3/11	22	jar, everted pointed rim, scar at neck/shoulder junction
15	1520	4052	2/5	23	jar, everted pointed rim, band of impressed decoration on int. lip
16	259	2020	4/15	23	jar, everted rounded rim, sharp int. carination at neck/shoulder, band of impressed decoration on int. lip
17	1149	4034	3/11	23	jar, everted pointed rim, sharp int. carination at neck/shoulder, band of 'reed' impressed decoration on int. lip (cf. genre 3)

18   6016   4087   3/11   23   jar, everted rounded ext. rilled rim, sharp int. carinations at lip/neck and neck/shoulder, band of 'reed' impressed decoration on int. lip

19   1170   4032   3/11   23   jar, everted rounded rim, band of 'reed' impressed decoration on int. lip

Fig. 201. Jars with loop handles (genre 24)

1   5828   2154   2/3   24   jar, vertical rounded rim, loop handle on shoulder, body diagonally finger streaked

2   3333   50006   2/7-9   24   jar, slightly everted pointed rim on vertical neck, loop handle at rim

3   4273   2154   2/3   24   jar, rounded vertical rim, splayed loop handle at rim

4   5575   2136   2/6   24   jar, everted rounded rim, ext. rim/neck finely grooved, ext. body and int. lip red slipped

5   5953   2138   2/7   24   jar, everted rounded rim, loop handle at shoulder, ext. red slipped

6   4977   5001   1   24   jar, vertical rounded rim, ext. lip/neck slurred, red painted rim and vertical stripes below

7   4844   50006   2/7-9   24   jar, everted rounded rim, loop handle at shoulder, irregular red painted stripes ext.

8   472   2051   2/9   24   jar, everted/vertical rounded rim, loop handle on shoulder, red painted stripe at rim/neck and vertical stripes below

Fig. 202. High-shouldered jars (genres 25 - 27>)

1   1442   4075   3/11   25   jar, no rim, high indented shoulder, ext. body diagonally finger streaked below indentation

2   1843   4009   4/15   25   jar, no rim, high indented shoulder, ext. body diagonally finger streaked below indentation

3   2150   4048   2/10   26   jar, everted rounded rim, pushed up rounded lugs on shoulder, red painted stripe on lip, ext. body red slipped

4   2448   2058   2/9   26   jar, everted rounded/pointed rim, int. carination at neck/shoulder, pushed up rounded lugs on shoulder

5   168   0000   0000   26   jar, everted rounded rim, scar at neck/shoulder join

6   80   0000   0000   26   jar, everted pointed rim, int. carination at neck/shoulder

7   8050   2154   2/3   26   jar, everted rounded rim, int. carination at neck/shoulder, ext. rim/neck slurred

8   898   4070   3/11   26   jar, everted rounded rim, int. carination at neck/shoulder

9   4398   1080   3/11   27   jar, everted rounded slightly down turned rim, scar at neck/shoulder join, moulded raised band on shoulder

10   70   0000   0000   27   jar, everted pointed rim, raised band of impressed decoration on shoulder

11   306   1026   4/15   27   jar, everted rounded thickened rim, band of impressed decoration on ext. lip

12   1072   4021   3/11   27   jar, everted rounded thickened rim, neck slurred

Fig. 203. Heavy high-shouldered jars (genre <27)

1   2509   4032   3/11   27   jar, everted rounded recessed rim

2   2541   0000   0000   27   jar, everted rounded rim, band of impressed decoration on ext. lip

3   2939   1075   3/12   27   jar, everted rounded recessed rim, bands of impressed decoration on ext. lip and shoulder

4   251   4002   4/15   27   jar, everted rounded recessed rim, impressed decoration on ext. lip

5   64   0000   0000   27   jar, everted bevelled rim, band of impressed decoration on ext. lip

6   408   4077   3/11   27   jar, everted rounded recessed rim, band of impressed decoration on ext. lip

7   2912   1076   3/12   27   jar, everted rounded rim, band of impressed decoration on ext. lip

8   61   0000   0000   27   jar, vertical bevelled rim, impressed bands of decoration on ext. lip and on shoulder

9   63   0000   0000   27   jar, in sloping int. recessed rounded/bevelled rim, bands of impressed decoration on ext. lip and on shoulder

Fig. 204. Everted and vertical rim jars (genres 28 and 29)

1   1255   2036   3/13   28   vertical perforated spout, flaring profile, front decorated and moulded to represent a face

2   2588   1076   3/12   28   jar, everted pointed rim, vertical flared false spout on shoulder, rounded body, probably omphaloid base (cf. Fig. 110), two round lugs on shoulder, two rounded ledge handles at waist, made in two halves. scars of join visible, ext. body and int. lip red burnished

3   906   4070   3/11   28   vertical flared perforated spout, ext. red burnished

4   2358   2047   3/11   28   jar, everted pointed rim, sharp int. carination at neck/shoulder, vertical partly perforated flared spout on shoulder, round body, ext. red burnished

5   1468   4020   3/11   28   jar, everted rounded rim, sharp carination at neck/shoulder, ext. red burnished

6   2338   2047   3/11   28   jar, everted pointed rim, ext. body and int. lip red burnished

7   97   0000   0000   28   jar, everted pointed rim, sharp carination at neck/shoulder, ext. body and int. lip red burnished

8   7984   2107   3/11   28   jar, everted pointed rim, int. carination at neck/shoulder, ext. body and int. lip red burnished

9   5681   4088   3/12   29   jar, near vertical rounded rim, ext. rim/neck finely grooved, ext. 'grain-wash' (?)

10   83   0000   0000   29   jar, slightly in sloping rounded rim

11	1601	4072	3/11	29	jar, vertical rounded rim, ext. groove about neck, 'grain -wash' ext. body and int. lip
12	1377	2107	3/11	29	jar, slightly in sloping rounded rim, banded 'grain-wash' ext. body and int. lip
13	138	0000	0000	29	jar, everted rounded/pointed rim, ext. body and int. lip 'grain-wash' (stance? cf. TUH204.11)
14	1094	4025	3/11	29	jar, near vertical rounded rim on slightly 'bowed' neck, reddish slip int./ext.
15	2309	4027	4/15	29	jar, vertical rounded rim on short neck, reddish slip int./ext.
16	1306	4019	3/11	29	jar, everted rounded/pointed rim on slightly in sloping short neck, banded 'grain-wash int./ext.
17	2860	1075	3/12	29	jar, everted rounded rim on near vertical neck, band of red paint about ext. lip, ext. traces of 'grain-wash'

Fig. 205. High-necked jars (genre 30)

1	1546	4053	2/1		jar, everted rounded slightly bulbous rim on tall 'bowed' neck, sharp carination at neck/shoulder, loop handle(s?) at neck/shoulder junction, surface int. and ext. red slipped and red polished
2	136	1002	0000		jar, no rim, tall vertical 'bowed' neck, traces of reddish slip ext., polished
3	5830	2154	2/3	30	jar, everted straight-necked rounded rim
4	129	1001	0000	30	jar, everted rounded rim
5	3004	4125	2/2	30	jar, rounded rim on everted tall neck, slightly recessed at lip and 'bowed' in neck, ext. lip slurred, ext. traces of reddish slip
6	1275	2030	3/11	30	jar, everted rounded rim on everted tall neck
7	215	2011	0000	30	jar, everted rounded rim, ext. reddish slipped
8	1117	4025	3/11	30	jar, rounded rim on straight everted neck, ext./int. reddish burnished
9	2311	4027	4/15	30	jar, rounded rim on slightly flared everted tall neck
10	1291	4019	3/11	30	jar, slightly everted rounded rim on slightly flared neck, ext. reddish slipped
11	1265	2033	3/11	30	jar, rounded rim on slightly 'bowed' tall neck, ext. body and int. lip reddish burnished
12	401	4077	3/11	30	jar, rounded rim of out sloping slightly 'bowed' rim, ext. body and int. lip reddish burnished
13	1085	4025	3/11	30	jar, rounded/pointed rim on flared tall neck, ext. sharp inverse carination at neck/shoulder, int. slurred, ext. body and int. lip reddish slipped, ext. narrow vertical stripes in pattern burnish
14	8	0000	0000	30	jar, rounded rim on flared tall neck, ext. pattern red slipped, int. red slipped

15	603	2041	3/11	30	jar, pointed rim on slightly 'bowed' flared neck, reddish slipped int./ext.
16	1036	4022	3/11	30	jar, rounded rim on flared tall neck, int. slurred, ext. reddish slipped
17	345	1032	4/14	30	jar, rounded rim on 'bowed' tall flared neck, int. slurred, ext. reddish slipped

Fig. 206. High-necked jars (genres 31 and 32)

1	1526	4052	2/5	31	jar, rounded rim on flared neck
2	72	0000	0000	31	jar, rounded/bevelled slightly down turned rim on flared neck
3	76	0000	0000	31	jar, rounded rim on flared neck
4	2299	2049	3/11	31	jar, rounded rim on flared neck
5	916	4072	3/11	31	jar, rounded rim on flared neck, ext. neck scored
6	2488	4085	2/6	31	jar, rounded rim on flared neck
7	298	1024	4/15	31	jar, rounded rim on bulbous flared neck
8	85	0000	0000	31	jar, rounded rim on flared neck, ext. neck slurred
9	2352	2047	3/11	31	jar, everted down turned rounded rim on near vertical neck, sharp carination at neck/shoulder, int. slurred
10	1398	4018	3/11	31	jar, rounded rim on flared neck, int. scar at neck/shoulder join, ext. groove below rim, ext. splashes of red paint, int. traces of red paint
11	7985	4037	3/11	31	jar, pointed rim on flared neck
12	1311	4019	3/11	32	jar, rounded rim on 'bowed' everted neck, ext. red slipped
13	219	2013	3/11	32	jar, everted recessed rounded rim on 'bowed' everted neck, ext./int. slurred
14	1292	4019	3/11	32	jar, rounded rim on flared neck, ext. red burnished, int. slurred
15	1406	4074	3/11	32	jar, rounded rim on 'bowed' neck, sharp carination at neck/shoulder
16	1559	4047	2/10	32	jar, rounded rim on 'bowed' neck
17	2760	4125	2/2	32	jar, no rim, 'bowed' neck, high loop handle, ext. reddish slipped and painted in narrow vertical stripes
18	2716	1076	3/12	32	jar, rounded everted rim on everted 'bowed' neck, sharp carination at neck/shoulder, ext. reddish slipped, traces of burnishing, int. painted in narrow vertical stripes
19	2957	1075	3/12	32	jar, everted rounded rim on 'bowed' neck, sharp int. carination at neck/shoulder, ext. red burnished
20	2946	1075	3/12	32	jar, pointed everted rim on 'bowed' everted neck, ext. red burnished and pattern burnished in near vertical stripes
21	198	4022	3/11	32	jar, pointed everted rim on 'bowed' everted neck, int./ext. reddish slipped
22	159	0000	0000	32	jar, rounded rim on 'bowed' neck

Fig. 207. Highnecked jars (genre 33)

1	7824	50005	2/7-9		jar, everted rounded slightly recessed rim on vertical neck, sharp int. carination at neck/shoulder, rounded body, flat base, raised band of moulded decoration about neck
2	2887	50000	2/7-9		jar, everted slightly recessed rounded rim on near vertical neck, band of 'reed' impressed decoration on top of finely grooved rim and at base of neck, ext. red slipped
3	6046	2122	2/8		jar, everted slightly recessed rounded rim on near vertical neck, int. scar at neck/shoulder join, band of 'reed' impressed decoration near base of neck
4	2778	1075	3/12	33	jar, no rim, no base, rounded body, ext. red slipped and net pattern burnished to below waist, horizontal burnishing to base
5	1841	4009	4/15	33	jar, no rim, no base, rounded body, reddish slipped ext. with net pattern burnish to waist, horizontally pattern burnishing to base
6	1683	4071	3/11	33	jar, no rim, no base, ext. reddish slipped with net pattern burnishing, int. scar at neck/shoulder join
7	2971	1075	3/12	33	jar, no rim, no base, rounded body, ext. reddish burnished with net pattern burnishing to below waist, horizontal pattern burnish below
8	2923	1076	3/12	33	jar, no rim, no base, rounded body, ext. reddish slipped with net pattern burnish from neck to waist
9	1735	4005	4/15	33	jar, no rim, no base, rounded body, ext. reddish slipped with striped pattern burnish from neck to waist
10	2830	1075	3/12	33	jar base, flat, ext. reddish slipped with net pattern burnish to near base, horizontal pattern burnish below to base

Fig. 208. High-necked jars with loop handles

1	7823	30014	4/15	jar, rounded slightly down pointing rim on flared neck, 2 flattened loop handles at waist, flat base, ext. rim/neck slurred, ext. red burnished
2	358	0000	0000	jar, rounded rim on flared neck, ext. red burnished
3	184	1004	0000	jar, no rim, narrow flared neck, flat base. ext. red burnished
4	1206	4029	3/11	jar, pointed slightly everted rim on straight everted neck, flat high loop handle, ext. red burnished
5	272	4008	4/15	jar, rounded everted rim on flared neck, int. scar at neck/shoulder join, flattened high loop handle
6	4932	31005	/20	jar, no rim, tall bulbous neck, high loop handle, int. scar at neck/shoulder join

7   4933 31005 /20   jar, no rim, no base, rounded body, high loop handle, ext.
                          reddish slipped

Fig. 209. High loop-handled juglets (genres 34 and 35>)

1   3003 4125 2/2   34   juglet, no rim, high doubled loop handle, ext. painted in
                            narrow near vertical red stripes
2   5824 2141 2/7   34   juglet, no rim, flared neck, high doubled loop handle,
                            band of impressed decoration on neck
3   2993 4125 2/2   34   juglet, everted pointed rim on flared neck, no handle
                            extant, ext. painted in vertical irregular red stripes
4   1778 4039 3/13   34   juglet, no rim, high doubled loop handle, ext./int. red
                            splash painted
5   1560 4047 2/10   34   jar, juglet, no rim, high doubled loop handle, ext. red
                            splash painted
6   788   2099 2/9   34   juglet, high doubled loop handle
7   958   4043 2/10   34   juglet, high doubled loop handle
8   3987 50008 2/7-9 34   juglet, no handle extant, everted rounded rim on short
                            slightly 'bowed' rim, bagshaped body, ext. red splash
                            painted in irregular vertical stripes
9   3824 4128 2/1   34   juglet, no handle extant, everted slightly recessed rim on
                            in sloping 'bowed' neck, sharp inverse carination at
                            neck/body junction, ext. red painted with near vertical
                            stripes, int. lip red splash painted
10 3354 50006 2/7-9 34   juglet, no handle extant, everted pointed slightly
                            recessed rim on in sloping slightly 'bowed' neck, sharp
                            inverse carination at neck/high shoulder junction, finely
                            grooved ext. lip, ext. red splash painted, int. trickles of
                            red paint
11 2728 50003 2/7-9 34   juglet, no handle extant, everted slightly recessed
                            rounded rolled rim from in sloping slightly 'bowed' neck,
                            sharp inverse carination at neck/shoulder junction, ext.
                            red polished, traces of slip int.
12 99   0000 0000   35   juglet, no rim, high loop handle, flat/rounded base, ext.
                            red burnished/polished
13 1303 4019 3/11   35   juglet, rounded rim on flared neck, high flat loop handle,
                            ext. red burnished/polished
14 105   0000 0000   35   juglet, pointed/rounded rim on flared neck, sharp
                            carination at neck/shoulder, high loop handle
15 1285 4019 3/11   35   juglet, rounded/pointed slightly recessed rim on everted
                            neck, high loop handle, ext. red burnished/polished
16 170   0000 0000   35   juglet, rounded/pointed everted rim, flat high loop
                            handle, ext. reddish slipped
17 895   4070 3/11   35   juglet, no rim, high loop handle, ext. red burnished
18 337   1030 4/15   35   juglet, no rim, high loop handle, ext. red burnished

19	104	0000	0000	35	juglet, no rim, low hollow base, high loop handle from near base, ext. red burnished
20	1201	4029	3/11	35	juglet, no rim, low hollow base, high loop handle from base, ext. red burnished
21	334	4016	3/11	35	juglet, pointed everted rim on slightly in sloping neck, sharp int. carination at neck/shoulder, high loop handle from base, ext. red burnished
22	122	1001	0000	35	juglet, no rim, high loop handle, ext. red polished

Fig. 210. High loop-handled juglets (no extant handles) (genre <35)

1	2357	2047	3/11	35	juglet, pointed everted rim, sharp carination at neck/shoulder, ext. lip reddish slipped, int. lip red burnished to int. carination
2	1397	4018	3/11	35	juglet, everted rounded rim, sharp carination at neck/shoulder, ext. lip reddish slipped, ext. body red burnished, int. lip red burnished to carination
3	833	4067	3/11	35	juglet, pointed rim on vertical neck, ext./int. neck reddish slipped, ext. body red burnished
4	870	4070	3/11	35	juglet, everted rounded/pointed rim, ext. lip reddish slipped, ext. body red burnished, int. lip red burnished, int. reddish slipped
5	1864	4008	4/15	35	juglet, rounded everted slightly 'bowed' rim, ext./int. reddish slipped
6	2297	2049	3/11	35	juglet, pointed everted rim, ext. neck reddish slipped, ext. body red burnished, int. neck red burnished, rest int. red slipped
7	1290	4019	3/11	35	juglet, pointed/rounded slightly recessed rim on vertical neck, ext. neck reddish slipped, ext. body red burnished, int. reddish slipped
8	1280	2030	3/11	35	juglet, pointed everted slightly recessed rim on flared neck, ext. neck reddish slipped, ext. body red burnished, int. reddish slipped
9	1265	2033	3/11	35	juglet, rounded everted rim on flared neck, ext. neck and int. reddish slipped, ext. body red burnished
10	1396	4018	3/11	35	juglet, pointed/rounded everted rim on flared neck, ext. neck and int. reddish slipped, ext. body red burnished
11	2377	2043	3/12	35	juglet, pointed/rounded everted rim on flared neck, ext. neck and int. reddish slipped, ext. body red burnished
12	1095	4025	3/11	35	juglet, rounded rim on flared neck, ext. neck reddish slipped, ext. body red burnished

Fig. 211. shallow burnished and polished bowls (genre 36>)

1	2395	2043	3/12	36	bowl, pointed in turned rim
2	1982	1003	0000	36	bowl, rounded in turned rim
3	54	0000	0000	36	bowl, rounded in turned rim

4	440	4083	2/6	36	bowl, rounded in rolled in turned rim, red polish int./ext.
5	2120	2114	2/7	36	bowl, rounded in turned rim, reddish slipped int./ext.
6	950	4043	2/10	36	bowl, bevelled in turned rim, ext. red polished, int. reddish slipped
7	3254	1086	2/7	36	bowl, rounded in turned rim, ?flat base, red polished int./ext.
8	127	1001	0000	36	bowl, rounded in turned rim, ext. red polished
9	1258	4079	2/7	36	bowl, rounded in turned rim, red polished int./ext.
10	3256	1086	2/7	36	bowl, pointed slightly in turned rim, red polished int./ext.
11	1911	2080	2/9	36	bowl, pointed in turned rim, red polished int./ext.
12	464	2076	2/8	36	bowl, rounded near vertical rim, rounded/flattened base, reddish polished (?)
13	1224	4037	3/11	36	bowl, pointed/rounded in turned rim, ext. red polished, int. lightly red polished
14	582	2015	4/15	36	bowl, rounded in turned rim, ext. red burnished/polished, int. reddish slipped
15	1801	2052	2/9	36	bowl, rounded in turned rim, ext./int. red polished
16	2142	4048	2/10	36	bowl, pointed in turned rim, slightly thickened body to int. inverse carination below lip, ext. red polished, int. reddish slipped
17	1756	2050	2/9	36	bowl, rounded in turned rim, ext. slightly carinated at waist, ext. red polished, int. light red polished
18	167	0000	0000	36	bowl, rounded slightly in turned rim, ext. red polished
19	4349	31005	/20	36	bowl, rounded vertical rim, int./ext. red burnished/polished
20	4695	50007		36	bowl, rounded rim
21	1977	1003	0000	36	bowl, rounded rim, int. red polished
22	182	1005	0000	36	bowl, rounded rim, int./ext. red polished
23	56	0000	0000	36	bowl, rounded rim, flat base, reddish polished (?)
24	4382	4125	2/2	36	bowl, rounded slightly out rolled rim, ext. red polished
25	3690	50001	2/7-9	36	bowl, rounded/pointed rim on slightly thickened body
26	128	1001	0000	36	bowl, pointed rim
27	1180	4032	3/11	36	bowl, rounded rim, ext. red polished
28	780	4065	2/1	36	bowl, pointed rim, ext./int. slight carination at waist, ext. red polished, int. light red polished
29	2555	50000	2/79	36	bowl, pointed slightly in turned rim, ext./int. slightly carinated at waist, ext. red polished, int. light red polished
30	785	2104	2/9	36	bowl, rounded vertical rim, ext. slightly carinated at waist, ext. red polished, int. light red polished
31	1552	4053	2/1	36	bowl, rounded rim, ext. slightly carinated at waist, ext. red polished, int. light red polished

32	3098	4125	2/2	36	bowl, rounded rim, ext./int. red polished
33	3765	50007	2/7-9	36	bowl, rounded/pointed slightly in turned rim
34	429	4066	2/1	36	bowl, rounded slightly bulbous rim, rounded base, ext. light red polished, int. red polished
35	1359	4019	3/11	36	bowl, rounded rim, ext. red polished, int. light red polished

Fig. 212. shallow bowls (genres <36-38)

1	2528	2116	2/4	36	bowl, rounded slightly in turned rim ext. red polished, int. light red polished
2	2136	4045	2/4	36	bowl, rounded rim
3	1444	4075	3/11	36	bowl, rounded rim
4	443	4083	2/6	36	bowl, pointed/rounded rim
5	420	4066	2/1	36	bowl, pointed slightly in turned rim, flat/rounded base
6	744	2112	2/7	36	bowl, rounded vertical rim, int./ext. red polished
7	2422	1053	3/11	36	bowl, rounded slightly everted rim
8	2756	4125	2/2	37	bowl, pointed rim, red burnished int./ext.
9	4463	4128	2/1	37	bowl, pointed rim, red burnished int./ext., scored pattern on base
10	145	1003	0000	37	bowl pointed slightly in turned rim, red burnished int./ext.
11	4018	31012	3/14	37	bowl, rounded rim, ext. reddish slipped, int. red burnished
12	3782	50004		37	bowl, rounded vertical rim, red burnished int./ext.
13	3159	4128	2/1	37	bowl, pointed slightly recessed and in turned rim, thickened body, red burnished int./ext.
14	5960	2138	2/7	37	bowl, rounded in turned rim, red burnished int./ext.
15	5741	1068	4/15	37	bowl, pointed/rounded rim, flattened base, red burnished int./ext.
16	549	1055	3/11	37	bowl, hollow/omphaloid base only, ext. red burnished
17	859	2091	2/7	38	bowl, cut formmade (?) rim
18	5174	4101	4/-	38	bowl, cut formmade (?) rim
19	2740	50003	2/7-9	38	bowl, cut formmade (?) rim
20	4685	50007	2/7-9	38	bowl, cut formmade (?) rim, thickened body
21	4962	4128	2/1	38	bowl, cut formmade (?) rim
22	5964	2159	2/1	38	bowl, cut formmade (?) rim, ext. red burnished
23	5269	4121	2/3	38	bowl, cut formmade (?) rim, flat stance
24	3876	50007	2/7-9	38	bowl, cut formmade (?) rim

Fig. 213. Medium shallow bowls (genre 39>)

1	4944	4128	2/1	39	bowl, rounded rim
2	1670	2064	2/9	39	bowl, rounded rim
3	2428	1053	0000	39	bowl, pointed slightly int. recessed rim, ext. red burnished, traces of pattern burnish
4	4194	30016	3/14	39	bowl, pointed slightly in turned rim, ext. red burnished

5	60	0000	0000	39	bowl, rounded rim
6	4089	3200	6/18	39	bowl, rounded rim
7	7860	2160	2/1	39	bowl, rounded rim, ext. and int. lip reddish slipped
8	3579	30008	4/15	39	bowl, rounded slightly in turned rim, ext. reddish slipped
9	5966	2159	2/1	39	bowl, rounded rim
10	1895	1035	2/13	39	bowl, rounded rim, int./ext. reddish slipped
11	5120	300017		39	bowl, rounded rim, ext./int. reddish slipped
12	4456	4128	2/1	39	bowl, rounded rim, thickened body
13	7969	4055	2/6	39	bowl, rounded rim
14	1868	4008	4/15	39	bowl, pointed rim, ext. lip and int. red burnished
15	5965	2159	2/1	39	bowl, rounded rim, int. lip reddish slipped
16	8051	0000	0000	39	bowl, rounded rim
17	3224	4128	2/1	39	bowl, rounded rim, ext. red burnished, int. reddish slipped
18	3090	4125	2/2	39	bowl, rounded rim, int./ext. red burnished
19	945	4043	2/10	39	bowl, pointed/rounded rim, drilled mendhole, ext. and int. lip reddish slipped
20	1575	4056	2/1	39	bowl, rounded rim, flat disc base
21	992	4022	3/11	39	bowl, rounded rim
22	5116	30017	3/13	39	bowl, rounded rim
23	1005	4022	3/11	39	bowl, rounded rim

Fig. 214. Medium shallow bowls (genres <39-41>)

1	1054	4021	3/11	39	bowl, pointed slightly int. recessed rim
2	2816	4125	2/2	39	bowl, pointed slightly int. recessed rim, thickened body
3	1589	4054	2/1	39	bowl, pointed/rounded rim, thickened body
4	2319	4024	3/11	39	bowl, pointed rim
5	2625	1069	3/13	39	bowl, pointed slightly everted rim
6	1842	4009	4/15	39	bowl, pointed rim
7	3255	1086	2/7	39	bowl, rounded in turned rim, ext. band of 'reed' impressed decoration below lip
8	3882	50007	2/7-9	39	bowl, pointed slightly int. recessed rim
9	2551	50000	2/7-9	39	bowl, pointed in turned rim, int. lip slurred
10	58	0000	0000	39	bowl, pointed in turned rim, slightly thickened body
11	57	0000	0000	39	bowl, rounded in turned rim
12	4697	50007		39	bowl, rounded in turned rim, ext. lip slurred
13	2345	2042	3/11	39	bowl, rounded in rolled rim
14	59	0000	0000	39	bowl, rounded rim, flattened base (?), ext. carinations
15	5017	50019	2/7-9	40	bowl, rounded rim, int./ext. band of red paint on lip appended by narrow red painted vertical stripes
16	2995	4125	2/2	40	bowl, rounded in turned rim, ext./int. red stripes along lip appended by narrow red painted vertical stripes
17	3229	4128	2/1	40	bowl, bevelled in turned rim, ext. red stripe along lip appended by narrow red painted vertical stripes

18	657	4079	2/7	41	bowl, rounded in turned rim, int./ext. slurred
19	2511	4023	3/11	41	bowl, rounded slightly in turned rim, int./ext. slurred
20	433	1050	0000	41	bowl, rounded/pointed rim, int./ext. slurred
21	2853	1075	3/12	41	bowl, pointed in turned rim, int./ext. slurred
22	2697	1076	3/12	41	bowl, rounded out rolled rim, int./ext. slurred
23	994	4022	3/11	41	bowl, rounded in turned rim, flat base, int. slurred
24	3694	50001	2/7-9	41	bowl, rounded in turned rim, int./ext. reddish slipped
25	2375	2043	3/12	41	bowl, rounded in turned rim, int./ext. slurred and reddish slipped
26	1286	4019	3/11	41	bowl, rounded rim, ext. reddish slipped

Fig. 215. Bowls (genres <41-45>)

1	7896	4104	2/3	41	bowl, rounded in turned rim, ext./int. red burnished
2	343	1032	4/14	41	bowl, rounded in turned rim, int./ext. red burnished
3	884	4070	3/11	41	bowl, rounded in turned rim, ext. red burnished, int. lip reddish slipped
4	1860	4012	3/11	41	bowl, rounded in turned rim, ext. red burnished, int. lip reddish slipped
5	218	0000	0000	41	bowl, rounded in turned rim, loop handle(s?) on shoulder/waist, ext. red burnished
6	1262	2033	3/11	41	bowl, rounded in turned rim on slightly thickened body, ext. red burnished
7	733	2090	2/9	42	bowl, rounded rim, ext. vertically finger streaked and red splash painted
8	2546	0000	0000	42	bowl, rounded rim, ext./int. red splash painted
9	53	0000	0000	43	bowl, pointed in turned rim, slight carinations at waist int./ext., red burnished int./ext.
10	2463	1066	2/13	43	bowl, rounded/pointed in turned rim, slight carinations at waist, ext./int. red burnished
11	2516	4023	3/11	43	bowl, rounded slightly everted rim, slight int./ext. carinations at waist, int. red burnished
12	1006	4022	3/11	43	bowl, pointed/rounded slightly everted rim, int./ext. carinations
13	2970	1075	3/12	44	bowl, rounded (?) slightly everted rim, ext. red/brown burnished
14	2689	1076	3/12	44	bowl, rounded slightly everted rim, ext. red burnished
15	2916	1076	3/12	44	bowl, rounded slightly everted rim, ext. red burnished, int. slurred, rounded base (?)
16	2678	1076	3/12	44	bowl, rounded rim, ext. red burnished, int. lip reddish slipped
17	2919	1076	3/12	44	bowl, rounded slightly everted rim, ext. red/brown burnished
18	2519	2116	2/4	45	bowl, rounded everted down turned rim, int./ext. dark purple slip, 'Esdraelon' ware

19 2937 4125 2/2 45 bowl, rounded bevelled/recessed down turned everted rim, raised oval knobs at waist, black/purple burnished int./ext., 'Esdraelon' ware

Fig. 216. 'Esdraelon' ware bowls (genre <45)

1 1584 4054 2/1 45 bowl, rounded everted rim, ext. black burnished, 'Esdraelon' ware

2 2414 1053 0000 45 bowl, pointed everted rim, ext. black burnished, 'Esdraelon' ware

3 1646 2062 2/9 45 bowl, rounded everted rim, ext. black burnished, 'Esdraelon' ware

4 1745 2050 2/9 45 bowl, rounded everted rim, ext. black/purple burnished, 'Esdraelon' ware

5 1513 4052 2/5 45 bowl, waist, raised oval knobs, ext. black burnished, 'Esdraelon' ware

6 2520 2116 2/4 45 bowl, rounded everted down turned rim with sharp int. carination below rim, int./ext. black burnished, 'Esdraelon' ware

7 1623 4061 2/1 45 bowl, rounded everted down turned rim, ext. dark purple burnished, 'Esdraelon' ware

8 2589 4125 2/2 45 bowl, rounded/pointed everted down turned rim from sharp int. carination at lip, raised oval knobs along slightly carinated waist, flat base, int./ext. black burnished, 'Esdraelon' ware

9 2994 4125 2/2 45 bowl, rounded in turned rim, raised oval knobs below rim, int. reddish burnished, ext. grey/reddish burnished, 'Esdraelon' ware

10 3078 2156 2/2 45 bowl (?), flat base, ext. black burnished, 'Esdraelon' ware

11 2638 2153 2/4 45 bowl (?), flat slightly hollow base, ext. black burnished, 'Esdraelon' ware

Fig. 217. Bowls (genres 46-48>)

1 2990 4125 2/2 46 bowl, rounded slightly flared rim, band of small raised round knobs at waist, int./ext. red/orange burnished

2 2539 0000 0000 46 bowl, pointed bevelled rim, row of small round knobs at waist, int./ext. red/orange burnished

3 5284 2139 2/6 46 bowl, pointed rim, row of small round knobs at waist, int./ext. red/orange burnished

4 2545 0000 0000 47 bowl, pointed in turned rim from ext. carination on shoulder, round pointed knob(s?) applied to shoulder, int. red burnished

5 4702 50007 2/79 47 bowl, rounded slightly in rolled rim, down turned round pointed knob(s?) on shoulder, ext. reddish slipped

6 4789 1081 2/7 47 bowl, rounded bulbous in turned rim, rounded ledge handle(s?) on shoulder

7	4026	31012	-/-	47	bowl, rounded in turned rim, rounded shallow ledge handle(s?) at shoulder
8	7990	2154	2/3	48	bowl, rounded everted rim from int. carination below lip, ext. lip/neck slurred, ext. body diagonally finger streaked
9	2566	0000	0000	48	bowl, everted slightly bulbous down pointing rim
10	1141	4046	2/4	48	bowl, rounded everted rim, ext. body red splash painted

Fig. 218. Bowls (genre <48>)

1	2301	4044	2/5	48	bowl, rounded bevelled everted slightly bulbous rim, ext. traces of reddish (painted?) wide vertical stripes
2	5587	2136	2/6	48	bowl, rounded everted rim, ext. sharp indentation at neck/shoulder, ext. neck slurred, ext. body diagonally finger streaked
3	269	4009	4/15	48	bowl, rounded everted bulbous rim, ext. body diagonally finger streaked
4	88	0000	0000	48	bowl, rounded slightly bulbous everted rim, ext. body diagonally finger streaked
5	238	2018	4/15	48	bowl, rounded everted rim
6	2873	50000	2/7-9	48	bowl, rounded everted rim from slight int. carination below rim
7	5992	4109	2/4	48	bowl, rounded everted rim from sharp int. carination, ext. sharp indentation at neck/shoulder, Int. lip slurred, int. diagonally finger streaked
8	3516	2153	2/4	48	bowl, rounded everted rim, ext. sharp indentation at neck/shoulder, ext. lip slurred, ext. body horizontally finger streaked
9	985	4050	2/7	48	bowl, rounded everted rim from sharp int. carination, ext. sharp indentation at neck/shoulder

Fig. 219. Bowls (genre <48)

1	5261	4121	2/3	48	bowl, rounded/rolled everted rim, traces of ext. indentation at neck/shoulder, ext. body crisscrossed finger streaked
2	5585	2136	2/6	48	bowl or hmj (?), (cf. also Figs 1512), pointed everted rim from sharp int. carination, ext. sharp indentation at neck/shoulder, ext. bands of 'punctate' and grooved decoration at shoulder, ext. lip red painted, body red splash painted (stance?)
3	5771	4125	2/2	48	bowl, pointed everted down turned bevelled rim from sharp int. carination, int./ext. lip slurred, red polished
4	3105	4125	2/2	48	bowl, pointed everted flared rim from sharp int. carination, red polished
5	8052	0000	0000	48	bowl, rounded down pointing bulbous rim from sharp int. carination, red polished

6   4522 2154 2/3   48 bowl, bowl, rounded recessed rim from sharp int.
                           carination
7   2129 4051 2/10 48 bowl, rounded slightly recessed everted rim from sharp
                           int. carination, rim red painted, red splash painted
                           int./ext.

Fig. 220. Bowls (genres 49 and 6 [cf. Figs 146-7])

1   4951 4128 2/1   49 bowl, rounded everted rim
2   4852 2148 2/5   49 bowl, pointed everted rim, band of incised/impressed
                           decoration about waist
3   6075 2135 2/8   6   bowl, rounded bevelled everted rim, ledge below ext.
                           rim
4   1790 4039 3/13 6   bowl, rounded bevelled everted rim from int. carination,
                           ext. traces of light reddish paint or slip
5   1796 4039 3/13 6   bowl, rounded doubly recessed everted rim on bulbous
                           neck, sharp ext. indentation below rim
6   4346 2148 2/5   6   bowl, bevelled rim on bulbous neck, ext. band of
                           impressed decoration below rim, pushed
                           up rounded lugs below rim
7   3546 1079 3/11 6   bowl, (stance?), bevelled slightly recessed rim on bulbous
                           neck, ext. groove or sharp
                           indentation below rim

Fig. 221. Heavy bowls with moulded decoration (genre 50>)

1   2476 4077 3/11 50 bowl, rounded bevelled rim, band of impressed
                           decoration along ext. lip
2   1214 4037 3/11 50 bowl, rounded/bevelled rim, bands of impressed
                           decoration along int./ext. lip
3   25   0000 0000 50 bowl, bevelled slightly in turned rim, band of impressed
                           decoration along ext. lip
4   597   1054 3/13 50 bowl, rounded recessed in turned rim, band of
                           impressed decoration along ext. lip
5   1428 4073 3/11 50 bowl, recessed splayed slightly in turned rim, band of
                           impressed decoration below ext. rim
6   353   1034 4/14 50 bowl, rounded recessed in turned splayed rim, bands of
                           impressed decoration along ext. lip and below rim
7   28   0000 0000 50 bowl, rounded recessed in turned splayed rim, bands of
                           impressed decoration along ext. lip
                           and below rim
8   35   0000 0000 50 bowl, rounded recessed in turned splayed rim, bands of
                           impressed decoration along ext. lip
                           and below rim
9   2534 0000 0000 50 bowl, rounded bevelled inturned splayed rim, band of
                           impressed decoration below ext. rim

Fig. 222. Heavy bowls with moulded decoration (genre <50>)

1	2346	2047	3/11	50	bowl, rounded rilled splayed rim, bands of impressed decoration along ext. lip and below rim
2	290	4007	4/15	50	bowl, rounded recessed in turned splayed rim, bands of impressed decoration along ext. lip and below rim
3	1229	4037	3/11	50	bowl, rounded bevelled in turned splayed rim, bands of impressed decoration along ext. lip and below rim
4	30	0000	0000	50	bowl, rounded recessed in turned splayed rim, bands of impressed decoration along ext. lip and below rim
5	2401	4036	3/11	50	bowl, rounded recessed in turned splayed rim, band of impressed decoration along ext. lip and below rim
6	1188	4029	3/11	50	bowl, rounded recessed in turned splayed rim, bands of impressed decoration along ext. lip and below rim
7	39	0000	0000	50	bowl, recessed in turned splayed rim, band of impressed decoration along ext. lip
8	33	0000	0000	50	bowl, rounded recessed in turned splayed rim, band of impressed decoration along ext. lip and band of impressed decoration diagonally across waist

Fig. 223. Heavy bowls with moulded decoration (genres <50 and 51)

1	47	0000	0000	50	bowl, rounded bevelled/recessed in turned splayed rim, ext. raised band of decoration
2	1028	4022	3/11	50	bowl, splayed in turned rim, bands of impressed decoration along ext. lip and in horizontal rows below rim
3	34	0000	0000	50	bowl, bevelled in turned splayed rim, bands of impressed decoration along int. and ext. lip and below ext. rim
4	1726	1034	4/14	50	bowl, rounded recessed in turned splayed rim, bands of impressed decoration on ext. lip and below rim
5	21	0000	0000	50	bowl, rounded recessed in turned splayed rim, bands of impressed decoration along ext. lip and below rim
6	2318	4024	3/11	50	bowl, rounded recessed splayed rim, impressed decoration along ext. lip and below rim
7	7986	1004	0000	51	bowl, recessed rim, band of impressed decoration beneath ext. rim

8	31	0000	0000	51	bowl, rounded in rolled rim, raised band of impressed decoration under ext. rim
9	2699	1076	3/12	51	bowl, rounded recessed splayed rim, ext. groove under rim, ext. raised band of impressed decoration
10	37	0000	0000	51	bowl, bevelled /rounded rim, ext. raised band of impressed decoration
11	4142	1078	3/12	51	bowl, recessed in turned splayed rim, ext raised band of impressed decoration
12	8053	0000	0000	51	bowl, rounded recessed in turned splayed rim, ext. raised band of impressed decoration

Fig. 224. Bowls (genres 52 - 54>)

1	4081	32006	-/18	52	bowl, out rolled rim on everted slightly bulbous body, ext. carination, int. reddish slipped
2	7952	0000	0000	52	bowl, beaded slightly recessed everted rim
3	2973	1075	3/12	52	bowl, beaded slightly recessed rim
4	746	2112	2/7	52	bowl, rounded/bevelled slightly everted rim
5	1530	4045	2/4	52	bowl, beaded slightly everted rim
6	2989	4125	2/2	52	bowl, rounded/bevelled slightly everted rim
7	4955	4128	2/1	53	bowl, rounded/bevelled rim, int. 'crazed'
8	3355	50006	2/7-9	53	bowl, rounded rim, high doubled loop handle, int. lip reddish slipped, int. 'crazed'
9	3049	4125	2/2	53	bowl, rounded rim, int. 'crazed'
10	2784	50001	2/7-9	53	bowl, rounded in turned rim with slight ext. carination, high doubled loop handle, int. lip reddish slipped, int. 'crazed'
11	3350	50006		53	bowl, beaded in turned rim, int. 'crazed'
12	3383	4117	2/4	53	bowl, beaded slightly everted rim, int. 'crazed'
13	1045	2117	2/7	54	bowl, pointed everted rim, int. lip scored, rounded base, int. 'crazed'
14	702	2093	2/9	54	bowl, pointed everted recessed rim, int. lip scored, int. 'crazed'
15	1407	4074	3/11	54	bowl, pointed everted recessed rim, int. lip scored, int. 'crazed'
16	1753	2050	2/9	54	bowl, pointed everted recessed rim, int. lip scored, int. 'crazed'
17	7987	2127	2/8	54	bowl, pointed everted recessed rim, int. lip scored, int. 'crazed'
18	4636	50006	2/7-9	54	bowl, pointed everted recessed rim, int. lip scored, int. 'crazed'
19	4629	50006	2/7-9	54	bowl, pointed everted recessed rim, int. lip scored, int. 'crazed'
20	1583	4056	2/1	54	bowl, pointed everted recessed rim, int. lip scored, int. 'crazed'

21	1674	2086	2/7	54	bowl, pointed everted recessed rim, int. lip scored, int. 'crazed'
22	8054	0000	0000	54	bowl, pointed everted recessed rim, int. lip scored, int. 'crazed'
23	1635	2062	2/9	54	bowl, pointed everted recessed rim, int. lip scored, int. 'crazed'
24	2323	4024	3/11	54	bowl, pointed everted recessed rim, int. lip scored, int. 'crazed'
25	166	0000	0000	54	bowl, pointed everted recessed rim, int. lip scored, int. 'crazed'

Fig. 225. Bowls (genre <54)

1	1230	4037	3/11	54	bowl, pointed everted recessed rim, int. lip scored, int. 'crazed'
2	1489	4057	2/5	54	bowl, pointed everted recessed rim, int. lip scored, int. 'crazed'
3	1922	2065	2/7	54	bowl, pointed everted recessed rim, int. lip scored, int. 'crazed'
4	1499	4058	2/1	54	bowl, pointed everted recessed rim, int. lip scored, int. 'crazed'
5	5849	2118	2/9	54	bowl, pointed everted recessed rim, int. lip scored, int. 'crazed'
6	712	2095	3/11	54	bowl, pointed everted recessed rim, int. lip scored, int. 'crazed'
7	51	0000	0000	54	bowl, pointed everted recessed rim, int. lip scored, int. 'crazed'
8	351	1034	4/14	54	bowl, pointed everted recessed rim, int. lip scored, int. 'crazed'
9	7988	0000	0000	54	bowl, pointed everted recessed rim, int. lip scored, int. 'crazed'
10	737	2090	2/9	54	bowl, pointed everted recessed rim, int. lip scored, int. 'crazed'
11	2942	1075	3/12	54	bowl, pointed everted recessed rim, int. lip scored, int. 'crazed'
12	8055	4043	2/10	54	bowl, pointed everted recessed rim, int. lip scored, int. 'crazed'
13	1636	2062	2/9	54	bowl, pointed everted recessed rim, int. lip scored, int. 'crazed'
14	752	2112	2/7	54	bowl, pointed everted recessed rim, int. lip scored, int. 'crazed'
15	800	2105	2/9	54	bowl, pointed everted recessed rim, int. lip scored, int. 'crazed'
16	640	4069	3/11	54	bowl, pointed everted recessed rim, int. lip scored, int. 'crazed'

17	713	2095	3/11	54	bowl, pointed everted recessed rim, int. lip scored, int. 'crazed'
18	55	0000	0000	54	bowl, pointed everted recessed rim, int. lip scored, int. 'crazed', flat base
19	2108	4081	2/6	54	bowl, pointed everted recessed rim, int. lip scored, int. 'crazed', rounded base (?)
20	1496	4058	2/1	54	bowl, pointed everted recessed rim, int. lip scored, int. 'crazed'
21	2472	4077	3/11	54	bowl, pointed everted recessed rim, int. lip scored, int. 'crazed'
22	50	0000	0000	54	bowl, pointed everted recessed rim, int. lip scored, int. 'crazed'
23	685	2093	2/9	54	bowl, pointed everted recessed rim, int. lip scored, int. 'crazed'
24	2376	2043	3/12	54	bowl, pointed everted recessed rim, int. lip scored, int. 'crazed'
25	525	2061	2/8	54	bowl, pointed everted recessed rim, int. lip scored, int. 'crazed'
26	2456	2066	2/8	54	bowl, pointed everted recessed rim, int. lip scored, int. 'crazed'
27	2302	4044	2/5	54	bowl, rounded thickened rim, int. lip scored, int. 'crazed'
28	1314	4019	3/11	54	bowl, pointed everted recessed rim, int. lip scored, int. 'crazed'
29	3171	4128	2/1	54	bowl, rounded thickened rim, int. 'crazed'

Fig. 226. Bowls (genres 55 and 56)

1	3669	4128	2/1	55	bowl, pointed everted recessed rim, int./ext. lip red painted with appended narrow vertical red stripes
2	1426	4073	3/11	55	bowl, pointed everted recessed rim, rounded base, int. ext. lip painted red, ext. red painted stripes to base
3	993	4022	3/11	55	bowl, pointed everted recessed rim, rounded base, int./ext. red painted narrow vertical stripes
4	2495	4033	3/11	55	bowl, everted pointed recessed rim, ext./int. lip slurred, int. red painted pattern from lip, ext. narrow red painted vertical stripes
5	1048	4021	3/11	55	bowl, everted pointed recessed rim, rounded base, ext. criss-crossed narrow painted stripes from lip to over base
6	287	4013	3/11	55	bowl, rounded everted recessed rim, int./ext. lip slurred, ext. vertical red painted stripes
7	5029	50019	2/7-9	55	bowl, pointed slightly recessed rim, ext. red stripe along lip with appended narrow red

					painted vertical lines, int. vertical red painted lines
8	1059	4021	3/11	55	bowl, rounded everted recessed rim, int. lip and ext. body slipped, ext. vertical and criss crossed red painted lines
9	3642	40008		56	bowl, rounded recessed rim, int. lip reddish slipped
10	3736	2152	2/5	56	bowl, pointed everted rim, int./ext. lip slurred, rounded base (?)
11	3520	2153	2/4	56	bowl, rounded recessed rim, rounded base (?)
12	4448	4128	2/1	56	bowl, rounded recessed rim, in./ext. lip reddish slipped, traces of slip int./ext. body
13	7678	31021	4/16	56	bowl, rounded recessed in turned rim, int. slipped
14	5652	2146	2/6	56	bowl, rounded everted rim
15	5677	4088	3/12	56	bowl, everted rounded recessed rim
16	2156	4048	2/10	56	bowl, rounded everted recessed rim
17	6124	2134	2/6	56	bowl, rounded everted recessed rim
18	854	2115	2/6	56	bowl, rounded everted rim with int. ridge
19	8056	0000	0000	56	bowl, rounded/pointed everted rim, int. lip and ext. body reddish slipped
20	216	2011	0000	56	bowl, rounded everted rim, int./ext. reddish slipped
21	2533	0000	0000	56	bowl, rounded everted recessed rim, int. reddish slipped, ext. red burnished
22	872	4070	3/11	56	bowl, rounded everted recessed rim, int./ext. red burnished
23	3065	2153	2/4	56	bowl, rounded everted recessed rim, int./ext. red burnished
24	598	1054	3/13	56	bowl, rounded everted slightly splayed rim
25	1313	4019	3/11	56	bowl, rounded everted recessed rim, int./ext. reddish slipped
26	4767	50001	2/7-9	56	rounded recessed rim
27	2440	4031	3/11	56	bowl, rounded everted recessed rim, int. lip and ext. red burnished, int. reddish slipped

Fig. 227. Bowls and platters (genres 57-59>)

1	1631	4061	2/1	57	bowl, rounded vertical rim with ext. recess, int./ext. red burnished
2	3845	4126	2/1	57	bowl, rounded vertical rim with ext. recess, int./ext. reddish slipped
3	123	1101	0000	58	bowl, rounded everted rim, double carination ext. waist, int./ext. red burnished
4	131	1002	0000	58	bowl, rounded everted rim, carination at waist, int. slurred, ext. red burnished
5	223	2013	3/11	58	bowl, rounded everted rim, double ext. carination at waist, int./ext. red burnished
6	1816	2018	4/15	58	bowl, rounded (?) everted rim, carination at waist, ext. red burnished

7 2104 1043 4/15 58 bowl, rounded everted rim, ext. carination, ext. red burnished

8 4654 31006 -/- 58 bowl, rounded everted rim, carination at waist, ext. reddish slipped, int. red burnished

9 1242 2036 3/13 58 bowl, rounded (?) everted rim, ext. carination

10 7931 0000 0000 58 bowl, rounded everted rim, ext. carination

11 278 4011 3/13 59 platter, pointed rim, sharp ext. carination, int. groove at base of lip, ext. grooves beneath carination

12 361 0000 0000 59 platter, rounded rim, carinated, int./ext. red burnished

13 3570 30008 4/15 59 platter, pointed/rounded rim, sharp carination, narrow int. groove at base of lip, int./ext. sharp carination, int./ext. red burnished

14 4102 30008 4/15 59 platter, rounded near vertical rim, sharp carination, int./ext. red burnished, int. radial pattern burnish

15 5213 31009 4/15 59 platter, rounded in rolled thickened rim, sharp carination, int./ext. red burnished

16 2537 0000 0000 59 platter, rounded thickened rim, ext. carination, int./ext. red burnished

17 608 1045 0000 59 platter, rounded rim, int. carination, int./ext. red burnished

Fig. 228. Platters (genre <59>)

1 7956 0000 0000 59 platter, rounded rim, on splayed body, int./ext. grooves at rim/body junction, int./ext. red burnished

2 291 4007 4/15 59 platter rounded rim, double ext. carination, ext. red burnished

3 7957 0000 0000 59 platter, rounded rim, int./ext. red burnished

4 5430 3201 6/17 59 platter, rounded in turned rim, flat base, horizontally pierced down turned lug at waist, int./ext. red burnished

5 1894 1033 4/14 59 platter, no rim, carination, down turned horizontally pierced lug at waist, ext. red burnished

6 349 1033 4/14 59 platter, no rim, carination, down turned horizontally pierced lug at waist, ext./int. red burnished with radial pattern burnish int., net pattern burnish ext. body

7 250 4002 4/15 59 platter, no rim, carination, down turned horizontally pierced lug at waist, ext. red burnished

8 1898 2000 0000 59 platter, rounded rim, carination, int./ext. red burnished

9 248 4002 4/15 59 platter, rounded rim, carination

10	205	2010	0000	59	platter, rounded rim, carination
11	2435	1062	0000	59	platter, rounded slightly everted rim/neck, carination, int. red burnished and pattern burnished, ext. red burnished
12	249	4002	4/15	59	rounded vertical rim, carination, ext. red burnished, int. slurred
13	2011	2011	0000	59	platter, rounded everted vertical rim, carination, ext. red burnished

Fig. 229. Platters (genre <59)

1	7955	0000	0000	59	platter, sloping rounded 'hammer' rim, int./ext. red burnished
2	147	1003	0000	59	platter, sloping rounded 'hammer' rim, int./ext. red burnished
3	6859	30012	4/15	59	platter, rounded in turned slightly recessed rim, carination, ext. body and int. lip red burnished, int. red pattern burnished
4	3297	30006	/17	59	platter, rounded inturned recessed splayed rim , drilled mend hole, ext. reddish slipped, int. red burnished
5	508	1052	3/13	59	platter, rounded sloping 'hammer' rim
6	3727	40016	-/-	59	platter, rounded in turned recessed splayed rim, int./ext. reddish slipped
7	3725	40016	-/-	59	rounded in and down turned recessed rim, int./ext. reddish slipped
8	360	0000	0000	59	platter, rounded splayed 'hammer' rim, int./ext. red burnished
9	3712	40016	-/-	59	platter, pointed recessed splayed rim
10	3713	40016	-/-	59	platter, rounded 'hammer' rim, ext. red burnished
11	4013	32007	-/18	59	platter, rounded 'hammer' rim on rounded in turned body, int./ext. red burnished

Fig. 230. Bowls (genre 60)

1	161	1004	0000	60	bowl, rounded everted rim ext. recessed, ext. reddish pattern slipped, int. reddish slipped
2	100	1000	0000	60	bowl, everted rounded rim ext. recessed
3	3584	30008	4/15	60	bowl, in turned rounded everted rim ext. recessed
4	3620	31003	-/17	60	bowl, rounded everted rim from sharp ext. indentation, int./ext. reddish slipped
5	3571	30008	4/15	60	bowl, rounded in turned rim from ext. high rounded indented shoulder
6	3466	30011	4/15	60	bowl, rounded everted ext. recessed rim, int./ext. dark red burnished
7	3475	30013	4/15	60	bowl, rounded everted rim ext. recessed, int./ext. reddish slipped

8	1376	2107	3/11	bowl, rounded splayed rim, ext. body and int. lip red burnished, traces of red slip int.
9	2691	1076	3/12	bowl, rounded everted 'hammer' rim
10	1981	1003	0000	bowl, rounded 'hammer' rim
11	506	1052	3/13	bowl, rounded 'hammer' rim
12	2505	4023	3/11	bowl, rounded recessed 'hammer' rim
13	1386	2107	3/11	bowl, rounded recessed ('hammer') rim, int./ext. reddish slipped

Fig. 231. Bowls

1	772	4065	2/1		conical bowl, rounded everted rim, int. ledge, ext. groove below lip
2	5035	50019	2/7-9		conical bowl, rounded slightly bulbous rim/neck
3	3302	50006	2/7-9		conical/rounded bowl, everted rounded out rolled rim, int. diagonally finger streaked
4	5074	32001	-/20		conical bowl, rounded rim, ext. lip reddish slipped, int. red burnished
5	805	0000	0000		conical bowl, rounded slightly recessed rim
6	1574	4056	2/1		conical bowl, rounded slightly bulbous rim
7	3606	40014	-/-		conical bowl, rounded/pointed rim
8	3608	40014	-/-		bowl, rounded rim, traces of ext. carination
9	1450	4075	3/11	[4]	bowl, recessed rim, band of impressed 'wavy' decoration along ext. lip
10	1223	4037	3/11		bowl, rounded recessed 'hammer' rim, ext. rounded knob below lip
11	5166	41014	-/-		bowl, recessed rounded rim, band of impressed decoration ext. lip
12	4232	40002	-/-		bowl, recessed rounded rim, ext. rounded knob below lip
13	7938	0000	0000		bowl, recessed rounded in rolled rim, ext. rounded knob under lip
14	210	2011	0000		bowl, rounded pointed sloping 'hammer' rim on bulbous neck
15	257	2020	0000		bowl, bevelled/recessed splayed in turned rim, loop handle at lip
16	300	1024	4/15		bowl, rounded pointed splayed rim, loop handle at rim

Fig. 232. Bowls

1	5188	50009	2/7-9	bowl, bevelled rim slightly out rolled, ext. red burnished
2	5500	2118	2/9	bowl, rounded pointed slightly splayed rim, band of 'reed' impressed decoration on ext. lip
3	5305	4121	2/3	conical bowl, rounded rim
4	8058	0000	0000	bowl/platter, rounded vertical rim
5	2431	1053	0000	platter, rounded rim, int./ext. reddish slipped
6	144	1003	0000	platter, pointed rim, carination, int./ext. reddish slipped
7	2841	1075	3/12	bowl, rounded in turned rim, ext. red burnished

8	4016	31012	3/14	bowl, rounded slightly recessed rim, int./ext. reddish slipped
9	4792	1067	4/15	bowl, rounded rim, int./ext. red burnished
10	318	4015	3/11	platter, rounded in turned rim, carination, ext. red burnished
11	161	1004	0000	bowl, rounded in turned rim, carination, band of impressed decoration ext. waist

Fig. 233. Bowls (genre 61)

1	1441	4075	3/11	[13] bowl, rounded ext. slightly recessed or grooved rim, ext. body and int. lip. 'grain wash'
2	5548	2145	2/6	bowl, rounded in turned rim
3	4128	50002	2/7-9	bowl, pointed in turned rim with ext. shallow grooves on lip
4	674	4068	3/11	[13] bowl, rounded in turned bulbous rim, int./ext. reddish burnished
5	4903	50011	2/7-9	bowl, rounded in and down rolled rim
6	7876	50003	2/7-9	bowl, rounded rim
7	4704	50007	2/7-9	bowl, rounded in pointed rim, ext. body and int. lip reddish slipped
8	4216	30007	4/15	61 bowl, rounded everted (out rolled) rim, high carinated/indented shoulder, ext. body and int. lip reddish slipped
9	5281	2139	2/6	61 bowl, rounded everted rim, high rounded shoulder, int./ext. red burnished
10	2458	1066	3/13	[58] bowl, rounded out rolled rim, ext. lip/neck red burnished, body slipped
11	162	1004	0000	bowl, everted rounded rim, ext. body and int. lip reddish slipped
12	1272	2034	3/13	bowl, everted rounded recessed rim
13	1943	2001	0000	bowl, everted rounded rim, int./ext. red burnished

Fig. 234. Bowls

1	29	0000	0000	bowl, recessed int. lipped rim, ext. band of impressed decoration on shoulder
2	700	2093	2/9	[4] bowl, bevelled in turned rim
3	8059	4109	2/4	bowl, recessed in turned rim on splayed neck/shoulder, ext. shoulder slurred, ext. band of impressed decoration on waist
4	2356	2047	3/11	bowl, rounded out rolled rim
5	7989	4128	2/1	bowl, pointed in turned rim from recessed high shoulder and carination, ext. lip red painted with appended irregular narrow vertical red painted stripes

6   3554 1079 3/12   bowl, everted pointed rim on high sharply indented
                            shoulder

Fig. 235. Spouts (genres 62 and 63) and 'churns'

1   4658 31006 -/20 62 flared spout, ext. slipped and painted with red stripes
2   2763 1075 3/12 62 spout, ext. red burnished
3   2556 50000 2/79 62 spout
4   3632 30005 /17/ 63 long spout, red burnished
5   1215 4037 3/11 63 long spout, red burnished
6   432   1050 0000 63 long down turned spout, red burnished
7   3236 4124 2/1   63 long up turned spout, red burnished
8   165   0000 0000   hmj/deep bowl, bevelled in turned rim, large 'trumpet'
                            spout beneath rim, int. lip and int.
                            lip of spout red painted, ext. traces of crisscross red
                            painted narrow lines
9   406   4077 3/11   rounded in turned rim, spout beneath lip, ext. int. vessel
                            red burnished
10   5796 2135 2/8
11   7822 0000 0000   'churn', flat end, loop handle mounted across axis of
                            vessel
12   7911 0000 0000   'churn', flat end, loop handle mounted across axis of
                            vessel
13   350   1034 4/14   loop handle (of 'churn'?)
14   1453 4020 3/11   loop handle (of 'churn'?), patched rounded perforation
                            beside handle

Fig. 236. Rounded horizontal decorated ledge handles (genre 64)

1   118   0000 0000 64 band of impressed decoration on edge
2   1547 4053 2/1   64 incised band of decoration on edge
3   2304 4044 2/5   64 band of impressed decoration on edge
4   771   4065 2/1   64 incised band of decoration on edge
5   5363 2134 2/6   64 band of impressed decoration on edge
6   1498 4058 2/1   64 handle slightly up turned, band of impressed decoration
                            on edge
7   8060 0000 0000 64 handle slightly up turned, band of impressed decoration
                            on edge
8   819   2089 2/9   64 heavy band of impressed decoration on edge
9   2517 4023 3/11 64 heavy band of impressed decoration on edge

Fig. 237. Ledge handles (genres 65 and 66)

1   5693 2127 2/8   65 slim rounded wavy edged handle
2   3894 50007 2/7-9 65 slim rounded wavy edged handle
3   868   2088 2/9   65 slim rounded wavy edged handle, vertical red painted
                            stripes on body of vessel and over
                            handle

4	5177	50009	2/7-9	65	slim rounded wavy edged handle
5	4507	4117	2/4	66	rounded up turned handle, incised decoration along edge and in arc above handle, splash painted and finger streaked
6	4293	2156	2/2	66	rounded up turned handle, incised decoration along edge and in arc above handle, splash painted stripes
7	2582	0000	0000	66	rounded up turned handle, incised decoration along edge and in arc above handle

Fig. 238. Rounded up turned ledge handles (genres 67 - <69>)

1	1784	4039	3/13	67	plain
2	3755	50007	2/7-9	67	plain
3	581	2078	2/10	67	plain
4	1205	4029	3/11	67	plain, stampseal impression on top
5	5287	4107	2/5	68	band of impressed decoration along edge and in arc above on body
6	2586	0000	0000	68	band of impressed decoration along edge and in arc above on body
7	7948	0000	0000	68	band of impressed decoration along edge
8	3758	50007	2/7-9	68	band of impressed decoration along edge
9	853	2115	2/6	69	arc of impressed decoration above handle on body
10	111	0000	0000	69	plain

Fig. 239. Ledge handles (genres <69 - 71)

1	8029	0000	0000	69	plain, end bulbous, finger streaked beneath
2	2486	4085	2/6	69	red painted stripes and finger streaking
3	6122	2118	2/9	69	red splash painted
4	2714	1076	3/12	69	red splash and stripe painted
5	2583	0000	0000	70	thin profiled scalloped beneath, arc of impressed ovals beneath
6	1600	2106	2/6	70	thin profiled scalloped beneath, arc of impressed ovals beneath
7	476	2051	2/9	70	thin profiled scalloped beneath, arc of impressed ovals beneath, wavy edge
8	7979	0000	0000	70	thin profiled scalloped beneath, arc of impressed ovals beneath, band of impressed decoration along edge, red painted stripes on body of vessel
9	307	1026	4/15	70	thin profiled scalloped beneath, arc of impressed ovals beneath, wavy edge, red splash painted
10	2581	0000	0000	71	lump handle

Fig. 240. Handles (genres 72 and 73)

| 1 | 1115 | 4025 | 3/11 | 72 | horizontally pierced lug on shoulder of vessel |

2	1250	2036	3/13	72	horizontally pierced lug on shoulder of vessel, ext. red burnished
3	1614	4072	3/11	72	horizontally pierced lug on shoulder of vessel
4	831	4085	2/6	72	loop handle
5	2098	2111	2/7	72	thick loop handle
6	457	1052	3/13	72	horizontally pierced lug on shoulder of vessel
7	101	1000	0000	72	horizontally pierced lug on shoulder of vessel
8	1040	4022	3/11	72	thick loop handle, body of vessel criss-cross pattern burnished
9	2460	1066	3/13	72	horizontally pierced lug on shoulder of vessel
10	2289	2049	3/11	72	vertically pierced lug, red burnished
11	7964	4016	3/11	72	horizontally pierced lug on shoulder of vessel, red burnished
12	892	4070	3/11	72	horizontally pierced lug on shoulder of vessel, red burnished
13	557	1065	2/7	72	vertically double pierced lug, vessel red burnished with stripy pattern burnish
14	4408	1080	3/11	73	horizontal ledge handle with band of incised decoration along edge, decoration runs onto body of vessel
15	116	0000	0000	73	up turned rounded ledge handle, band of impressed decoration along edge continuing in bands over body of vessel

Fig. 241. Ledge handles (genres 74 - 76)

1	1052	4021	3/11	74	rounded slightly up turned, 'grain wash'
2	505	1052	3/13	74	rounded thin, oval blank stamped impression on top, 'grain wash'
3	252	4022	4/15	74	rounded up turned, scalloped beneath, red burnished
4	2298	2049	3/11	74	rounded up turned slightly bulbous, red painted stripes
5	264	4005	4/15	74	rounded up turned, traces of three oval impressions beneath
6	157	1004	0000	75	rounded up turned wavy edge, flat base
7	357	0000	0000	76	rounded up turned wavy and impressed edge
8	4544	1077	3/12	76	rounded wavy/impressed edge
9	3426	60013	-/-	76	rounded up turned wavy/impressed edge
10	348	1032	4/14	76	rounded, impressed band along edge

Fig. 242. Handles (genres 77 and 78)

1	2139	4045	2/4	77	pushed up rounded lug, red splash painted and finger streaked
2	1518	4052	2/5	77	pushed up rounded lug, stabbed pattern
3	1836	4009	4/15		doubled loop handle
4	1625	4061	2/1		up turned indented lug
5	2936	4125	2/2	[78]	flattened loop handle on waist of vessel, red burnished

6	973	4043	2/10	[78]	flattened high loop handle, red burnished
7	803	2105	2/9	[78]	flattened high loop handle, red burnished
8	1019	4022	3/11	[78]	flattened high loop handle, red burnished
9	7980	0000	0000		rounded scalloped beneath, wavy impressed pattern on edge
10	2585	0000	0000		rounded up turned edge, plain
11	7981	0000	0000		rounded up turned scalloped beneath, wavy/impressed on edge
12	3794	30004	-/17		rounded horizontal, pushed up impressed decoration on edge
13	3183	30004	-/17		[EB IV] vestigial' ledge handle, impressed design
14	356	0000	0000		rounded horizontal, wavy pushed up impressed design along edge, traces of red paint on white slip

Fig. 243. Decorated body sherds (genres 79 - 81)

1	1143	4046	2/4	79	red splash paint, finger streaked
2	1216	4037	3/11	79	red splash paint, finger streaked
3	3219	1084	2/7	79	red splash paint, raised band of impressed decoration
4	2669	4125	2/2	79	red splash paint, band of impressed decoration
5	2891	50001	2/7-9	79	red splash paint, finger streaked, band of impressed decoration
6	2134	2055	2/9	79	red splash paint, finger streaked, band of impressed decoration
7	7975	0000	0000	79	red splash paint, finger streaked, band of impressed decoration
8	3054	4125	2/2	80	raised band of impressed decoration
9	5314	2123	2/9	80	raised band of impressed decoration, black burnished
10	2577	0000	0000	80	raised band of impressed decoration
11	1698	2097	2/7	81	variant of genre 79
13	2127	2059	2/10	81	variant of genre 79
14	1591	4054	2/1	81	variant of genre 79
15	1916	2080	2/9	81	variant of genre 79
16	946	4043	2/10	81	variant of genre 79
17	1602	4072	3/11	81	variant of genre 79
18	974	4043	2/10	81	variant of genre 79

Fig. 244. Decorated body sherds (genres 82 - 84, 33)

1	1814	2018	4/15	82	raised band(s) of 'reed' impressed decoration, red painted vertical stripes
2	588	2075	2/10	82	raised band(s) of 'reed' impressed decoration, red painted vertical stripes
3	7960	2071	2/9	82	raised band(s) of 'reed' impressed decoration, red painted vertical stripes
4	1177	4032	3/11	82	raised band(s) of 'reed' impressed decoration
5	7962	0000	0000	82	double raised band of 'reed' impressed decoration

6	7963	0000	0000	82	double raised band(s) of 'reed' impressed decoration, one band in 'chevron' pattern
7	2023	4002	4/15	33	red criss-cross pattern burnished
8	8061	0000	0000	83	'grain wash'
9	1486	4020	3/11	33	red criss-cross pattern burnished
10	580	2078	2/10	84	bands of impressed decoration
11	2574	0000	0000	84	bands of impressed decoration
12	2475	4077	3/11	84	bands of impressed decoration
13	7977	0000	0000	84	bands of impressed decoration
14	1370	4074	3/11	84	bands of impressed decoration
15	698	2093	2/9	84	bands of impressed decoration
16	397	4077	3/11	84	bands of impressed decoration
17	7978	0000	0000	[94]	red painted crisscross stripes
18	1281	4019	3/11		red painted stripe with appended narrow stripes

Fig. 245. Bases (genre 85>)

1	7872	50006	2/7-9	85	pedestalled, flat, finger streaked
2	6072	2135	2/8	85	pedestalled, flat
3	3106	4125	2/2	85	pedestalled, hollow
4	5540	2123	2/9	85	pedestalled, flat, finger streaked, impressed decoration
5	2563	50000	2/7-9	85	pedestalled, hollow, impressed decoration
6	2718	1076	3/12	85	pedestalled, flat, impressed decoration
7	5657	4112	2/7	85	pedestalled, flat, finger streaked, impressed decoration

Fig. 246. Bases (genre <85)

1	3358	50006	2/7-9	85	pedestalled, flat, base ridged
2	5038	50019	2/7-9	85	pedestalled, flat
3	1572	4056	2/1	85	pedestalled, flat
4	1332	2038	3/11	85	pedestalled, flat
5	2569	0000	0000	85	pedestalled, flat
6	5509	2118	2/9	85	pedestalled, flat
7	3502	50008	2/7-9	88	pedestalled, flat
8	5806	2154	2/3	85	pedestalled, flat, finger streaked and splash painted in vertical stripes
9	3679	4128	2/1	85	pedestalled, flat, finger streaked and splash painted
10	4922	50011	2/7-9	85	pedestalled, flat, splash painted
11	1733	1034	4/14	85	pedestalled, flat, splash painted
12	1142	4046	2/4	85	pedestalled, flat, splash painted
13	1634	2062	2/9	85	pedestalled, flat, splash painted
14	1523	4052	2/5	85	pedestalled, flat, splash painted

Fig. 247. Bases (genre 86 and 87)

1	5486	4123	2/4	86	flat concave profile, finger streaked
2	6051	4088	3/12	86	flat concave profile, impressed decoration
3	5821	2141	2/7	86	flat concave profile

4	4525	2154	2/3	86	flat concave profile
5	2651	50003	2/7-9	86	flat concave profile, finger streaked, band of incised decoration
6	3766	50007	2/7-9	86	flat concave profile
7	2890	50001	2/7-9	86	flat concave profile
8	3246	1081	2/7	86	flat concave profile, band of incised decoration
9	1140	4046	2/4	86	flat concave profile
10	707	2093	2/9	87	flat, red splash painted, impressed decoration
11	2117	2065	2/7	87	flat, red splash painted
12	2146	4048	2/10	87	flat (hollow), red splash painted
13	742	2112	2/7	87	flat, red splash painted
14	2538	0000	0000	87	flat, red splash painted
15	944	4043	2/10	87	flat, red splash painted
16	2570	0000	0000	87	flat, red splash painted
17	2116	2065	2/7	87	flat, red splash painted
18	413	4077	3/11	87	flat, red splash painted, impressed decoration

Fig. 248. Bases (genres 88 and 89>)

1	871	4070	3/11	88	omphaloid, red burnished
2	1405	4018	3/11	88	omphaloid, red burnished
3	7965	2075	2/10	88	omphaloid, red burnished
4	565	1065	2/7	88	omphaloid, red burnished
5	1964	4016	3/11	88	omphaloid, red burnished
6	880	4070	3/11	88	omphaloid, red burnished
7	1261	2033	3/11	88	omphaloid, red burnished
8	1247	2036	3/13	88	omphaloid, red burnished
9	1000	4022	3/11	88	omphaloid, reddish slipped
10	2173	1061	3/11	88	omphaloid, reddish slipped
11	670	4068	3/11	89	flat, red painted stripes
12	4537	1077	3/12	89	flat, red painted stripes
13	792	2099	2/9	89	flat, red painted stripes
14	1368	4074	3/11	89	flat, red painted stripes
15	1232	4037	3/11	89	flat, red painted stripes
16	466	2076	2/8	89	flat, red painted stripes
17	604	2041	3/11	89	flat, red painted stripes
18	1692	4071	3/11	89	flat, red painted stripes

Fig. 249. Bases (genres <89 - 91>)

1	2571	0000	0000	89	flat, red painted stripes
2	2562	50000	2/7-9	89	flat, red painted stripes
3	932	4072	3/11	89	flat, red painted stripes
4	143	1003	0000	89	flat, red painted stripes
5	209	2011	0000	90	pedestal, hollow based, scored
6	5603	2137	2/6	90	pedestal, hollow based, red slipped
7	1132	4025	3/11	90	pedestal

8	1925	2065	2/7	90	pedestal
9	7356	6001	[5/0]	91	[EB IV] flat, steep sided
10	6461	41020	[5/0]	91	[EB IV] flat, steep sided
11	2126	2059	2/9	91	flat, steep sided
12	8062	0000	0000	91	flat, steep sided
13	7347	40008	[5/0]	91	flat, steep sided

Fig. 250. Bases (genres <91 and 92>)

1	7839	4001	4/15	91	flat, steep sided
2	7838	4001	4/15	91	flat, steep sided
3	2549	2090	2/10	91	flat, steep sided
4	7840	4001	4/15	91	flat, steep sided
5	1451	3001	0000	91	flat, steep sided, red burnished
6	1854	2010	0000	91	flat, steep sided, red burnished
7	255	4002	4/15	91	flat, steep sided
8	158	1004	0000	91	flat, steep sided, red burnished
9	173	0000	0000	91	flat, steep sided, red burnished
10	2771	1075	3/12	92	flat, heavy raised horizontal bands of impressed decoration
11	1485	4020	3/11	92	flat, heavy raised horizontal bands of impressed decoration
12	1446	4075	3/11	92	flat, heavy raised horizontal bands of impressed decoration

Fig. 251. Bases (genres <92 and 93)

1	706	2096	2/9	92	flat, heavy raised horizontal bands of impressed decoration
2	4927	50011	2/7-9	92	flat, heavy raised horizontal bands of impressed decoration
3	877	4070	3/11	93	flat, 'grain-wash'
4	957	4043	2/10	93	flat, 'grain-wash'
5	1338	1045	0000	93	flat, 'grain-wash'
6	1682	4071	3/11	93	flat, 'grain-wash'
7	4832	30019	3/13	93	flat, 'grain-wash'
8	286	4016	3/11	93	flat, 'grain-wash'
9	275	1022	0000	93	flat, 'grain-wash'
10	523	2061	2/8	93	flat, 'grain-wash'

Fig. 252. Bases (genre 94)

1	175	1005	0000	94	flat, red painted criss-cross pattern
2	274	1022	0000	94	flat, red painted criss-cross pattern
3	1998	1005	0000	94	flat, red painted criss-cross pattern
4	256	4002	4/15	94	flat, red painted criss-cross pattern
5	2554	50000	2/7-9	[?]	flat, mat impressed base [stage 1?]
6	8063	0000	0000		rounded, pattern burnished (stage 1?)

Fig. 253. Flat juglet bases (cf. genre 35 [Figs 204-5])

1	405	4077	3/11	35	red burnished/polished
2	346	1032	4/14	35	red burnished/polished
3	2321	4024	3/11	35	red burnished/polished
4	692	2093	2/9	35	red burnished/polished
5	2518	4023	3/11	35	red burnished/polished
6	477	2051	2/9	35	red burnished/polished
7	183	0000	0000	35	red burnished/polished
8	703	2096	2/9	35	red burnished/polished
9	160	0000	0000	35	red burnished/polished
10	1371	4074	3/11	35	red burnished/polished
11	1179	4032	3/11	35	red burnished/polished
12	753	2101	3/13	35	plain
13	2335	2047	3/11	35	plain
14	262	4005	4/5	35	plain
15	206	2010	0000	35	plain
16	2361	2047	3/11	35	reddish slipped
17	919	4072	3/11	35	reddish slipped
18	224	2013	3/11	35	reddish slipped
19	2379	2043	3/12	35	red burnished/polished
20	1488	4020	3/11	35	reddish slipped

Fig. 254. Various vessels

1	8064	0000	0000	[33] hmj, bevelled slightly everted rim, ext. pattern burnished
2	7863	1061	2/8	heavy deep bowl, rounded rim, int. carination, ext. band of impressed decoration below lip
3	3745	40016	-/-	deep bowl or jar, everted rounded bevelled and ext. rilled rim
4	1581	4056	2/1	jar, rounded slightly everted rim from in sloping neck
5	3228	4128	2/1	jar, everted pointed recessed rim on 'bowed' neck
6	3616	40014	-/-	heavy jar, rounded rim on short vertical neck, ext. reddish slipped
7	8065	0000	0000	jar, everted rounded rilled rim, ext./int. reddish slipped
8	1099	4025	3/11	jar, everted pointed rim, sharp carination at neck/shoulder, ext. and int. lip red burnished
9	400	4077	3/11	jar, rounded everted rim, int./ext. red burnished
10	718	2096	3/11	jar, rounded everted rim, ext./int. red burnished
11	7944	0000	0000	jar, pointed everted rim, sharp int. carination at neck/shoulder

Fig. 255. Various vessels

1	430	4066	2/1	jar, no rim, slurred neck/shoulder junction, ext. red burnished, int. red slipped
2	1322	2032	3/11	jar, everted rim (?), ext. red burnished

3	93	0000	0000	jar, rounded everted rim, rounded lug(s?) with three oval impressions beneath at waist
4	5020	50019	2/7-9	jar, rounded everted rim, impressed 'wavy' decoration along ext. lip
5	811	2105	2/9	bowl ('conique'?), everted bevelled 'hammer' rim, impressed 'wavy' decoration along ext. lip, ext. red burnished
6	689	2096	2/9	heavy deep bowl, recessed rounded splayed rim with ext. groove below lip, band of 'wavy' impressed design along ext. lip
7	1360	4019	3/11	small bowl, rolled 'hammer' rim, flat loop handle from lip to base, rounded base, ext. red burnished, int. slurred
8	8066	0000	0000	bs, red painted stripes
9	1979	1003	0000	bs, band of impressed decoration
10	1902	2000	0000	bs, band of impressed decoration
11	4179	40018	-/-	bs, red painted net pattern in vertical registers on cream slip (?) [fb = genre 34]
12	5196	50009	2/7-9	pot stand, rounded slurred rims

For Figures 256 - 260, G = Tell Um Hammad corresponding genres; St = relative stage at Tell Um Hammad

no.	C	G	St	Description

Fig. 256 Ruweiha: surface collection

1	R26	1	2	hmj, rounded rim with finely grooved band, 'bowed' shoulder, band of heavy impressed decoration on shoulder
2	R24	1/80	2	bs, shoulder, band of heavy impressed decoration
3	R19	1/80	2	bs, shoulder, band of heavy impressed decoration
4	R21	1/80	2	bs, shoulder, band of heavy impressed decoration
5	R20	2?	2	hmj, bevelled rim, band of heavy punctate decoration below rim
6	R18	2?	2	hmj, bevelled rim, band of heavy punctate decoration below rim
7	R	16	2	jar, bevelled rim on in-sloping 'bag'-shaped shoulder, band of impressed decoration on shoulder/neck
8	R	16	2	jar, rounded slightly everted rim on in-sloping 'bag'-shaped neck
9	R	16	2	jar, bevelled rim on in-sloping neck, band of heavy impressed decoration on shoulder/neck

10   R   16?   2   jar, rounded int. recessed rim on in-sloping neck, band of impressed decoration below rim

Fig. 257 Ruweiha: surface collection

1   R16   16?   2   jar, bevelled/pointed rim on in-sloping neck, heavy band of impressed decoration below rim

2   R27   16?   2   jar or deep bowl/pithos, bevelled rim on in-sloping neck, neck slightly 'bowed' and crimped at shoulder, band of thumb-impressed decoration at shoulder/neck junction

3   R22   16?/1?   2   jar or hmj, pointed rim on in-sloping neck, band of deeply impressed decoration below rim

4   R28   16   2   jar, rounded everted rim on in-sloping neck, finely grooved on rim and upper neck, ext. 'finger-streaked' and painted with rough horizontal bands of red

5   R12   16   2   jar, rounded rim on in-sloping neck, band of impressed decoration at neck/shoulder junction

6   R3   16   2   jar, rounded everted slightly int. recessed bulbous rim, ext. band of impressed decoration at neck/rim junction

7   R4   16?   2   jar, rounded out-rolled rim on everted bulbous neck, band of impressed decoration at neck/shoulder junction

Fig. 258 Ruweiha: surface collection

1   R11   16   2   jar, rounded slightly bevelled rim on bulbous vertical neck

2   R13   19?   2   jar, rounded/pointed everted rim on 'bag'-shaped body, sharp int. carination at neck/shoulder junction

3   R   22   2   jar, rounded slightly recessed everted rim

4   R   64   2   duck-billed up-turned ledge handle, 'finger-streaked' beneath, band of impressed decoration on leading edge running on to body of vessel

5   R   64   2   rounded up-turned ledge handle, band of impressed decoration on leading edge

6   R   67/69 2   plain rounded up-turned ledge handle

7   R   68   2   rounded up-turned ledge handle, band of punctate decoration on leading edge

8   R   64   2   rounded up-turned ledge handle, band of punctate decoration on leading edge

9   R   64   2   rounded up-turned ledge handle, band of punctate decoration on leading edge

10   R   35   2-3 high loop-handled juglet, red burnished

11   R25   35   2-3 high loop-handled juglet, red burnished

| 12 | R | 80? | 2 | bs, twin bands of deep thumb-impressed decoration, incised band beneath, dark burnished surface |

Fig. 259 Ruweiha: surface collection

1	R	45	2	bowl, 'Esdraelon' ware
2	R8	48	2	bowl, rounded everted rim
3	R10	48	2	bowl, rounded slightly bevelled everted rim, sharp int. carination, red polished surface
4	R7	48	2	bowl, rounded/pointed everted rim, sharp int. carination, red polished
5	R2	48	2	bowl, rounded everted rim, ext. lip finely grooved, body horizontally 'finger streaked'
6	R23	48/49?	2	bowl, everted pointed rim, ext. lip finely grooved, band of impressed decoration on shoulder, ext. body painted with irregular horizontal red stripes
7	R	cf.Fig. 231:1?	2	bowl, conical body, band of impressed decoration beneath rim

Fig. 260 Ruweiha: surface collection

1	R1	53	2	bowl, rounded/slightly bevelled rim, int. lip slurred, int. 'crazed'
2	R14	53	2	bowl, rounded rim, int. lip slurred, int. 'crazed'
3	R15	53	2	bowl, rounded rim, int. lip slurred, int. 'crazed'
4	R6	36	2	bowl, rounded vertical rim, rounded/flattened base, highly red burnished ext, traces of black ash on lip
5	R5	36?	2	bowl, rounded rim, rounded base
6	R9	43	3	bowl, rounded/pointed vertical rim, ext. slight carination, ext. red burnished
7	R29	cf.Fig. 235:11-14	3?	churn, flat end, doubled loop handle in line with body near end
8	R	cf. Fig. 235:11-14	3?	churn?, loop handle near end of vessel
9	R	85	2	base, pedestal with heavy impressed decoration
10	R	?	2	base, vertical sides, slipped
11	R	86	2	base, incised decoration along bottom
12	R	?	?	base, hollow, rough lumpy 'bag'-shaped body
13	R	86?	2	base, splayed foot, reddish slip ext.
14	R	?	?	base, hollow
15	R	88?	2	hollow base, ext. highly red burnished

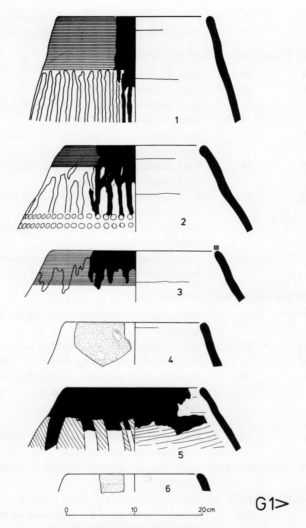

Fig. 139. Pottery catalogue: genre 1

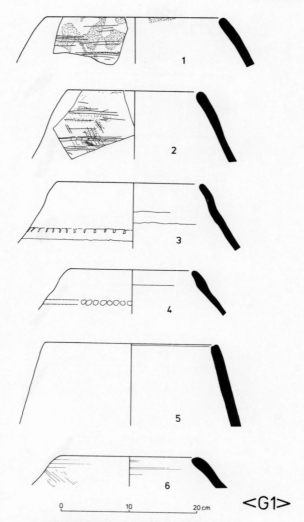

<G1>

Fig. 140. Pottery catalogue: genre 1

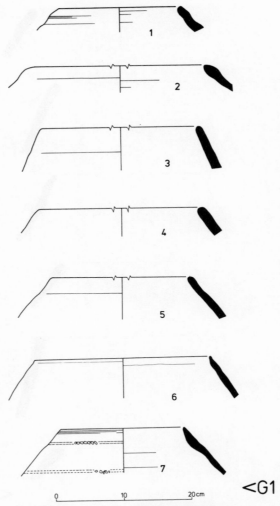

Fig. 141. Pottery catalogue: genre 1

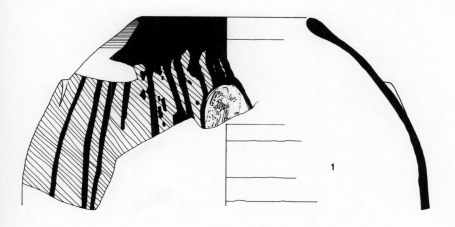

1

G 1/2

Fig. 142. Pottery catalogue: genre 1/2

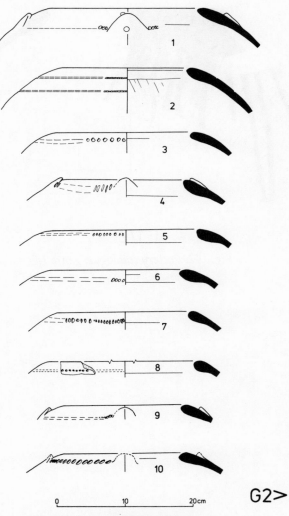

Fig. 143. Pottery catalogue: genre 2

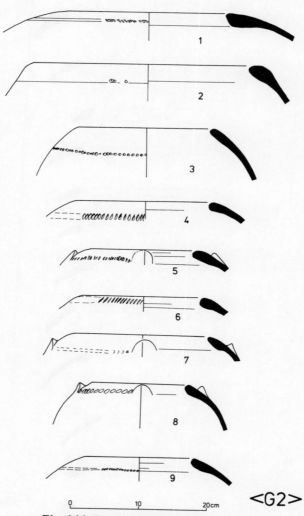

<G2>

Fig. 144. Pottery catalogue: genre 2

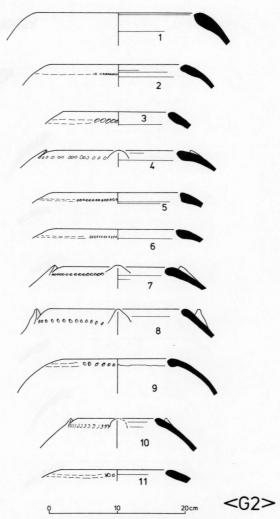

<G2>

Fig. 145. Pottery catalogue: genre 2

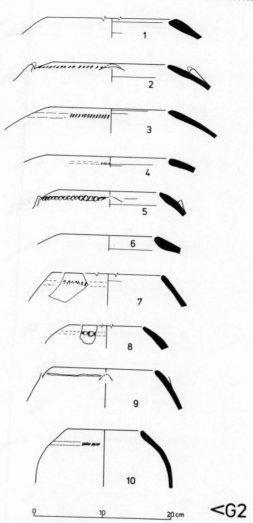

Fig. 146. Pottery catalogue: genre 2

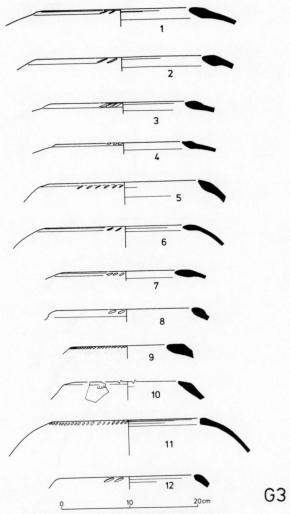

Fig.147. Pottery catalogue: genre 3

G3

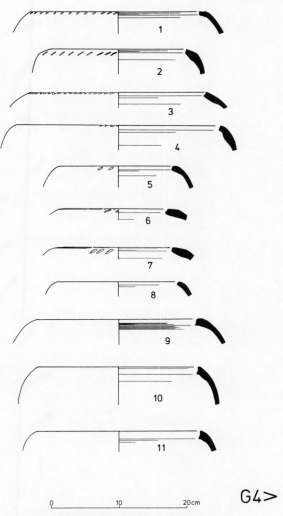

G4>

Fig.148. Pottery catalogue: genre 4

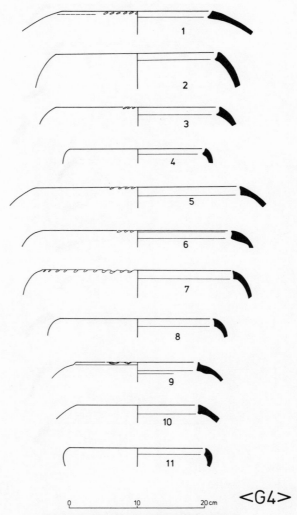

<G4>

Fig.149. Pottery catalogue: genre 4

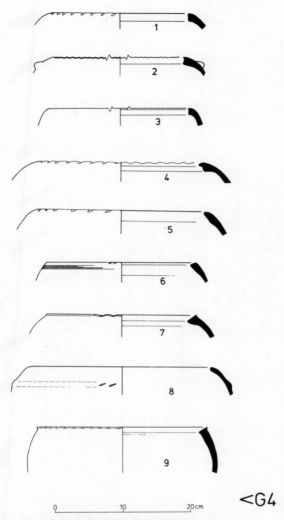

Fig.150. Pottery catalogue: genre 4

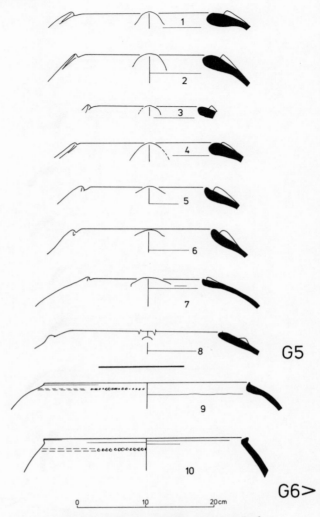

Fig.151. Pottery catalogue: genres 5, 6

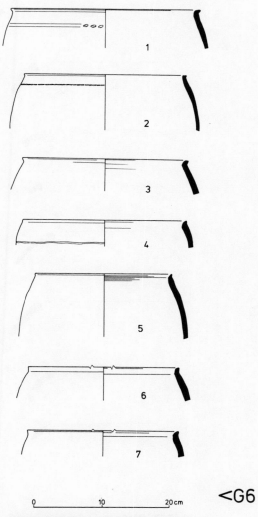

Fig.152. Pottery catalogue: genre 6

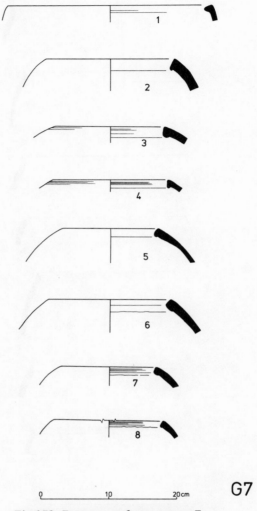

Fig.153. Pottery catalogue: genre 7

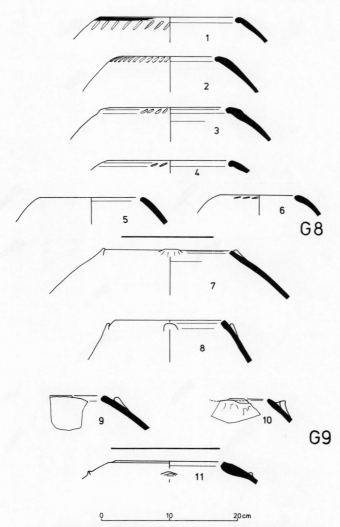

Fig.154. Pottery catalogue: genres 8, 9, unclassified

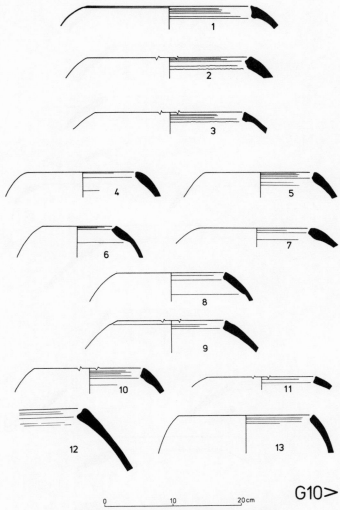

Fig.155. Pottery catalogue: genre 10

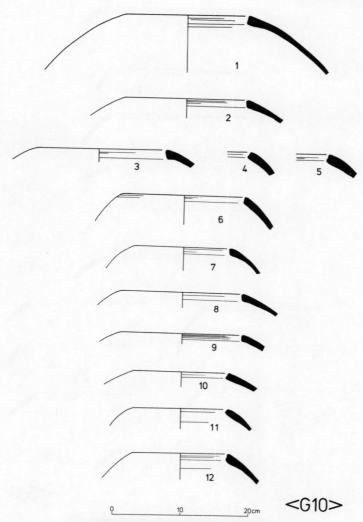

<G10>

Fig.156. Pottery catalogue: genre 10

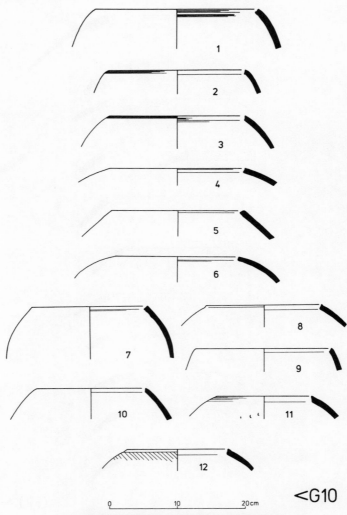

Fig.157. Pottery catalogue: genre 10

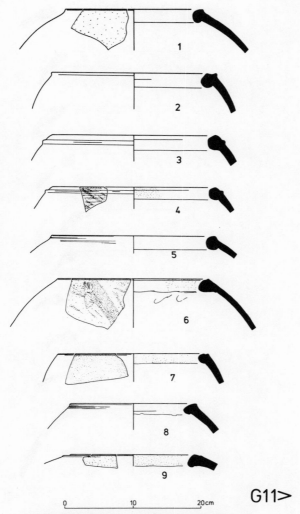

G11>

Fig.158. Pottery catalogue: genre 11

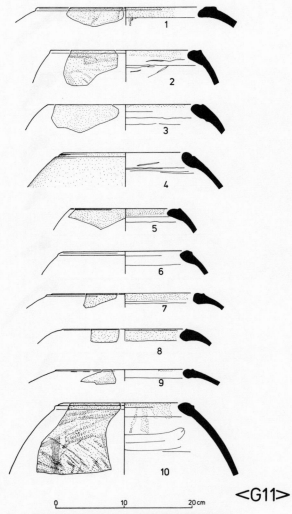

<G11>

Fig.159. Pottery catalogue: genre 11

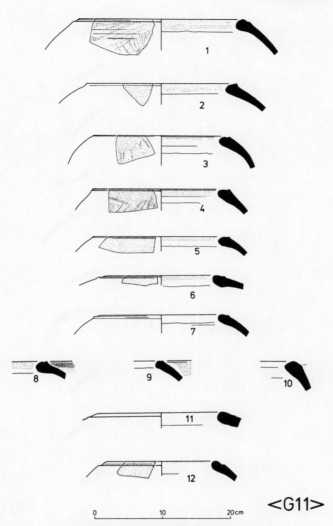

<G11>

Fig.160. Pottery catalogue: genre 11

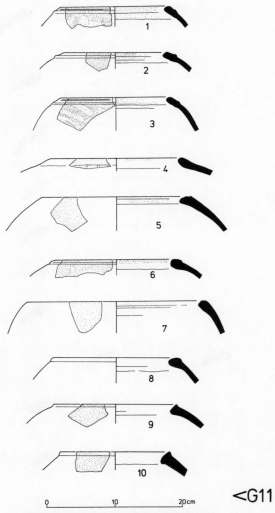

<G11

Fig.161. Pottery catalogue: genre 11

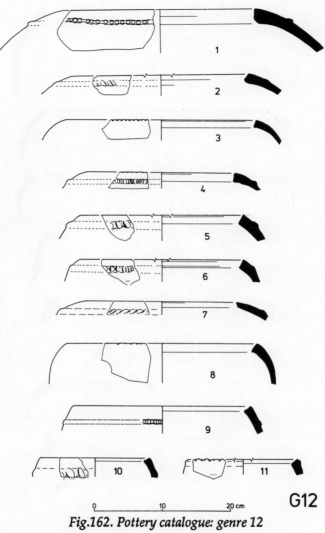

Fig.162. Pottery catalogue: genre 12

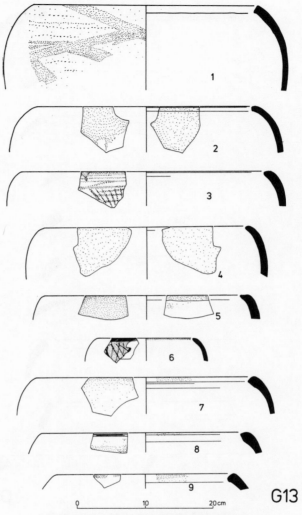

Fig.163. Pottery catalogue: genre 13

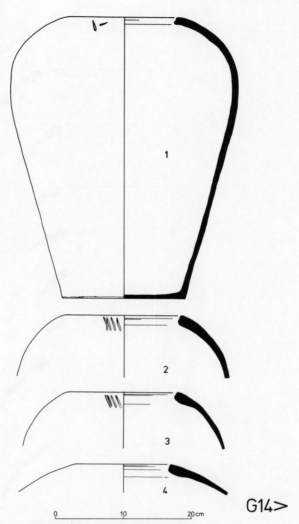

Fig.164. Pottery catalogue: genre 14

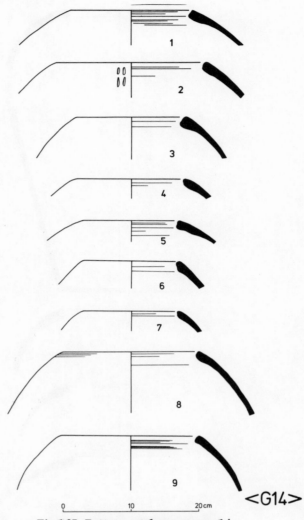

<G14>

Fig.165. Pottery catalogue: genre 14

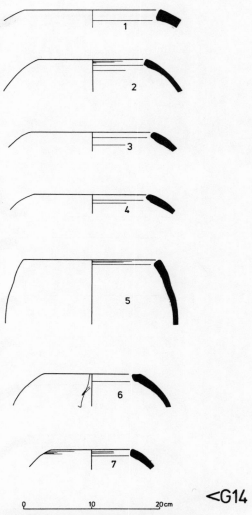

<G14

Fig.166. Pottery catalogue: genre 14

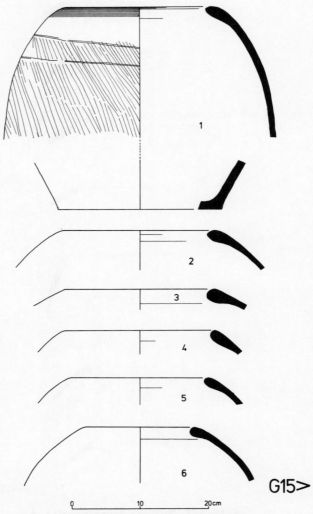

Fig.167. Pottery catalogue: genre 15

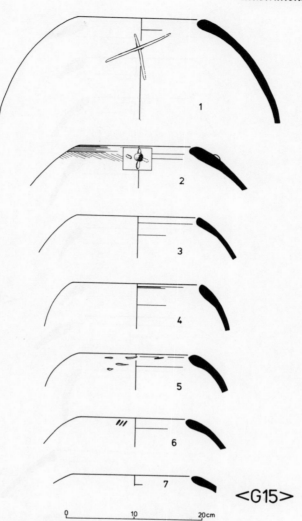

Fig. 168. Pottery catalogue: genre 15

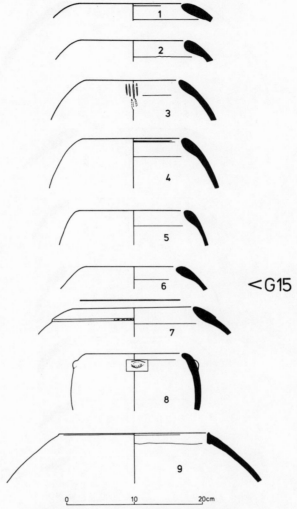

Fig. 169. *Pottery catalogue: genre 15*

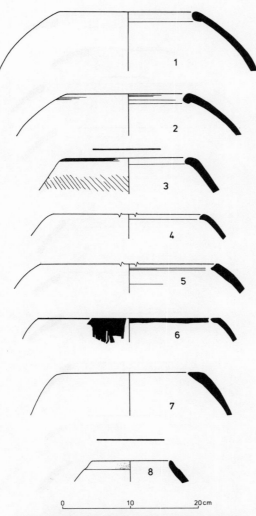

Fig. 170. Pottery catalogue: unclassified

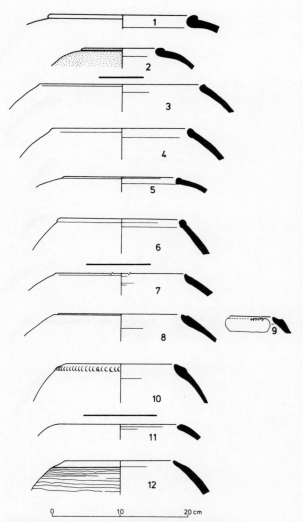

Fig. 171. Pottery catalogue: unclassified

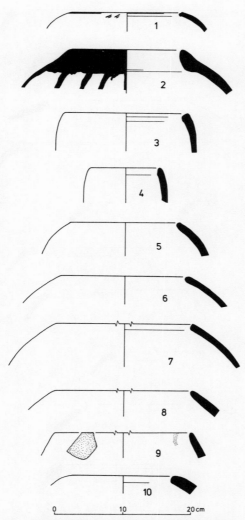

Fig. 172. Pottery catalogue: unclassified

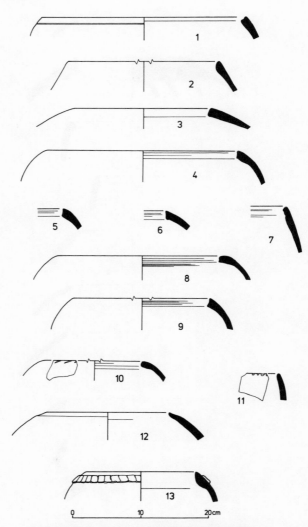

Fig. 173. Pottery catalogue: unclassified

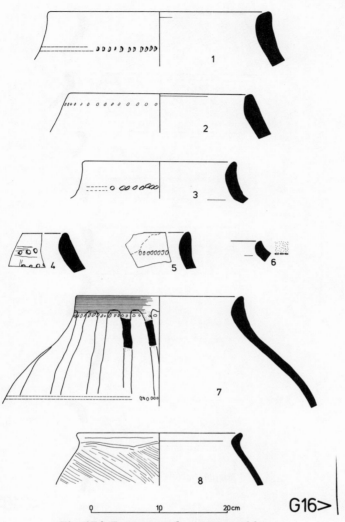

Fig. 174. Pottery catalogue: genre 16

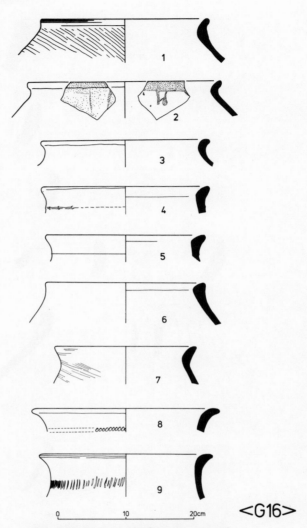

<G16>

Fig. 175. Pottery catalogue: genre 16

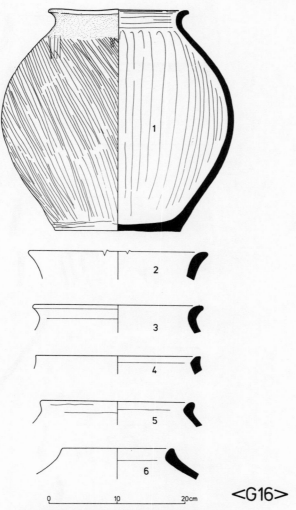

<G16>

Fig. 176. Pottery catalogue: genre 16

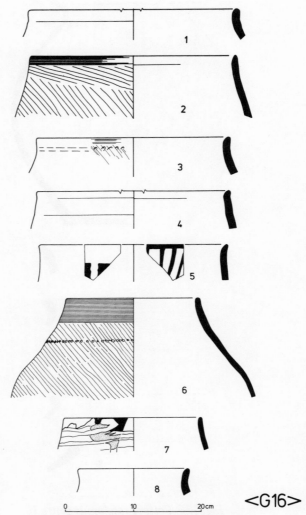

Fig. 177. Pottery catalogue: genre 16

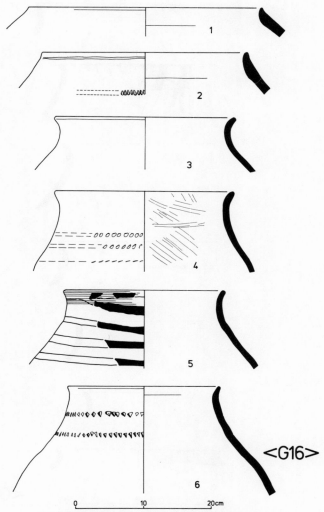

<G16>

Fig. 178. Pottery catalogue: genre 16

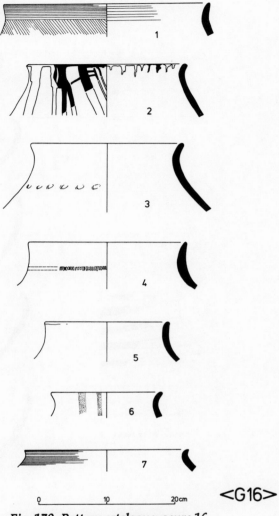

Fig. 179. Pottery catalogue: genre 16

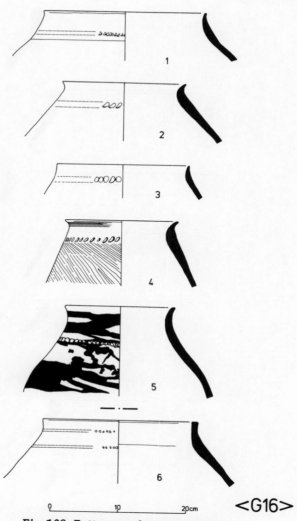

<G16>

Fig. 180. Pottery catalogue: genre 16

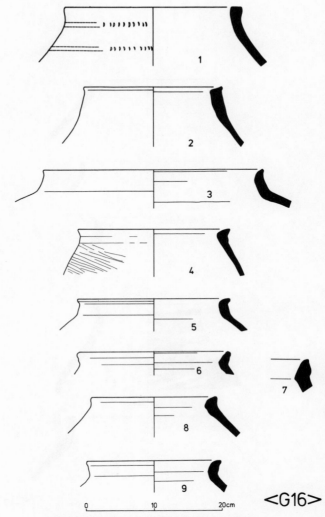

Fig. 181. Pottery catalogue: genre 16

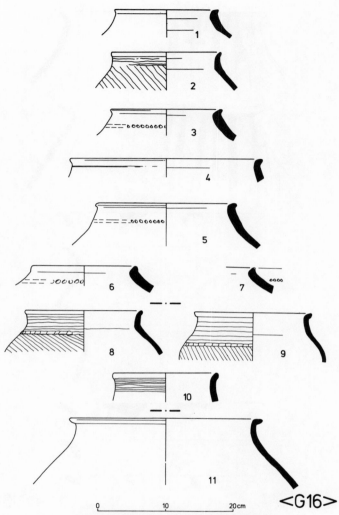

Fig. 182. Pottery catalogue: genre 16

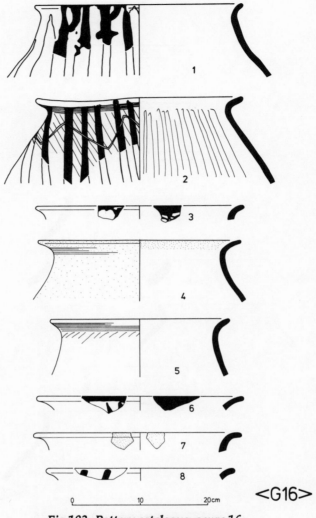

<G16>

Fig.183. Pottery catalogue: genre 16

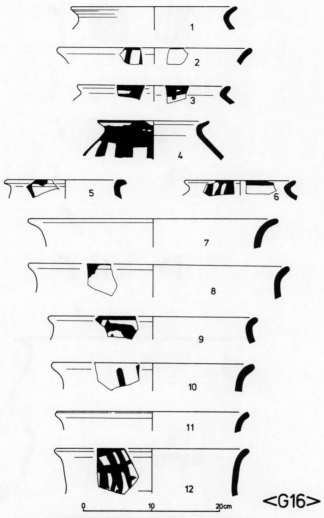

<G16>

Fig.184. Pottery catalogue: genre 16

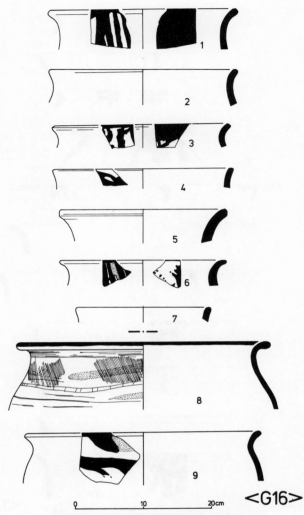

Fig.185. Pottery catalogue: genre 16

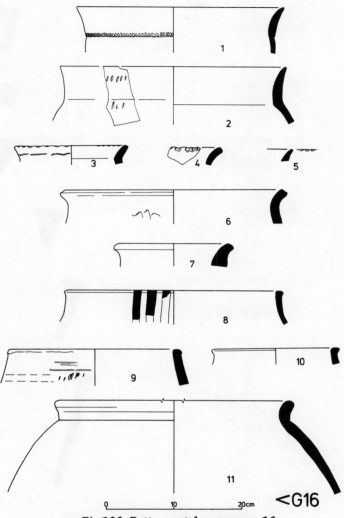

Fig.186. Pottery catalogue: genre 16

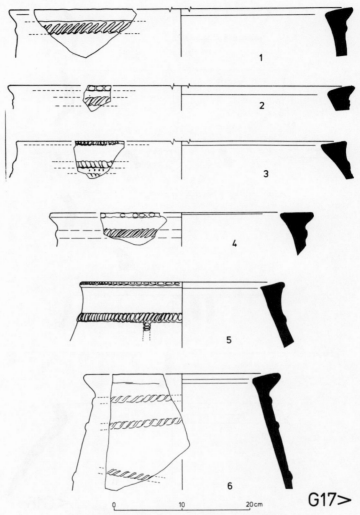

Fig.187. Pottery catalogue: genre 17

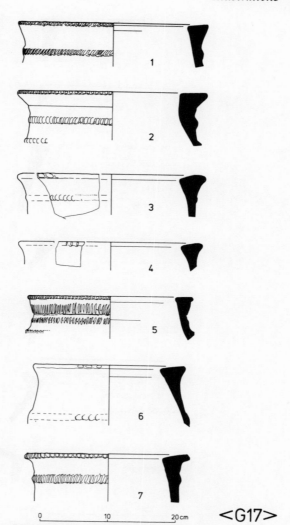

<G17>

Fig.188. Pottery catalogue: genre 17

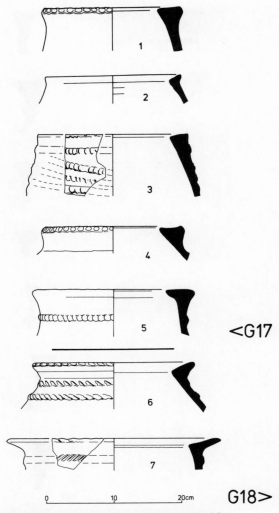

Fig.189. Pottery catalogue: genres 17, 18

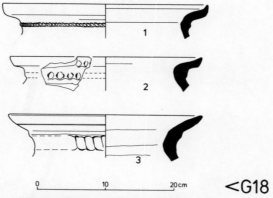

Fig.190. Pottery catalogue: genre 18

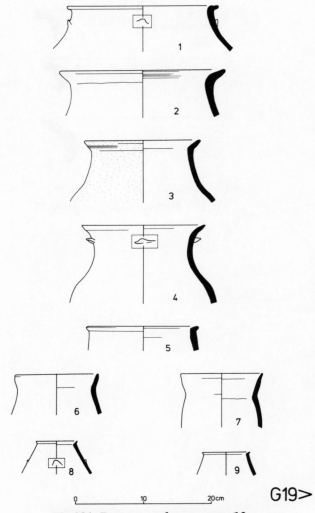

Fig.191. Pottery catalogue: genre 19

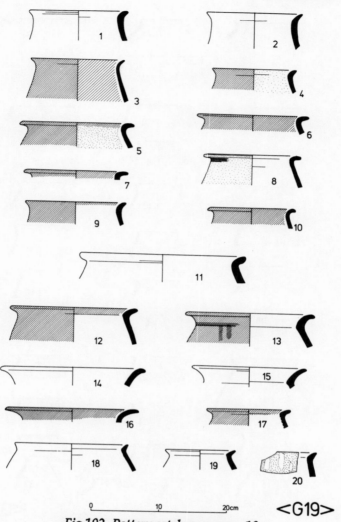

Fig.192. Pottery catalogue: genre 19

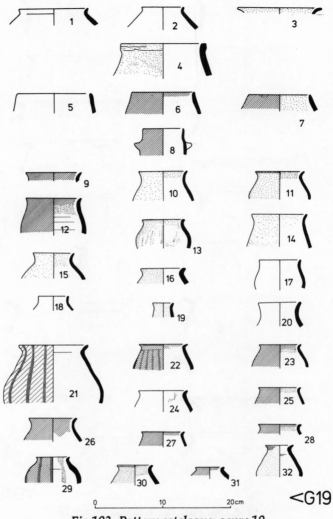

Fig.193. Pottery catalogue: genre 19

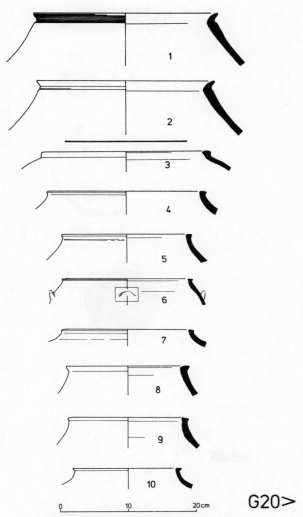

Fig.194. Pottery catalogue: genre 20

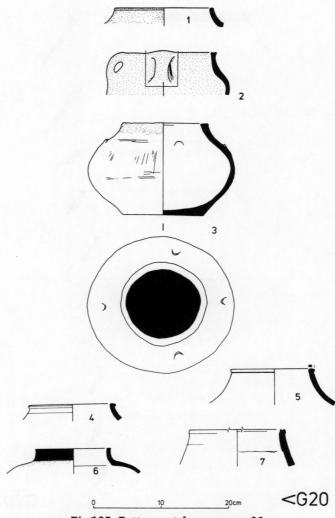

Fig.195. Pottery catalogue: genre 20

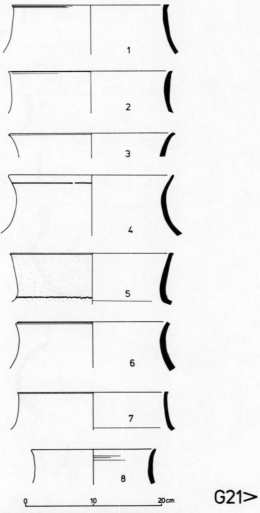

G21>

Fig.196. Pottery catalogue: genre 21

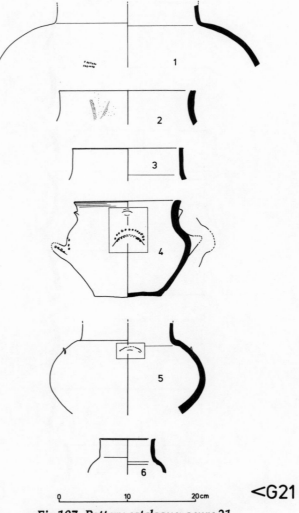

Fig.197. Pottery catalogue: genre 21

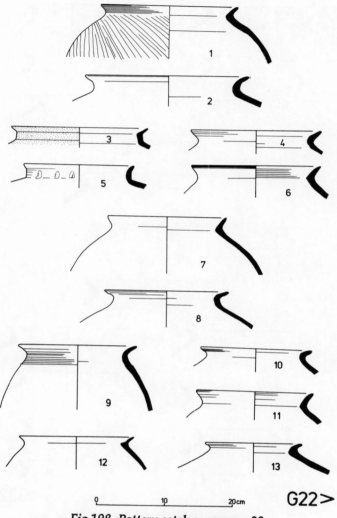

Fig.198. Pottery catalogue: genre 22

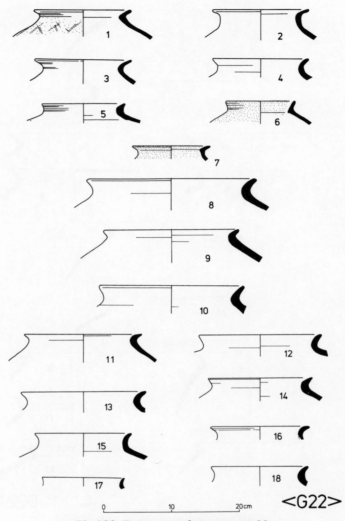

Fig.199. Pottery catalogue: genre 22

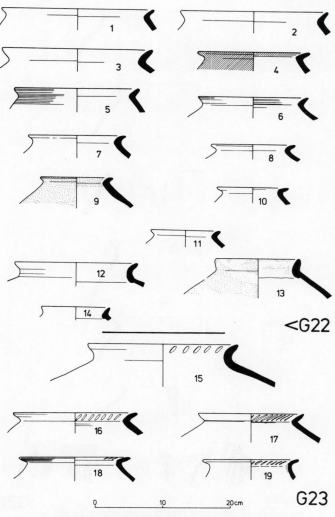

<G22

G23

Fig.200. Pottery catalogue: genres 22, 23

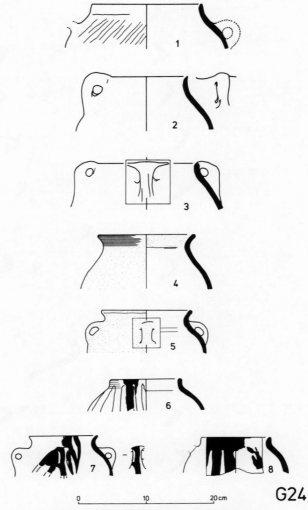

Fig.201. Pottery catalogue: genre 24

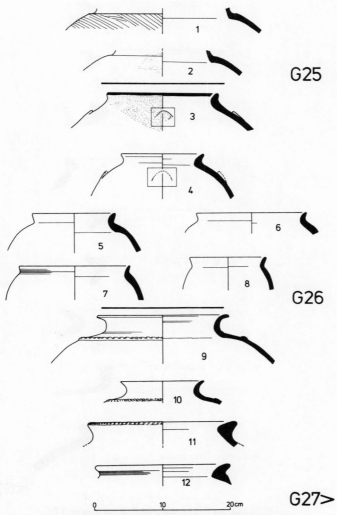

Fig.202. Pottery catalogue: genres 25, 26, 27

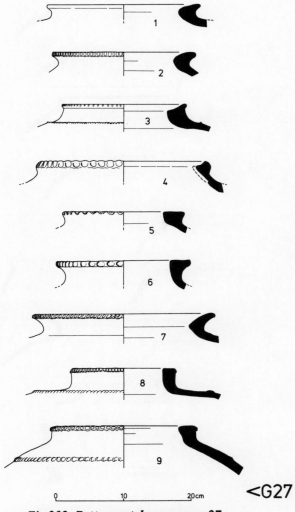

Fig.203. Pottery catalogue: genre 27

<G27

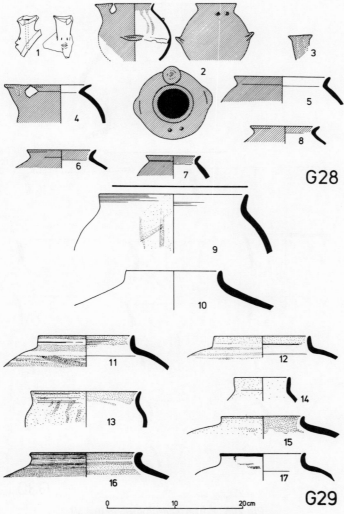

G28

G29

0   10   20 cm

Fig.204. Pottery catalogue: genres 28, 29

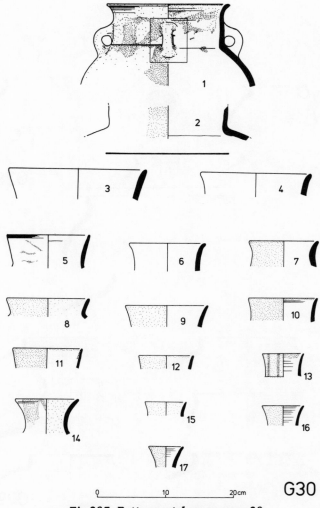

Fig.205. Pottery catalogue: genre 30

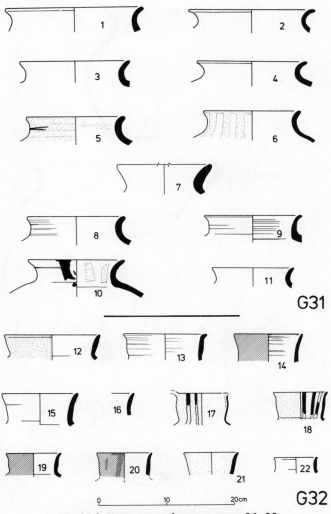

Fig.206. Pottery catalogue: genres 31, 32

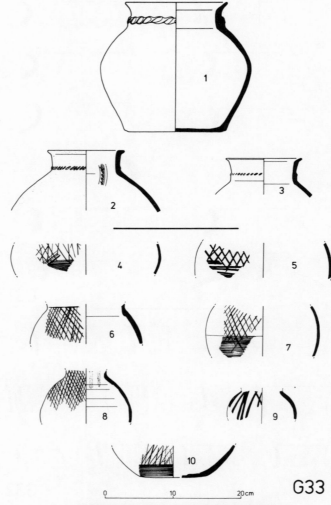

Fig.207. Pottery catalogue: genre 33

G33

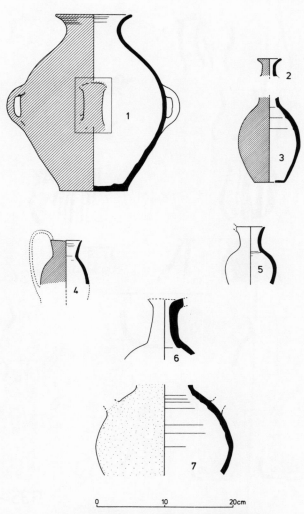

Fig.208. Pottery catalogue: unclassified

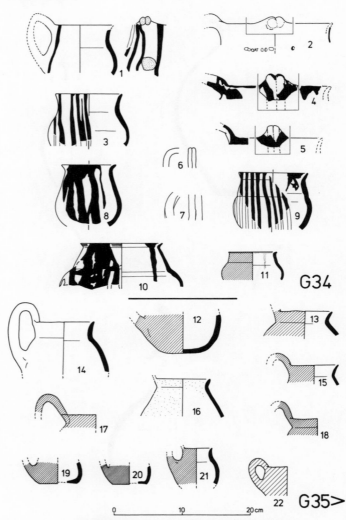

Fig.209. Pottery catalogue: genres 34, 35

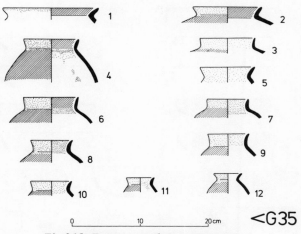

Fig.210. Pottery catalogue: genre 35

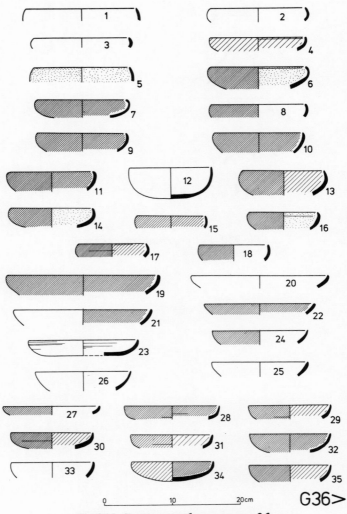

Fig.211. Pottery catalogue: genre 36

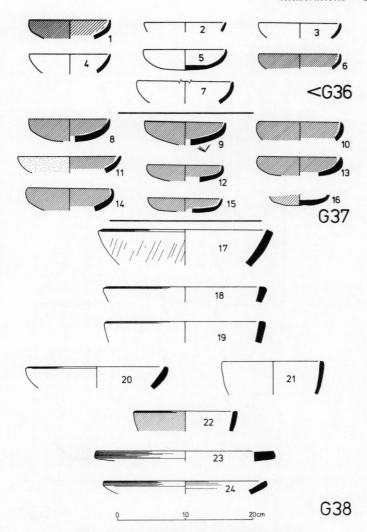

Fig.212. Pottery catalogue: genres 36, 37, 38

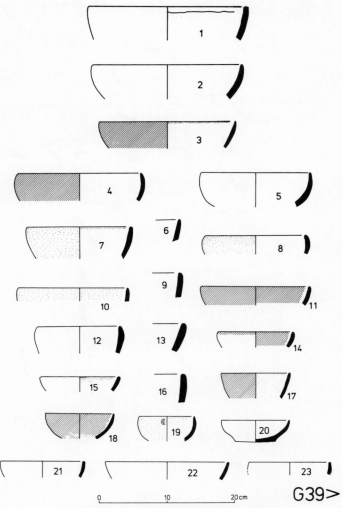

Fig.213. Pottery catalogue: genre 39

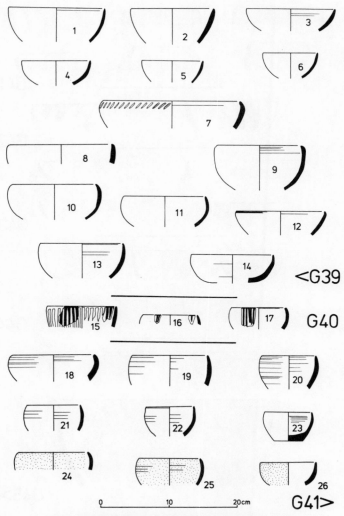

Fig.214. Pottery catalogue: genres 39, 40, 41

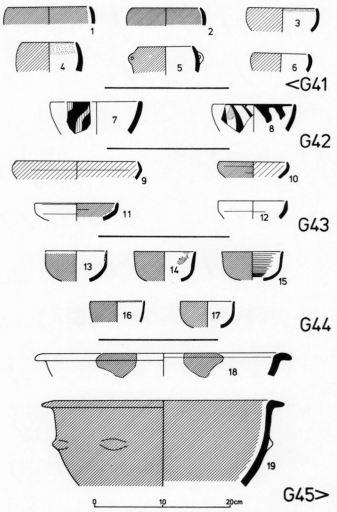

Fig.215. Pottery catalogue: genres 41, 42, 43, 44, 45

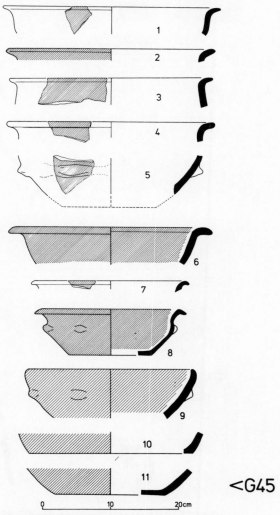

<G45

Fig.216. Pottery catalogue: genre 45

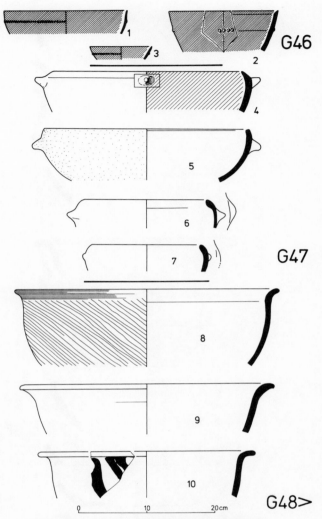

Fig.217. Pottery catalogue: genres 46, 47, 48

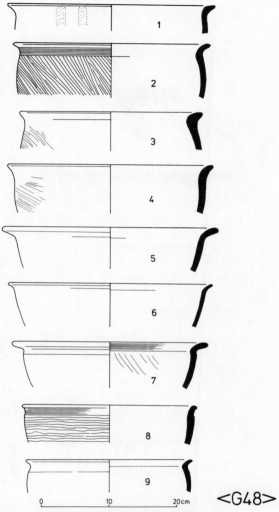

<G48>

Fig.218. Pottery catalogue: genre 48

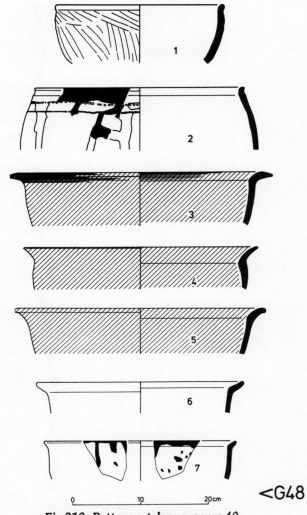

<G48

Fig.219. Pottery catalogue: genre 48

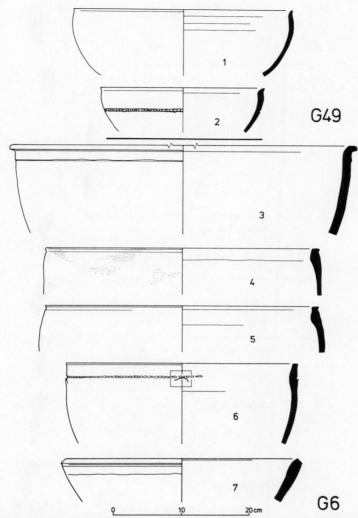

Fig.220. Pottery catalogue: genres 49, 6 (large range: see also Figs 151, 152)

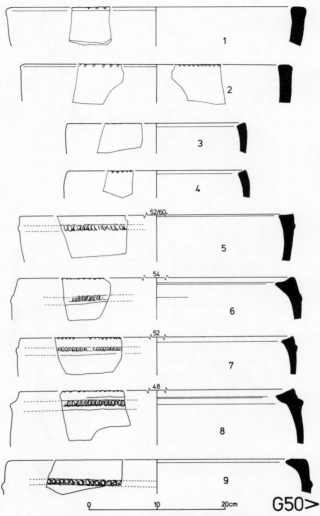

Fig.221. Pottery catalogue: genre 50

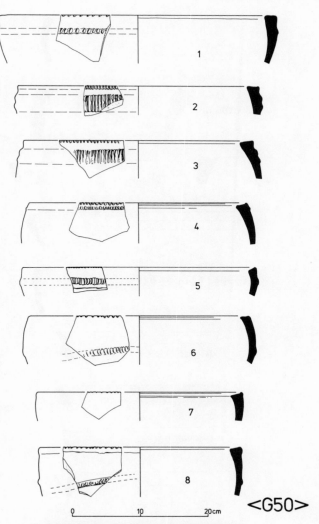

<G50>

Fig.222. Pottery catalogue: genre 50

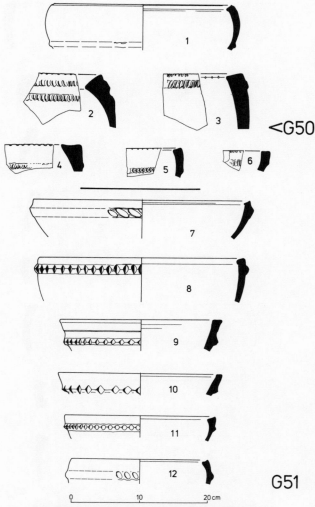

Fig.223. Pottery catalogue: genres 50, 51

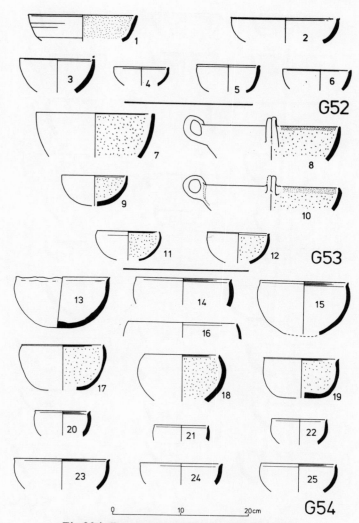

Fig.224. Pottery catalogue: genres 52, 53, 54

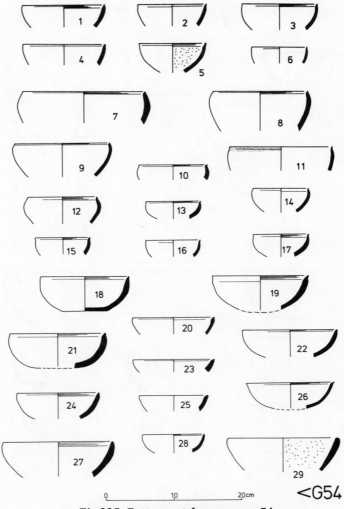

Fig.225. Pottery catalogue: genre 54

<G54

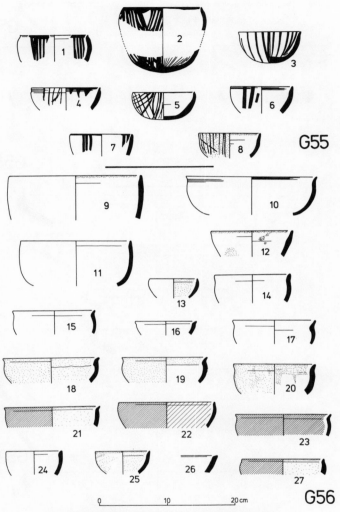

Fig.226. Pottery catalogue: genres 55, 56

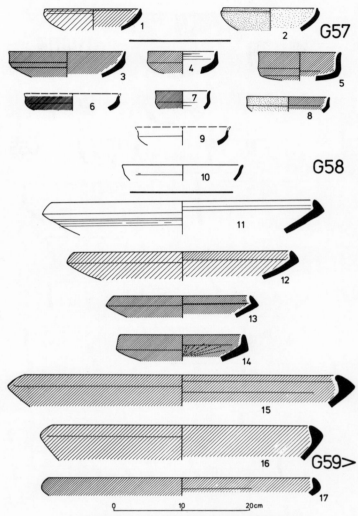

Fig.227. Pottery catalogue: genres 57, 58, 59

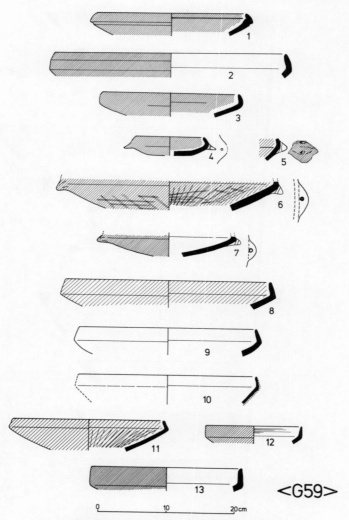

Fig.228. Pottery catalogue: genre 59

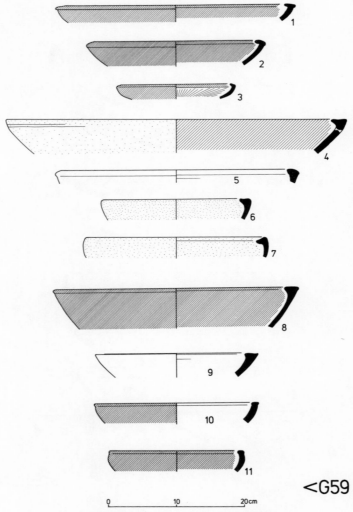

Fig.229. *Pottery catalogue: genre 59*

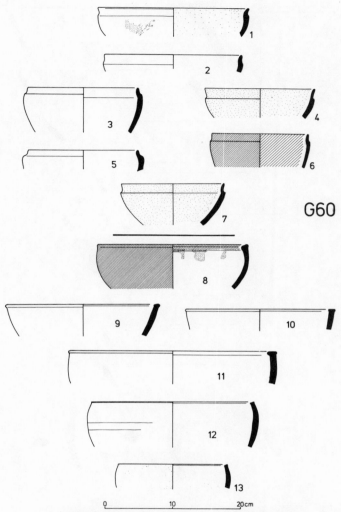

G60

Fig.230. Pottery catalogue: genre 60, unclassified

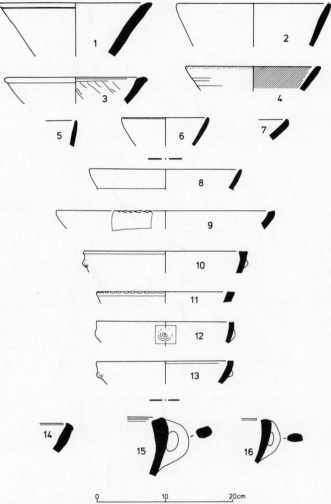

Fig.231. Pottery catalogue: unclassified

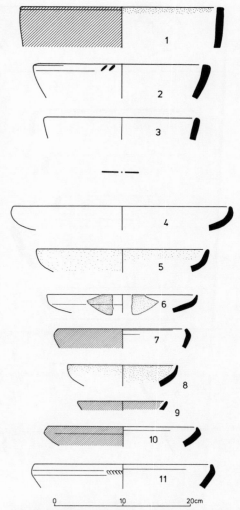

Fig.232. Pottery catalogue: unclassified

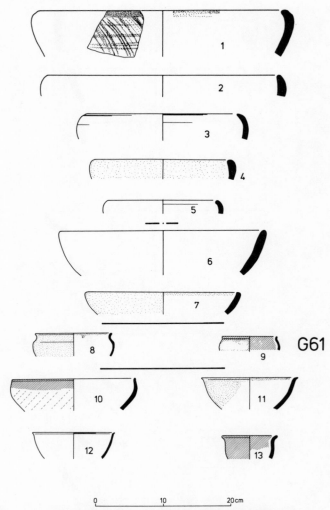

G61

Fig.233. Pottery catalogue: genre 61, unclassified

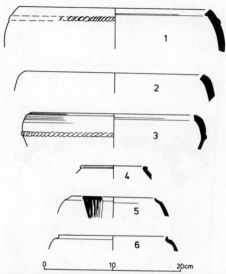

Fig.234. Pottery catalogue: unclassified

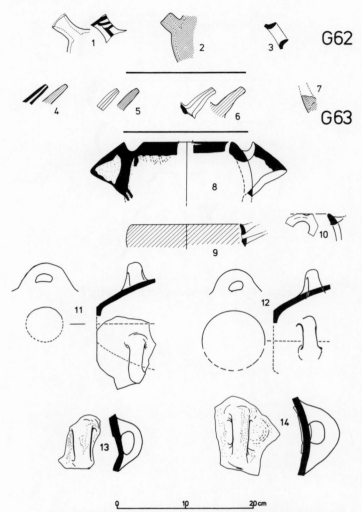

Fig.235. Pottery catalogue: genres 62, 63, unclassified

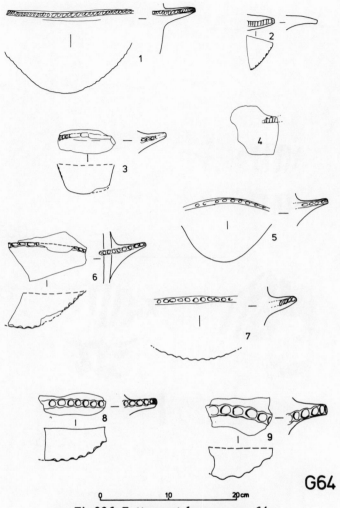

G64

Fig.236. Pottery catalogue: genre 64

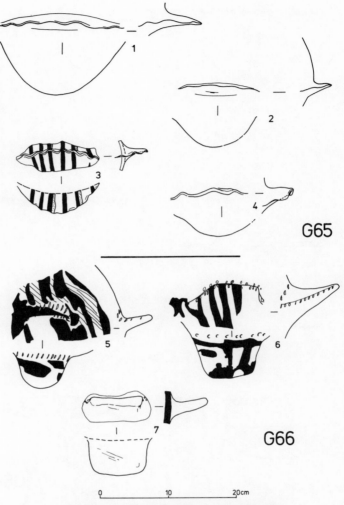

Fig.237. Pottery catalogue: genres 65, 66

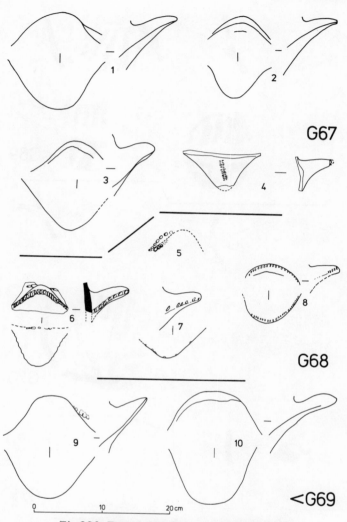

G67

G68

<G69

Fig.238. Pottery catalogue: genres 67, 68, 69

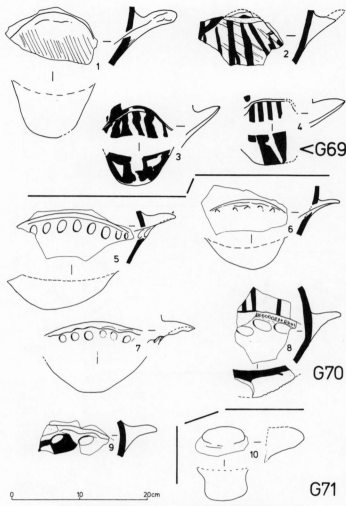

Fig.239. Pottery catalogue: genres 69, 70, 71

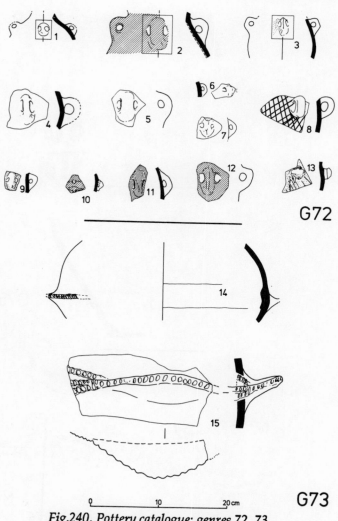

Fig.240. Pottery catalogue: genres 72, 73

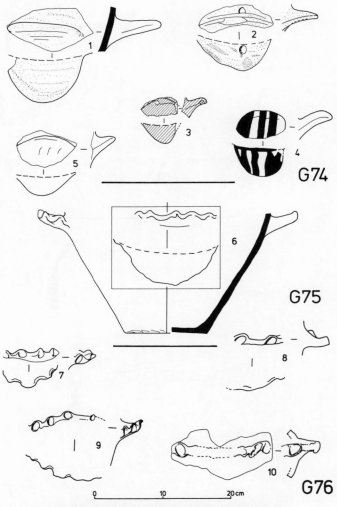

Fig.241. Pottery catalogue: genres 74, 75, 76

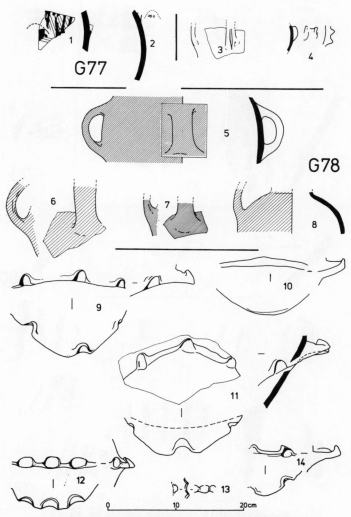

G77

G78

Fig.242. Pottery catalogue: genres 77, 78, unclassified

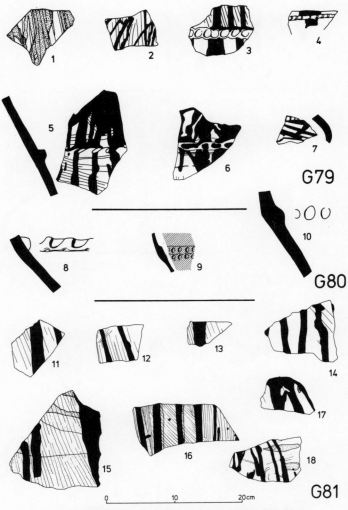

Fig.243. Pottery catalogue: genres 79, 80, 81

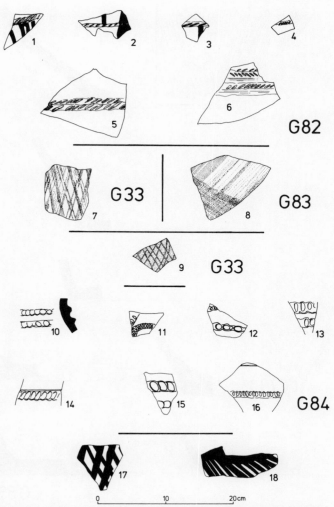

Fig.244. Pottery catalogue: genres 82, 33, 83, 84, unclassified

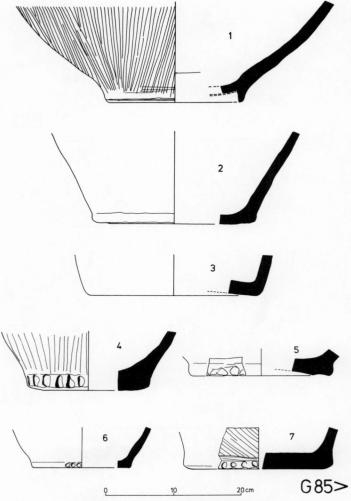

Fig.245. Pottery catalogue: genre 85

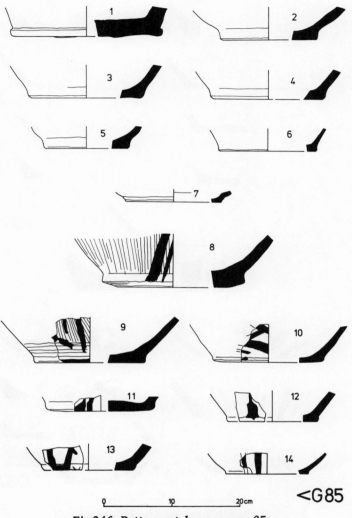

Fig.246. Pottery catalogue: genre 85

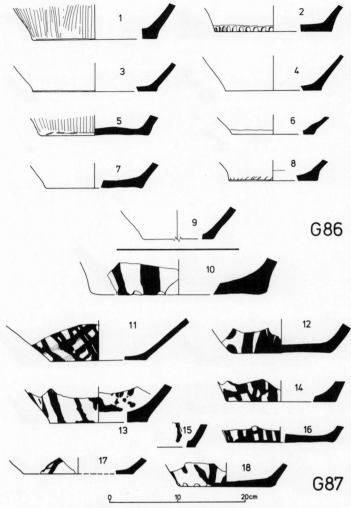

Fig.247. Pottery catalogue: genres 86, 87

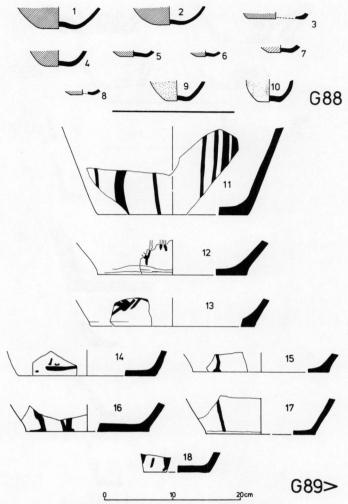

Fig.248. Pottery catalogue: genres 88, 89

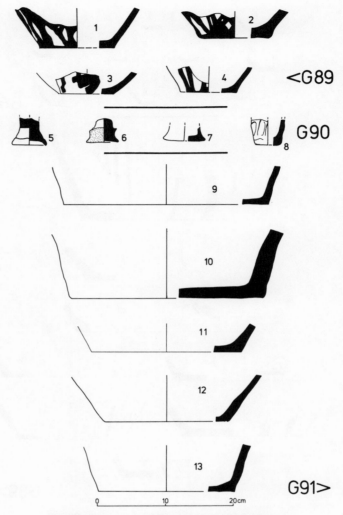

Fig.249. Pottery catalogue: genres 89, 90, 91

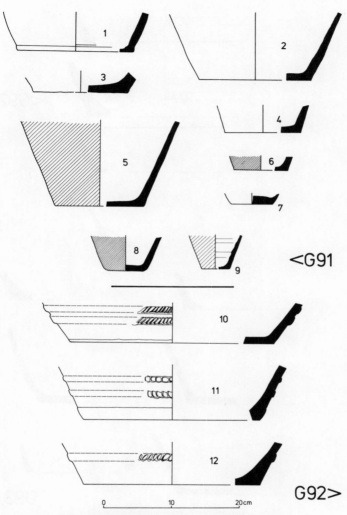

Fig.250. Pottery catalogue: genres 91, 92

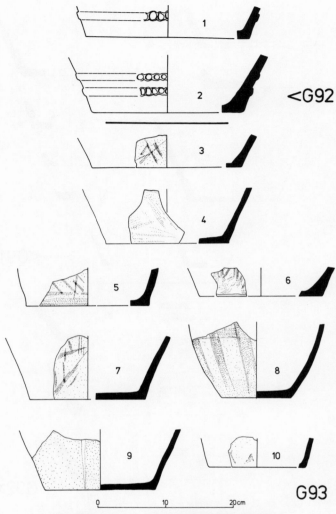

Fig.251. Pottery catalogue: genres 92, 93

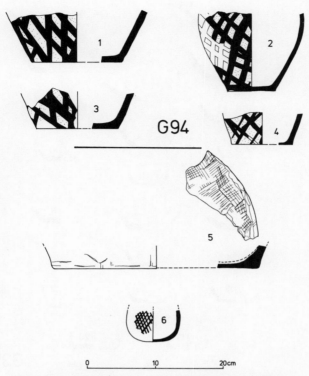

Fig.252. Pottery catalogue: genre 94, unclassified

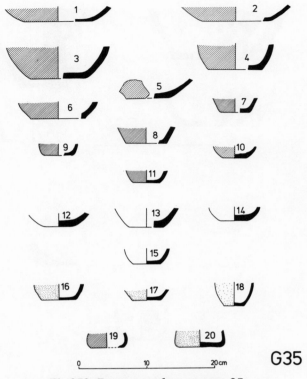

G35

Fig.253. Pottery catalogue: genre 35

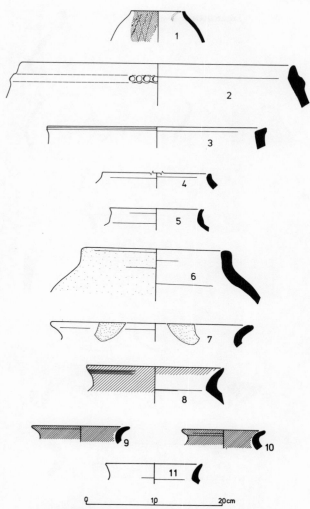

Fig.254. Pottery catalogue: unclassified

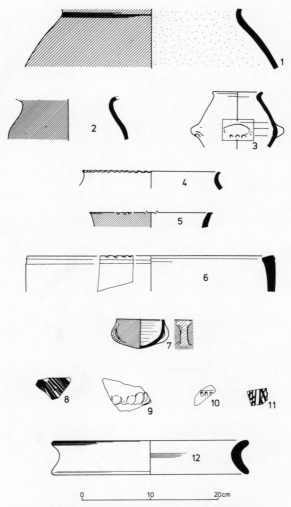

Fig.255. Pottery catalogue: unclassified

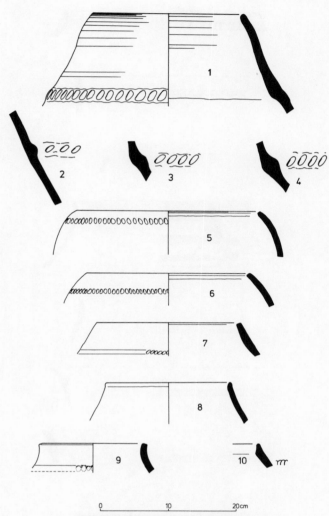

Fig.256. Ruweiha: surface pottery

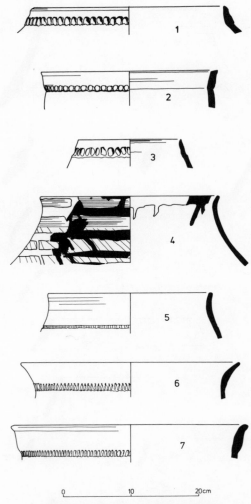

Fig.257. Ruweiha: surface pottery

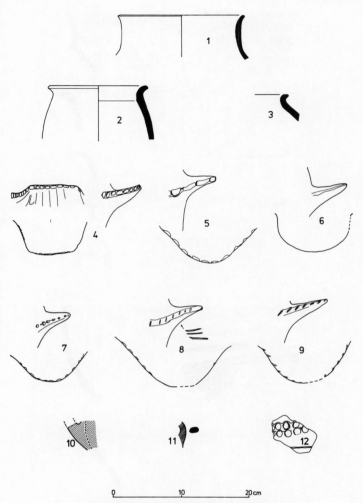

Fig.258. Ruweiha: surface pottery

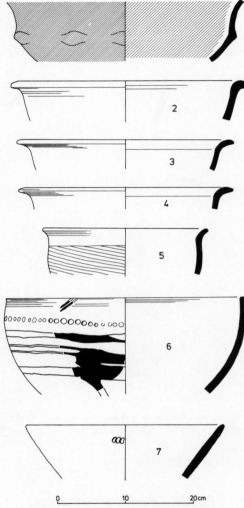

Fig.259. Ruweiha: surface pottery

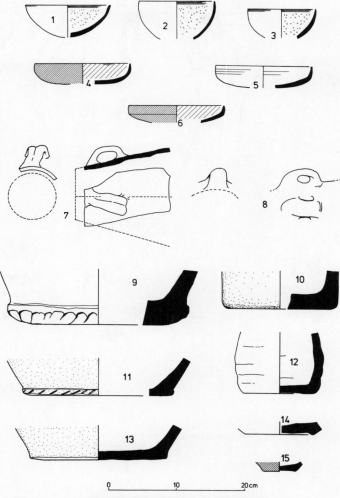

Fig.260. Ruweiha: surface pottery

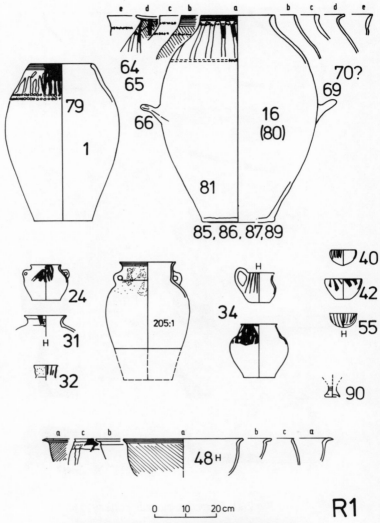

Fig.261. Repertoire R1: 'Chalcolithic' style

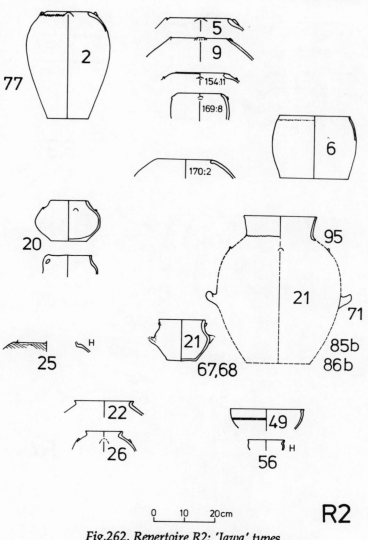

0   10   20cm

R2

Fig.262. Repertoire R2: 'Jawa' types

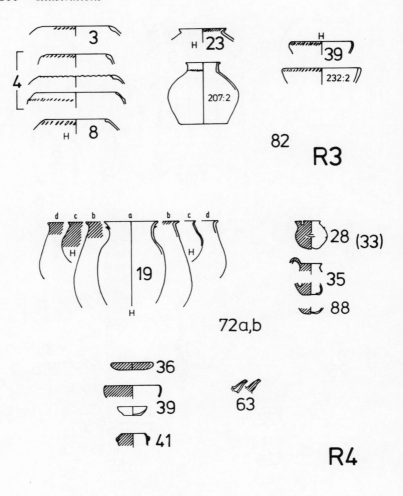

Fig.263. Repertoires R3 and R4

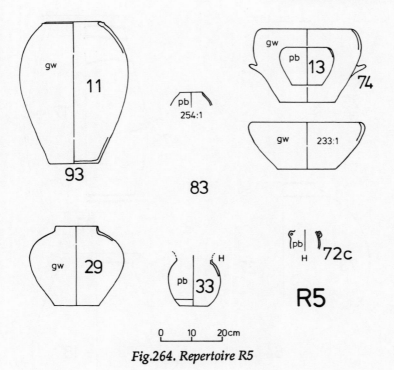

0   10   20cm

Fig.264. Repertoire R5

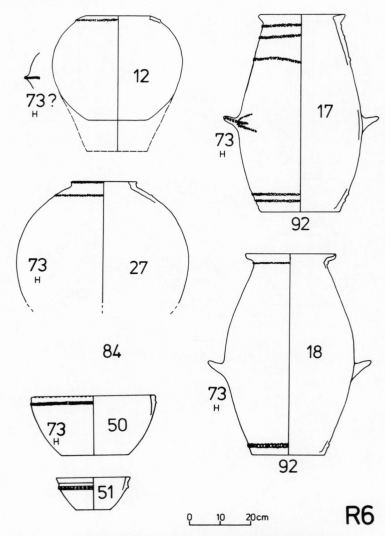

Fig.265. Repertoire R6: 'Northern Chalcolithic' style

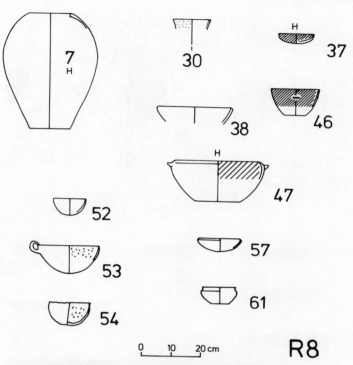

R8

Fig.266. Repertoire R8 (miscellaneous styles)

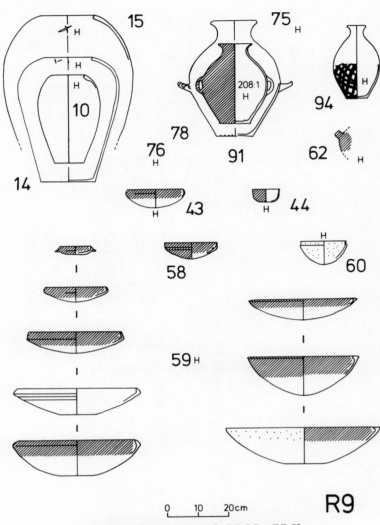

Fig.267. Repertoire R9: EB I B - EB II

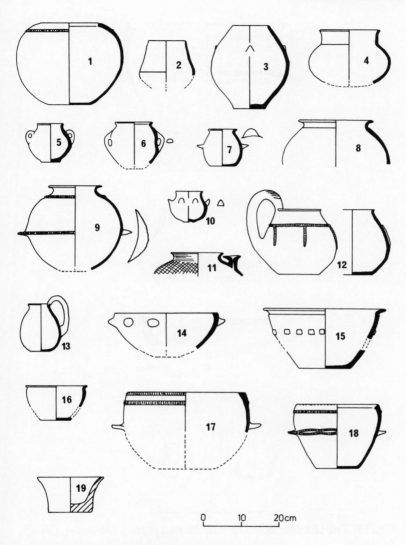

Fig.268. Tell Um Hammad pottery (Mellaart)

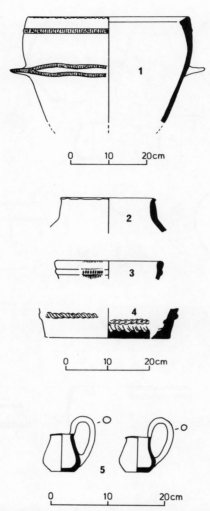

Fig.269. Tell Um Hammad and Tell Mafluq pottery (Mellaart, Glueck, Tubb)

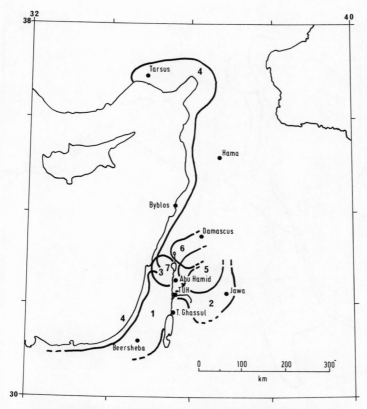

Fig.270. Map: possible source areas for pottery repertoires

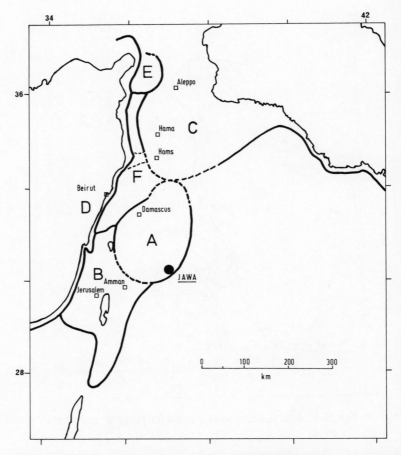

Fig.271. Map: Jawa: distribution of pottery parallels (repertoires and genres)

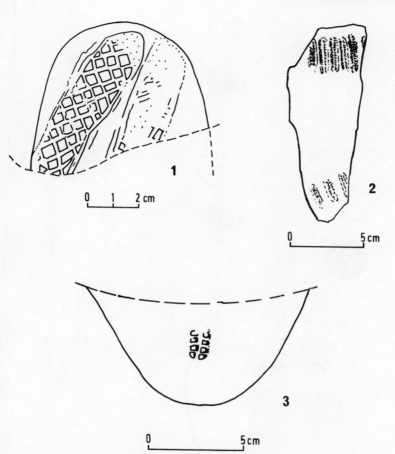

Fig.272. Stamp seal impressions

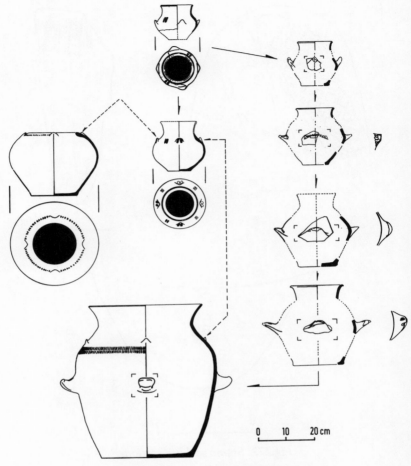

Fig.273. Jawa: genres A and B

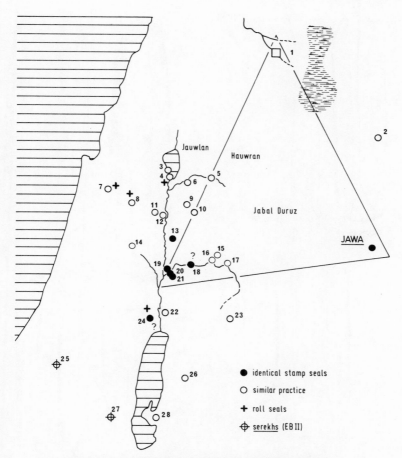

Jauwlan

Hauwran

Jabal Duruz

JAWA

● identical stamp seals

○ similar practice

✚ roll seals

⊕ serekhs (EB II)

Fig.274. Distribution of stamp seal impressions

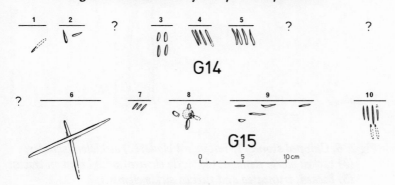

G14

G15

0   5   10 cm

Fig.275. 'Potter's marks'

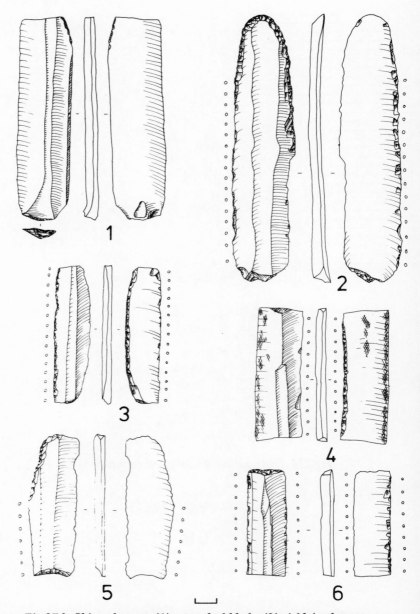

Fig.276. Chipped stone: (1) retouched blade; (2) sickle/endscraper;
(3) backed sickle element; (4) sickle element with bitumen traces;
(5) backed, truncated and turned sickle element;
(6) truncated sickle element

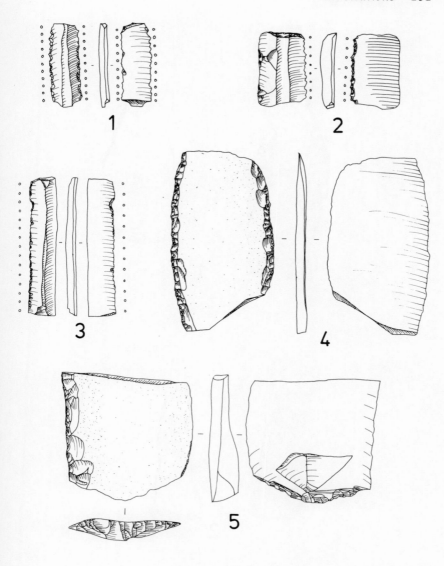

Fig.277. Chipped stone (EB I/II): (1) denticulated sickle element;
(2) denticulated sickle element; (3) sickle element;
(4), (5) tabular scrapers

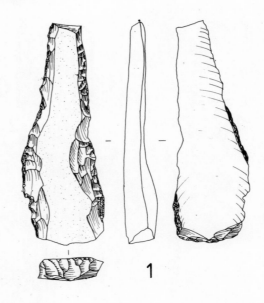

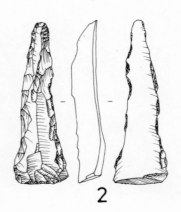

Fig.278. Chipped stone (EB I/II): (1) tabular scraper; (2) perforator

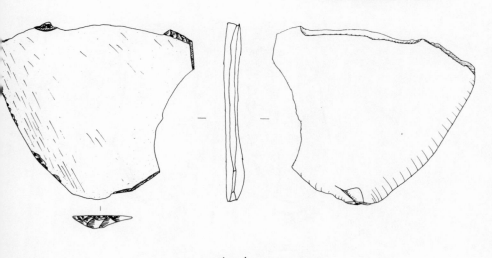

Fig.279. Chipped stone (EB I/II): tabular scraper

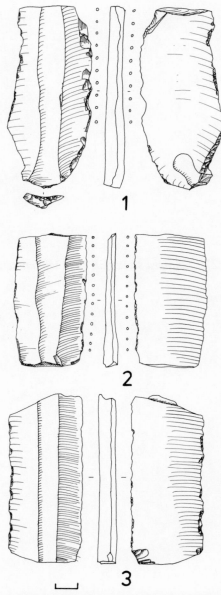

Fig.280. Chipped stone (EB IV): (1) sickle blade; (2) sickle blade; (3) used blade

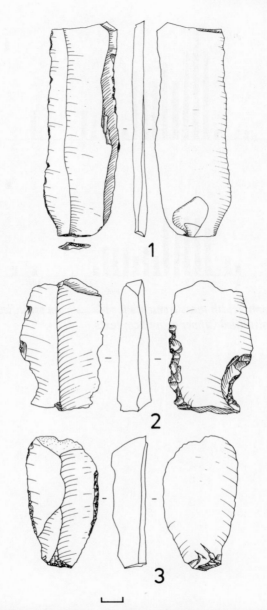

Fig.281. *Chipped stone (EB IV): (1) used blade; (2) denticulated flake;*
    (3) retouched flake

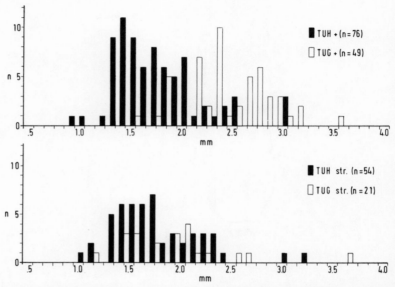

Fig.282. Graph: width measurements for blades from stratified (lower graph) and unstratified (upper graph) contexts

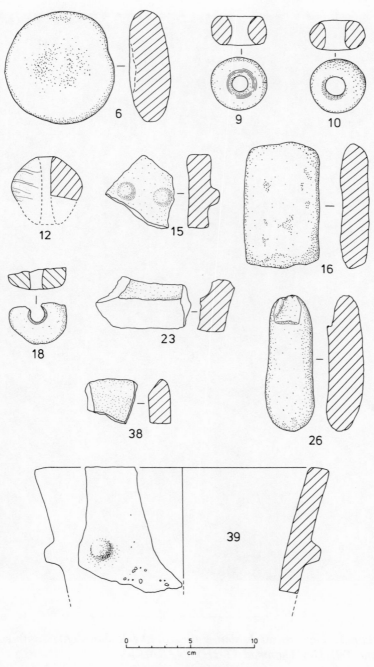

Fig. 283. Other finds

0 ⌊_____⌋ 10 km

Plate 1. The central Jordan Valley at the Jordan-Zerqa confluence and Tell Um Hammad (TUH): NASA/RBV

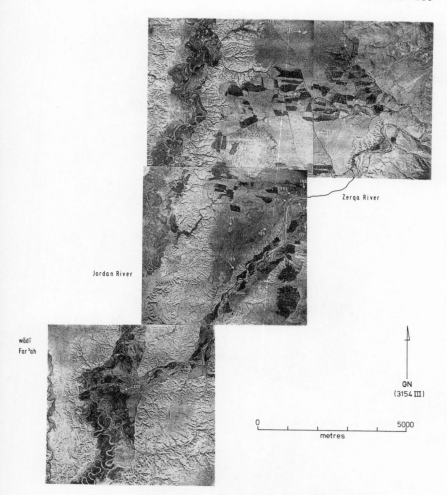

Plate 2. The 'Zerqa Triangle' and Tell Um Hammad after Glueck 1951

Plate 3. Pottery: (1) 'churn' fragment (cf. Fig. 235: 14); (2) mat-impressed base (cf. Fig. 252: 5); (3) mat-impressed base from Ruweiha

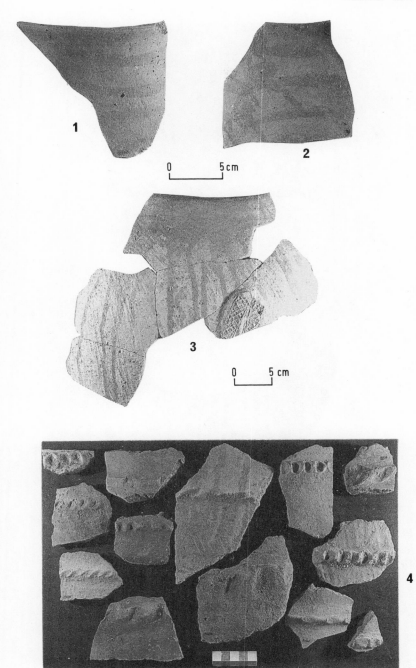

Plate 4. Pottery: (1) genre 1, 'trickle paint' (cf. Fig: 178: 5); (2) 'trickle paint' (= genre 16) from Ruweiha (cf. Fig. 257: 4); (3) genre 1/2, 'trickle paint' and 'finger-streaking', stamp seal impressions on pushed up lug handle (cf. Fig. 137); (4) genre 79 (scale 5 cm) (cf. Fig. 243)

Plate 5. Pottery: (1) stamp seal impressions from Jawa (cf. Betts [ed.] 1991: Fig. 160); (2) genre/type AA from Jawa (cf. Betts [ed.] 1991: Fig. 110: 3, 4)

Plate 6. Pottery: (1) genre 17 (cf. 187: 5); (2) genre 50 (cf. Figs 221-3); (3) genre 54 (cf. Fig. 224: 13); (4) genre 55 (cf. Fig. 226: 2); (5) genre 55 (cf. Fig. 226: 3)

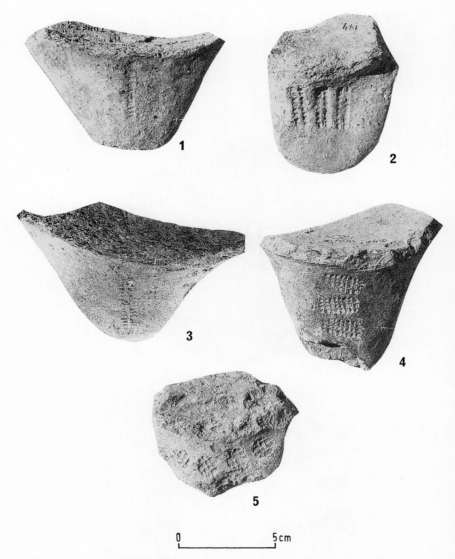

Plate 7. Ledge handles with stamp seal impressions: (1 - 4) Um Hammad; (5) Tell Mafluq

Plate 8. (1) stamp seal impressions on a holemouth jar of genre 2 (cf. Fig. 143: 1); (2) stamp seal impressions on a holemouth jar of genre 1/2 (cf. Pl. 4: 3; Figs 142, 272); (3) 'reed' impressed bands on genre 82 (cf. Fig. 244: 5); (4) stabbed impressions on genre 21 (cf. Fig. 197: 1); (5) 'reed' impressed bands (cf. Figs 147, 148: 1-7, 154: 1-6)

Bibliography

ABBREVIATIONS

AAA *Liverpool Annals of Archaeology and Anthropology*
AAAS *Annales Archéologiques Arabes Syriennes*
AASOR *Annual of the American Schools of Oriental Research*
ADAJ *Annual of the Department of Antiquities of Jordan*
AJA *American Journal of Archaeology*
ATLAL *The Journal of Saudi Arabian Archaeology*
BAR *British Archaeological Reports*
BASOR *Bulletin of the American Schools of Oriental Research*
BiArR *Biblical Archaeological Review*
CNRS *Centre National de la Recherche Scientifique*
IEJ *Israel Exploration Journal*
IFAPO *Institut Français d'Archéologie du Proche Orient*
JAOS *Journal of the American Oriental Society*
JESHO *Journal of Economic and Social History of the Orient*
JNES *Journal of Near Eastern Studies*
JPOS *Journal of the Palestine Oriental Society*
PEFQS *Palestine Exploration Fund Quarterly Series*
PEQ *Palestine Exploration Quarterly*
QDAP *Quarterly of the Department of Antiquities in Palestine*
RB *Revue Biblique*
ZDPV *Zeitschrift des Deutschen Palästina Vereins*

BIBLIOGRAPHY

Abu Hamid: Village du 4e millénaire de la vallée du Jourdain, (1988), (Centre Culturel Français et Département des Antiquités de Jourdaine) Amman.

Amiran, R. (1968). 'Chronological Problems of the Early Bronze Age', *AJA*, 72, 316-318.

Amiran, R. (1969). *Ancient Pottery of the Holy Land from its Beginnings in the Neolithic Period to the End of the Iron Age*, Jerusalem: Massada Press.

Amiran, R. (1970). 'The Beginnings of Urbanization in Canaan', in Sanders (ed.) (1970), 83-100.

Amiran, R. (1977). 'Pottery from the Chalcolithic Site near Tell Delhamiya, and some Notes on the Chalcolithic-Early Bronze 1 Transition', *Eretz Israel* 13, 48-56.

Amiran, R. (1978). *Early Arad I: the Chalcolithic settlement and Early Bronze city*, Jerusalem: Israel Exploration Society.

Amiran, R. (1981). 'Some Observations on Chalcolithic and Early Bronze Age Sanctuaries and Religion', in Biran (ed.) (1981), 47-53.

Amiran, R. (1986). 'The Fall of the Early Bronze Age II City of Arad', *IEJ*, 36, 74-6.

Amiran, R. and Porat, N. (1984). 'The Basalt Vessels of the Chalcolithic Period and Early Bronze Age I', *Tel Aviv*, 11, 3-19.

Anati, E. (1963). *Palestine before the Hebrews: a history, from the earliest arrival of man to the conquest of Canaan*, London: Cape.

Anati, E. (1971). 'Excavations at Hazorea, in the Plain of Esdraelon, Israel', *Origini*, 5, 59-148.

Andrae, W. (1938). *Das Wiedererstandene Assur*, Leipzig: Hinrichs Verlag.

Avi-Yonah, M. and E. Stern (eds) (1977). *Encyclopedia of Archaeological Excavations in the Holy Land*. Oxford: Oxford University Press.

Baird, D. (1987). 'A preliminary analysis of the chipped stone from the 1985 excavations at Tell esh-Shuna North', *ADAJ*, XXXI, 461-80.

Bar-Adon, P. (1980). *The Cave of the Treasure*, Jerusalem: The Israel Exploration Society.

Beale, T. W. (1978). 'Bevelled Rim Bowls and their implications for changes and economic organization in the later fourth millennium BC', *JNES*, 37, 289-313.

Beit-Arieh, I. (1984). 'New Evidence on the Relations between Canaan and Egypt during the Proto-Dynastic Period', *IEJ*, 34, 20-23.

Beit-Arieh, I. (1986). 'Two Cultures in Southern Sinai in the Third Millennium BC', *BASOR*, 263, 27-54.

Bender, F. (1968). *Geologie von Jordanien* (English edn 1974), Berlin: Beitr. 3, Regionalen Geol. d. Erde, Bd 7.

Ben-Tor, A. (1966). 'Excavations at Horvat Usa', *'Atiqot*, 3 (Hebrew Series, English Summary), 1-3.

Ben-Tor, A. (1973). 'Excavations at Two Burial Caves at Azor', *Qadmoniot*, 6, 48.

Ben-Tor, A. (1975). 'Two burial caves of the Proto-Urban period at Azor, 1971', *Qedem*, 1, 1-53.

Ben-Tor, A. (1978). *Cylinder Seals of Third-millennium Palestine*, Cambridge, Mass.

Betts, A. V. G. (1986). *The Prehistory of the Black Desert, Transjordan: an analysis*, unpubl. Ph. D. thesis, University of London.

Betts, A. V. G. (in press). 'Tell el-Hibr: a rockshelter occupation of the 4th millennium BC in the Jordanian badiya', *BASOR*.

Betts, Alison [V. G.], Helms Svend [W.], and William and Fidelity Lancaster (1991). 'The Burqu`/Ruweishid Project: Preliminary Report on the 1989 Field Season', *Levant*, 23, 7-28.

Betts, A. V. G. (ed.) (1991). *Excavations at Jawa 1972-1986*, Edinburgh: Edinburgh University Press.

Betts, A. V. G. and Helms, S. W. (in press). *Excavations at Tell Um Hammad 1982-1984. The Late Assemblages (EB IV/Iron Age)*, Edinburgh: Edinburgh University Press.

Bikai, P. M. (1978). *The Pottery of Tyre*, Warminster: Aris and Phillips.

Biran, A. (ed.). (1981). *Temples and high places in biblical times: proceedings of the colloquium in honor of the centennial of Hebrew Union College - Jewish Institute of Religion, Jerusalem 14-16 March 1977*, Jerusalem: Nelson Glueck School of Biblical Archaeology of Hebrew Union College - Jewish Institute of Religion.

Bliss, F.J. (1894). *A Mound of Many Cities*, London.

Braemer, F. (1984). 'Prospections archéologiques dans le Hawran (Syrie)', *Syria*, 61, 219-50.

Braemer, F. (1988). 'Prospections archéologiques dans le Hawran. II. Les reseaux de l'eau', *Syria*, 65, 99-137.

Braidwood, R. J. and Braidwood, L. S. (1960). *Excavations in the Plain of Antioch. I*, Chicago: University of Chicago Oriental Institute Publications 61.

Braidwood, R. J. and Willey, G. (eds) (1960). *Courses Towards Urban Life*, Chicago: Chicago University, Oriental Institute Studies in Ancient Oriental Civilisations, No. 31.

Braun, E. (1984). 'Yiftah'el', Notes and News, *IEJ*, 34, 191-4.

Braun, E. (1985). *En Shadud. Salvage Excavations at a Farming Community in the Jezreel Valley, Israel*, Oxford: BAR Int. Ser. 249.

Braun, E. (1987). 'Book Reviews' (Review of Hanbury-Tenison 1986), *Mitekufat Haeven: Journal of the Israel Prehistoric Society*, 20, 186-90.

Braun, E. (1989a). 'The Problem of the Apsidal House: New Aspects of Early Bronze I Domestic Architecture in Israel, Jordan, and Lebanon', *PEQ*, 1-43.

Braun, E. (1989b). 'The transition from the Chalcolithic to the Early Bronze Age in northern Israel and Jordan: is there a missing link?', in de Miroschedji (ed.) (1989), 7-27.

Braun, E. (1990). 'Basalt Bowls of the EB 1 Horizon in the Southern Levant', *Paléorient*, 16, 87-96.

Broshi, M. and Tsafrir, Y. (1977). 'Excavations at Zion Gate, Jerusalem', *IEJ*, 27, 28-37.

Broshi, M. and Gophna, R. (1984). 'The Settlements and Population of Palestine During the Early Bronze Age II-III', *BASOR*, 253, 41-53.

Callaway, J. A. (1964). *Pottery from the Tombs at 'Ai (et-Tell)*, London: Quaritch.

Callaway, J. A. (1972). *The Early Bronze Age Sanctuary at Ai (et- Tell)*, London: Quaritch.

Callaway, J. A. (1980). *The Early Bronze Age Citadel and Lower City at Ai (et-Tell)*, Cambridge Mass.: American Schools of Oriental Research.

Caneva, I. (1973). 'Note sull'industria litica de Arslantepe', in A. Palmieri (1973), 55-228.

Cauvin, J. and Sanlaville, P. (eds). (1981). *Préhistoire du Levant*, Paris: CNRS.

Cauvin, J. and Aurenche, O. (eds). (1985). *Cahiers de l'Euphrate 4*, Paris: Publication de l'URA 17.

Cauvin, J. and Stordeur, D. (1985). 'Une occupation d' époque Uruk en Palmyrene: le niveaux supérieur d'el Kowm 2 -Caracol', in Cauvin and Aurenche (eds) (1985), 191-205.

Chazan, M. and Lehner, M. (1990). 'An Ancient Analogy: Pot Baked Bread in Ancient Egypt and Mesopotamia', *Paléorient*, 16/2, 21-35.

Childe, V. G. (1950). 'The Urban Revolution', *Town Planning Review*, 21, 3-17.

Commenge-Pellerin, C. (1987). *La poterie d'Abou Matar et de l'Ouadi Zoumeli (Beersheva) au IVe millénaire avant l'ère chrétienne*, (Les Cahiers du Centre Recherche Français de Jerusalem, vol. 3), Paris: Association Paléorient.

Contenson, H. de (1956). 'La céramique chalcolithique de Beersheba; étude typologique', *IEJ*, 6, 163-79, 226-38.

Contenson, H. de (1960). 'Three Soundings in the Jordan Valley', *ADAJ* 4/5, 12-98.

Crowfoot Payne, J. (1948). 'Some Flint Implements from 'Affula', *JPOS*, 21, 72-79.

Crowfoot Payne, J. (1960). 'Appendix I: Flint Implements from Tell al-Judaidah', in Braidwood and Braidwood (1960), 525-39.

Crowfoot Payne, J. (1983). 'Appendix C: The Flint Industries of Jericho', in Kenyon and Holland (1983), 622-759.

Dayan, Y. (1969). 'Tell Turmus in the Huleh Valley', *IEJ*, 19, 65-78.

Dever, W. G. (1980). 'New Vistas on the EB IV ('MB I') Horizon in Syria-Palestine', *BASOR*, 237, 35-64.

Dollfus, G. and Kafafi, Z. (1986). 'Abu Hamid, Jordanie. Premiers résultats', *Paléorient*, 12, 91-100.

Dollfus, G. and Kafafi, Z. (n.d.). *Abu Hamid. Mission jordano- française*, Yarmuk University/CNRS.

Dothan, M. (1957). 'Excavations at Meser: 1956. Preliminary Report on the First Season', *IEJ*, 7, 217-28.

Dothan, M. (1959a). 'Excavations at Horvat Beter (Beersheba)','*Atiqot*, 2, 1-42.

Dothan, M. (1959b). 'Excavations at Meser: 1957. Preliminary Report on the Second Season', *IEJ*, 9, 13-29.

Dothan, M. (1971). 'The Late Chalcolithic Period in Palestine - Chronology and Foreign Contacts', *Eretz Israel*, 10, 126-31(Hebrew), xii-xiii (English Summary).

Dubertret, C. and Dunand, M. (1954/5). 'Les Gisements Ossifers de Khirbet el-Umbachi et de Hébariye (Safa)', *AAAS*, 4-5, 59-76.

Duckworth, R. (1976). 'Appendix C: Notes on the Flint Implements from Jawa', in Helms (1976b), 31-5.

Dunand, M. (1937). *Fouilles de Byblos. I. 1926-1932*, Paris: Geuthner.

Dunand. M. (1973). *Fouilles de Byblos. V*, Paris: Adrien Maisonneuve.

Ehrich, R. W. (ed.) (1965). *Chronologies in Old World Archaeology*, Chicago: University of Chicago Press.

Eisenberg, E. (1989). 'The Chalcolithic and Early Bronze Age I occupations at Tel Teo', in Miroschedji (ed.) (1989), 29-40.

Eitan, A. (1969). 'Excavations at the Foot of Tel Ras ha`ayin','*Atiqot*, 5, 49-68.

Elliott, C. (1977). 'The Religion of the Ghassulians c. 4000-3000 B.C.', *PEQ*, 3-25.

Elliott, C. (1978). 'The Ghassulian Culture in Palestine; Origins, Influence, and Abandonment', *Levant* 10, 37-54.

Engberg, R. M. and Shipton, G. M. (1934). *Notes on the Chalcolithic and Early Bronze Age Pottery of Megiddo*, Chicago: C.U.P.

Epstein, C. (1978). 'A New Aspect of Chalcolithic Culture'. *BASOR* 229, 27-45.

Epstein, C. (1985a). 'Pithat ha-Yarmuk', in Notes and News, *IEJ*, 35, 56-7.

Epstein, C. (1985b). 'Dolmens excavated in the Golan', '*Atiqot*,17, 20-58.

Esse, D. L. (1984). 'Archaeological Mirage: reflections on Early Bronze I C in Palestine', *JNES*, 43, 317-30.

Esse, D. L. (1989). 'Secondary State Formation and Collapse in Early Bronze Age Palestine', in de Miroschedji (ed.) (1989), 81-96.

Fitzgerald, G. M. (1934). 'Excavations at Beth Shan 1933', *PEFQS*, 66, 123-4.

Fitzgerald, G. M. (1935). 'The Earliest Pottery of Beth Shan', *The Museum Journal*, 24, 5-22.

Friberg, J. (1984). 'Numbers and Measures in the Earliest Written Records', *Scientific American*, Feb., 78-85.

Fugmann, E. (1958). *Hama: Fouilles et recherches 1931-1938: II1. L'architecture des périodes préhellénistiques.* Copenhagen: Nationalmuseet.

Garrod, D. (1934). 'Notes on the Flint Implements', in Engberg and Shipton (1934), 78-91.

Garstang, J. (1932). 'Jericho, City and Necropolis', *AAA*, 19, 3-22.

Garstang, J. (1935). 'Jericho, City and Necropolis, Fifth Report', *AAA*, 22, 143-84.

Garstang, J. (1936). 'Jericho, City and Necropolis: Reports for the Sixth and Concluding Season, 1936', *AAA*, 23, 67-100.

Garstang, J. (1937). 'Exploration in Cilicia', *AAA*, 24, 53-68.

Garstang, J. (1953). *Prehistoric Mersin: Yümük Tepe in Southern Turkey*, Oxford: Clarendon Press.

Glueck, N. (1943). 'Three Israelite Towns in the Jordan Valley: Zarethan, Succoth, Zaphon', *BASOR*, 90, 2-12.

Glueck, N. (1945a). 'A Chalcolithic settlement in the Jordan Valley', *BASOR* 97, 10-22.

Glueck, N. (1945b). 'A settlement of Middle Bronze I in the Jordan Valley', *BASOR*, 100, 7-13.

Glueck, N. (1951). *Explorations in Eastern Palestine, IV. Parts 1 and 2*, (AASOR, 25-28).

Gophna, R. (1979). 'Two Early Bronze Age Basalt Bowls from the Vicinity of Nizzanim', *Tel Aviv*, 6, 136-7.

Gophna, R. (1984). 'The Settlement Landscape of Palestine in the Early Bronze Age II - III and the Middle Bronze Age II', *IEJ*, 34, 24-31.

Gophna, R. (1990). 'The Early Bronze Age I Settlement at `En Besor Oasis', *IEJ*, 40, 1-11.

Gophna, R. and Sadeh, S. (1988-9). 'Excavations at Tel Tsaf: an early chalcolithic site in the Jordan Valley', *Tel Aviv*, 15- 16, 3-36.

Gordon, R. L. and Villiers, L. E. (1983). 'Telul edh-Dhahab and its Environs. Survey of 1980 and 1982: Preliminary Report', *ADAJ* 27, 275-89.

Grant, E. and Wright, G. E. (1938). *Ain Shems Excavations. Part IV (Pottery) (Plates)*, Biblical and Kindred Studies, No.7, Haverford College, Haverford.

Gustavson-Gaube, C. (1985). 'Tell esh-Shuna North 1984: a Preliminary Report', *ADAJ*, 29, 43-87.

Gustavson-Gaube, C. (1986). 'Tell esh-Shuna North, 1985: A Preliminary Report', *ADAJ*, 30, 69-113.

Hadidi, A. (ed.) (1982). *Studies in the History and Archaeology of Jordan I*, Amman: Department of Antiquities.

Hadidi, A. (ed.) (1987). *Studies in the History and Archaeology of Jordan III*, Amman, London and New York: Department of Antiquities and Routledge and Kegan Paul.

Hanbury-Tenison, J. W. (1986). *The Late Chalcolithic to Early Bronze I Transition in Palestine and Transjordan*, Oxford: BAR Int. Ser. 311.

Hanbury-Tenison, J. W. (1987). 'Jarash Region Survey, 1984', *ADAJ*, 31, 129-57.

Hanbury-Tenison, J. W. (1988), 'A Late Chalcolithic Bowl-stand from Pella, Jordan', *PEQ*, 100-1.

Hanbury-Tenison, J. W. (1989a). 'Desert Urbanism in the Fourth Millennium?', *PEQ*, 55-63.

Hanbury-Tenison, J. W. (1989b). 'Jabal Mutawwaq 1986', *ADAJ*, 33, 137-44.

Helms, S. W. (1976a). *Urban Fortifications of Palestine During the Third Millennium BC*, unpubl. Ph.D. thesis, University of London.

Helms, S. W. (1976b) 'Jawa Excavations 1974 - a preliminary report', *Levant*, 9, 21-35.

Helms, S. W. (1983). 'The EB IV (EB-MB) Cemetery at Tiwal esh- Sharqi in the Jordan Valley, 1983', *ADAJ*, 28, 55-85.

Helms, S. W. (1984a). 'Excavations at Tell Umm Hammad esh-Sharqiya in the Jordan Valley, 1982', *Levant*, 16, 35-54.

Helms, S. W. (1984b). 'The Land behind Damascus: urbanism during the 4th millennium in Syria/Palestine', in Khalidi (ed.)(1984), 15-31.

Helms, S. W. (1986). 'Excavations at Tell Um Hammad, 1984', *Levant*, 18, 25-50.

Helms, S. W. (1987a). 'Jawa, Tell Um Hammad and the EB I/late Chalcolithic landscape', *Levant*, 19, 49-81.

Helms, S. W. (1987b). 'A Question of Economic Control during the Proto-Historical Era of Palestine/Transjordan', in Hadidi (ed.) (1987), 41-51.

Helms, S. W. (1989). 'An EB IV Pottery Repertoire at Amman, Jordan', *BASOR*, 273, 17-36.

Helms, S. W. (1990). *Early Islamic Architecture of the Desert. A bedouin station in eastern Jordan*, Edinburgh: Edinburgh University Press.

Helms, S. W. (in press). 'The "Zerqa Triangle": a preliminary appraisal of protohistorical settlement patterns and demographic episodes', (IVth Conference on the History and Archaeology of Jordan, Lyon 1989 = Studies in the History and Archaeology of Jordan IV).

Hennessy, J. B. (1967). *The Foreign Relations of Palestine during the Early Bronze Age*, London: Quaritch.

Hennessy, J. B. (1969). 'Preliminary Report on a First Season of Excavations at Teleilat Ghassul', *Levant*, 1, 1-24.

Hennessy, J. B. (1982). 'Teleilat Ghassul: Its place in the archaeology of Jordan', in Hadidi (ed.) 1982, 55-8.

Holland, T. A. (1983). 'Appendix M: Stone Mace-heads', in Kenyon and Holland (1983), 804-13.

Homès-Fredericq, D. and Franken, H. J. (1985). *Argile, source de vie: sept millénaires de ceramique en Jordanie*, Brussels and Tongeren: Musées Royaux d'Art et d'Histoire and Provinicaal Gallo-Romeins Museum.

Hours, F. (1979). 'L'industrie lithique de Saida-Dakerman', *Berytus*, 27, 57-76.

Ibrahim, M, Sauer, J. and Yassine, K. (1976). 'The East Jordan Valley Survey, 1975', *BASOR*, 222, 41-66.

Kafafi, Z. (1982). *The Neolithic of Jordan (East Bank)*, (Inaugural-Dissertation, Berlin).

Kantor, H. J. (1965). 'The Relative Chronology of Egypt with that of other parts of the Near East', in Ehrich (1965), 1- 27.

Kaplan, J. (1958a). 'Excavations at Wadi Rabah', *IEJ* 8, 149-60.

Kaplan, J. (1958b). 'Excavations at Teluliot Batashi in the Vale of Sorek', *Eretz Israel* 5: 9-14 (Hebrew), 83-84 (English Summary).

Kaplan, J. (1963). 'Excavations at Benei Beraq 1951', *IEJ*, 13,300-12.

Kaplan, J. (1969). "Ein el-Jarba. Chalcolithic Remains in the Plain of Esdraelon', *BASOR*, 194, 2-39.

Kempinski, A. (1978). *The Rise of Urban Culture: The Urbanization of Palestine in the Early Bronze Age, 3000-2150 B.C.*, Jerusalem.

Kempinski, A. (1983). 'Early Bronze Age Urbanization of Palestine: Some Topics in a Debate', *IEJ*, 33, 235-41.

Kenyon, K. M. (1960). *Excavations at Jericho. I*, London: British School of Archaeology in Jerusalem.

Kenyon, K. M. (1965). *Excavations at Jericho. II*, London:British School of Archaeology in Jerusalem.

Kenyon, K. M. (1974). Review of de Miroschedji 1971, *Biblica*, 55, 88-90.

Kenyon, K. M. (1981). *Excavations at Jericho. III*, London: British School of Archaeology in Jerusalem.

Kenyon, K. M. and Holland, T. A. (1982). *Excavations at Jericho. IV*, London: British School of Archaeology in Jerusalem.

Kenyon, K. M. and Holland, T. A. (1983). *Excavations at Jericho. V*, London: British School of Archaeology in Jerusalem.

Khalidi, T. (ed.) (1984). *Land Tenure and Social Transformation in the Middle East*, Beirut: American University of Beirut.

Kochavi, M. (1969). 'Excavations at Tel Esdar', *'Atiqot*, 5, 14-48.

Koeppel, R. (1940). *Teleilat Ghassul II: compte rendu des fouilles de l'Institut Biblique Pontifical 1932-36*, Rome: Institut Biblique Pontifical.

Kroeper, K. (1989). 'Palestinian Ceramic Teapots in Pre- and Protodynastic Egypt', in de Miroschedji (ed) (1989), 407-22.

Lapp, P. W. (1968). 'Bab edh-Dhra' Tomb A 76 and Early Bronze I in Palestine', *BASOR*, 189, 12-41.

Lapp, P. W. (1970). 'Palestine in the Early Bronze Age', in Sanders (ed.) (1970), 101-131.

Lee, J. R. (1973). *Chalcolithic Ghassul: new aspects and master typology*, unpubl. Ph.D. thesis, Hebrew University.

Leonard, A. (1983). 'The Proto Urban/Early Bronze I Utilization of the Kataret es-Samra Plateau', *BASOR*, 251, 37-60.

Leonard, A. (1989). 'A Chalcolithic' Fine Ware' from Khirbet es-Samra in the Jordan Valley', *BASOR*, 276, 3-14.

Leonard, A. (n.d.). *Preliminary Plates from the 1953 Sounding in the Jordan Valley conducted by James Mellaart* (= AASOR forthcoming).

Levy, T. E. (1986). 'The Chalcolithic Period', *Biblical Archaeologist*, 49, 82-108.

Levy, T. E. (ed.) (1987). *Shiqmim I*, Oxford: BAR Int. Ser. 356.

Levy, T. E. and Rosen, S. (1987).'The Chipped Stone Industry at Shiqmim', Chapter 10 in Levy (ed.) (1987).

Loud, G. (1948). *Megiddo II - Seasons of 1935-1939*, (University of Chicago Oriental Institute Publications LXII), Chicago: Chicago University Press.

Mabry, J. (1989) 'Investigations at Tell el-Handaquq, Jordan (1987-88)', *ADAJ* 33, 59-95.

Macalister, R. A. S. (1902). 'First Quarterly Report on the Excavations at Gezer', *PEFQS*, 34, 317-75.

Macdonald, E. (1932). *Beth Pelet II, Prehistoric Fara*, London: British School of Archaeology in Egypt.

Mallon, A., Koeppel, R, and Neuville, R. (1934). *Teleilat Ghassul I*, (Comptes rendus des fouilles l'institut biblique pontifical, 1929-1932), Rome: Scripta Pontifici Instituti Biblici.

Maqdissi, M. al-. (1984). 'Compte rendu des traveaux archéologiques dans la Ledja en 1984', *Berytus*, 32, 7-17.

Maqdissi, M. al-. (1988). 'Moumassakhin 1987, poterie du Bronze ancien IV', *Syria*, 65, 410-12.

Maqdissi, M. al-. (1990). 'Moumassakhin 1988', *Syria*, 67, 459-61.

Marquet-Krause, J.(1949). *Les fouilles de 'Ay (et-Tell). 1933- 1935: La résurection d'une grande cité biblique*, (Institut Français d'Archéologie de Beyrouth. Bibliotheque archéologique et historique 45), Paris: Geuthner.

Mathias, V. and Parr, P. J. (1989). 'The Early Phases at Tell Nebi Mend: A Preliminary Account', *Levant*, 21, 13-32.

McCartney, C. (in press). 'Preliminary Report of the 1989 Excavations at Site 27 of the Burqu'/Ruweishid Project', *Levant*, 24.

McConaughy, M. (1979). *Formal and Functional Analysis of Chipped Stone Tools from Bab edh-Dhra'*, unpubl. Ph.D. thesis, Ann Arbor.

McCreery, D. W. (1981). 'Flotation of the Bab edh-Dhra' and Numeira Plant Remains', in Rast and Schaub (eds) (1981), 165-69.

McNicoll, A., Smith, R. H. and Hennessy, J. B. (1982). *Pella in Jordan 1*, Canberra: Australian National Gallery.

Mellaart, J. (1956). 'The Neolithic Site of Ghrubba', *ADAJ*, 3, 24-30.

Mellaart, J. (1962). 'Preliminary Report of the Archaeological Survey in the Yarmuk and Jordan Valley', *ADAJ*, 6-7, 126-32.

Mellaart, J. (1966). *The Chalcolithic and Early Bronze Ages in the Near East and Anatolia*, Beirut: Khayats.

Mellaart, J. (1975). *The Neolithic of the Near East*, London: Thames and Hudson.

Mesnil du Buisson, R. du (1935). *La site archéologique de Mishrife-Qatna*, Paris: Boccard.

Millard, A. R. (1988). 'The bevelled-rim bowls: their purpose and significance', *Iraq*, 50, 49-57.

Miroschedji, P. R. de (1971). *L'Epoque Pré-urbaine en Palestine*. Paris: Cahiers de la Revue Biblique 13, Paris: Gabalda.

Miroschedji P. [R] de (1989). *L'urbanisme de la Palestine a l'âge du bronze ancien. Bilan et perspectives des recherches actuelles*. (Actes du colloque d'Emannus [20-24 octobre 1986]). BAR Int. Ser. 527 (i, ii), Oxford.

Moormann, F. (1959). *Report to the Government of Jordan on the Soils of East Jordan* (Report No. 1132, FAO/59/86239), Rome.

Nasrallah, J. (1938). 'Présentations et Communications', *BSPF*, 35, 250.

Nasrallah, J. (1948a). 'Une station ghassoulienne du Hauran', *RB*, 55, 81-103.

Nasrallah, J. (1948b). 'Peignes à corder de Eneolithique Syrien', *BSPF*, 45, 398-401.

National Water Master Plan. Hashemite Kingdom of Jordan (1977). (Federal Republic of Germany GT 2).

Nissen, H. J. (1985). 'The Emergence of Writing in the Ancient Near East', *Interdisciplinary Science Reviews*, 10, 349-61.

North, R. (1961). *Ghassul 1960 Excavation Report*, (Analectica Biblica 14), Rome: Pontifical Biblical Institute.

O'Connell, M. G. and Ross, D. G. (1980). 'Tell el Hesi', *PEQ*, 73-91.

Oren, E. and Gilead, I (1981). 'Chalcolithic Sites in Northeastern Sinai', *Tel Aviv*, 8, 25-49.

Palmieri, A. (1973). 'Scavi nell'area sud-occidentale di Arslantepe', *Origini*, 7, 55-228.

Palmieri, A. (1981). 'Excavations at Arslantepe (Malatya)', *Anatolian Studies*, 31, 101-19.

Parr, P. J. (1956). 'A Cave at Arqub el-Dhahr', *ADAJ*, 3, 61-73.

Perrot, J. (1955). 'The Excavations at Tell Abu Matar, near Beersheba', *IEJ*, 5, 17-40, 73-84, 167-189.

Perrot, J. (1961). 'Une tombe à ossuaires à Azor', *'Atiqot*, 3, 1-83.

Perrot, J., Zori, N. and Reich, Y. (1967). 'Neve Ur, un nouvel aspect du Ghassoulien', *IEJ*, 17, 201-32.

Potts, D. (1981). 'The Potters Marks of Tepe Yahya', *Paléorient*, 7, 107-22.

Prag, K. (1971). *A Study of the Intermediate Early Bronze - Middle Bronze Age in Transjordan, Syria and Lebanon*, unpubl. D.Phil. dissertation, Oxford.

Prag, K. (1974), 'The Intermediate Early Bronze Middle Bronze Age: an Interpretation of the evidence from Transjordan, Syria and Lebanon', *Levant*, 6, 69-116.

Pritchard, J. B. (1958). *The Excavation at Herodian Jericho, 1951*, New Haven: American Schools of Oriental Research, (AASOR, 32-3).

Rast, W. E. (1980), 'Palestine in the 3rd millennium. Evidence for Interconnections', *Scripta Mediterranea*, 1, 5-20.

Rast, W. E. and Schaub, R. T. (1980). 'Preliminary Report of the 1979 Expedition to the Dead Sea Plain, Jordan', *BASOR*, 240, 21-61.

Rast, W. E. and Schaub, R. T. (eds) (1981). 'The Southeastern Dead Sea Plain Expeditions: an Interim Report of the 1977 Session', *AASOR*, 46.

Richard, S. (1980). 'Towards a Concensus of Opinion on the End of the Early Bronze Age in Palestine - Transjordan', *BASOR*, 237, 5-34.

Richard, S. (1987). 'The Early Bronze Age. The Rise and Collapse of Urbanism', *Biblical Archaeologist*, 50, 22-43.

Roaf, M. (1990). *Cultural Atlas of Mesopotamia and the Ancient Near East*, Equinox: Oxford.

Rosen, S. A. (1982). 'Flint Sickle-blades of the Late Protohistoric and Early Historic Periods in Israel', *Tel Aviv*, 9, 139-45.

Rosen, S. A. (1983a). *Lithics in the Bronze and Iron Ages in Israel*, unpubl. Ph.D. thesis, University of Chicago.

Rosen, S. A. (1983b). 'The Canaanean Blade and the Early Bronze Age', *IEJ*, 33, 15-29.

Rosen, S. A. (1983c). 'Tabular Scraper Trade: a model of material cultural dispersion', *BASOR*, 249, 79-86.

Rosen, S. (1985). 'The En Shadud Lithics', Appendix B in Braun (1985).

Rosen, S. (1989). 'The Analysis of Early Bronze Age Chipped Stone Industries: A Summary Statement', in Miroschedji (1989), 199-222.

Saidah, R. (1979). 'Fouilles de Sidon-Dakerman: l'agglomeration chalcolithique', *Berytus*, 27, 29-56.

Salah, M. M. and Dakkak, A. R. (1974). 'Digital Model for predicting the runoff from rainfall for Zerqa River Watershed', *Dirasat* (Jordan University) Nos 1 and 2.

Saller, (1964/5). 'Bab edh-Dhra'', *Liber Annuus*, 15, 137-219.

Sanders, J. A. (ed.) (1970). *Near Eastern Archaeology in the Twentieth Century, (Essays in Honor of Nelson Glueck)*, New York: Doubleday.

Schaub, R. T. (1981). 'Patterns of Burial at Bab edh-Dhra' and Ceramic Sequences in the Tomb Groups at Bab edh-Dhra', in Rast and Schaub (eds) (1981), 44-68, 69-118.

Schaub, R. T. (1982). 'The origins of the Early Bronze Age walled town culture of Jordan', in Hadidi (ed.) (1982), 67-75.

Schaub, R. T. (1987). 'Ceramic Vessels as Evidence for Trade Communications during the Early Bronze Age in Jordan', in Hadidi (ed.) (1987), 247-50.

Schaub, R. T. and Rast, W. E. (1984). 'Preliminary Report of the 1981 Expedition to the Dead Sea Plain, Jordan', *BASOR*, 254, 35-60.

Schick, T. (1978). 'Flint Implements' in Amiran (1978), 58-63.

Seger, J. D., Baum, B., Borowski, O., Cole, D. P., Forshey, H., Futato, E., Jacobs, P. F., Laustrip, M., O'Connor Seger, P., and Zeder, M. (1990). 'The Bronze Age settlements at Tell Halif: Phase Ii excavations, 1983-1987', *BASOR Supplement*, 26, 1-32.

Selin, E. and Watzinger, C. (1913). *Jericho - die Ergebnisse der Ausgrabungen*, Leipzig.

Smith, R. H. (1973). *Pella of the Decapolis*, The College of Wooster.

Stekelis, M. (1935). *Les monuments mégalithiques de Palestine*, Paris: Masson.

Sürenhagen, D. (1978). *Keramikproduktion in Habuba Kabira-Süd*, Berlin: Bruno Hessling.

Sukenik, E. (1936). 'Late Chalcolithic Pottery from Affuleh', *PEFQS*, 68, 150-4.

Sukenik, E. L. (1948). 'Archaeological Investigations at Affula', *JPOS*, 21, 1-9.

Sussman, V. and Ben-Arieh, S. (1966). 'Ancient Burial in Giv'atayim', *'Atiqot*, 3 (HS), (ES 4).

Tadmor, M. and Prausnitz, M. (1959). 'Excavations at Rosh Hanniqra', *'Atiqot*, 2, 72-88.

Tubb, J. N. (1990). *Excavations at the Early Bronze Age Cemetery of Tiwal esh-Sharqi*, London: British Museum.

Tubb, J. N. and Dorrell, P. G. (1991). 'Tell es-Sa'idiyeh: Interim Report on the Fifth (1990) season of Excavations', *Levant* 23, 67-86.

Tubb, J. N. and Wright, M. W. (1985). 'Excavations in the Early Bronze Age Cemetery of Tiwal esh-Sharqi. A Preliminary Report', *ADAJ*, 29, 115-30.

Tufnell, O. (1958). *Lachish IV. The Bronze Age*, London: Oxford University Press.

Tzori, N. (1958). 'Neolithic and Chalcolithic Sites in the Valley of Beth Shan', *PEQ*, 44-51.

Unger-Hamilton, R. (1991). 'The Microwear Analysis of Scrapers and 'Sickle Blades', Chapter 6 in Betts (ed.) (1991).

Ussishkin, D. (1980). 'The Ghassulian Shrine at En-Gedi', *Tel Aviv*, 7, 1-44.

Valla, F. (1978). 'Essai de typologie des objets de silex lustré de Susiane', *Paléorient*, 4, 325-34.

Vaux, R. de (1951). 'La troisième campagne de fouilles a Tell el- Far'ah, près Naplouse - la nécropole', *RB*, 58, 566-93.

Vaux, R. de (1952). 'La quatrième campagne de fouilles a Tell el- Fara'ah, près Naplouse', *RB*, 62, 541-89.

Vaux, R. de (1955). 'Les Fouilles de Tell el-Far'ah, près Naplouse, cinquième campagne', *RB*, 62, 541-89.

Vaux, R. de (1957). 'Les fouilles de Tell el-Far'ah, près Naplouse, sixième campagne', *RB*, 64, 552-88.

Vaux, R. de (1961). 'Les fouilles de Tell el Far'ah, rapport préliminaire sur les 7ème, 8ème, 9ème campagnes 1958-1960', *RB*, 68, 557-92.

Vaux, R. de (1970). 'Palestine during the Neolithic and Chalcolithic Periods', *The Cambridge Ancient History*, I, 1, 499-538.

Vaux, R. de (1971). 'Palestine in the Early Bronze Age'. *The Cambridge Ancient History*, I, 2A, 208-37.

Vaux, R. de and Steve, A. M. (1947). 'La première campagne de fouilles a Tell el Fara'ah, près Naplouse', *RB*, 54, 394-433.

Vaux, R. de and Steve, A. M. (1948). 'La seconde campagne de fouilles a Tell el-Far'ah, près Naplouse', *RB*, 55, 544-80.

Vaux, R. de and Steve, A. M. (1949). 'La deuxième campagne de fouilles a Tell el-Far'ah, près Naplouse: la nécropole', *RB*, 56, 102-38.

Waechter, J. (1958). 'Flint Implements', in Tufnell (1958), 325-27.

Wirth, E. (1971). *Syrien: eine geographische Landeskunde*, Darmstadt: Wissenschaftliche Buchgesellschaft.

Wright, G.E. (1937). *The Pottery of Palestine from the Earliest Times to the End of the Early Bronze Age*, (American Schools of Oriental Research), New Haven: Publications of the Jerusalem School.

Wright, G. E. (1958). 'The Problem of the Transition between the Chalcolithic and Bronze Ages', *Eretz Israel*, 5, 37-45.

Wright, G. E. (1961). 'The Archaeology of Palestine', in Wright (ed.) (1961), 73-112.

Wright, G. E. (1971). 'The Archaeology of Palestine from the Neolithic through the Middle Bronze Age', *JAOS*, 91, 282-93.

Yassine, K. (1985). 'The Dolmens: Construction and Dating Reconsidered', *BASOR*, 259, 63-9.

Yassine, K. (ed.) (1988). *Archaeology of Jordan: Essays and Reports*, Amman: University of Jordan.

Yassine, K., Ibrahim, M. and Sauer, J. (1988). 'The East Jordan Valley Survey, 1976', in Yassine (ed.) (1988), 187-207.

Yeivin, M. S. (1967). 'A New Chalcolithic Culture at Tel `Erany and its Implications for Early Egyptian-Canaanite Relations', Jerusalem: *Fourth World Congress of Jewish Studies*-Papers, 45-8.

Yeivin, S. (1961). *First Preliminary Report on the Excavations at Tell "Gat" (Tell Sheykh 'Ahmad el-Areyney, Seasons 1956- 1958)*, Jerusalem: Dept. of Antiquities.

Yeivin, Z. (1977). 'El-Mahruq, Khirbet', in M. Avi-Yonah and E. Stern (eds) (1977), 766-8.